ENCHANTED GROUND

ENCHANTED GROUND

REIMAGINING JOHN DRYDEN

Edited by
Jayne Lewis and Maximillian E. Novak

Published by the University of Toronto Press in association with
the UCLA Center for Seventeenth- and Eighteenth-Century Studies and
the William Anderson Clark Memorial Library

© The Regents of the University of California 2004
Toronto Buffalo London
Printed in Canada

ISBN 0-8020-8940-2

Printed on acid-free paper

UCLA Center / Clark Series

National Library of Canada Cataloguing in Publication

Enchanted ground : reimagining John Dryden / edited by Jayne
Lewis and Maximillian E. Novak.

(UCLA Center / Clark series)
Includes bibliographical references and index.
ISBN 0-8020-8940-2

1. Dryden, John, 1631–1700 – Criticism and interpretation.
2. Dryden, John, 1631–1700 – Political and social views.   3. Dryden,
John, 1631–1700 – Dramatic works.   I. Lewis, Jayne Elizabeth
II. Novak, Maximillian E.   III. William Andrews Clark Memorial
Library.   IV. University of California, Los Angeles. Center for 17th-
& 18th-Century Studies.   V. Series.

PR3424.E53 2004   821′.4   C2004-900945-1

This book has been published with the help of a grant from the UCLA Center
for Seventeenth- and Eighteenth-Century Studies.

University of Toronto Press acknowledges the financial support for its
publishing activities of the Government of Canada through the Book Publishing
Industry Development Program (BPIDP).

University of Toronto Press acknowledges the financial assistance to its
publishing program of the Canada Council for the Arts and the Ontario
Arts Council.

Contents

Figures

Acknowledgments

The essays in this volume grew out of a series of lectures given at the William Andrews Clark Memorial Library on 27–8 October and 1–2 December 2000 in celebration of the tercentenary of John Dryden's birth. The lectures were followed by long and lively discussions with members of the audience, and the final versions of many of these essays were unquestionably shaped by the interactions between the speakers and such Dryden scholars as Douglas Canfield, Vinton Dearing, Wallace Maurer, and Alan Roper, who also chaired one of the sessions. The editors are grateful for all of those who participated in a remarkably stimulating discussion of Dryden for our new century. The lectures were sponsored by UCLA's Center for Seventeenth- and Eighteenth-Century Studies, and we wish to thank the director, Peter Reill, and the entire staff of the center, particularly Marina Romani. We are also indebted to the entire staff of the William Andrews Clark Memorial Library and its librarian, Bruce Whiteman, for providing a perfect atmosphere for the intellectual exchanges that eventually became the finished essays in this volume.

Held at the research base for *The Works of John Dryden (California Dryden)*, the lectures were, at least partly, a celebration of the completion of the final volume of this twenty-volume enterprise. Critics often simply credit the founding editors, Edward Hooker and H.T. Swedenberg, as a shorthand for all of the editors who have worked on these volumes, despite the astonishing work of Alan Roper and, finally, Vinton Dearing over the years as managing editors. We include the entire edition under the abbreviation *California Dryden*, but in appreciation, we would like to list the editors who have worked on individual volumes: A.B. Chambers, Vinton Dearing, William Frost, George Guffey, Edward Hooker, John

Loftis, Earl Miner, Samuel Monk, Dougald MacMillan, Wallace Maurer, Maximillian Novak, David Rodes, Allan Roper, H.T. Swedenberg, and John Harrington Smith. Working with this community of scholars and helping to put the individual volumes into final form for almost the entire history of the edition has been Geneva Phillips. All of those with an interest in English poetry, drama, and criticism, and particularly scholars working in the late seventeenth century, owe these editors a significant debt. Finally, we wish to thank Johanna Schwartz for her heroic assistance in preparing this volume, and Charles Stuart for his meticulous work as it went to press.

JAYNE LEWIS
MAXIMILLIAN E. NOVAK

Contributors

SHARON ACHINSTEIN is presently Lecturer in English at Oxford University and Fellow of St Edmund Hall. She has recently published a study of Restoration polemics and poetry, *Literature and Dissent in Milton's England*, and is currently working on a project on early feminisms from the Levellers to Locke.

JENNIFER BRADY is Professor of English at Rhodes College. She is co-editor of Ben Jonson's 1616 Folio and of *Literary Transmission and Authority: Dryden and Other Writers*.

LEO BRAUDY is University and Bing Professor of English at the University of Southern California. Among other books, he is the author of *Narrative Form in History and Fiction: Hume, Fielding, and Gibbon* and *The Frenzy of Renown: Fame and Its History*. His most recent book is *From Chivalry to Terrorism: War and the Changing Nature of Masculinity*.

DIANNE DUGAW is Professor of English at the University of Oregon. Her most recent book is *'Deep Play' – John Gay and the Invention of Modernity*. Her CD, *Dangerous Examples – Fighting and Sailing Women in Song*, is based on her earlier *Warrior Women and Popular Balladry, 1650–1850*.

DEBORAH PAYNE FISK is an Associate Professor of Literature and an Affiliate Professor of Theatre at American University. A specialist on Restoration and eighteenth-century drama, Professor Fisk has published numerous articles in addition to editing *The Cambridge Companion to English Restoration Theatre*. She has forthcoming a volume, *Four Libertine*

Plays from the Restoration, and has recently agreed to co-author a new textbook, tentatively entitled *A Cultural History of the Theatre*. Professor Fisk also directs and does dramaturgy; she is the Humanities Research Consultant at The Shakespeare Theatre in Washington, DC.

DAVID HALEY is the author of *Shakespeare's Courtly Mirror* and *Dryden and the Problem of Freedom: The Republican Aftermath, 1649–1680*. Professor Haley, who teaches at the University of Minnesota, is completing a book on the community in Shakespeare's earlier plays.

BLAIR HOXBY is Associate Professor of English at Yale University. He is the author of *Mammon's Music: Literature and Economics in the Age of Milton*. He is now writing a study of tragic drama – including the sung and the sacred varieties – in seventeenth-century England, France, Italy, and Spain. It is entitled *Baroque Tragedy: Passion and Performance, 1630–1750*.

MARGERY KINGSLEY is an Associate Professor of English at Cameron University in Lawton, OK. She is the author of *Transforming the Word: Prophecy, Poetry, and Politics in England, 1650–1742* in addition to several essays on John Dryden. She is currently working on a study of inheritance and the commercial production of history in the Restoration and early eighteenth century.

RICHARD KROLL is Professor of English at the University of California, Irvine. Apart from articles on philosophy, print culture, the novel, and Pope, his books include *The Material Word: Literate Culture in the Restoration and Early Eighteenth Century* and (as editor) *Philosophy, Science, and Religion in England, 1640–1700* as well as two volumes of reprinted essays on the eighteenth-century novel. The essay in this volume will eventually form part of a book on Restoration drama and seventeenth-century economic theory tentatively entitled *Poltical Economy and Restoration Drama*.

JAYNE LEWIS is Professor of English at the University of California, Irvine. She is the author of *The English Fable: Aesop and Literary Culture, 1651–1740* and *Mary Queen of Scots: Romance and Nation*, and of essays on Dryden, Richardson, Defoe, Finch, and others.

MICHAEL MCKEON teaches British literature at Rutgers University in New Brunswick, NJ. He is the author of *Politics and Poetry in Restoration*

England and *The Origins of the English Novel*, and the editor of *Theory of the Novel*. He is currently completing a book entitled *The Secret History of Domesticity: Public, Private, and the Division of Knowledge.*

MAXIMILLIAN E. NOVAK is Professor Emeritus in the Department of English at UCLA. He has written widely on Dryden, Restoration drama, eighteenth-century fiction, and Defoe, and most recently published his biography, *Daniel Defoe Master of Fictions.* He was an editor of volume ten in *The California Edition of the Works of John Dryden,* joint editor of volume thirteen, and associate editor of volume seventeen in that edition.

CEDRIC D. REVERAND II is George Duke Humphrey Distinguished Professor of English at the University of Wyoming, where his research focuses on both English literature and the fine arts in the seventeenth and eighteenth centuries. He is the author of numerous articles on Dryden, as well as *Dryden's Final Poetic Mode: The 'Fables.'*

SUSAN STAVES is the author of *Players' Scepters: Fictions of Authority in the Restoration* and *Married Woman's Separate Property in England, 1660–1833.* With John Brewer she has edited and contributed to *Early Modern Conceptions of Property,* and with Cynthia Ricciardi she has edited Elizabeth Griffith's *Delicate Distress.* In 2001 she retired from Brandeis University, where she was Paul Proswimmer Professor of the Humanities. Her current book project is a literary history of women's writing in Britain from 1660 to 1785.

JAMES GRANTHAM TURNER is Professor of English at the University of California, Berkeley, and has taught at Oxford, Sussex, Liverpool, Virginia, Northwestern, and Michigan. In addition to editing *Politics, Poetics and Hermeneutics in Milton's Prose* with David Loewenstein, Robert Paltock's *Life and Adventures of Peter Wilkins,* and *Sexuality and Gender in Early Modern Europe: Institutions, Texts, Images,* he has written numerous articles on seventeenth- and eighteenth-century culture and four books: *The Politics of Landscape: Rural Scenery and Society in English Poetry, 1630–1660; One Flesh: Paradisal Marriage and Sexual Relations in the Age of Milton; Libertines and Radicals in Early Modern London: Sexuality, Politics and Literary Culture, 1630–1685;* and *Schooling Sex: Libertine Literature and Erotic Education in Italy, France, and England, 1534–1685.*

JAMES A. WINN is the author of *John Dryden and His World* and *'When*

Beauty Fires the Blood': Love and the Arts in the Age of Dryden. A professional flautist, he has a lifelong interest in studies of the relations between music and poetry. He serves as Chairman of the Department of English at Boston University.

STEVEN ZWICKER is Stanley Elkin Professor of Humanities at Washington University, St Louis. In addition to his books on Dryden, he has written on Marvell, Milton, and, more broadly, on the encounter between literature and politics in early modern England. He is currently preparing a *Companion to John Dryden* for Blackwell.

ENCHANTED GROUND

Introduction

JAYNE LEWIS AND MAXIMILLIAN E. NOVAK

Happiness was never to be found;
But vanish'd from 'em, like Enchanted ground.
Religio Laici (ll. 28–9)

Passion's too fierce to be in Fetters bound,
And Nature flies him like Enchanted Ground.
Aureng-Zebe (Prologue, ll. 9–10)

When John Dryden died on 1 May 1700, few would have contested the proposition that he had been the greatest poet of the last forty years of the century. He was given a glorious funeral. His body was put on display at the College of Physicians, and on 13 May a procession of approximately fifty coaches made their way to Westminster Abbey to see him interred in that enchanted ground between the poets Geoffrey Chaucer and Abraham Cowley. A magnificent eulogy was pronounced by Samuel Garth, one of the leading poets of the end of the century, and a chorus of singers, accompanied by a small orchestra, sang an ode by Horace rather than religious hymns. So many people crowded into the Abbey that some critics complained it resembled a mob scene.[1] Among the many elegies printed on the occasion was a volume of nine poems by women taking the roles of the Muses. So transformed, each lamented the poet's death, enumerated his accomplishments, and bewailed the loss suffered by English literature at his passing.[2]

In the centuries since grief wrought these metamorphoses, however, it has become apparent that Dryden in some important sense did not pass away at all. On the contrary, he has enjoyed a long and healthy afterlife, as these fifteen essays, written on the three hundredth anniversary of his death, bear witness. While no one represented in this collection would presume to impersonate a muse, and while many maintain a robust scepticism about his methods and motives, all pay tribute to a Dryden very much alive to today's critical imagination. Taken together, more-over, these essays suggest that Dryden's enduring vitality is owing to something other than the lifelong consistency of aims and attitudes dis-cernible in most writers of his magnitude. In Dryden's unique case, it would appear that it is the very difficulty in discovering any single, immutable thread to bind his vast oeuvre together that continues to pro-voke fascination, speculation, and debate. As a poet, critic, dramatist, and translator – and as a sycophant and a satirist – Dryden was nothing if not a shape-shifter, and he was so in ways that transcended even the extraordinary social and political pressures of his times. The amazing versatility of his pen was matched only by the transformational energy that shapes individual works, from heroic dramas that stage unresolved (and thus dynamic) arguments between competing moral, emotional, and political claims to the great satires, epitomized in *Absalom and Achi-tophel*, that are charged as much with the seductive power of what they oppose as with the fervour of their explicit moral positions.

When in Dryden we do encounter a recurrent motif, it's unlikely to strike us as an authorial signature in any conventional sense. The reader of *Religio Laici*, for example, early encounters the image of 'enchanted ground,' invoked to describe the 'happiness' of certitude, which as Dry-den reckons it, fled the antique seekers of religious truth. Seven years before, Dryden's Prologue to his great heroic tragedy *Aureng-Zebe* had already conjured the image of enchanted ground, but there it had signalled aesthetic frustration, limning the realm of 'nature,' which evades any poet who permits himself – as Dryden of course did – to be fettered by rhyme. Within Dryden's work, in other words, the image of enchanted ground is itself enchanted ground, its connotations ever slip-ping from an aesthetic (and tragic) register to a philosophical and reli-gious (hence implicitly comic) one. Yet, this slippage is itself mar-vellously constant. For all its variability, Dryden's work is invariably engaged in a quest for political, artistic, religious, and even moral stabil-ity, and it is the tragicomic futility of this quest that in fact constitutes the voice we take to be enduringly his. This, we suppose, is the secret of his attraction for readers of the present day, and so in good conscience we borrow the figure of enchanted ground to describe the body of Dryden's work as a whole, both in itself and as that work is inevitably experienced by those who venture onto its capricious and beguiling terrain.

When we turn to the illustrious facts of Dryden's life – the facts celebrated by his contemporaries at his death – we find the aptness of this epithet confirmed, not least because of the singular, and inherently revisionary, range of Dryden's achievement. He had succeeded Sir William Davenant as Poet Laureate in 1668, and held that position for twenty years until politics dictated that he be replaced by his old enemy, Thomas Shadwell. By the time of his death, he had written some twenty-eight works for the stage – comedies, tragedies, heroic plays, masques, and operas – which made him a dominant force in the drama of the period. Although there had been important critical statements before he published his essays and prefaces, he left a body of literary criticism, written in his wonderful prose style, that made criticism into both a personal statement and an art form. And then there was the poetry. He was never a sublime poet in the grand style of John Milton, but as T.S. Eliot was to remark, Dryden was the first poet who made English poetry speak in ordinary speech.[3] This in itself is a potent legacy, and it allows us to regard Dryden as the first truly modern poet, even as his heroic preoccupations and moral idealism link him to the classical past.

In addition to being Poet Laureate, Dryden also held the office of Historiographer Royal, and in that position wrote political pamphlets in defence of the government and translated one major historical work from the French. He had read and, what is more important, he had thought more deeply about history, politics, theology, and literature than all but a few of his contemporaries. Only John Milton and Andrew Marvell, with both of whom he had worked in the same office during the Interregnum, might have been his match, but Milton died in 1674 and Marvell four years later. Dryden's learning was sometimes a point of complaint. Critics mocked Dryden's allegorical poem *The Hind and the Panther* (1687), Jonathan Swift deriding it as 'intended for a complete abstract of sixteen thousand schoolmen, from Scotus to Bellarmine.'[4] After Dryden's death Daniel Kenrick defended him against a contemporary poet who opined that, so far as he was concerned, had other English poets read all the books that Dryden had read, 'he saw no reason but that their verse might be as good.'[5] As Kenrick maintained, what was important was not that Dryden was so learned, but that he had so entirely transmuted the substance of his learning into the brilliant shadow of poetry.

Of course, Dryden's critics hardly needed any particular grounds to attack him. In the popular imagination he was strongly identified with

Bayes, the clumsy, foolish, but oddly fascinating playwright and poet of Buckingham's *The Rehearsal* (1671), and through this transformation he came to represent the very concept of the poet for the period.[6] For many, from the members of the Rota group early on in his career to Jeremy Collier at the end of the century, Dryden was an object of satire, and in these battles he gave better than he received, creating, in his verbal assault upon the comic playwright Thomas Shadwell, *Mac Flecknoe*, the wittiest and one of the wisest commentaries on the pretensions of the artist and bad art ever written. And Dryden was not only responsible for the most deft satire of his time; he also 'Englished' the Roman satirists, then converted his poetic insights into satire in an unforgettable essay on the form. Even so, by the end of the seventeenth century, those the satire had left cold could enjoy the wonderful narrative poems of his late *Fables*, where metamorphosis doubles as theme and poetic method.

Dryden's unusual combination of intellectual range and stylistic versatility easily accounts for the great influence he exerted on Alexander Pope in the eighteenth century, on John Keats in the nineteenth, and on T.S. Eliot in the twentieth. Closer to his own day, it led George Farquhar to deem his writing uneven; Samuel Johnson gave the same opinion, but he nevertheless – and perhaps for this very reason – found Dryden a greater poet than Pope. 'His works abound with knowledge, and sparkle with illustrations,' wrote Johnson. 'There is scarcely any science or faculty that does not supply him with occasional images and lucky similitudes; every page discovers a mind very widely acquainted both with art and nature, and in full possession of great stores of intellectual wealth.'[7] That he deserves such homage and revaluation there can be no doubt. Dryden could be daring; he could be emotional; he was witty in an age that treasured wit; he had a great gift for new and revealing images; but most of all, he could write a poetry that asked his readers to respond emotionally to ideas. Although not a few efforts have been made to disparage his status within the past decades,[8] the editors of *Enchanted Ground* are convinced that each generation will discover new aspects of John Dryden's writings to admire, and it was in this conviction that we invited the contributors to this volume to examine and reconsider a variety of ways in which Dryden will remain a living and powerful literary force in our new century.

Since Dryden was a public poet commenting on matters of national concern even before he became Poet Laureate to the monarchies of Charles II and James II, we have divided the essays that make up *En-*

chanted Ground into two sections, the first involving politics and society, and the second treating problems of aesthetics in the various forms (poems, plays, songs) to which Dryden turned his talents throughout his long career. We have done so in the full understanding that Dryden was always an artist, even in the writings he produced slavishly at the behest of his superiors, and that he was always the subtle social and political thinker even in what might at first appear to be a simple lyric, fable, or translation. His indefatigably engaged intelligence could hardly escape either intellectual or artistic involvement with the explosive changes of his time. In turn, this involvement helped to generate the kinetic multiplicity of voices, creeds, attitudes, and practices that in some sense *is* Dryden and that, at the very least, has kept him an object of enchantment down to the present day.

Part I: Enchanted Ground: Dryden, Politics, and Society

In his position as Historiographer Royal after 1668, Dryden became the official apologist for the Stuarts in all matters of politics. During this time, famously or infamously, he published two religious confessions: *Religio Laici* in 1682 and *The Hind and the Panther* in 1687. Composed on the perilous cusp of private conviction and public statement, these two poems embrace two very different creeds, the former Anglican and the latter Roman Catholic. Though they straddle Dryden's conversion to Rome, they have come to stand not for the poet's spiritual growth but instead for his ability to entertain multiple truths and perspectives. This is not only a religious and philosophical feat but a social and political one as well, and if it is exemplified in the diametrical differences between the two poems, it is also anticipated in *Religio Laici* itself, whose earliest lines invoke the image of 'enchanted ground' to describe the chimerical path inevitably trodden by ancient seekers of truth.

As the political dimensions of his poetry reveal, Dryden himself was more ancient than modern in this respect. His social and political writing proved ground every bit as enchanted as the 'happiness' that eluded the pagan pursuers of 'supernatural light,' the 'happiness' of certainty ever shifting into new mirages as convincing as the ones they replaced. In exploring Dryden's relationship to politics and society, the first eight essays in this collection themselves pursue the phantasms of conviction, and as a result they sometimes conflict with one another. As Laureate and Historiographer Royal, Dryden was almost always forced to take sides. Yet even in poems as committed as *The Hind and the Panther* he seems to have found truth – and therefore certainty – elusive.[9] Whereas a contemporary like Milton shifted emphasis from the formerly integrated and ideal body of truth to the worldly labour of piecing it together again, Dryden preferred the dialogic juxtaposition of multiple internally coherent truths. This is the system at work in critical pieces like his *Essay of Dramatick Poesie* (1665–7), whose rhetoric works not by the assertion of a single truth (or even, as Milton had, a single truth about truth), but rather through the performance of multiple propositions. This peculiar alchemy is both an internal feature of individual works and the composite effect of many of Dryden's works taken together, and it is the signal characteristic of his social and political expression. Hence, insofar as the authors of these essays focus upon individual poems, plays, or critical statements, they are inclined to disagree with one another. Yet, from the perspective, dramatic and argumentative, that Dryden built over the course of his literary career, each speaks a truth.

The first essay with the title 'John Dryden and Politics' appeared at the end of the nineteenth century.[10] Dismissing the uncritical approval of Edmond Malone and the attempts at historical impartiality of Sir Walter Scott, its author, Alexander Beljame, attacked Dryden as a despicable example of the writer's subservience to his superiors. Both Dryden and his contemporary critics were caught up in a dialectic of ideologies that have, to a certain extent, collapsed, at least as doctrinaire possibilities in our modern world. As an observer of his time, Dryden could have seen the emergence of the ideological conflicts that were to dominate the following centuries. In sects such as the Levellers and the Diggers, he could have observed the possibilities of political and economic egalitarian movements, and with the emergence of Louis XIV's France, a powerful, absolute monarchy that seemed to offer ascendancy in both the cultural and military spheres. In the philosophies of Thomas Hobbes, James Harrington, and, eventually, John Locke, he could have seen the formation of the varieties of theoretical positions that were to dominate English politics. And in the contemporary accounts of the brief reign of the fisherman, Tomasso Masaniello, in Naples during 1647, he would have been able to learn of the terrifying spectre of complete anarchy.[11] Indeed, the middle and close of the seventeenth century was a time of such intellectual ferment that, towards the end of the period, Jonathan Swift could find in the whirl of contemporary ideas the whiff of insanity. This, in turn, led him to the ironic proposal of urg-ing the employment of the insane as citizens who would be capable of making valuable contributions to the society.

The essays in this volume tend rightly to avoid easy solutions to questions about Dryden's beliefs, preferring 'thick descriptions' of Dryden's milieu and complex readings of Dryden's arguments. A relatively short time ago, close examinations of Dryden's writings during the period following the Glorious Revolution of 1688 led to the surprising realization that Dryden carried his Jacobite sympathies further than had previously been thought. Today, in studies such as Paul Hammond's *Dryden and the Traces of Classical Rome*, it is clear that, even in his most speculative pieces in poetry and prose, Dryden did not foresee any easy solutions for the English political establishment – that is, a simple restoration of James II to the throne or a reinstitution of the policies that brought about his removal.[12] But it is difficult to know whether one must seek the 'real' Dryden in his early period, when, as Richard Kroll suggests in this volume, following Sir William Davenant, he was upholding high ideals of heroic virtue, or in his later years, when he was throwing out suggestions about the excellence of republics and searching for a concept of the perfect Member of Parliament.

Perhaps the search for Dryden's 'real' political stance is misplaced. Because he loved the excitement of ideas and, as Samuel Johnson suggested, they inspired his best writing, Dryden seemed most comfortable when he was playing one idea against another, utilizing the sceptical method of which he and his age was so fond. He filled his heroic plays with debates about virtue, self-interest, and the nature of the state. He was a brilliant satirist, but it is not certain that the kind of moral certitude required of the satirist was his most comfortable stance as a writer.[13] As has been suggested, the four-way debate of his *Essay of Dramatick Poesie* was surely more natural to him than the dogmatism and the single-minded certainty of which he complained in his remarks on translating Lucretius.

Dryden's view of politics and society was inevitably conditioned by his conception of history (which, for the most part, as Michael McKeon has shown, tended to draw upon cyclic imagery whatever doubts he may have about the possibility of complete restorations)[14] and morality. At the same time, the growing tendency in the age towards a progressive theory of history had to form one of those 'inner dialogues' that spurred Dryden's mental processess.[15] He continued to believe that a right view of history could teach and carry conviction. 'All History,' he

wrote in his 'Life of Plutarch' (1683), 'is only the precepts of Moral Philosophy reduc'd into Examples: *Moral Philosophy* is divided into two
parts, *Ethicks* and *Politicks*; the first instructs us in our private offices of
virtue; the second in those which relate to the management of the Com-
mon-wealth.'[16] One of the key words in this passage is 'examples,' for
Dryden functioned as an artist and a thinker on the premise that past
examples will always provide us with ways of behaving in the present and
for the future. The conviction that there was a continuity between past
and future and that it could be shaped by example gave to Dryden's
writing an immediacy which we have lost in the modern period, yet
there was also something frantic in the way in which this method of
thinking (it was closer to an emotional way of apprehending experience) was being tested constantly by the events of Dryden's time. It
was not only the Popish Plot that stirred an atmosphere of hysteria; in
Dryden's own 'Dedication' to the *History of the League* (1684), his attitude towards contemporary politics shows similar signs of becoming un-
glued.[17] Having popularized the 'parallel' poem in *Absalom and Achitophel*, which, typically enough for Dryden, linked past and present, he
seemed genuinely disturbed that the Whigs could come up with historical examples that were equally compelling. Though, in the years after
the Glorious Revolution, he depicted William III as a usurping tyrant,
the departure of James II for the Continent, despite all the disillusion-
ment it caused him, was certainly a boon to his creativity as a thinker on
moral, political, and historical themes.

Perhaps it is too hard on Dryden to demand some of the historical
insights that three centuries of hindsight have produced. It should be
enough to have what he has given us – brilliant writings that are the
product of his intellectual and artistic engagement with his times. He
thought as a poet, and politics might easily be conceived as part of the
'enchanted ground' in which he placed his allegorical figures in *Albion
and Albanius*. He lived through a civil war, the beheading of a monarch,
the successful reign of the leader of the rebellion, the restoration of a
monarch, two rebellions against his successor (the first a failure and the
second a success) and he ended his life as a kind of exile within his own
country, professing a religion that aroused hatred in the majority of
Englishmen and espousing political convictions that to all but the small
number of defenders of an exiled royal family appeared to be a lost
cause. Such a brief outline of the politics of the Interregnum and Restoration not only omits many of the major political crises through which
Dryden lived but also does not touch at all upon the social and intellec-

tual ferment of the time – matters that tend to interest us far more than the dynastic changes of the period. What were people thinking and feeling? What was happening in the culture? If England was to emerge as the great commercial power of the world after the decline of Holland, how did all the new, imported luxury goods influence the ways in which people saw their world? And how were poetry and drama reflecting such matters?

In the first essay in this collection, 'Dryden and the Consumption of History,' Margery Kingsley focuses on Dryden's most vituperative satire, *The Medall* (1682), by way of discussing his attitude towards the culture of the Restoration. After briefly considering the poem as history in the manner of Dryden's *Absalom and Achitophel*, she turns to the problem of the particular medal that is the subject of Dryden's poem. During the Restoration, the study of coins and medals was given a new status. Such objects possessed a permanence that written histories lacked, and it was argued at the time that the study of Greek and Roman coins could provide a better insight into ancient culture. Under such circumstances, the medal commemorating the first earl of Shaftesbury and the jury that, despite all the pressure from the court, refused to find him guilty of treason appeared, in Dryden's eyes, to represent a falsification of true history.

Kingsley then demonstrates Dryden's anxiety about the ways in which the artefacts and material goods produced by a commercial society may control the historical record. The medal is viewed by Dryden as the worthless product of an artisan culture, and as Kingsley demonstrates, Restoration England produced all kinds of transgressive artefacts – cheap pottery depicting the monarch, playing cards illustrating the events of the Popish Plot – all of which had the potential to destabilize the meaning of history and politics. In contemporary satires, Shaftesbury, who died in Holland not long after he fled England, was seen as continuing to spread infection through his rotting body, and Dryden reveals a similar fear of the contagion of Whig ideas. But as Kingsley suggests, in his prophecy of future strife, Dryden seems to accept the inevitability of an England, exhausted by the conflict of ideas and cultures, settling into a political situation that will have to accept debate and uncertainty as part of the political scene.

Leo Braudy's 'Dryden, Marvell, and the Design of Political Poetry' considers the entire range of Restoration politics in a contrast between the two great political poets of the Restoration, John Dryden and Andrew Marvell. In his view of the history and politics behind the two poets,

Braudy attempts to refute the arguments of the historian Lawrence Stone, who claimed that nothing very permanent happened with the revolutions of 1642 and 1688 because the machinery that saw the triumph of the parliamentary system during the nineteenth century was not yet in place. Braudy finds this excessively sceptical. If the party system that governed Parliament from the nineteenth century until our time was not in place, there was nevertheless a cultural awareness of what was happening. Everyone knew that the beheading of Charles I in 1649 changed the face of politics in England forever, and Parliament knew that it had created a king with the Convention Parliament in 1689. Both Marvell and Dryden played significant but very different roles in creating this cultural awareness.

Braudy contrasts Marvell's critical intelligence with Dryden's tendency to see a design and a spiritual force behind events. Both were interested in the nature of the state, but each viewed it differently. Examining their poems to Cromwell, Braudy points to Marvell's view of Cromwell from the standpoint of character and the historical moment, in contrast to Dryden's examination of design and signs in Cromwell's rise to power. Dryden looks to the past for historical models by which to view the monarchy of Charles II, and so becomes the propagandist for what he conceives as an ideal state; he believes that fallen nature can be restored. Marvell, the brilliant critic of Charles II and his monarchy, creates a fallen pastoral world that might be partially redeemed by some form of democracy.

In her essay 'Dryden and Dissent,' Sharon Achinstein turns to problems of violence and agression, which she sees throughout Dryden's poetry but most particularly in *The Hind and the Panther* with its Fable of the Swallows and Fable of the Pigeons. She focuses on Dryden's attitude towards the Dissenters in the society of the Restoration, those who refused to accept the doctrines of the Church of England and suffered various kinds of legal punishments, including imprisonment and death. Although James II attempted to win the Dissenters over to his side by his Declaration of Indulgence in 1687, many remained suspicious of James's motives and refused to associate themselves with his attack upon the power of the Church of England. Achinstein demonstrates Dryden's continuing antipathy towards the Dissenters and his subtle critique of James's policies.

Pointing to various passages that are critical of both the Dissenters and the Church of England in *The Hind and the Panther*, Achinstein underscores the images of violence and predation, and the debates over transubstantiation that involved accusations of cannibalism – all of which she defines as 'food issues.' What lay behind this, for Dryden, was a fear of the ways in which religion and the Bible were taken over by each Dissenter in 'a nightmare of unbounded consumption.' Achinstein explores various types of images arising out of the economics of consumption in the period as Dryden encountered them, from concepts of the fungibility of money to Locke's notion of the self as a form of property, concluding that Dryden was engaged in managing the social trauma that dominated the period.

Like Achinstein's piece, Michael McKeon's essay, 'The Politics of Pastoral Retreat: Dryden's Poem to His Cousin,' is a wide-ranging consideration of politics, but this time the focus is on a poem included in *Fables Ancient and Modern*, published in the year of the poet's death. Since 'To My Honour'd Kinsman' comes so late in Dryden's career as a writer of political poetry, it has the advantage of allowing an overview of all that came before. McKeon treats the work as a pastoral as well as a kind of fable and allegory. Although the poem shifts from the private to the public about halfway through, McKeon attempts to show how it gathers force by a process of 'spatial thickening' that functions to recapitulate Dryden's engagement with the political history of the period.

Through an insightful close reading of the poem against the politics of England following the Treaty of Ryswick (1697), which ended nine years of war with France, McKeon shows convincingly how Dryden turned to Parliament as the force that would oppose the standing army that ambitious monarchs always treasured. Instead of a direct attack upon William III, Dryden chooses to recall his family's opposition to Charles I at the beginning of the seventeenth century. Through this excursion into history, Dryden attempts to define the function of Parliament and does so in a way very different from his pro-monarchical stance at the time of the Exclusion crisis twenty years before. Now, just a few years before his death, Dryden extols the power of Parliament and, as McKeon argues, seems to foresee the eventual triumph of Parliament as the seat of future power.

No less about politics but different in approach is David Haley's 'Dryden's Emergence as a Political Satirist.' This essay traces the steps by which Dryden, who was thought of by contemporaries as a brilliant dramatist and a daring and innovative poet but not particularly partisan, transformed himself into the most powerful and witty poetic spokesman for the court party and the most savage adversary of the opposition forces led by the first earl of Shaftesbury. Haley examines Dryden's life and attitudes for clues to this transformation. He sees Dryden not as the time-serving minion of the court whom Beljame treated with such contempt, but as a writer struggling to find his own attitudes at a time of flux. He also argues that the true beginning of Dryden's satiric poetry came with the Prologue to *The Loyal General* in 1679.

Haley views Dryden as something of an outcast within the milieu where he had cast his lot. Perhaps because he had once been a supporter of Cromwell or perhaps because of a certain shyness in his character, the great court poets John Wilmot, second earl of Rochester, and Sir Charles Sedley never accepted him, despite his position as Poet Laureate. And, indeed, Dryden never quite fit in. His image of continuity in government was shattered by the removal of Clarendon in 1667, and for someone who was supposed to uphold the establishment of both church and state, Dryden showed an intense dislike of the Anglican clergy. But Dryden had always believed in the moral basis of art, and his turn to political satire was part of his adherence to this belief. If his satiric genius may have pleased the court and made him more acceptable, Dryden was actually an artist and thinker undergoing a process of evolution. It is not certain that the same court would have entirely appreciated his eventual turn to religious themes.

In 'The Political Economy of *All for Love*,' Richard Kroll discusses Dryden's play in terms of a lost concept of a world of high heroism. Looking back to the writings of Sir William Davenant, Dryden's predecessor in the Laureateship and a collaborator with Dryden in the adaptation of Shakespeare's *The Tempest* to the Restoration stage, Kroll argues a self-consciousness about such a world. Davenant passed on to Dryden a concept of drama that was at once highly political and yet sceptical about the possibilities of achieving successful political resolutions. The audience experienced dramatic works in which ideals of loyalty to the sovereign and morality were undercut by doubts about the nature of power.

Kroll argues that *All for Love,* Dryden's play about the final hours of Antony and Cleopatra, partakes of many of these aspects of Davenant's drama of uncertain political power and that it is staged with a sense of nostalgia. The world of the present is 'Well Lost' (as the subtitle suggests) because the new world of commercial enterprise has already made the heroic world obsolete, hence the static quality of the play with its visual imagery and tableaux. Octavius, who is made to represent the new world of buying and selling, is entirely absent from Dryden's play, and what the audience is given is a tragedy highly conscious of its status as a play. In a wonderful image, Kroll suggests that it is as if Dryden's

Antony and Cleopatra were marooned in a world still on the gold standard, a past of golden dreams of love and friendship to be replaced by a new milieu of credit and paper money. In some sense, at the end, when Cleopatra arranges herself and the already dead Antony so that they seem to be alive as ideal monarchs, they are acting in a play for which there is no functioning audience. Kroll sees the very language of the play as contributing to a lack of present action. The love of Antony and Cleopatra drives the play forward, but from the very start these characters appear to belong to history.

At first glance Susan Staves's coupling of John Dryden and Edward Gibbon in 'Wit, Politics, and Religion' might seem strangely arbitrary. Certainly, the translator of Virgil and other poets writing in Latin was deeply involved in the classical past, but his interests were a far cry from those of the author of *The Decline and Fall of the Roman Empire*. But Staves is mainly interested in the somewhat odd combination of wit and religious thought that appears in both writers. It should be said at once that Staves's Gibbon is far from the 'notorious infidel' whom Boswell identified with a satanic hatred of religion.[18] Instead we are presented with a writer of a witty turn of mind who was nevertheless deeply interested in religion itself and the actions of the early Church. Both, she suggests, were fascinated by theology, and although Gibbon turned around on his youthful conversion to Catholicism after a period of what we would call reprograming, he remained a practising Christian. She picks up Dryden at a time when he was defending the Catholic Church and delivering not-so-subtle attacks upon both the Church of England and the Dissenters in *The Hind and the Panther*, and Gibbon in his treatment of two crucial moments in the history of the Church: Constantine's declaration favouring Christianity in the fourth century and the conversion of the various tribes in eastern Europe.

Both have in common the theme of problematic conversions, for despite James II's presentation of his Declaration of Indulgence as an act of toleration, the majority of Englishmen, both the followers of the Church of England and the Dissenters, viewed James's action as an effort to convert the nation to Catholicism. Approaching these moments of crisis from a modern and a contemporary perspective, Staves discovers a number of ironic parallels. Gibbon depicted a situation in the Roman Empire that saw the Latin Church accept the Nicene Creed, which rejected what became the Arian heresy – the belief that Jesus was not of the same substance with God the Father. In *The Hind and the Panther*, Dryden has the Hind (the Catholic Church) accuse the

Panther (the Church of England) of reviving the Arian heresy. In turn, the Church of England ridiculed various doctrines of the Catholic Church as violations of the First Commandment and even, as Achinstein also suggests, as a form of cannibalism. Although both Dryden and Gibbon took these controversies seriously, they approached them with wit and humour, using a tone of argument that was common enough in religious dispute yet suspect both then and now. If Gibbon refrained from using anything so witty as Dryden's beast fable, he cannot help but find some aspects of Catholicism absurd and exploits an overarching irony in treating the fact that the barbaric tribes had, by seeming 'accident,' been converted to a Christianity that had the Arian heresy as a tenet of its faith. In her conclusion, Staves, with considerable wit of her own, weighs the entire problem of the difficult mixture of wit and religion.

In its scepticism, the final essay in this section, Steven Zwicker's 'How Many Religions Did John Dryden Have?' stands in contrast to Staves's discussion. Whereas Staves demonstrates the fascination for religion during the age in even so vilified a figure as Gibbon, Zwicker finds echoes of other voices, particularly that of Robert Boyle, in what is supposed to be so confessional a poem as Dryden's *Religio Laici*. As Zwicker demonstrates, Dryden's contemporaries were aware of his borrowings and found it a cause for suspicion that the author of such a salacious play as *Mr. Limberham* and the purveyor of such sharp anticlericism in *Absalom and Achitophel* should suddenly emerge as a commentator on religious subjects.

Zwicker shares the suspicions of a number of Dryden's contemporaries, raising questions about his many borrowings. Looking behind Dryden's indebtedness to the arguments of Boyle, Stillingfleet, and John Tillotson, he asks whether the use of voices other than his own does not suggest certain contradictions behind Dryden's attempts at a spiritual stance. Where Dryden seems most comfortable in his *Religio Laici* is in the vehemence of his attack upon the sects of Nonconformity; where he seems least at ease is in speaking of his own beliefs. While trying to gain the 'enchanted ground,' the supernatural authority, as well as the respectability, of religion, Dryden, Zwicker argues, was pushing the political agenda of the Stuarts. After the Glorious Revolution, he was only too happy to return to the anticlericism of his earlier writings.

Part II: The Grounds of Enchantment: Dryden and the Arts

The baroque arts, in England and elsewhere, were happily black. In pursuit of unholy power, they compelled stunned 'admiration' and arrested time into a tableau, transforming spirit into substance, incoherence into form. The essays in the second half of this collection ask how Dryden's literary art trafficked with its visual and musical counterparts in the second half of the seventeenth century; they thus, perforce, look into the grounds of enchantment common to all of the expressive and rhetorical practices of that era. And not only of that era. Remarkably, the authors of these essays often find *themselves* on enchanted ground, their professional scepticism detained in dialogue with some of the more baffling and seductive, if timely, tricks of Dryden's trade.

It was, as we have already noted, in his prologue to *Aureng-Zebe* that Dryden first summoned the figure of enchanted ground. This, he supposed, is what 'nature' must be for the poet who attempts to capture it in the 'fetters' of rhyme, and he repudiated those fetters accordingly. He did so, however, in perfect iambic couplets, the form that persists through *Aureng-Zebe* and on through the decades, and so his verse performs the aesthetic problem at issue within it. In the preface to *Aureng-Zebe*, Dryden traces such paradoxes to history; 'betwixt two ages cast,' neither ancient nor modern, the poet has no choice but to malinger on enchanted ground, and this perception shadows the second half of this collection, as in fact does *Aureng-Zebe* itself. As many of our contributors discover, such paradoxes are the ironic essence of Dryden's poetic and conceptual coherence, and managing them became the precondition of his art. Again and again, provocative self-contradiction is deemed central to Dryden's vision, and is seen to organize, if not motivate, his transactions with other representational modes. Nor do such tensions merely animate Dryden's language. Here a dynamic, centripetal, and magically affirmative doubt turns out to be deeply characteristic of the artist himself, apparent in everything from his regenerative ambivalence to the literary past to the constitutive ambiguities of his eroticism. Not, however, content to probe the mysterious core of Dryden's art, our contributors also measure that art's periphery, tracing its extraordinary porosity sometimes to his often enigmatic collaborations with other artists, past and present, and sometimes to the mystical sisterhoods he sealed between the literary, dramatic, visual, and musical arts.

As they chart the enchanted ground that gave rise to works from *Aureng-Zebe* to *Alexander's Feast*, the authors of these last seven essays find it difficult to explain Dryden within an entirely rational model of literary history. They foreground the eerie suspensions of time we encounter in his poetry and plays and even in his prose, the supernatural potential buried in his techniques of spatial embodiment, his mysteriously vital affinities with other authors. Consequently, while previous

generations of critics have tended to refer Dryden's art to specific, presumably unrepeatable and untranscendable political and historical situations, our contributors sometimes employ unorthodox tools to gauge
the forces of attraction and influence at play in all his work. Whether it
is by invoking the vocabularies of unconscious abjection and sexual stu-
pefaction or by conceding the preternatural efficacy of music, our
authors mix spiritual, psychological, and emotional apprehensions of
Dryden's achievement with traditional methods of historical analysis.

One recurrent theme in these essays, for instance, is the infamous
instability of Dryden's authorial identity. His voice was always an enclitic
one, ever stimulated by, or attached to, someone else's. Conspicuous
in everything from occasional poetry through dramatic reworkings of
Shakespeare to the late translations, Dryden's shape-shifting has been
variously interpreted as a vestigial form of postmodernism, as a political
strategy, and as the artefact of a precarious juncture in literary and
national history. If, the story goes, we cannot find one unified and consistent Dryden even within a single poem or play – let alone across his
literary career – this may nonetheless be explained historically or bio-
graphically, or at the very least with recourse to practical paradigms of
cultural history. The essays here, however, seek other ways of interpret-
ing the internal conflicts into which Dryden seems to vanish, yet which
also keep him perennially present to us. Jennifer Brady, for instance,
finds Dryden's drama driven by the preconscious and prehistorical
urgency of sympathetic identification. Other contributors detect a similar urgency in Dryden's day-to-day involvement with his contemporaries.
Deborah Payne Fisk alludes to it in her study of Dryden's collaborations
with other theatre people, while James Winn and Dianne Dugaw do the
same in their studies of his long infatuation with contemporary music.
Meanwhile, those who focus on Dryden's relationships with his precursors are compelled to postulate a kind of wrinkle in historical time.
Brady thus suggests that Dryden's 1679 adaptation of Shakespeare's
Troilus and Cressida not only staged his own sense of belatedness to his
Jacobean predecessors but discovered that sense of belatedness already
present in them. Cedric Reverand II follows the game of literary *fort-da*
Dryden liked to play with precursors such as Shakespeare and Jonson
until the present could not be told from the past.

If Dryden's contemporary collaborations show him at his most secure
and accomplished, his negotiations with those who came before him
prove darker, more fraught and complex. But in either case, the effect
was to extend Dryden's own life, both synchronically and diachronically.

His authority is here understood as distributed in his own time, across a range of artistic activities, and projected backward through time, as his often paradoxical involvements with earlier writers revivify them and render Dryden a vital presence within his own, and England's, literary past. In Dryden's art we thus encounter not only the shades of the other arts of the Restoration but also the ghosts of his own predecessors, at once transfixed and animate. Finally, we encounter Dryden too, the composite of the many spectres aflicker throughout his work.

At least some of these effects may be attributed to the transitional character of Dryden's historical moment, which hosted endless colloquies between magic and science, sacred kingship and political contract, the semi-mystical modulations of the Caroline stage and the pragmatic clamour of a commercialized marketplace. Our essayists attend to these colloquies and show how they shaped Dryden's art, reinforcing its paradoxes and motivating intricate collaborations with the exploratory forms of painting and music. But of more interest than historical and cultural mandates are the singularly beguiling symbolic strategies Dryden devised in response to them; these, like visual images and musical notes, purport to travel back and forth between the material and immaterial worlds. Dugaw thus underscores the ways in which the words of Dryden's songs call on the finally 'suprarational' powers of music to realize their epistemological directives, while Blair Hoxby shows how plays like *Aureng-Zebe* mysteriously transform speech into the visible gestures of baroque fresco. James Winn's discussion of Dryden's songs merges with those very songs; hence, a compact disc accompanies his contribution to this collection, transmuting critical discourse into actual melody in a process that mimics the one at work in Dryden's own poetry. In James Grantham Turner's analysis of Dryden's mixed attitudes towards the fleshly charms, we find the eroticism of language inseparably fused with that of the author (and, ultimately, with that of the reader), so that words themselves become volatile atoms in a fiery fantasia that steadily consumes itself, only to be reborn into its own parodic opposite. Indeed, the hybrid symbolic forms that Dryden devised are here often seen as inherently self-reflexive. Besides verging on emotion, sensation, and dream, they produce complex figures of self-reference that, while they seem to suspend action, are also magically dynamic. Hoxby thus delineates Dryden's theatre as one whose topic – and topos – is its own illusion; Reverand and Brady show how his translations and revisions of earlier poets and dramatists are equally transfigurations of the modern author himself.

Under the late Stuart kings, of course, magic also made for potent political metaphor, and the arts of the English Restoration remain fundamentally political ones. Consequently, the reflexivity that characterizes Dryden's art is never autotelic or self-enclosing; it is as much a dynamic refraction of the power struggles within the human arena as it is a commentary upon its own procedures. Because its concern, as Hoxby points out, is ultimately with the production and reproduction of culture, Dryden's baroque art is finally an art less of reference (self- or otherwise) than of referendum. Its concerns are fundamentally communal and its significances are incessantly ironized through their exposure to the other systems of meaning with which they knowingly share place. In other words, here – as in the critical heritage *Enchanted Ground* extends – Dryden's art remains a profoundly and instructively ethical one. Its interesting incoherence is both the sign and the source of an awareness of otherness, both in the other and in the artist himself.

Nevertheless, the otherness so central to Dryden's poetry, plays, and prose is also sometimes a property of the 'things above us' that Dryden first invoked in 1677.[19] The essays in the second half of this collection respect the sway held by such 'things.' Many of them capture Dryden's ambivalence towards certain transcendental forms of otherness, be they dead fathers like Shakespeare or the celestial spirit of music. Yet this very ambivalence is what has guaranteed Dryden's own afterlife for centuries of readers: it is his dialogues with alternative – non-linguistic and irrational – realms of meaning, not his submission to them, that has kept him interesting, and hence vitally present to us.

Brady's 'Anxious Comparisons in John Dryden's *Troilus and Cressida*' paints a nuanced portrait of Dryden's vexed relationship to the English literary past, as registered in his 1679 rewriting of Shakespeare's play. Brady sees Dryden's bond with the notionally superior Jacobeans as a 'depressive' one – so much so that it is best interpreted by means of Freud's famous essay 'Mourning and Melancholia,' a work that captures the surprising affinity for melancholy and moral criticism, satire and abjection, we also find in Dryden's revision of *Troilus and Cressida.* Freud's subject was, of course, Shakespeare's Hamlet, whose purgatorial wanderings in his own psyche delineate deeply human problems of attachment. But Dryden's transformation of a more obscure script also discloses the dynamics of melancholy, this time on a historical axis that intersects with the psychological one. In Brady's view, this under-read (and under-appreciated) treatment of the understudies of the Trojan Wars inherits the very anxieties about succession and inferiority that ought to be its own, and the result is a constant deferral of authorial melancholy. Consequently, within the play itself conflicts of individuation are resolved not through Oedipal assertion but rather via what Brady deems 'pre-Oedipal' expressivity, registered most vividly in Dryden's feminization of the traditionally paternalistic Hector. Brady takes note of the rather shocking appearance of Shakespeare's ghost upon the stage to seal a system of melancholic ideation whose structure actually suspends the very laws of temporal descent that torment it.

Brady summarizes this suspended space with a line from *Aureng-Zebe* that often appears in this collection: 'betwixt two Ages cast.' For Brady, Dryden's place betwixt two ages both irritates and impels him, prompting him at last to barter one version of history for another. Dryden's 'fears about succession,' so easily and customarily referenced to the Stuart predicament, are here both stimulated and resolved within an ultimately supernatural literary history, and this opens them up to psychological analysis. In shifting the frame of that analysis from the Oedipal to the pre-Oedipal, Brady gains access to some of the unconscious patterns within the arts of the Restoration – their status as a state of mind. At the same time, she captures Dryden's own participation in a literary history understood less as a series of ages than as a hall of mirrors that infinitely repeats the ghostly contents of a less-than-conscious mind.

A similar vision informs Reverand's 'Dryden and the Canon: Absorbing and Rejecting the Burden of the Past.' As Reverand's title implies, Dryden's art is at once intimate with and alienated from the literature that embodies and represents the past. For Dryden, consequently, the past is better understood in spatial terms than in temporal ones – as, for example, a 'literary estate' inherently susceptible to improvement. While Reverand's Dryden is on the whole less fretful than Brady's, he is no less involved with his own predecessors, sometimes retaining and relinquishing them in the same literary gesture, or devising new genres like the rhymed heroic plays with the double intention of creating a new form for himself and insisting on that form's ancient provenance. However contradictory such gestures and formal innovations might appear, Reverand sees them as simultaneous rather than alternating. They are instances of the ambivalence that animates Dryden's art, and they mark its unique polytemporality, its eerie capacity to inhabit more than one moment in time. The result is a literary career best charted via a kind of critical geography, as opposed to, say, a critical historiography. It is as such a geography that Reverand proposes analysing Dryden's own theory of contemporary literary practice in light of how that practice turned out. This is not to say that the particular qualities of Dryden's historical moment can be ignored; on the contrary, Reverand sees the Restoration theatre's revivalist bent as a key source of the ambiguity between present and past that Dryden exploited. Reverand's own discussion moves chronologically across Dryden's theoretical statements about his forerunners, but the double thrust of his art – retrospective and prospective – is here seen to have lasted over decades.

Both Fisk's study of the practical associations that shaped Dryden's career as a playwright and Blair Hoxby's essay arrive at strikingly similar visions of his suspense between two different moments in the history of drama – pre–Civil War theatre and its Restoration successor. In '"Betwixt two Ages cast": Theatrical Dryden,' Fisk uses Dryden's negotiations with musicians, actors, and other playwrights to reveal some of the fault lines within 'the marriage of the old and the new' that shapes plays from *Cleomenes* to *Amphytrion*. Fisk notices the peculiar sense in which Dryden's relatively advanced age at the time of the Restoration created a ghostly affinity with the Caroline playwrights and even with Shakespeare, one that shaded his pragmatic theatrical activities. She also reminds us that Dryden was a shareholder in the theatre, but even this practical and commercial role contributed to his uniquely suspended and dispersed authorial identity, fostering an exceptionally deep identification with other playwrights, actors, theater managers, and even stage designers. These identifications freed him to create a uniquely self-referential theatre not unlike the one Hoxby describes, in which 'stage technology' can be exploited 'if not to shape form, then at least to suggest metaphoric possibilities about the form itself.' The backward-bending infinity implicit in this mode of self-reference corresponds to that built into the trans-historical and collaborative aspects of Dryden's authorship.

The strange stasis we find in so much of Dryden's work is the subject of Hoxby's analysis of the dramaturgical practices (and innovations) that shape one of his most impressive tragedies, *Aureng-Zebe*. In 'Dryden's Baroque Dramaturgy: The Case of *Aureng-Zebe*,' Hoxby foregrounds the continuities between Dryden's play and a Continental baroque theatre smitten with the possibilities of extending the human body as far into space as possible, and thus devoted to a literalization of perspective, an epistemology of admiration, and a semiotics of exteriorized passion. Hoxby explores the rhetorical potential embedded in the baroque stage as actors and actresses 'freeze themselves momentarily into works of visual art' while the suspense of action provides the very fibre of that action.

With suspense at the centre of Dryden's art, we again find ourselves hovering outside time. As plays like *Aureng-Zebe* virtually personify this realm, a new didacticism emerges, one uniquely conscious of its own strategies of emotional solicitude and pretence, and thus devoted to a poetics of self-reference borrowed from architecture and the visual arts. *Aureng-Zebe* thus blends the physics of presentation with the metaphysics of self-conscious representation, and for the spectator this creates an experience more akin to walking through a building than to what we normally think of as a dramatic sequence. The result is a mode of cultural reproduction whose essence is memory, substitution, and performance – the elements of theatre itself. In turn, this understanding of Dryden's baroque dramaturgy not only produces a new reading of *Aureng-Zebe*; it also secures the play's transitional place in Dryden's own oeuvre, casting it as a work of equipoise that contains both past and future theatrical structures and practices in its processes of exteriorization and stasis, even as mind and voice materialize in an enveloping illusion of body.

Dryden collaborated not only with other theatre people but also with musicians, but his musical associations have long been overlooked in favour of his more visible negotiations with painting. Both Dugaw and Winn, however, revitalize our understanding of his language by exploring its affinities with its 'acknowledg'd Siste[r],' music, the least tangible of the baroque arts. Dugaw's essay, '"The ~~Rationall~~ Spirituall Part": Dryden and Purcell's Baroque *King Arthur*,' looks beyond the local conditions of Restoration theatre to identify Dryden with the Continental – and, significantly, the Catholic – baroque, in which music participates, but whose special qualities it also exemplifies. The 'pan-sensory, multimedia' nature of much of Dryden's own poetry and drama following his conversion to Rome reveals a striving towards the realm of spirit, away from text, reason, logic, and sequence and towards the associative sphere most closely approximated in and by music. The resulting referential structure is one that engages the senses to produce a world as immanent as it is material. Dugaw finds it most fully embodied – and examined – in *King Arthur*, Dryden's 1691 collaboration with Henry Purcell, where music turns out to be both actor and metaphor, an allegory of faith performed equally in the mind, body, and (most important) spirit of its auditor. Dryden's coinciding 'rhetorics of music and spectacle' summon a 'complex world of planed realities' not unlike the pictorial and architectural one of Hoxby's *Aureng-Zebe*. And when Dugaw goes so far as to call the consequent aesthetic 'sensuous and bi-gendered,' she invokes the pre-Oedipal resolutions of psychic trauma Brady tracks in *Troilus and Cressida*. At once approximated in Purcell's music and produced through that music's literal attachment to Dryden's language, this ultimately spiritual domain of converging realities reveals the sensibility of incarnation – of suspended disbelief and metaphysical guidance whose past and future are present all at once.

While more sceptical of Dryden's investment in music, Winn nonetheless also places that investment at the centre of his interpretation of Dryden's art. Like Dugaw, Winn looks away from the more obvious properties of baroque music (for example, its obsession with system) to the lyrical qualities critics have been slow to appreciate. 'Dryden's Songs' begins with the premise that Dryden's intimate knowledge of music organized much of his poetry. In turn, several vocal recordings accompany Winn's essay, inviting readers not merely to entertain its argument, but actually to experience it. In Winn's view, Dryden developed an analogical understanding of the relationship between words and music in response to the transitional nature of Restoration music, most particularly the late-seventeenth-century convergence of English song traditions with contemporary popular taste for the new. At the same time, the songs in Dryden's plays approach the condition of magic, conspiring – as, for instance, in *The Indian Queen* (1664) – to create a suspended and hypnotic state that can convey 'Aerial Spirits' both thematically and semiotically, moving the play itself farther and farther from the material world. While Dugaw's Dryden embraces this movement, and sees it as consistent with the invocation of the body (and bodily modes of representation) ever central to his art, Winn's Dryden is ultimately encumbered by it, as inclined to see music as a limitation as to exploit its possibilities. In the end, refusal to attribute profound significance to music, even scepticism about its monitory power, provides an ironic and self-questioning foundation for Dryden's literary practice. As dramatic and rhetorical as it is lyrical, the ensuing dialogue holds his art aloft from one end of his career to the other. For Winn it is apotheosized in *The State of Innocence*, where musical contrasts embody temptation at one and the same time that they embody resistance to it.

As Winn recognizes, Dryden's musicality was entwined with his eroticism, which has also tended to discourage critical attention over the last three centuries. In the final essay in this collection, Turner is determined to redress this wrong. '"Thy Lovers were all untrue": Sexual Overreaching in the Heroic Plays and *Alexander's Feast*' revisits several key texts in the Dryden canon to find his eroticism omnipresent but also ambivalent, a libidinal force that is at once imperious and repudiated, celebrated and ironized. For Turner, these dualities commingle at the heart of Dryden's art, culminating in the *Secular Masque*'s infamous expulsion of Venus. Equally the source of violence and creativity, veracity and fiction, Eros finds in Dryden a priest of two minds: thus, while works from the overblown *Conquest of Granada* to the wraithlike *Secular Masque* stage the 'cult of erotic sublimity' that flourished throughout the Restoration, Dryden is also compelled to convert the libidinal into the aesthetic, and to redouble the idiom of sexual heroism back upon his own verbal art.

Turner points out that these reflexes are not just a property of Dryden's work but also created a unique critical environment, occasioning an efflorescence of pornographic parodies even as they prompted other readers to embrace Dryden's eroticism. In either case, the boundary between Dryden's venereal paradigms and their unpredictable reception is erased, and this erasure is figured in works like the ubiquitous *Aureng-Zebe*. In Turner's estimation, this play's improbable fusion of Cartesian physiology and Lucretian epistemology creates a distinctive semiotic in which literal and metaphorical references are reversed, figures from Dryden's earlier poetry inverted, and satiric and celebratory orientations towards the 'erotic sublime' prove impossible to differentiate. In turn, this ambiguity bears directly on what we might call Dryden's literariness. Indeed, his style as both a writer and a reader of other writers enacts a drama of transgression that has powerful implications for an understanding of the entire 'literary system of the Restoration.' In this system, eroticism and criticism are intricately entwined; both the subject of criticism and its object experience the same vertiginous inversions and transpositions at the heart of erotic experience. It may be that such inversions are the secret of the near-mythic vitality celebrated in all of the essays that follow. They remain the ground of our enchantment three centuries after Dryden cast (and retracted) his final spell.

Notes

1 See James Winn, *John Dryden and His World* (New Haven: Yale University Press 1987), 512–13, and note 80, 627. See also the irreverent account by George Farquhar, *Works*, ed. Shirley Strum Kenny, 2 vols. (Oxford: Clarendon Press 1988), 1:358–9 and Ned (Edward) Ward, *The London Spy*, ed. Arthur Hayward (London: Cassell 1927), 296–300. Dryden's body was initially put in a hum-

ble grave and later disinterred at the request of the earl of Dorset. The William Andrews Clark Memorial Library has a manuscript listing the expenses paid for the funeral.

2 *The Nine Muses. Or Poems upon the Death of the Late Famous John Dryden* (London 1700).

3 *Selected Essays* (New York: Harcourt Brace 1942), 267–70.

4 *A Tale of a Tub*, in *The Prose Writings of Jonathan Swift*, ed. Herbert Davis, 14 vols (Oxford: Blackwell 1939–68), 1:41.

5 Daniel Kenrick ['On John Dryden'], William Andrews Clark Memorial Library, MS, K36M1, fol 1.

6 See, for example, John Dunton, *A Voyage Round the World* (London 1691), 1:154. 'Let's step up a little to Wits Coffe-house, and present our Service to mr. *Laureat* – that was – what in the same Religion for a whole three or four years together! indeed Mr. Bays 'tis unconsionable.' See also Hugh Macdonald, *John Dryden: A Bigliography of Early Editions and of Drydeniana* (Oxford: Clarendon Press 1939), 259–62.

7 'Life of Dryden,' in *Lives of the Poets*, ed. George Birkbeck Hill, 3 vols. (Oxford: Clarendon Press 1895), 1:417.

8 For a recent attack upon Dryden as a poet who lacked the human touch of a Shakesepare and whose excellence lay mainly in an ability to write an occasional good line, see Barbara Everett, 'Unwritten Masterpiece ... Dryden's Hamlet,' *London Review of Books* 23 (4 January 2001), 29–32. This essay is very much in the manner of F.R. Leavis in its insistence on imposing one standard of artistic taste on a writer who aimed at something entirely different.

9 For a recent attempt to interpret *The Hind and the Panther* in terms of commentaries on the *Canticles*, see Anne Barbeau Gardiner, *Ancient Faith and Modern Freedom in John Dryden's The Hind and the Panther* (Washington, D.C.: Catholic University Press of America 1998), passim. Although Gardiner has suggested new layers of meaning to the poem, it may be said that while she has added to our understanding of the complexity of the work, she has not succeeded in making it less ambiguous.

10 It first appeared in *Le Public et les Hommes de lettres en Angleterre au Dix-huitième Siècle* in 1881.

11 There was fear of a collapse into anarchy in England in 1659 through the 'Quaker menace,' but the famous example of such an event for readers in England and Europe would have been Masaniello's astonishing revolt of 1647 accompanied by widespread executions, including some members of the nobility. See Ronald Hutton, *The Restoration* (Oxford: Clarendon Press

1985), 52–4, and Rosario Villari, *The Revolt of Naples*, trans. James Newell and John Marino (London: Polity Press 1993), passim.

12 Paul Hammond, *Dryden and the Traces of Classical Rome* (Oxford: Clarendon Press 1999). See especially 222–3, where he finds that Dryden's translation of the *Aeneid* often offers a 'teasing interplay of similarity and difference between English and Roman history' and where he discovers 'complex and to some degree self-deconstructing' elements in Dryden's methods. On the other hand, Hammond (278) notes the frequent repetitions of variations of the word 'restore' in writings of 1697. The seeming contradictions may be seen as aspects of intellectual play in Hammond's Derridean interpretation of Dryden.

13 In his Dedication of *Plutarch's Lives* he complained of living in an age 'only fit for Satyr.' *The Works of John Dryden*, ed. E.N. Hooker, H.T. Swedenberg, Jr, et al., 20 vols. (Berkeley: University of California Press 1956–2000), 17:229 (hereafter cited as *California Dryden*).

14 See McKeon, *Politics and Poetry in Restoration England* (Cambridge: Harvard University Press 1975), 174–5, 237–41, 261–6. McKeon (19) quotes Earl Miner's observation that there were progressive elements within the larger system.

15 Hammond's phrase, *Dryden and the Traces of Classical Rome*, 285.

16 *California Dryden* 17:274.

17 Not satisfied with seeing endemic conspiracies among the Dissenters and those he considered to be republicans, Dryden seems to believe that the League functioned less as a parallel historical example than as a direct, seemingly compulsive, model for the actions of Shaftesbury and those involved in the Rye House Plot.

18 See James Boswell, *Laird of Auchinleck 1778–1782*, ed. Joseph Reed and Frederick Pottle (New York: McGraw Hill 1977), 144.

19 'The Author's Apology for Heroic Poetry and Poetic Licence.' *California Dryden* 12:95.

PART I

ENCHANTED GROUND

chapter one

Dryden and the Consumption of History

MARGERY KINGSLEY

Perhaps Dryden's most famous statement about history – it is certainly his most quoted – is the passage from his 'Life of Plutarch' in which he lays out his theory of historical parallel. History, he says, 'helps us to judge of what will happen by showing us the like revolutions of former times ... [because] nothing can come to pass, but some President of the like nature has already been produc'd.' Men and women can therefore 'apply examples, and by them foretell, that from the like Counsels will probably succeed the like events ... [a]nd thereby ... [we can] be instructed ... what to avoid and what to choose.'[1] Given the popularity of this example, it is not too surprising that most studies of Dryden and the past talk of Dryden's 'use' of history as a pedagogical and persuasive tool; his appropriation of earlier events and images and his colonization of earlier texts become at once a means of authorizing his own creative and polemical enterprises and a means of containing a past that, for the Restoration, often threatened to spill into the present in a most distressing way.[2] Like the curio cabinets that reduced the exotic places of the world to parlour decorations, the literary integration of the past into present text made it knowable and thus controllable, or so the argument goes.

Judged by those standards, *The Medall* is in many ways an unmitigated disaster. A poem that, in the view of Philip Harth and others, was intended to provide closure to the Exclusion crisis, it repeatedly descends to a vituperative name-calling that seems not so much to contain past conflict as it does to epitomize and incite the rhetoric of political violence. Parodying the medal struck by George Bower in 1682 to commemorate the earl of Shaftesbury's release from the Tower, Dryden's

piece first paints a vicious picture of Shaftesbury as a eunuch and hypo-
crite, then attacks the city of London for its support of the Whigs; moreover, it does so in terms that, far from providing closure or containment,
sparked a series of nasty rebuttals that, if anything, prolonged and pro-
tracted the debate. And for most serious Dryden scholars, the poem has
typically proved a bit of an embarrassment. Dryden's contemporary
Samuel Pordage was probably the first to discuss its so-called limitations,
describing it as a 'slovenlier Beast' than *Absalom and Achitophel*.[3] Since
then, critics have generally felt compelled to apologize for a poem that
by many accounts is crasser and more vulgar than Dryden somehow
ought to be, and the mandatory recounting of rumours that Charles II
might have had something to do with the writing of the poem always
seems to function in part as an excuse for the piece, implying that the
fault may not have been Dryden's alone. Most studies that deal with Dryden and the Exclusion crisis allot *The Medall* only a third of the space
devoted to *Absalom and Achitophel*, if in fact they deal with it at all. And if
they do discuss it, they often do so in the context of a reassuring reference to Dryden's theory of satire, implying that he did not really believe
in the harsh polemical style that the poem adopts.

It is, of course, possible to read *The Medall* as a shorter and less elegant version of *Absalom and Achitophel*. Like the earlier poem, after all,
The Medall is about history, and more specifically about succession –
about, that is, the transfer of political, ideological, and material inheritance from one generation to the next. Shaftesbury's medal, 'grav'd'
by the 'Arbitrary Crowd ... their Conquest to record,' is implicitly set
against a proper succession ('natural inheritance') represented by
James, duke of York; by engendering the Exclusion crisis, Dryden would
seem to argue, Shaftesbury has set himself up as a fraudulent monarch
threatening both a divinely ordained transfer of power and 'the Government and the benefit of Laws ... which we desire to transmit to our Posterity.'[4] In the process, he becomes an Adamic antitype: like Adam he
has sinned and passed on his sin to generations who 'curse the Woes
that must descend on all' as a result of his original transgression (*M*, 1.
262). By thus usurping, as it were, the historical record in its image of
Shaftesbury as king ('Shaftesbury victorious'), the medal threatens to
leave behind a distorted image of the past, constructing an implicitly
false record of the present. The medal, Dryden tells us, is 'counterfeit'
and so corrupts the future through its own transmission to posterity,
much as the seduction of Monmouth/Absalom in *Absalom and Achitophel*
threatens a second fall of man.

Yet *The Medall* is not *Absalom and Achitophel* redux. Nor is its primary concern simply to contain the transgressive history represented by the medal that informs it. If *Absalom and Achitophel*'s satiric fascination with inheritance gone bad represents the generic tendency of satire 'to debase metaphors of false conveyance,' as Michael Seidel has suggested, *The Medall*, on the other hand, would seem rather to express an anxiety about the increasing effectiveness of material and commercial remains that are all too real as vehicles for the transmission of history and the creation of political continuity.[5] Explicitly an artefact of the market-place, the medal is 'a Monster' that defies the monarch's official con-struction of history; at home in the transgressive world of 'Fayrs [and] Theatres' it seemingly subverts attempts to define the future according to the order of human, natural, or divine law (*M*, ll. 4, 5). In fact, it is the medal's very material presence that enables a disconcerting power to claim for itself the status of history and thereby propagate the chaos it represents upon posterity; when Shaftesbury has finally died, Dryden suggests, his followers will wear his segmented remains in thumb-rings to remind them of their loyalty to his cause. Thus, in fact, *The Medall* would seem to explicitly address not the use or containment of history, but the rather more awkward ability of our material past to construct our future. In Dryden's 'Life of Plutarch,' after all, history is colonizer as well as colonized, determining our choices for the future through its record of the past – a point that hardly needed to be made to English-men convinced by the Exclusion crisis that the rebellion of '42 had in-scribed recurring internecine conflict on their political landscape. And as *The Medall* itself reminds us, such concerns were frequently exacer-bated by the increasing awareness that history itself was hardly essential or absolute, but rather a construction produced by many of the same market forces that shaped British colonial enterprises abroad – another representation of the same economic interest that so often seemed in the period to subvert both political and textual authority. In Dryden's poem, after all, the Shaftesbury medal is fraudulent and misleading, not only because it is politically 'wrong' but because it is commercially successful.

Thus, in a sense, it is the very refusal of *The Medall* to extricate itself from the often grotesque and disturbing material conditions of the soci-ety that produced it, or to elevate itself, like *Absalom and Achitophel*, to theoretical discussions of providence and history, that make it a useful corrective to so much of what has been said about Dryden as a thinker and a historian. And that in turn suggests that perhaps the problem of our embarrassment with *The Medall* does not lie entirely with Dryden's poem, but rather stems at least in part from our own mistaken perceptions of who Dryden ought to be, politically and aesthetically. By voicing concerns about the chaotic power of political belief realized as material inheritance in *The Medall*, Dryden does not simply offer yet another defence of rightful succession but rather addresses a problem particular to the late 1670s and early 1680s – the perceived inability to circumscribe the relationship among historical text, material, and belief (political and religious) in the face of political divisions and the period's increasing investment in the political and economic construction of history itself. And as he does so, he does not seek merely to contain the material of history or the political opposition that threatens to usurp that history, but rather to rework the relationship between text and historical artefact, adapting rather than controlling the rhetoric of his Whig opponents and ultimately confessing his own implication in the socio-economic construction of both text and history.

Dryden, of course, was hardly the first to talk of history as the transmission of political and religious belief from one generation to the next, nor was he alone (even in the Restoration) in figuring both as the inheritance of material goods. After the death of Cromwell in 1658 and the subsequent collapse of the Commonwealth, those in favour of a restoration – advocates, as they saw it, for a legitimate succession – had sought to contain the historical forces of opposition represented by the Good Old Cause. They did this by aligning its rhetoric with that of religious fanatics and condemning both as the product of an ineffective theory of language that saw words as things and political philosophy as a destructive and illegitimate material inheritance. Ridiculing the radical prophets of the 1650s who insisted that their texts had special status as creating and created Word (and thus had the ability to construct history – past, present and future), royalists attacked fanatics as those who 'cheat themselves with Words, mistaking them for Things,' and more than one royalist pamphlet of the day figured both radical beliefs and opposition politics as commercial goods – the material evidence of self-degradation through participation in commercial and artisan culture.[6] Several pieces of the 1660s referred to those who opposed a monarchy restored as swineherds driving pigs to a market no longer interested in the product they were trying to sell.

Thus, in the late 1650s and early 1660s, satiric fake wills, in particular, were a common means of suggesting both the debasing materiality and inherent self-interest of the Good Old Cause, ridiculing the implied inability of Commonwealth citizens to successfully transmit their beliefs or ensure their historical continuity. One such piece, purportedly the will and last testament of the regicide John Bradshaw, lumps together Bradshaw's 'Goods and Chattels, Lands and Hereditaments' with his 'Religion, Charity and Mercy' effectively equating them; all are to go together to his 'dearly beloved Pimp, Mr. Nedham,' suggesting among other things that Bradshaw's beliefs were the ill-gotten gain of his ideological prostitution – his prominent role, that is, in the trial and execution of Charles I.[7] Likewise, in *The Lamentation of a Sinner* (another purported Bradshaw will), the inheritance of political and religious ideology realized as material goods can result only in the shame of the heir and the annihilation of the cause. There Bradshaw leaves 'ten pound for the erecting of two poles, on which each of Vanes and Needhams Heads may be placed, for to demonstrate (truer than any Weathercock) which way the wind blows.'[8] Amidst the optimism of the early Restoration, such pieces enabled the argument that it was the force of human economies, the laws of economic transaction upheld by a purportedly legal document (the mock will), that would render the 'stuff' of radical political opposition worthless, and so neither a threat to the restoration of social order nor a vehicle for alternative versions of either past or future. The failure of the political and religious values advocated by Bradshaw – the ideological inheritance of his followers – ironically comes to rest in their own legal but self-defeating transmission as inherited goods; the inheritance of Vane and Nedham, after all, leaves them incontrovertibly dead and thus incapable of either telling their history or using their version of that history to influence the societies of the future.

Dryden's *Medall* is not a mock will, but it does take as its subject a material object that, like the inheritance of Bradshaw, represents both an alternative history and an alternative succession. And in the tradition of these early mock wills, Dryden does seek to punish and contain Shaftesbury by transforming the man into material. Shaftesbury is a trumpet, a 'Bagpipe,' and most famously a 'Vermin, wriggling in th' Usurper's Ear' (*M*, ll. 35, 31). Meanwhile the very casting of the Whigs' commemorative medal has already rendered living political and religious beliefs into a historical artefact, the carefully crafted but worthless product of artisanal culture. In sitting for the medal, and permitting its production, Shaftesbury has become it, and so has transformed himself into an 'Idol' that is 'base ... counterfeit and light' – the empty, reified, and corrupted object of misguided religious belief (*M*, ll. 7, 9).

But in its celebration of Shaftesbury's acquittal, that base and counterfeit idol also becomes for Dryden the symbol of the erosion of the
boundaries between obedience and transgression, value and worthlessness, which in his 'Life of Plutarch' form the very basis of our ability to
judge the past – to decide 'what to avoid and what to choose.' In fact,
Dryden's continual juxtaposition of medal and coin suggests that its
commemorative and commercial status has effectively confused the
notion of both intrinsic and official value. As a souvenir, its memorial
function transcends its moral and political value; as a counterfeit, its
role is to defeat attempts to distinguish between that which is valuable
and that which is not. At the same time, the medal itself celebrates the
corruption of law (Shaftesbury's acquittal): the jury in the Shaftesbury
case 'chaw / The prickles of unpalatable Law,' and ultimately in Dryden's eyes make an erroneous decision in order to ease their own dis-
comfort, while:

> The Witnesses, that, Leech-like, liv'd on bloud,
> ... when they fasten'd on *their* fester'd Sore,
> Then, Justice and Religion they foreswore;
> Their Mayden Oaths debauch'd into a Whore.
> (*M*, ll. 147–8, 149–53)

Even the marketplace, which had once claimed the power to perform judgment where civil law could not, has been transformed into
the transgressive and undiscriminating space of the mob itself, driven
not by public judgment but by private interest. The Whigs, according
to Dryden, have threatened the law and taken 'the license of traduc-
ing the Executive Power' by producing the medal, in part because of
the promise of economic advantage. 'The Graver' of the medal, Dryden reminds us, 'has made a good Market of it,' and '*English* Ideots
run in crowds to see' the commemorative piece, implying significant
economic return (*M*, 38, l. 2). As a result, the inherent baseness of the
'counterfeit' coin, which should by law be banned from circulation,
is overshadowed by its commercial value; its natural value has been
'inhanc'd' by the demands of the mob, the marketplace, and the engraver who stands to profit, rendering it both valuable and lasting, and
a significant means of transmitting the political opposition that it represents. If the gift of a pole for Vane's and Needham's heads ensures
their silence by rendering them dismembered corpses, Dryden's sug-
gestion that Shaftesbury's followers will wear his segmented remains in

thumb-rings reminds readers that even death and corpses have a material and commemorative value.

In fact, the level of anxiety the Shaftesbury medal creates suggests that if past opposition figured as material inheritance was not a problem for the parodies of 1660, by 1682 the containment of opposition rhetoric based merely on its metaphorical status as commercial and material object – dead, reified, and worthless – seemed a lot less tenable. And that itself was undoubtedly because, by the 1680s, Restoration attitudes towards material culture and material history were clearly changing. While Restoration royalists continued to dismiss the debasing stuff of artisanal culture and belief, they were also very much aware that history itself was increasingly defined for those who studied it by its material evidence. Whereas even earlier antiquarian works like William Camden's *Remains Concerning Britain* (1605) had emphasized the importance of collecting words, symbols, and sayings for transmission to future generations assuming in part that the history of a culture inheres in the words it leaves behind, the latter half of the seventeenth century developed a far greater interest in the collection and preservation of cultural material as a means of recording history. The late seventeenth century's fascination with antiquities and exotica, fetishized in the curio cabinets of the wealthy and institutionalized (and often commercialized) in the public collection, provides testimony to the new centrality of material remains in the historical record.[9] No longer detritus clogging the wheels of true history, material objects came to be seen as vital to the transmission and continuity of history itself, and that, as Dryden's *Medall* suggests, meant a pressing need for royalists to re-evaluate the relationships they had drawn among text, belief, and material culture.

So thorough was the invasion of the historical record by material culture that by 1697 John Evelyn, a long-standing supporter of Stuart monarchy, could carefully elaborate upon the superiority of the metallic records of coins and medals to the paper records left behind by writers and historians. 'What's now become,' he asks in his *Numismata*,

> of so many antient Books as once filled those Noble and Royal Libraries at *Pergamus* and *Alexandria*? 'Tis deplorable even to consider what irreparable loss the Learned World has suffered by so many Conflagrations and other funest [*sic*] Accidents, as have not only dissipated, but quite consum'd infinite numbers of Volumnes [*sic*]; so as of all that Noble and Venerable Store, so very few in comparison are left us, that there is hardly to be found a *Manuscript* in the whole World which can honestly pretend to above eight

hundred, or a thousand years Antiquity, and to have so long escap'd the
rage of Fire, Wars, or (what is worse) barbarous Ignorance, and Fanatick
Zeal: whilst Medals ... have surviv'd, and outlasted the most antient Records, and transmitted to us the knowledge of a thousand useful things of
twice a thousand years past.[10]

Having, like many of his contemporaries, lived through both the
'Fanatick Zeal' of the civil wars and the conflagration of 1666, Evelyn is
all too sensitive to the precariousness of paper records and the unreli-
ability of words, and as a true historian conscious of his dual role as
examiner of the past and repository of his own culture's knowledge, he
embraces coins and medals, which offer the potential of both a longer
memory and a further-reaching audience.

And, indeed, Evelyn's understanding of the nature of historical records was perhaps inevitable, given that, compared to previous English
wars, the period 1640–60 was remarkable simply for the sheer amount
of 'stuff' it had left behind, the material remainders (and reminders) of
civil trauma. We are, thanks to the work of recent scholars, very much
aware of the Restoration creation of public spectacle as a means of
memorializing the conflicts of the civil wars; the coronation celebration
of Charles II, plans to build a monument to Charles I, the redecoration
of country houses, and the drama of the period both in the theatre and
in the streets: all served as important venues for the public exhibition of
material culture.[11] But in many ways the public spectacle of the period
was merely an occasional manifestation of a more far-reaching trend:
the overt politicization of material goods like the Shaftesbury medal.
Thus, just as pervasive and perhaps more insidious were the smaller
remains of the day made possible and popular at the end of the seventeenth century by new technologies and expanding domestic markets:
prints, pottery, jewellery, playing cards, and medals among them. These
goods infiltrated what was by most accounts not yet the domestic sphere,
and as they did so, they actively refuted the basic assumptions of the
mock wills of 1660. Nearly ubiquitous and often quite valuable, these
political objects provided a means by which material inheritance could
in fact influence the course of history and the nature of society.

In many ways, in fact, the medal struck by Bower to commemorate the
Shaftesbury verdict was part of an explosion of material goods specifically designed to participate in the construction of the political arena.
Commemorative medals themselves, though they date from classical
antiquity, were of fairly recent popularity in England. Charles I was an

avid collector of ancient and modern coins and medals, and perhaps
the first in England to recognize the full political potential of such commemorative pieces;[12] as the first English monarchs to issue commemorative medals on a regular basis, both Charles I and Charles II celebrated
the important achievements of their reigns with official strikings in an
attempt to influence popular opinion and to leave behind a material
record for the persuasion of posterity. The seventeenth century also saw
the refinement of slipware production and the introduction of delft-
ware to England from the Netherlands, which made it possible to deco-
rate earthenware with more precise designs and more realistic
representations,[13] while the rapid expansion of the printing press, precipitated to some extent by the civil wars, made printed goods like playing cards (which could be used to convey a political message) both
more accessible and more affordable. Under the pressure of the political strains of the civil war period, such goods became a popular means
of memorializing both political events and political allegiances.

Of course, the availability of such goods did not necessarily mean
total anarchy. Despite Dryden's complaint in *The Medall*, most of the
goods produced during the Restoration seem to have been authorized
in some form by the Stuart government. Like the exhumed and segmented corpses of Cromwell and Bradshaw that adorned the spikes of
the Tower of London – the momento mori that reminded a precariously
balanced England of what it could once again become and what would
happen if it did – many commercial goods were carefully constructed
and framed by a restored monarchy. In fact, despite royalist jibes at the
materiality of Commonwealth culture, the monarchy itself was an active
participant in the early souvenir business, exploiting the continuity of
material culture as a means of establishing a historical record and prop-
agating the image of Stuart government. A slipware dish made around
1660 seems clearly intended to remind royalists of their blessings.
Depicting a highly stylized Prince Charles hiding in an oak tree, it celebrates the miracle of the prince's escape after the Battle of Worcester;
the British lion and unicorn surround the tree, both reminding viewers
of the inherent authority of the restored king and hinting at the danger
from ravenous wild animals that made his survival all the more obviously
an example of divine providence in action.[14] Another platter of the
period depicts Archbishop William Juxon placing the crown on the
head of Charles II, thus not only memorializing the coronation celebration itself but also reiterating the symbolic continuity of the Stuart monarchy inherent in Juxon's very person: it had been Juxon who had

prayed with Charles I on the morning of his execution, and it was Juxon who anointed the son of the deceased monarch some eleven years later.[15] Even a pack of playing cards dating from the 1670s announces its royalist agenda by depicting on the face of individual cards satirical representations of Commonwealth personalities and events. The ace of spades bears the motto 'Bradshaw, the Jaylor, and the Hangman keepers of the liberty of England,' and depicts the two latter with noose and manacles appearing before John Bradshaw seated on the throne of state. The ace of clubs, subtitled 'A Free state or a tolleration for all sort of Villany,' shows armed Commonwealth members in-vading a home in the background while in the foreground a lecherous roundhead attempts to rape a (presumably loyalist) woman whose anguish is indicated by her desperate struggles to wrench herself away from him.[16] For the royalist owners of such goods, the transformation of belief into material substance was hardly destructive, but rather seemed, if anything, both a powerful reminder of personal beliefs and political allegiances and a potent means, as Evelyn suggests, of transmitting those loyalties to children and posterity.

But as the concerns that Dryden voices in the *The Medall* might suggest – concerns about the potential of such material remains to obfuscate the distinction between law and chaos, value and worthlessness – such goods were at best ambivalent signifiers, challenging through their very being traditional constructions of the origins and representation of political authority and thereby in a sense the narrative of official history. Dryden's point, after all, is not simply that the Shaftesbury medal is bad because it depicts Shaftesbury in a favourable light. That is certainly part of the problem, but Dryden's more fundamental concern seems rather to be that the very essence of the medal as a manufactured, portable, and transferrable object involves it in an economy of production, exchange, and inheritance that ultimately destabilizes political meaning. The engraver is blamed for usurping the creative power of God, working on the medal 'four [days] more than God to finish *Adam* took,' and for producing and marketing the medal in a way that misrepresents its intrinsic value, making it 'so golden to the sight, / [but] so base within, so counterfeit and light'; at the same time, Dryden expresses concern that the very dating of the medal will create a new historical iconography for future generations, for 'the Day, Month, Year, to the great Act are join'd: / And a new Canting Holiday design'd' for future celebration (*M*, ll. 19, 8–9, 16–17).

Even the most royalist of goods, in fact, could be accused of such subversive tendencies; and, notably, their popularity among royalists dates not from the Restoration but from the Commonwealth period, when they created a private space where official culture could be resisted while opposition could be memorialized and fostered. A locket made during the Commonwealth, for example, contains on one side a picture of the martyred Charles I, on the other a future Charles II; it was most likely intended to be worn secretly (or closed) as a reminder of a promised continuity and a means of memorializing and transmitting history and political belief in the face of Commonwealth authority.[17] Likewise, supporters of Charles I issued commemorative medals after his death, both defying parliament's seizure of prerogative and undermining the efficacy of public conformity to official representation.[18] And as they moved the representation of political authority from public to private space, such goods also questioned the locus of political authority, suggesting in part that power might stem as much from the act of memorializing it as it does from its public execution. In some sense, the most striking thing about the two plates, for instance, is the size of the name of the potter at the bottom of the slip decoration; the unusually prominent and self-conscious reminder of the origins and production of the political artefact actually destabilizes its image and obfuscates its representation of authority, for it seems ultimately unclear whether the king has authorized the plate or if plate and potter have lent legitimacy to the monarchy. Thus, in a sense, the very nature and construction of these goods, whatever their political agenda, inherently served to blur the line between obedience to power and power itself, loyalty and transgression, order and chaos.

Like other objects that served both as political commodity and domestic memento, moreover, the medal that is the subject of Dryden's poem not only literalized the metaphoric link between belief and material product but in a sense perpetuated the prophetic ability to enact history, in part because of the economic status that such goods achieved. Such pieces, that is, were commodity goods in a time of expanding markets and increased affordability, and it could be quite profitable to produce both them and the destabilizing history they represented, even (perhaps especially) when they defied official culture. As Dryden's poem reminds us, the medal commemorating Shaftesbury's acquittal was a commercial success, selling out so quickly that many of his followers were unable to obtain them. Cheap engravings of Oliver Cromwell and Thomas Fairfax were listed in print shop catalogues through the 1660s, often right alongside those depicting Charles I,

Charles II, and Catherine of Braganza, which suggests that the market
rendered the trade worthwhile, whatever the potential risk.[19] Thus, the
value of many of these objects lay not in their loyalty to official history,
or even in an inherent material worth, but in their perceived potential
to subvert official culture. Many of them were actually quite crude, suggesting that their aesthetic and monetary value lay in their political content, not their craftsmanship.

At the same time, the late-seventeenth-century infatuation with collecting (often itself pursued through inheritance or the dissolution of
inherited estates) had the further effect of validating and disseminating
even the most politically transgressive of goods by insisting that the
value of an object inheres not in its conformation to authority or even in
its value at the moment of production, but rather in its status as historical record, transcending, at least at one level, the particulars of its political engagement. In *Numismata*, Evelyn discusses medals that he regards
as collectible and insists that he will 'mention the Names of those that
are Conspicuous for their Virtue and Worth, as well as Notorious for
their Villanies and Ambition; all of them Matter and Argument for
Medal of great Use in good History, and by no means to be neglected or
slighted of the curious and diligent Collector.'[20] As collectibles, that is,
medals like Dryden's are subject to a logic of valuation, exchange, and
dissemination that supersedes their initial market value and subsequent
political value because of their inherited historical status. The result was
that medals and other historical goods did not simply condemn the stuff
of opposition history but, rather, made it more valuable. Even text, as a
material, exchangeable, collectible commodity, took on a kind of value
as an object, as the Thomason tracts might suggest. Thus, opposition
rhetoric itself could ironically assume a greater value as a historical
object than it had originally as a polemic. As a result, these material
goods ultimately disseminated opposition politics through the marketplace and perpetuated alternative history and opposition belief in a way
that, for royalists at least, threatened to overwhelm the future.

Thus, the Shaftesbury medal was in fact merely one of a myriad of
commercial objects that enabled a kind of domestic resistance to official
culture. Some of these goods were actually preserved and inherited
from the Commonwealth period – an effective means of keeping the
history and the potential of the Good Old Cause alive. A crude slipware
jug, made in 1656, was a practical solution to the plea for perseverance
uttered by Nonconformists like Milton and Bunyan. Decorated with the
motto 'FAST AND PRAY AND PRAY/ AND PITTY THE POOR AMEND THY/

LIFE AND SENNE NO MOR,' it provided a potent daily reminder of the reformist agenda of religious radicals during the 1650s.[21] Likewise, medals produced by Parliament after 1642 celebrated parliamentary revolt; the most famous bears a picture of Charles I on the obverse and Parliament (albeit led by the king) on the reverse.[22] Other goods produced after the Restoration merely defied official control in constructing their own versions of historical events. A number of medals from 1678 depicted the murder of Sir Edmund Berry Godfrey in an attempt to advance rumors of the Popish Plot, and of course the Shaftesbury medal that is Dryden's subject also rejected an official history that cast Shaftesbury inexorably in the role of villain.[23] Like other goods that memorialized an unofficial history, opposition medals defied the logic of the mock wills of 1660 in part because rather than serving (like Vane's and Nedham's heads) as a means of signifying public judgment, their private nature defied the signs of public spectacle, the outward signifiers of loyalty and transgression, and hence rendered the functions of public display and public judgment shifting and unreliable.

In short, by the time Dryden published *The Medall* in 1682, political mementos had come to suggest the impotence of early royalist attacks on 'hard words' and opposition ideology, transforming the material inheritance they represented from the worthless ruin of the Good Old Cause to a valuable means of memorializing and spreading it. And so, during the Exclusion Crisis, when opposing parties accused each other of being heirs to civil-war parliamentarians and loyalists, they invoked a metaphor that was all too potentially literal and all too dangerously close to achieving the very effect of political continuity it had originally been intended to defy. For many royalists, exclusionists were not simply Good Old Cause lookalikes, the whimsical results of evolutionary convergence. Rather, they were quite explicitly the sometimes figurative and often literal heirs and successors of the earlier rebels of 1642, recipients of a grim political, ideological, and material inheritance that offered a grotesque parody of the legitimate succession that royalists sought to defend. The author of *Presbytery Rough-Drawn* describes the Good Old Cause as a self-procreating Hydra that might have been killed but for the leniency of Charles II. Instead it lives on and multiplies, 'ev'ry Neck a thousand Heads thrusts out,' and the exclusionists are merely those appendages 'that succeed [the] Monsters [Cromwell and his followers] in their Crimes.'[24] Likewise, a 1681 edition of *The Last Will and Testament of that Monstrous, Bloody, Tyrannical, Crual and Abominable Parliament dissembled at Westminster, May 15, 1648* (a 1648 pamphlet reprinted in 1660 and 1681) suggests that the Whigs of 1680 are in fact the 'Heirs and true Sons of [the] Rebellion, Treason, Murder, and Theft' represented by the Long Parliament.[25] In the context of the rapid proliferation of consumable and transmittable material history, claims that the events of 1679–81 were directly descended from the conflicts of the civil wars seem not so much a figurative stretch as an honest assessment of the effect of the material conveyance of ideology.

Not surprisingly, then, the early 1680s saw a revival of both reprinted and original mock wills that made exactly that point. *The Last Will and Testament of That Monstrous ... Parliament* bequeaths MPs, figured as various parts of a corpse, to their several fates; Parliament leaves its 'procreating Member, Mr. *Henry Martin* to the mercy of the spiritual Bawds, Whores, and Strumpets, to be cured of the Pox,' while other unnamed members, materialized into disjointed 'Toes little or great, Fingers and Thumbs, Legs and Arms of what Joynt or Bone soever,' are variously left either 'to seek them a new Jerusalem in some of the Western Islands' or 'to be transported with all their pamphlets and manuscripts to Amsterdam, there to remain till the Lord hath need of them, as Instruments to punish some other Nation.'[26] Likewise in his supposed last will and testament, printed for [Samuel] Ward in 1682, the earl of Shaftesbury himself declares:

> Then for my *Polish Crown*, that pretty thing,
> Let M[onmouth] take't, who longs to be a *King*,
> His *empty Head* soft Nature did design
> For such a *light* and *airy Crown* as mine.
> With my *Estate* I'll tell you how it stands,
> *Jack Ketch* must have my *Cloaths*, the *King* my *Lands*.[27]

Many of the mock wills of the early 1680s, moreover, were far more conscious and anxious than their predecessors about the potential of material remains as historical and political objects to propagate the very beliefs and ideologies that they supposedly rendered worthless. By 1682, royalists in particular seemed only too poignantly aware of the ability of the market to make something of nothing. In *The Last Will and Testament of Anthony King of Poland*, Shaftesbury reluctantly bequeaths 'The Carcass of his Plot' to Charles II, with the promise that 'In a Consumption the poor thing doth lie, / And when I'm gone, 'twill pine away and die.'[26] But dead bodies as we now know have their own value and their own ability to overrun the boundaries of the texts and histories that seek to contain them, thus the author depicts Shaftesbury worrying:

> Let not my Quarters stand on City Gate,
> Lest they new *Sects* and Factions do create;
> For certainly the Presbyterian Wenches
> In Dirt will fall to *Idolize* my *haunches.*[29]

In this case, Shaftesbury's own supposed concern with the effect of his material remains suggests the all-too-real ability of the memorializing object to perpetuate and even proliferate the beliefs it represents. Shaftesbury's dismembered corpse breeds not maggots but political and religious factions, which the author finds even more invasive and pestilent, as the corpse is eroding social order as it decays. And so Shaftesbury reluctantly bequeaths the nation he has corrupted to its rightful owner, Charles II, but only after it has been ruined to the extent that its transmission must necessarily create problems for the inheritor:

> To good *King Charles* I leave (though, faith, 'tis pity)
> A poison'd Nation, and deluded City,
> Seditions, Clamours, Murmurs, Jealousies,
> False Oaths, Sham-Stories, and Religious Lies.[30]

The document gives to Charles what is rightfully his, but instead of the promise of proper authority restored it can offer only a vision of a diseased and poisoned nation threatening the future of Stuart monarchy, and it suggests that even the text itself cannot stop that process of corruption and transmission.

By 1682, then, Dryden's assertion that the casting of the Shaftesbury medal represents material history and material inheritance gone haywire – escaping from the bounds that should confine it safely to the past and imposing its all-too-literal shape and form upon the future – was part and parcel of indelible economic and political changes in the English material landscape. Hence the problem for Dryden, as it is posed in part by the mock wills of the period, is not to find a means of containing or discrediting the Shaftesbury medal as a genuine vehicle for the creation of alternative history, but rather to develop an understanding of both social text and social order that can thrive on the disruptive legacy which the medal ensures.

In a world in which writing itself has become both collectible and a commodity good given value in part by the political faction and resistance to authority that spurs it on, text cannot simply assert hegemony through its containment of material opposition. At the same time, by 1682, the unfolding of the Exclusion crisis and the subsequent vindication of Shaftesbury and the Whigs had made royalists more aware than ever that hegemony itself was a dangerous double-edged sword; in presenting an image of Shaftesbury as king, the very medal that Dryden ridicules offered a potent reminder that the difference between opposition to power and power itself is tenuous at best. In fact, in the wake of the Exclusion crisis, Dryden's rhetoric insisted that it was conservatism that sought to resist a monolithic Whig culture: in the 'Life of Plutarch,' after all, it is the Whigs who attempt to control history, producing 'large Volumes of State Collections, and Church Legends, stuff'd with detected forgeries in some parts, and gaping with omissions of truth in others.'[31] And so, faced with both the impracticability of textual hegemony and its potential dangers, Dryden's position in *The Medall* is not so much the voice of cultural authority as it is that of the poet ambivalently learning to negotiate the rhetorical strategies of opposition politics through the language of material culture.

Thus, if Dryden does seek, as some have suggested, to invoke the allusive language of prophecy at the end of his poem, predicting England's future and warning of calamities to come, his is not the prophecy of the civil wars that early Restoration royalists rejected as 'hard words,' a prophecy that claimed its own hegemonic power to reform society by eliminating transgression and disobedience. Dryden himself ridicules prophetic inspiration earlier in the poem; part of the problem with Shaftesbury is that he epitomizes 'Hypocritique Zeal,' having 'cast himself into the Saint-like mould; / Groan'd, sigh'd and pray'd, while Godliness was gain; / The lowest Bagpipe of the squeaking Train' (*M*, ll. 38, 33–5). Thus, Dryden's own foreknowledge is presented, as Phillip Harth has argued, as a common-sense vision of a political fate that any reasoning individual might foretell.[30] 'Without a Vision Poets can fore-show / What all but Fools, by common Sense may know,' and Dryden's elaborated projection of a country at war with itself seems not an inspired rhetoric that imposes divine law and creates a society of the elect, but merely the logical conclusion of present political controversy (*M*, ll. 287–8). In the future that Dryden foresees, opposition cannot be magically whisked away by textual claims to prophetic inspiration, but rather remains a constant scar on the English political landscape.

Even Dryden's poem itself, in fact, seems self-consciously limited by an awareness of the inability of text to contain material culture or smooth away the deep divisions of Restoration society. In a 1966 article, 'The Design of Dryden's *The Medall*,' A.E. Wallace Maurer argued that Dryden's poem is structured in such a way that it effectively creates its own version of the Shaftesbury medal, literally inscribing first the obverse, a portrait of Shaftesbury, then the reverse, a prospect of the city of London; Dryden's medal (*Medall*), as Maurer points out, is merely the version that royalists would like to see, erasing the original medal's figuration of Shaftesbury as king and rendering him 'Vermin' instead.[33] But if Dryden does attempt to create through his poem an alternative medal more palatable to the royalist cause, the result is at best an imperfect and biased version of the object itself: Dryden's portrait of Shaftesbury as 'an Eunuch,' 'a Pigmee,' 'a gross Cheat,' and a 'Wretch turn'd loyal in his own defence' may contain a grain of truth, but it is ultimately no more accurate and no less divisive than the Bower medal's celebratory pose (*M*, ll. 23, 27, 43, 51). Corrupted by the Restoration 'fall of language,' which Richard Kroll has so aptly described, Dryden's *Medall* duplicates rather than transcends the partisan strife that informs it.[34] Thus, for Dryden, it seems, text cannot contain material opposition but only reiterate it.

Yet Dryden's poem is not, I would contend, dark or hopeless, or even ultimately disgusted with a material world that continually overflows its historical boundaries; the poem ends, after all, not in chaos but catharsis, with an exhausted nation thrown upon 'a rightful Monarch's Breast.' In an England ensured of the inheritance of political strife by both the material goods of history and an emerging party politics, Dryden may have understood that political hegemony conceived of as monolithic ideology was no longer possible, nor its methods ultimately conducive to social order. But that meant for him that the role of polemic was not to suppress difference or opposition – a strategy that can only lead, as we have seen, to an underground economy and martyrology that merely strengthens it – but rather to make hidden insurrection public and common, freeing it from the economics of collecting and resistance and thereby transforming it from political subversion to cultural difference. The final image of peace and security results only from a war of material words – a seventeenth-century version of Lyotard's image of history as contending assertions. Peace will come only after every side has had its say:

> The *Presbyter*, puft up with spiritual Pride,
> Shall on the Necks of the lewd Nobles ride:

His Brethren damn, the Civil Pow'r defy;
And parcel out Republique Prelacy.
But short shall be his Reign; his rigid Yoke
And Tyrant Pow'r will puny Sects provoke;
And Frogs and Toads, and all the Tadpole Train
Will Croak to Heav'n for help, from this devouring Crane.
                                        (*M*, ll. 298–305)

And so strife will continue, Dryden asserts, until the nation tires of jabbering and controversy, ironically suggesting that it is the very articulation of difference as material (pamphlet) culture that will ultimately lead to social order and continuity; the material production of difference seems in many ways more conducive to future stability than does the ascendence of any particular political stance.

Significantly, then, the end of the poem does not try to insist that Shaftesbury's opposition to the Stuarts must fail based on the inherent materiality with which Dryden has graced it throughout the piece. If anything, in fact, it seems to take all too seriously the possibility that Shaftesbury might actually succeed in disrupting a peaceful succession, indulging in a long description of what might happen 'if true succession from our Isle should fail' (*M*, l. 289). The future that he depicts, moreover, is one marked by the very propagation of corrupted material inheritance that both Dryden himself and the anonymous author of *The Last Will and Testament* had so feared, but it is propagation figured as the public exposure of private and concealed infection:

The swelling Poyson of the sev'ral Sects,
Which, wanting vent, the Nations Health infects,
Shall burst its Bag; and fighting out their way
The various Venoms on each other prey.
                                        (*M*, ll. 294–7)

Ironically, in *The Medall*, it is the very act of propagation – the fact that opposition and the objects that represent it become not dead and hence devoid of meaning or empty of symbolic value, but rather spread and proliferate – that leads to a rightful succession, a rightful inheritance; 'halting Vengeance,' as it spreads, will eventually '[overtake the] Age,' and it is the country's 'wild Labours, wearied into Rest' that will eventually bring relief (*M*, ll. 320–1). If Shaftesbury is Adam, as Dryden suggests, condemning his progeny to a tainted future, his fall is rendered (however reluctantly) a *felix culpa* by its very commonality; because it is the common inheritance of all mankind, the gross material of history generated by his transgression ultimately transmits Shaftesbury's corruption to heirs who curse their legacy, thus enabling their redemption. At the same time, the ending, though optimistic, suggests not so much resolution as fatigue – a cessation of hostilities without the reconciliation of opposition. The country has not resolved its differences, it has merely gotten tired, and the material and dialectic propagation of history, figured now as poisoned speech and text, is not antithetical but necessary to that process.

Thus, I would suggest, *The Medall* is a poem that ultimately both confesses the power of the material object to construct history and dramatizes its own conversion into 'hard words' (material object), though not without profound ambivalence. We can, I think, see Dryden's attempt to create his own medal in part as a means of articulating the poem's public status as a cultural artefact, and one that does not so much contain difference as preserve the opposition it ironically represents; in a political environment in which the real threat seemed not so much Whig opposition but a Whig control of power, the poem seeks to articulate and dramatize a means by which the subversive potential of material culture (resisting as it does a monolithic history) enables historical (and royalist) continuity. But at the same time, *The Medall*'s concluding vision of 'rest' suggests that by 1682 Dryden also had enough distance from his own role as polemicist and public historian to appreciate the value of silence. *The Medall*'s final vision of an exhausted and quiet nation underscores the value of moments when language, both as text and as object, fails; the end of the poem represents a country too tired to speak and therefore unable to propagate its history, blessedly caught in a transitory moment where past, present, and future coexist and are therefore blissfully meaningless. For a tired Dryden, aware of the necessity of polemically constructed history but also conscious of its dangers, silence is a precious commodity, all the more valuable for the noisy material of the marketplace that consistently threatens to overwhelm it.

Notes

1 John Dryden, 'Life of Plutarch.' *The Works of John Dryden*, ed. E.N. Hooker, H.T. Swedenberg, Jr, et al., 20 vols. (Berkeley: University of California Press 1956–2000), 17:270–1 (hereafter cited as *California Dryden*).

2 David Kramer has made the most extensive use of this metaphor in *The Imperial Dryden: The Politics of Appropriation in Seventeenth-Century England* (Athens: University of Georgia Press 1994), but Phillip Harth also refers to Dryden's 'use' of history in *Pen for a Party: Dryden's Tory Propaganda in Its Contexts* (Princeton: Princeton University Press 1993), 186. Richard Kroll also takes the materials and images of history as discrete collectibles that Dryden forges into a poetic grammar in *The Material Word: Literate Culture in the Restoration and Early Eighteenth Century* (Baltimore: Johns Hopkins University Press 1991).

3 Samuel Pordage, *The Medal Revers'd. A Satyre against Persecution* (1682), 2–3.

4 Dryden, *The Medall. California Dryden*, 2:39. All further reference to the poem (abbreviated *M*) will be to this edition and will be cited within the text by line number or page number as appropriate.

5 Michael Seidel, *Satiric Inheritance, Rabelais to Sterne* (Princeton: Princeton University Press 1979), 23.

6 Samuel Butler, *Characters* (Cleveland: Press of Case Western Reserve University 1970), 156.

7 *Bradshaw's Ghost*, 3rd ed. (1659), 18.

8 *Lamentation of a Sinner* (1659), 4.

9 See, for example, *The Origins of Museums: The Cabinet of Curiosities*, ed. Oliver Impey and Arthur MacGregor (Oxford: Clarendon Press 1985).

10 John Evelyn, *Numismata. A discourse of Medals Ancient and Modern* (London 1697), 2.

11 Important studies in this vein include Jonathan Sawday, 'Re-Writing a Revolution: History, Symbol, and Text in the Restoration,' *The Seventeenth Century* 7 (1992), 171–99 and J. Douglas Stewart, 'A Militant, Stoic Monument: The Wren-Cibber-Gibbons Charles I Mausoleum Project: Its Authors, Sources, Meaning, and Influence,' in *The Restoration Mind*, ed. W. Gerald Marshall (Newark: University of Delaware Press 1997).

12 'The Visual Image of Charles I,' in *The Royal Image: Representations of Charles I*, ed. Thomas Corns (Cambridge: Cambridge University Press 1999), 187.

13 Griselda Lewis, *A Collector's History of English Pottery* (New York: Viking Press 1969), 23–4, 35.

14 Ibid., 26.

15 Ibid.

16 Edmund Goldsmid, *Explanatory Notes of a Pack of Cavalier Playing Cards Temp Charles II. Forming a Complete Political Satire of the Commonwealth* (Edinburgh: E&G Goldsmid 1886).

17 Joan Evans, *A History of Jewellery 1100–1870* (London: Faber and Faber 1953), plate 115.

18 See Peacock, 'Visual Image of Charles I,' 199.
19 Alexander Globe, *Peter Stent, London Printseller, circa 1642–1665* (Vancouver: University of British Columbia Press 1985), 60–1.
20 Evelyn, *Numismata*, 176.
21 Lewis, *History of English Pottery*, 25.
22 Peacock, 'Visual Image of Charles I,' 194.
23 Evelyn, *Numismata*, 171–4.
24 *Presbytery Rough-Drawn. A Satyr. In Contemplation of the Late Rebellion* (London 1683), 12.
25 *The Last Will and Testament of that Monstrous, Bloudy, Tyrannical, Cruel, and Abominable Parliament*, 3rd ed. (London 1681), 1.
26 Ibid., 2.
27 *The Last Will and Testament of Anthony King of Poland* (London: 1682), 2.
28 Ibid., 3.
29 Ibid.
30 Ibid.
31 Dryden, 'Life of Plutarch,' 236.
32 Harth, *Pen for a Party*, 186.
33 A.E. Wallace Maurer, 'The Design of Dryden's *The Medall*,' *PLL* 2 (1966), 293–304.
34 Kroll, *Material Word*, 305.

chapter two

Dryden, Marvell, and the Design of Political Poetry

LEO BRAUDY

Some thirty or forty years ago, literary scholars were still doing backflips trying to fit political satire – that notoriously allusive genre – into the canons of New Criticism, which demanded that lasting poetic value should be judged by the internal dynamics and 'tensions' of a poem rather than any relation to the world in which it appeared. Since then, an appreciation for the historical context of literature of all sorts has become more widespread in interpretive circles. Few would today presume to make purely architectonic and aesthetic readings of poems, especially those of the Restoration, so many of which wear their relevance to immediate issues on their sleeves.

But that openness to history has only rarely been reflected in an openness to literature by historians of either events or ideas. So far as disciplinary boundaries are concerned, they tend to move on separate tracks, assuming a hierarchy of knowledge in which literature is either at the bottom or irrelevant. Writers of fiction are said to be 'influenced' by philosophers; Defoe never shows up as a crucial way station between Locke and Hume, or Pope between Shaftesbury and Adam Smith. Similarly, Linda Colley makes a brief gesture towards the seventeenth-century context at the beginning of *Britons: Forging the Nation, 1707–1837*, but her main focus, as her title indicates, begins with the eighteenth century, and, for all her claim to be a revisionist historian using 'new' sources, her material is overwhelmingly drawn from explicitly intended statements of political partisanship or theory.[1] The Jacobite Rebellion, as seen from the perspective of *Tom Jones*, for example, makes no appearance, nor does *Waverly*, for that matter, or Uncle Toby's attitudes towards the wars of William III and Louis XIV.

This prejudice owes a significant debt to the codificaiton of intellectual disciplines begun in the eighteenth century, and it is particularly
ill-suited for understanding the relationship between literature and politics in the proto-disciplinary world of the Restoration. I therefore use
the word 'design' in my title for as many resonances as I can wring out
of it: poetic design in terms of structure and use of language; political
design in the poet's intention to change the minds of his audience or to
make their inchoate opionions into a patter; artistic design as an allusion to the analogies between poetry, painting, and theatre.

Similarly, I would like to emphasize Marvell and Dryden centrally as
political poets in themselves, while at the same time I want to stress that
the contrast between their work, their careers, and their ideas of what a
poet does emblematically embodies two very different sorts of cultural
meaning, under construction during the Restoration and with a long
history ever since. In short, instead of seeing poetry as a merely reflective version of political events and ideas, or even as a quintessential commentator upon them, I seek to restore some of the actual balance of
poetry and politics in the period – the interwined aesthetic/political
project.[2]

The primary cultural and political events in seventeenth-century
England were, of course, the Civil War and the execution of Charles I.
The restoration of Charles II to the throne seemed to promise that the
breach in time caused by these tumultuous events would be restored
along with the gap in dynasty. But, throughout the Restoration and into
the eighteenth century, the question of what England was and what it
meant to be English became explicitly crucial to the entire literate culture and thereby to the shape of any vision of the English future. In such
important national crises as the Great Plague and Great Fire of London
(1665–6), the naval defeats of the Second Dutch War (1666–7), the agi-
tation around the Popish Plot (1679–81), the rebellion of the duke of
Monmouth (1685), and the Glorious Revolution (1688), political positions that had previously been implicit had to be said out loud and even
argued.

Political argument in the past, especially argument about foreign
affairs, had often been considered treason by those in power. Thus
there was little precedent for political poetry – that is, a poetry that
dealt with contemporary issues, let alone current events. Instead, the
political poetry that did exist usually took the classic forms of satire and
panegyric that reached for some timeless rhetorical standard of either
praise or invective. But with the outpouring during the Civil War of a

pamphlet literature arguing every political, social, and religious nuance, the question might reasonably arise: Can there be a political poetry steeped in immediate events, a poetry more akin to a newspaper, at a time when newspapers themselves – in the form of couriers and coronatos – are just starting to appear?

To use the terms of the anthropologist Edward Hall, seventeenth-century England was changing from a 'high context' culture to a 'low context' culture, from a culture homogeneous enough that little had to be explained, to one in which an increasing number of assumptions had to be made more explicit and defended. The change had been in process since Elizabethan theatre first began to appeal to an audience that did not necessarily have to know how to read. It gathered force when the Stuarts and their supporters sponsored a theory of monarchical divine right that would not have to be stated if it were not in the process of being discarded. But with the expansion of literacy and the growth of publishing possibility nurtured by the Civil War, the urge to political argument increased much more rapidly. The monarchy could no longer be considered an unquestionably central cultural institution, and it would become even less so in 1714, when the German-speaking George I ascended the throne.

In the late seventeenth and early eighteenth century, then, for the first time in English history, there was a growing population of literate and even educated people who did not share the political and social assumptions of the former literate class. In this shift from a more homogeneous to a more varied cultural context, new rules and new rule-givers emerged. Culture began to be defined less as the natural possession of a class whose literacy was a mark of its power and more as a potential consensus of all those who could read and write (or at least argue), and thereby either be, or potentially be, citizens.

In the absence of a traditional language of political argument, it was literature, with its ready supply of allusions and effects, that principally supplied the armoury of discussion. With uncertain steps, political-language was distinguishing itself from what we would call literature, as well as gathering strength from it. New styles of controversy had emerged from the Civil War, and during all the most important political situations of the period, as well as many minor moments, the use of literary language, and language in general, to change minds was crucial. At the same time, a new generation of linguistic theorists, like John Wilkins, for whom the questions of linguistic authority and cultural authority were closely connected, set about exploring the history and logic of language itself. A 'language class' was coming into being. Its origins were in older groups, whose literacy was traditionally part of their political power, but for this new class literacy was the way to power.

In the political poetry of Dryden and Marvell, we can observe two very different responses to these changes: Dryden, the aspiring member of the gentry, virtually invents an ideology of naturalized monarchy to teach aristocrats and monarchs (along with their supporters) how to be what they seemed to be. His efforts respond to the dilemma of an aristocratic class whose sense of their own social relevance was getting less and less secure. By contrast, Marvell, the dissenter and anti-monarchist, writes a poetry and prose that seeks to be in 'opposition' stylistically as well as politically. He shows how the history and traditions of literature – so promoted and discussed by Dryden – might be seen instead as a partisan language, asserting both aristocratic decorum and moral sway, by pretending to be natural and innate.

The dilemma that both Marvell and Dryden in their different ways address is, once again, the gap made in history by the Civil War, the execution of Charles I, and especially the reign of Cromwell as Lord Protector. It is essentially the problem of continuity in history: not just the Elizabethan lyric issue of the pressure of onrushing Time, but what particularly is this time, or, as Marvell says of Cromwell, ''tis the most which we determine can, / If these the times, then this must be the man.'[3]

Sixteenth-century dynastic history, following the lead of Polydore Vergil among others, was set up as inevitably issuing in the grandeur and royal descendants of the present. Earlier seventeenth-century historiography, like that of Edmund Bolton, revived more cyclical models of decline and resurgence, and both agreed that there is a God of history. But it is precisely the search for this God in history, or any principle of continuity, that animates so much of the political poetry of both Marvell and Dryden. Can God or Providence or any other unitary concept justify or explain what otherwise appear to be chasms, disruptions, and discontinuities – the 'great gulf' or 'sad vacuum' left in the historical registers of the Civil War, as Thomas Fuller called them in 1661. How, in their own terms, could the times be 'restored' or 'redeemed'? What is the connection between the history that has happened and the mind that attempts to understand it and, not incidentally, to present that understanding in the forms and patterns of poetry?

Both Marvell and Dryden recognize that history after the death of Charles is different from history before, Marvell in 'An Horatian Ode' more intrigued by the death of Charles and Dryden in *Astraea Redux* and other early poems focusing poetically on new beginnings. Yet for both it is also crucially the frame of political institutions that has been broken, the frame that had been thought eternal and now turns out to be made by men – and if man-made, perhaps now man-remade.

The traditional consensus and frame of belief presided over by royal institutions has been shown by the new situation to be filled with conflicts that need to be fought out or adjudicated. What now? The scope of individual will, in other words, has become a political and poetic issue: Can I, can you, can anyone, even the monarch, have an effect on the form of things?

One central contrast between Dryden and Marvell is over the issue of will. It is Dryden's view that power expressed as authority (for example, in 'Absalom and Achitophel') is the ultimate stabilizer and structure of the universe, while it is Marvell's that power should be faced frankly as political give and take. For Dryden, politics should bear the emblematic marks of its heavenly descent, handed down from the divine to the human, while for Marvell, its essence is dissent, the cut and parry between human beings on Earth.[4]

With this new stress on will in time, the relation between the form of history and the form of poetry, between the poet's creation of a poem deliberately drawing upon tradition and the public man's establishment of order within the state, is therefore not merely metaphoric and analogous. In fact, to call it metaphoric is a way of diminishing the cultural in favour of the political event. Let's compare the view, handily represented by Lawrence Stone in J.G.A. Pocock's volume *Three British Revolutions*, that the Civil Wars were essentially 'unsuccessful' because these rebellions didn't directly accomplish anything immediately really lasting and tangible. But to what extent had the ideas shaped an evolution within which they could be appreciated?[5]

Stone's argument in effect tries to have it both ways. First, he claims that the ideas could not be effective until the political structures were 'ready' (as they would be by the nineteenth century, when classes and interests had evolved enough). Then, he takes the other side of the question: nothing new really happened with the Glorious Revolution, for example, because similar ideas and acts had existed before, his example being that in 1485 a king, Henry VII, was virtually elected by Parliament.

The difference between these two moments of history, however, is that what happened in 1485 was not perceived as a permanent act of parliamentary aggrandizement, or perhaps no one was interested in perceiving it that way, while with the Civil War and the Glorious Revolution, the summoning of a new monarch was explicitly interpreted as an act of parliamentary power. Stone's conflation of the two reflects the historian's typical undervaluing of myth, imagery, propaganda, and nostalgia – all cultural formations – as mere dress-up for the essential political and economic structures, and it ignores the power of ideas within a culture to have some actual effect.

For Dryden and Marvell, however, the political and the cultural have a more reciprocal relation. Whatever had been materially or structurally accomplished by the Civil War, a large space had been opened for the discussion and exploration of political, economic, and social issues. Contrary to Stone's purely political point of view, all values were up for grabs, to be reinterpreted.

In such an open interpretive space, the question of self-consciousness is crucial. This is where cultural nationalism can be distinguished from political nationalism and its claim to be related to actual power. Cultural nationalism relies on self-consciousness in individuals and in classes, as well as in the country at large. The two kinds of nationalism proceed at different rates. Perhaps a theorist of self-consciousness (rather than a political scientist) would be willing to say that they first spring from an individual's sense of difference and identity, especially someone forced by the Civil War to question in himself an unexamined and therefore 'innate' belief that owed more to memories of Gloriana and *Henry V* than to reality.

Cultural self-awareness of this sort is therefore, I would argue, necessarily prior to political or economic awareness – and they, in turn, depend upon it for their own validation. Christopher Hill has hinted at this when he writes that dreams of an anti-Catholic international crusade loom larger in popular consciousness than economic considerations at the end of the First Dutch war. Although Hill adds the economic and social detail that the Fifth Monarchy Men's greatest supporters were clothiers, the sense in which one kind of explanation can be reduced or subordinated to the other remains appropriately problematic, especially since the imperial goals of the First Dutch War qualify it as early evidence of a self-conscious political nationalism.[6]

In this heady atmosphere, both Marvell and Dryden are preoccupied by the dual question of how to design or frame the state and how to design or frame their poems. In accordance with their own temperaments and politics, they come up with very different conclusions that are connected to their ideas of what poetry and poets should be, as well as the shape of their own poetic careers.

Dryden, in attempting to re-establish the legitimacy of the royalist view of history to accompany the pragmatic restoration of the monarchy, succeeds paradoxically in establishing instead the primacy of a certain sort of heightened language we call literary and a sense of public character we call not the monarch but the poet. Marvell, by contrast, with his energetic scepticism, focuses on the inadequacy of language and linguistic traditions to account fully or even with minimal adequacy for historical events. He thereby exposes the actual historicity of what Dryden claims to be the natural order of things.

Both Dryden and Marvell, then, in their different ways and – it is not too extreme to say – their different politico-poetic ideologies, perceive the potential for a cultural nationalism in which the idea of England can permeate all classes independent of their degree of actual political participation. Many writers, especially historians and political scientists, have wondered why England never had a revolution as violent as the French. Part of the reason, I suggest, is this seventeenth-century exploration and establishment, by supporters of the monarchy and of Parliament alike, of a sense of cultural belonging, which in other countries, including France, was still confined to particular bureaucratic, military, and religious classes. One implication of the arguments of the Civil War – although admittedly it took a while to sort itself out – was that both Dissenters and Anglicans, parliamentarians and royalists, could with some justification claim the precedent of English history to say they were truly Englishmen. The 'seismic rift' Lawrence Stone sees through the seventeenth century and which he is then so puzzled to see disappear, is therefore from this point of view the first step in its own disappearance. When arguments are equally good although seemingly opposed, there comes a point when another generation sees how they can be shared.

The role of both Marvell and Dryden in this change cannot be minimized as 'merely' literary, for they help establish the language within which such different views can be articulated. For Marvell, Cromwell as ruler, as 'equal subject,' and in the 'Death of O.C.' as loving father and friend furnishes a model that lays the groundwork for subsequent efforts to define what a ruler or patriot king should be, even among those whose views on specific policies might be totally opposed to his. At the same time, Marvell's own introduction of himself as a speaker in the 'First Anniversary' indicates how the way has been prepared for the poet to put himself forward not as someone whose authority over the verse should be likened to that of the monarch over the country, but as a representative citizen inspired by Cromwell's example. Here he ventures forward as the kind of political and moral poet he might be (but never actually became, except as a satirist), as if emerging from the woods around Appleton House to celebrate Maria Fairfax's ability to harmonize nature. The possibility (he doesn't say he's totally sure) is that Cromwell combines grace and power; and this grace, this spiritual anointing, is not imaged (as it was in *Eikon Basilike*) in terms of the king as Christ's vicar undergoing Christ's sufferings, but as the benediction of privacy and personal life.[7]

Less so than in the 'Horatian Ode,' but still significantly, Marvell's view of Cromwell in both the 'First Anniversary' and 'A Poem upon the Death of O.C.' is presented as a question of shifting perspectives. In one of the most striking images, he at first mourns over the dead body of Cromwell, its life gone, and then sees it as even greater than when alive: 'The tree ere while forshortened to our view, / When fall'n shews taller yet than as it grew' (ll. 269–70). That Marvell has chosen to emphasize the particular aspects of Cromwell that raise the question of kingship, as well as the difficulty of comprehending them as a whole, is made even clearer when we compare the poem the twenty-seven–year-old Dryden also wrote, to his later embarrassment, as an elegy on Cromwell's death, 'Heroique Stanzas.'[8]

Dryden and Marvell see many of the same characteristics in Cromwell as worthy of poetic treatment. According to Dryden, Cromwell is 'the *Confidant* of *Nature,*' and words like 'authentick' and 'intuition' appear often. Yet Dryden looks as well for the lineaments of a commanding face, as in royal portraits of old, and celebrates the sway that face exacts: 'His countenance did imprint an awe' (l. 73).

While in some basic sense Marvell is interested in what the 'new' ruling personality of Cromwell means for the individual nature that has been liberated by the Civil War and the execution of Charles, Dryden in contrast fixes his attention specifically upon the ruler as a figure separated from ordinary human nature by power and position. This is not to say that Dryden believes that the monarch is not human, for something of human nature has to be recuperated into Dryden's image of kingship in order for it to be politically effective. Thus, after Cromwell's death, Dryden makes a specific issue in his poem of the superfluousness of praise. Cromwell is complete in himself and needs nothing more. The function of the praising poem, according to Dryden, is to reveal and publicize what already exists. The poet, in short, claims to discover nothing and to interpret nothing; he just sets the hero in the proper 'poetic' context to be understood.

Dryden's Cromwell is intuitive in his insight into others, and close to nature in his fortune and success. He differs decisively from Marvell's version in his connection to 'design.' For Marvell in the 'Horatian Ode' and to a lesser extent in 'First Anniversary,' Cromwell's great virtue is that the arc of his career is not related to a specific premeditation or orderly plan but is instead the emanation of a more complex, dimly perceived movement of history that may be beyond the power of human reason to discover. Like the discursive complex narrative pattern of 'Appleton House,' which begins by mocking the kind of architect who models his houses on his own brain, such a 'frame' owes as much to the changeableness of nature and the ability to respond to opportunity as it does to the royalist idea of Cromwell as Machiavellian bogeyman. Charles I, as many have noted, appears in the 'Horatian Ode' in a tableau, while Cromwell is in constant motion. Charles's power, such as it is, partakes of the ideal stasis of theatrical order, while Cromwell seems to be the progenitor of a new style of narrative connection. Unlike Dryden's more stately language, Marvell's shifts and moves. While Dryden seeks to discover the true shape of order, Marvell explores its variety. Neither simile nor typology is truly his mode, because they stop language in the act of discovery to celebrate an externally fetched pattern.

This emphasis may help to explain why Marvell's admirers are so confused that he does not follow the traditional model of a poetic career. It is precisely that a poetic career, with its stages and teleologies and classical sources, its necessary invocations of tradition and past ancestors, goes against Marvell's basic sense of the contingency of language and career and time itself. Dryden from the very first, however, seeks to have the graces of accident mingle directly with the power of precedent and premeditation. His early poem in praise of the poetry of his cousin Sir Robert Howard, for example, affirms his own sense of historical pattern: 'this is a piece too fair / To be the child of Chance, and not of Care' (ll. 29–30).[9] As such a line implies, Dryden is the chief initiator and prime definer of the idea of poetic professionalism for the modern period, as Ben Jonson had embodied it for the Elizabethans: the reader must know that all was done on purpose, with the best materials, in the appropriate amount of time, and delivered to the wise patron who commissioned it – even while the work can be appreciated by the wider audience who might eavesdrop on the transaction.

Accordingly, however much Dryden might not want to participate in the argument over tactics in 'Heroique Stanzas,' he still affirms Cromwell's ability to control events, with the appropriate caveat: 'And yet *Dominion* was not his Designe' (l. 37), although a few lines later: 'Yet still the *faire Designment* was his own' (l. 96). Here the curse of Machiavellian premeditation is taken off by making an analogy between political design and what a painter does in planning his work – the *disegno* emphasized by Vasari as the great accomplishment of Michelangelo, even though someone else might supply the colours. This softer order, 'the providence of wit' as Dryden calls it in the poem to Howard, makes the design of the political man not analogous to the impositions of tyranny but to the patterns of artistic harmony.[10]

Dryden's public pose for the poetic is in marked contrast to Marvell's emphasis on withdrawal and retirement, even when contemplating public issues, and the way he finds thematic strength in the realms of privacy and individual domestic nature. Their attitudes towards the pastoral fall into a similar pattern. For Marvell, the pastoral world is fallen, violated by History, embodying an innocence and purity that we not only cannot regain but also perhaps should not, because in the present it is a false and delusionary ideal. For Dryden, however, the pastoral ideal is restorable. The Golden Age can come back to earth, as he emphasizes in his poems on the accession of Charles II, although not without a cautionary note. For in those poems he becomes not just the panegyrist of Charles, but he also – in a role he will continue throughout his career – takes on the task, previously the province of humanist moralists, of creating a heuristic position for his poetry by which to teach the young monarch just what it means to be a king in this new day and age. In this task the qualities Dryden praised in the dead Cromwell are not forgotten, for Dryden is the fashioner of a new royalist ethos, not merely the propagandist of a pre-existing one.

As Marvell does when he faces the execution of Charles I and the advent of Cromwell, Dryden also discovers an empty space at the centre of national life where once the monarch had stood. At the Restoration a new royal body occupies that space, but how is it to be justified? For a complex of political and financial reasons, many of those who supported Cromwell combined with his antagonists to bring about the Restoration of Charles II. But this was primarily a restoration of kingship, not the specific person of Charles, except to the extent that he was, in fact, the genealogical heir. Legally defined kingship might therefore seem to be the same as it was before the disruption of the Interregnum.

But what political and cultural kingship might entail, and what kind of royal character Charles ought to have, becomes the business of Dryden and others to create, as much as, with even more premeditation a century later, the Founding Fathers decided that the personality of George Washington was the most suitable among them to fill a similar gap in American society left by the toppling of George III.

At the Restoration, then, the reality of kingship was not as much an issue as was the personality and character of the king, just as it had been under Cromwell. And the focus was much more an interplay between the king's private nature and his public role than the strictly separated realm of the medieval two bodies, or the Stuart theory of divine right, might have suggested.[11]

Some of the crucial elements in this redefinition are connected with Dryden's dubbing of Charles as David in *Astraea Redux*, much as Marvell had earlier described Cromwell. By this and other means, Dryden manages to bestow on Charles II some of the virtues of Cromwell's individuality while adding to them the boon of being hereditary ruler as well, connected to and justified by time rather than (like Cromwell) unprecedented and outside time. Charles's restoration is thus imaged as both a return and a new beginning. Charles is both the fruit of the past order as well as a youthful newcomer, relatively unconnected with past quarrels and animosities. As Dryden presents him, the points of behaviour to which he tacks in his voyage towards restoration are not those of his father but of the Roman emperors, especially those, such as Otho, Galba, and Piso, with a special connection to English history.

Dryden's Charles in *Astraea Redux* is both the person who *is* king and the person who *ought* to be king, not only by heredity but more dramatically by both knowledge and will: 'Thus banish'd *David* spent abroad his time, / when to be God's Anointed was his Crime' (ll. 79–80). Dryden, like his readers, knows full well that David was in exile because there was a conflict between the genealogical royal line of Saul and his own anointment by Samuel as the 'true' king. (In other words, David is more a Cromwell than a Charles.) But he calls Charles David to emphasize that Charles carries *both* genealogical sanction and divine justification. In addition, Charles has suffered and learned: 'Recov'ring hardly what he lost before, / His right indears it much, his purchase more' (ll. 85–6). While in exile, that is to say, he has learned the secrets of other monarchs in order better to rule himself. Kingship with such an apprenticeship is not just an emanation of one's own nature. It, like the poetic inspiration that requires care to be made into real poetic language, is something that must be learned well: 'To bus'ness ripened by digestive thought / His future rule is into Method brought' (ll. 89–90). Thus, through the ministrations of Dryden, divine right theory must be modified to assimilate the need that 'Scepters' [be] train'd' (l. 97).

To sharpen the contrast I am trying to draw here, I would characterize Dryden as the shaper of a poetic language that in connotation as well as content supports established power, while Marvell's language by the same token is critical of established power by being critical of established generalizations, genres, and tropes. In this way, for example, Dryden's reflexive verbs swallow up and redouble his meaning, as in 'To His Sacred Majesty': 'Born to command the Mistress of the Seas, / Your thoughts themselves in that blue Empire please' (ll. 99–100); or Charles calling the fleet in *Annus Mirabilis*: 'He in himself did whole Armado's bring' (l. 54); or, near the end of his life, in 'To My Honour'd Kinsman, John Driden': 'Safe in our selves, while on our selves we stand' (l. 146). Marvell's reflexive verbs by contrast tend to trap and undermine direct statement: '(so I myself deceive)' in 'The Coronet'; Charles I chasing himself to 'Carisbrooke's narrow case' in the 'Horatian Ode'; or Damon the Mower slashing his ankle with his own scythe, 'the mower mown.'

The contrast here is between Dryden's construction of a royalist self-sufficiency ('Full of your self you can admit no more' as he says in 'To His Sacred Majesty') and Marvell's sense of, and greater interest in, the difficulty of consistency, in both politics and human nature. For Dryden individual nature, especially that of monarchs, must be subdued to and justified by pre-existing models. The inconsistencies of the ideal person are thus purged in order to allow the symbolic person to be primary, just as in *Absalom and Achitophel* what would otherwise seem to be Charles II's private sexual life, suitable primarily for gossip, becomes yet another aspect of his relation to his great forerunner – once again, David.

As the Restoration honeymoon quickly ends and politics heat up in the mid-1660s, Marvell thus naturally gravitates to a satiric view of political events and personalities because of its emphasis on the difficulty of making everything fit together, its preoccupation with the unfortunate lapses and normal incoherence of reality. What makes this jaundiced view more than the potshots and innuendo that characterize so much of Restoration satire is Marvell's emphasis on the interrogatory role of satiric poetry as opposed to the celebratory stance of royalist panegyric. For Dryden, the poem affirms a pre-existing political order. For Marvell, it is a place within which to think out politics.

The years 1665-7 make a convenient, even a remarkably coincidental, crux for delving into some of these issues. In these years the newly re-established political coherence falls apart with two events of 1666 – the battle with the Dutch fleet at Lowestoft and the Fire of London that followed upon the heels of the Plague. The round of catastrophes begins with Marvell's return to England in January of 1665 after serving as a secretary for two years on an embassy to Russia, Sweden, and Denmark.

That January the English had provoked the Dutch into war by attacking their ships. Later, in the spring, plague began to rage in London. On 3 June the English fleet decisively defeated the Dutch at Lowestoft; but they failed to pursue their advantage, and in 1667 the Dutch returned the favour with a humiliating defeat of the English fleet. This defeat was a few years in the future, however, and at the time the 1665 victory of Lowestoft was celebrated everywhere. The duke of York, who led the fleet, had pictures of each of his senior officers painted by Sir Peter Lely, the court painter, while Edmund Waller, the favourite court poet, who had been in exile with Charles in France, wrote 'Instructions to a Painter,' a poem in a very up-to-date Italian poetic form directing an imaginary painter to depict the grand naval triumph in the appropriate heroic style.

Almost immediately, however, the political opposition, until now fairly scattered and without a central issue, seized on this victory – and this poem – as a way of uniting themselves and attacking their opponents. Otherwise submerged issues – What is the Dutch War for? How does it help England? What is the foreign policy of the king's government? Are his ministers capable of carrying it out? Should they? Who is responsible? – were brought together in an effort to tear the veil of triumph and victory away from the battle and show it in its true and much more corrupt light. Later, Waller's poem would generate second, third, and more advices to painters to paint what really happened, instead of what – these poems claim – the royalists wanted the public to think happened. Political argument has in a sense been born, through the medium of poetry, a poetry that contradicts another poem and its view of reality.

A year after the Battle of Lowestoft, and after the French had joined the war against England on the Dutch side, the English fleet under Albemarle, the hero of the Restoration, was severely damaged. The Fire of London occurred a few months afterward, and Dryden published *Annus Mirabilis*, a poem to celebrate 1666, the 'year of wonders' (and take the curse off the 666 'year of the beast'), by considering both this most recent phase of the war and the fire as evidence of the miraculous way England under Charles II's leadership had survived and grown, a phoenix from the ashes. In December Samuel Pepys, working in the embryonic bureaucracy of the Naval Office, received a manuscript of the 'Second Advice.' Perhaps then it was the combined weight of both Waller's and Dryden's celebrations that brought forth the opposition responses. Although it was vitally important that the professed response be to Waller and to the strategy and epistemology of painting rather than to Dryden's poetic conflation of the contemporary and the classical, it was the combination of their poetic and political ideologies that was the target.

What specifically was Marvell's role in the composition of the various Advices to a Painter is hard to specify. For my purposes here and, I would argue, for Marvell's as well, the question of individual authorship is irrelevant – and may itself be part of the polemic of collective authorship (and collective responsibility) as opposed to Dryden's perpetual and cherished analogies of monarch and poet.

Like the easy classical parallels and smooth imagery of *Annus Mirabilis*, Waller's poem assumes the transparent and immediate relation of verbal instruction to visual image, and visual image to actual event. But to the extent that Marvell believes that poetry is about language in process, he cannot accept Waller's poem on the aesthetic level. Furthermore, he understands the political ideology imbedded in that aesthetic – an ideology of the natural, the innate, and the universal. The Painter poems that Marvell either wrote or collaborated on are therefore the explicit politicization of the preoccupation with subjectivity already present in his pastoral lyrics and a politicization of what is otherwise a matter of personal perspective in the Cromwell poems. They represent a coming together of what was previously separate in Marvell's poetry and perhaps in his life as well, a reintegration that resembles the hope expressed in the 'Horatian Ode' that the sources of Cromwell's new energy were in a private sensibility, close to nature, that could be turned to benefit the public good.

The reaction to Waller's poem brings to the surface attitudes that had been submerged by the Restoration settlement, a reaction that is less an event than the interpretation of an event. Interpretation itself has again become an issue, as it had been in the Civil War, not now so much the big issues of the origins of monarchy and Parliament as more immediate questions – the competency of particular ministers and military men, the secret treaties, the machinations of the court:

'Tis not, what once it was, the *World*;
But a rude heap together hurl'd;
All negligently overthrown,
Gulfes, Deserts, Precipices, Stone.
('Upon Appleton House,' ll. 761–74)

Some have interpreted the envois in the Painter poems to imply that
Marvell is still a monarchist, reserving Charles as blameless in a kind of
'evil ministers' trope. But they more likely show disdain for his oblivious-
ness to the necessary details of rule, through either airy nonchalance or
the kind of tunnel vision illustrated in 'Last Instructions' when 'by a
weak Taper's light' Charles mistakes an allegory for a naked woman
seeking pleasure with him (ll. 885–906).

Perhaps then it is appropriate that so far as we know, Marvell wrote
prose, and little or no poetry, in the last decade of his life, although he
was continually credited with any anonymous anti-royalist satire that
rose above the common ruck. As the 'Horatian Ode' and his later works
so amply demonstrate, his sense of the essence of political, sublunary
poetry was that it ought to have no essence and to search for none. Its
ideal instead was a truth of earthly inconsistency, poetically discovered,
formed, and held together – much like the constant negotiation view of
politics that would ultimately make opposition to the court patriotic
rather than treasonous.

For Dryden, the prime function of poetry was not to analyse the
incompletenesses and uncertainties of reality, but to fulfil and restore
them to their ideal forms. Unlike Milton's criticism of epic analogy in
Paradise Lost or Marvell's epic parody in the Painter poems, Dryden's
invocation of classical analogies, as in *Annus Mirabilis*, is meant to run
smoothly. As a professional poet, he aimed to give good value for his
words, and for good value metaphors and images should work, not
undermine themselves. The goals of his poetry were thus to make language and value as invariable as possible, to embed them in nature, and
to identify that nature with royalism in poetry as well as in politics. But
Marvell is always too aware not only of the specifics of political issues but
also, first, of the difficulty of actually saying something true in language,
and second, of the manipulations that can be made with it. His most
direct object of attack was therefore not Dryden himself so much as Dryden's virtual creation of this ideology of innateness and naturalness, the
ideology of no ideology.[12]

It was essential to this ideology of innateness that the poetry of praise, which was so often its usual mode, claim that it never created value, only discovered it. You have it already, says Dryden to Sir Robert Howard, to Charles II, to Eleonora, and to a host of others. But still the poet has a crucial role to play. The poetry of praise, by the right person, became essential to the new publicity of proper value, a publicity that even the monarchy needed. Dryden's poet in this sense becomes an intermediary, a specialist in the public sphere, and so his public career has to be fashioned and frequently alluded to as well, his wrestlings with poetic and political issues, his relation to the greats of the past. This is a central function of Dryden's prefaces, which display not only his Virgilian career in a timeless world of poetic greatness but also his elemental importance in his own culture. How often was Dryden's name before the public eye in books, and how infrequently was Marvell's, unless in disguise or masquerade.

Marvell died, possibly of foul play, in 1678, just as the Popish Plot unfolds. Dryden lived twenty-two years more to 1700, long enough for him to realize that it was not political kingship itself with which he was so enamoured, but primarily that of Charles II. With William III, the identification of poetry and politics that Dryden assumed was innate and natural had evaporated for him, and the only monarch Dryden would recognize as a cultural figure was himself. This is the legacy he hands down to Pope, the Romantics, and all other poets who have sought an identity themselves as the unacknowledged legislators of the world. In that view, poetic power, the power of language to find the eternal essences of the world, is what counts in both eternity and history. They, in a sense, have given us much of the material and many of the assumptions on which our own profession of literary interpretation is based. Marvell's scepticism about poetic language, his use of it as an instrument of understanding, his insistence that it reflect complexity rather than subdue it to tradition or precept – that legacy in its turn has influenced much of what we enjoy of political democracy.

Notes

1 (New Haven: Yale University Press 1992), passim.
2 I take as one of the most searching examples of the latter perspective Steven Zwicker's *Lines of Authority: Politics and English Literary Culture, 1649–1689* (Ithaca: Cornell University Press 1993). Zwicker focuses on the 'polemicization of English literary culture' from the Civil War to the Glorious Revolu-

tion and what effect they may have had in shaping opinion. I agree entirely
with that, but my theme here is, in the case of Marvell and Dryden, how
tenuous any distinction is between the poems as poetry and the poems as
political statement

3 'The First Anniversary of the Government under His Highness the Lord
   Protector, 1655,' ll. 143-4, Andrew Marvell: *The Poems and Letters*, ed. H.M.
   Margoliouth, 3rd ed. (Oxford: Clarendon 1971), 106. Future citations to
   Marvell's poetry are to this edition and will be included in the text.

4 For an account of the question of will and action in human affairs from the
   perspective of Cromwellians and others after the Restoration, see Christopher Hill, *The Experience of Defeat: Milton and Some Contemporaries* (New York:
   Viking 1984).

5 Lawrence Stone, 'The Results of the English Revolutions of the Seventeenth
   Century,' in J.G.A. Pocock, ed. *Three British Revolutions: 1641, 1688, 1776*
   (Princeton: Princeton University Press 1980), 23–108. Should Marvell himself, who has poetic heirs in the twentieth century, but few or none in the
   eighteenth and nineteenth centuries, be considered equally unsuccessful?

6 Christopher Hill, 'A Bourgeois Revolution?' in Pocock, ed., *Three British
   Revolutions*, 127.

7 Other aspects of the 'First Anniversary' similarly turn away from Stuart
   images of power: the emphasis on music (one of Cromwell's passions, rather
   than painting or theatre) especially invokes the spiritual rather than the
   visual as an analogue of order. The discursus on the fall of Cromwell's coach
   thus becomes Marvell's own version of a Rubens-like apotheosis of otherwise
   worldly events, rendered more through feelings than details.

8 'Heroique Stanzas to the Glorious Memory of Cromwell,' *The Works of John
   Dryden*, ed. E.N. Hooker, H.T. Swedenberg, Jr, et al., 20 vols. (Berkeley: University of California Press 1956–2000), 1:11–16. Further citations to Dryden's
   poetry will be to this edition (hereafter cited as *California Dryden*) and will be
   included in the text. Steven Zwicker intriguingly compares 'Heroique Stanzas' and 'An Horatian Ode' from a somewhat different perspective in *Politics
   and Language in Dryden's Poetry: The Arts of Disguise* (Princeton: Princeteon
   University Press 1984), 70–84.

9 'To my Honored Friend, Sir Robert Howard.' *California Dryden*, 1:17–20,
   ll. 29–30.

10 Dryden combines painting and politics here, as he does poetry and politics
   in the Howard poem.

11 With the Glorious Revolution it would result in a change in the idea of kingship altogether. See Lois G. Schwoerer, 'The Bill of Rights: Epitome of the
   Revolution of 1688–89,' in Pocock, *Three British Revolutions*, 224–43.

12 J.G.A. Pocock comments that, 'If oligarchy by its nature does without ideology, ideology can nevertheless play a significant role among those who wish
to attack oligarchy from the outside' (*Three British Revolutions*, 16). But the
professed absence of ideology serves nicely as a shield, especially at a time
when explicit ideologizing takes up so much intellectual space in the minds
of the opposition.

chapter three

Dryden and Dissent

SHARON ACHINSTEIN

The Hind and the Panther is a work haunted by violence, an allegory through whose many cracks violence leaks out. The two titular figures, despite their courtesy, wage war by words; their animal kingdom is ever a world of aggression, malice, and cunning, where bloody religious factions are filled with hate and vengeance. Within Dryden's interpolated tales, the Fable of the Swallows and the Fable of the Pigeons, the final brutality and horror linger well beyond the telling. What violence lies at the core of the poem may not be masked by the patina of fable; it is elemental and positively everywhere.

Dryden is a master of the rhetorical and literary means by which to convert violence into pleasure; this, a habit born of an age in which the literal violence of civil war and decapitation of a king were readily converted into discursive violence of polemical pamphleteering, satiric poetry, and the iconic images of heroic, if bloody, martyrdom. These impulses to surrogate violence charge the literary methods of which Dryden was to become a master. His balance and antithesis of his sublime couplets serve to resolve aggression to aphorism, and his sharp, killing portraits and caricatures (*Absalom and Achitophel, The Medall*) elicit savage laughter. Dryden has often been called a poet of moderation; and yet, his irenicism, his search for (as he phrases it in *Religio Laici*) '*Common quiet*,'[1] are also daring explicit political positions on the question of violence, an attempt to assimilate the experience of social disruption which had produced the era of civil war. In an age when the political contract of the sovereign's protection in exchange for the subject's obedience was deemed by some to have been broken, violence was not remote from England's past nor its future. In several different ways, the drama of early modern social relations, emblematized in the traumatic history of the civil war years, provides the general framework for Dryden's literary aggression. In an age when dramatic shifts in the nature of the social, religious, and economic orders were registered in the complex political disputes over sovereignty and toleration, a position of non-violence could signify a desire to resolve – or to deny – those very real conflicts. The language of moderation in religion and politics could serve both to make visible and to distort fundamental social change.

In his poetics of conflict Dryden returns again and again to familiar figures, the Dissenters, often associated in his writing with violence. All Dissenters – those adherents of radical sectarian religion as well as members of that more moderate but (to Dryden) even more dangerous group, the Presbyterians – remained for Dryden a consistent source of anxiety and site of blame over his writing life between 1660 and 1688. For Dryden, Dissenters were the source of civil violence; they also represented that which was impossible to assimilate in the sociality: private, rather than public, authority. While Dryden's religious poetry has been understood in intellectual history through the binary rubric of authority versus private reason, I am interested in those social pressures and anxieties that motivated such binary representations of religious conflict and the specific metaphoric shapes they took in his writing. While Dryden's *The Hind and the Panther* attempts concord, it concludes with threats. The poetics of violence emerges out of the unassimilable experience of ruptures in the sociality, specifically its democratic and acquisitive elements, for which no discursive solution can avail.

Dissent

Dryden is jarringly clear in his views about those Protestant Nonconformists who refused to come into the Church of England after Parliament voted Uniformity in 1662. He repeatedly took digs at Nonconformists through the 1660s and 1670s from the perspective of an Anglican royalist. Even the Catholic Dryden, sharing with the Nonconformists adherence to a religion practised by a minority in England, can barely withhold his contempt. In *The Hind and the Panther*, the sectarian radicals are the lowest of the low; as 'A slimy-born and sun-begotten Tribe' (3:132, Pt. 1, l. 311) they are barely discernible as creatures vested with God's care. To figure his human concerns in bestial form, in fable, is to denote their degradation. But these fanatics are beyond artistic representation, 'nor will the Muse describe' them, he writes (3:132, Pt. 1, l. 310) of these 'gross, half-animated lumps' (3:132, Pt. 1, l. 314). Although Dryden's conversion to Catholicism did not change his fundamental views on Dissenters, his political rhetoric had to change regarding them once James, challenging Anglican power, suspended the Test laws and gave his Indulgence to Dissenters and Catholics alike in the spring of 1686. Because of James's volte-face, one of Dryden's critics called *The Hind and the Panther* a 'Poor ill-timed Poem!'[2] At this time, the Poet Laureate took the unusual gesture of reaching out to Dissenters in the Preface to his poem.

Dryden was keenly aware that the Dissenters, especially Whigs, had not universally taken to James's Indulgence; we know now, as he might not have known then, the depth of Nonconformist dissatisfaction with the Royal Dispensation. The experience of the king's declaration, indeed, transformed many Dissenters into Whigs. The Quaker leader William Penn was a leading supporter, yet although there were some Nonconformist addresses to James, citizens had reason to suspect these were solicited by the king's men, as George Savile, marquis of Halifax, put it in *A Letter to a Dissenter*, 'These Bespoken Thanks are little less improper than Love Letters that were Sollicited by the Lady to whom they are to be Directed: so, that besides the little ground there is to give them, the manner of getting them, doth extreamly lessen their Value.'[3] A number of leading Nonconformist ministers, Richard Baxter and John Howe among them, chose not to cooperate with the expressions of gratitude; indeed, they refused to subscribe to the Address when it was offered them, and spoke against the 'Dispensing power,' although there was pressure on them to sign.[4]

Against this background, Dryden makes a special point of the particular relevance of Dissenters in his Preface to the Reader of *The Hind and the Panther*: 'For at this time of day to refuse the Benefit [of Indulgence] and adhere to those whom they have esteem'd their Persecutors [the Church of England], what is it else, but publickly to own that they suffer'd not before for Conscience sake, but only out of Pride and Obstinacy ... if they can go so far out of Complaisance to their old Enemies, methinks a little reason should perswade 'em to take another step, and see whether that wou'd lead 'em.' Sensitive to the risks of the growing Whig political alliance between Dissenters and Anglicans, Dryden scolds Dissenters to remember the history of their persecution at the hands of Anglicans. Rather, they owe obedience to 'their Native Sovereign: who expects a Return in *Specie* from them' (3:120–1).

Dryden's opening remarks to Dissenters only go so far towards reconciliation; they were a token gesture that gave Dryden a chance to defend
freedom of 'conscience'; but, as I shall suggest later, this defence is also
liable to ambiguous interpretation. If Dissenters were an explicit audience for his Preface, Dryden's hasty revisions did little to mitigate his
harsh representation of them in the body of his poem; indeed, *The Hind
and the Panther* could only have hardened Whigs – Dissenters and Anglicans alike – against him. The radical sectarians would have been outside
the intended audience; even Independents and Presbyterians shared
Dryden's extreme antisectarian sentiments. The poem's aim was not
necessarily to gain converts to Catholicism, nor simply to temper the
enthusiasm of the hotter Catholics. In the poem, Dryden subtly shows
his fury at James for his fickleness. But, most importantly, Dryden is also
courting those conservative Anglicans who might share his exasperation
over the Church's inability to contain Dissent and to uphold Uniformity; allaying their fears about Catholics at home; and startling them by
exposing that their own principles inevitably lead to dissent and rebellion.[5] Indeed, his main argument to discredit the Established Church
rests upon its likely disloyalty and its inability to control dissent, here
seen as a fundamental, structural weakness.

The poem is, within its polemical context, unusually violent in its
imagery. By framing his argument in a world of beasts, Dryden's *The
Hind and the Panther* drew upon a rich tradition of politically coded writing. His representational mode also offered a vehicle in which violence
did not have to be displaced. After all, the animal world is a world of
cruelty and strife; it is in animals' natures to prey upon one another
without mercy. Yet the specific forms of that violence bear analysis. The
danger of predation, specifically, of being eaten, is a particularly notable
form of threatened violence iterated throughout the poem. So the Presbyterian, that 'insatiate' Wolf (3:127, Pt. 1, l. 153), can only act according to his low nature; Bears and Boars signifying Independents and
Baptists are also predatory ravagers. Dryden emphasizes their crimes as
those of hunger and consumption: 'muzl'd though they seem, the
mutes devour' (3:127, Pt. 1, l.159); the wolfish race 'Appear with belly
Gaunt, and famish'd face' (3:127, Pt. 1, l. 161), as Dryden evokes the
familiar stereotype of the 'minced' Puritan.[6] If predatory consumption
is the trademark of Nonconformists, so too is it a characteristic of the
Anglican Church in *The Hind and the Panther,* where hunger is also an
ambition for power: 'More liberty begets desire of more, / The hunger
still increases with the store' (3:138, Pt. 1, ll. 519–20). Violent predation

becomes the menace of the Fable of the Pigeons, where the Anglican
Buzzard 'waits the falling feast' (3:200, Pt. 3, l. 1288). In the Pigeon
fable, those figures of Anglicans, the 'sort of *Doves*' (3:189, Pt. 3, l. 946)
are themselves emblematized by their hunger and mismanagement of
food: 'They drunk, and eat, and grudgingly obey'd. / The more they
fed, they raven'd still for more' (3:189, Pt. 3, ll. 963–4). Dryden even
makes a joke of the Anglican rejection of the Eucharist by explaining
that these 'gourmands,' however, prefer 'Bran' to 'Flow'r' (3:190, Pt. 3,
ll. 969, 985). The sharp contrast between the Panther and the Hind is
drawn in the Hind's invitation to a very simple dinner:

> 'Tis true, coarse dyet and a short repast,
> (She said) were weak inducements to the tast
> Of one so nicely bred, and so unus'd to fast.
> But what plain fare her cottage cou'd afford,
> A hearty welcome at a homely board
> Was freely hers.
>
> (3:159, Pt. 2, ll. 672–7)

As the threat of being eaten becomes the consistent trope through
which the problems of dissent and religious heterogeneity are bodied
forth, so there is another theme of eating in this poem: the Eucharist.
The Hind and the Panther do share a meatless 'Lenten sallad' (3:161,
Pt. 3, l. 27), but the poem in several different places also defends a
Meaty Supper, the theology of Real Presence in the sacrament. Dryden chooses the Aesopian Fable of the Dog and his Shadow, where the
dog loses his mutton by snapping at his image in a pool of water, as the
discursive form to represent his theological stance. This is an emblem
of the 'Follies of unbridled desire.'[7] As Jayne Lewis has explained, this
tale is also pliable to theological controversy surrounding the symbolic
meaning of the Eucharist in *The Hind and the Panther*. The debate over
transubstantiation had many contours since the first Protestant Reformers challenged the meaning of the Lord's Supper, and disputes
over this rite concerned the central topics of religious controversy in
the early modern period: the office of the priesthood; the presence of
Christ in a community; the purpose of formal ritual in achieving grace;
the signs of contract between humans and God; as well as the relation
between the material world and the world of magic. During the Civil
War period, with the official proscription of the Anglican Prayer Book
for fifteen years, the habit of public reception of the sacrament was in

abeyance.[8] Dryden's poem arouses the chief component of Eucharistic anxiety, that is, the debate over figuration. In Protestant reading, the meaning of the sacrament was to be commemorative, and typological, and Protestant defences insisted upon figural readings in the 1680s.[9] Catholic response defended the literal, a mysterious interpretation.

Certainly there is overlap in the discourses of violent predation and Eucharistic anxiety, as is evident in the future Archbishop John Tillotson's 1684 attack on transubstantiation as a form of cannibalism. The latitudinarian Tillotson proposed that the Catholic doctrine of the Eucharist rested upon an absurdity, that Christ's words could not be taken literally, for that would lead one to believe Christ endorsed cannibalism: 'And the impiety and barbarousness of the thing is not in truth extenuated, but onely the appearance of it, by its being done under the *Species of Bread and Wine.* For the thing they acknowledge is really done, and they believe that they verily eat and drink the natural flesh and bloud of Christ. And what can any man do more unworthily towards his Friend? How can he possibly use him more barbarously, than to feast upon his living flesh and bloud?'[10] In 1661, the young Tillotson had attended the Savoy conference on liturgical reform as a minor player, as a member of the Presbyterian delegation: his later enemies did not forget his youthful alliance, which created his comprehensionist sympathies after his elevation in the Anglican Church.[11] In defending against Tillotson's charge, the Roman Catholic Joshua Bassett, like Dryden a recent Catholic convert, who became Master of Sidney Sussex College, Cambridge, under James II, considered the truth of the doctrine to be beyond the narrowness of any human imagination, and therefore he would accept the mystery on faith:

> But sure if this Doctrine *be true*, then it is impossible that it should be barbarous, except our Saviour himself, who commanded it, and is there voluntarily present in it, should have instituted a barbarous Sacrament; which, whether our Discourser [Tillotson] can believe, I know not; but sure I am, if the Doctrine be *not* true, it cannot be barbarous to eat him in *imagination* only, except our Discoursers opinion be also barbarous ... The Barbarousness therefore objected by our Discourser (supposing this eating were according to his false Conceptions) proceeds from the narrowness of his own thoughts, who would judge, and measure the Civility and Reason of the whole World, according to the Customs (it may be) of his own little Province.[12]

This interchange over the alleged cannibalism of the sacrament is symptomatic of the violence of predatory consumption that is written all over *The Hind and the Panther.* Dryden never specifically refutes the Anglican charges that the Catholic interpretation of the Host was 'barbarous,' but rather displaces that charge onto the violent behaviour of his enemies. The literal hunger of Presbyterian and Anglican groups results in their figural portraits as cannibals.

Reading and Eating

However proximate these different, shall we say, *food issues* are, there is, I suggest, a strong link between the predatory violence of sectarianism and pious Eucharistic defence. That link may be illuminated by moving beyond the moment of controversy to consider the larger structures of understanding that motivate these figures and reveal them to be symptomatic concerns. Dryden asks these emblems of eating – whether of the good or bad kind – to work a second shift. Not only does he direct them to the defence of the Host in his sacramental theology, but these metaphors of eating very often denote *reading* as well. 'What I desire the *Reader* should know concerning me, he will find in the Body of the Poem; if he have but the patience to peruse it' (3:119), Dryden asserts in his Preface to *The Hind and the Panther,* words curiously evoking the powerful language of the Eucharist. Theology and social commentary coexist in these metaphors.

In his portrait of ravenous dissent, Dryden offers a special case of the worry, present since the Reformation, about scriptural exegesis by the all and many. Over the long period of the Reformation, there was a change in the purpose of scriptural exegesis, as the catechistical mode was displaced by theological or exegetical habits, modes oriented towards the consumption of texts, enabling equal and regular access to texts, and the formation of habits of discrimination in reading. Dryden's opposition to the swarm of interpreters newly empowered by Protestant bibliolatry is often confused with antipopulism, yet his is not antipopulism in any simple sense. Rather, Dryden's terror of the Many-Headed Reader is linked to a cluster of associations in the economic register that evoke the dangers of fungibility, interchangeability, and, in short, warn against commodity consumption. Dryden's strategy of distinguishing authority from its opposite governs the prospect of social order in his poems, and his political ideas take the specific form of an observation on the excess of social mobility advanced by a particular historical mode of religion, for which dissent becomes the sign.

In *Religio Laici*, Dryden uses economic metaphors to narrate the history of how people wrested religious authority away from the priests: 'That what they thought the *Priest's*, was *Their* Estate,' Dryden writes in evoking the spectre of the great transfer of Church wealth into private hands. He describes the motive to directly consume what had before been mediated by authorized figures: 'every man who saw the Title fair / Claim'd a Child's part, and put in for a Share' (2:121, ll. 391, 394–5). However, for Dryden, the people's assuming an economic agency does not represent a triumph of right, but rather a nightmare of unbounded consumption. Again, *Religio Laici*:

> The Book thus put in every vulgar hand,
> Which each presum'd he best cou'd understand,
> The *Common Rule* was made the *common Prey;*
> And at the mercy of the *Rabble* lay.
>   (2:121, ll. 400–3).

The '*Common Rule*,' perhaps the 'Golden Rule' of the Bible, that doctrine of the reversibility of good acts, has disintegrated into a terrifying fantasy of social levelling. The double sense of the word 'common' articulates a double threat: that of accessibility through dissemination, and that which is low or vulgar. With the pun on '*common Prey*,' or common prayer, the language of predatory relation depicts reading in all its brutal carnality. If the language is that of commodity consumption, then indeed the voracious, hungry, physical need-driven acts classify the consumers as rank sensualists 'preying' on their victims:

> The tender Page with horney Fists was gaul'd;
> And he was gifted most that loudest baul'd:
> The *Spirit* gave the *Doctoral Degree*:
> And every member of a *Company*
> Was of *his Trade*, and of the *Bible free*.
> Plain *Truths* enough for needfull *use* they found;
> But men wou'd still be itching to *expound*:
> ....
> This was the Fruit the *private Spirit* brought;
> Occasion'd by *great Zeal*, and *little Thought*.

> While Crouds unlearn'd, with rude Devotion warm,
> About the Sacred Viands buz and swarm,
> The *Fly-blown Text* creates a *crawling Brood*;
> And turns to *Maggots* what was meant for *Food*.
> *A Thousand daily Sects rise up, and dye;*
> *A Thousand more the perish'd Race supply.*
>   (2:121, ll. 404–10, 415–22)

These class attacks, plain for all to see, resolve into a quotable aphorism, a linguistic normalization, impersonally marking an allegedly universal truth to which all can assent. By comparing this disturbing social arrangement to corrupted nature, Dryden makes the rejection of dissenting bibliophilia, with its 'private reason,' seem inevitable, which it was not. In glossing this passage, Earl Miner's text calls attention to *Hudibras*, where a similar image of texts and maggots is to be found:

> Religion spawn'd a various Rout,
> Of Petulant Capricious Sects,
> The Maggots of Corrupted Texts,
> That first Run all Religion down,
> And after every swarm its own.
> For as the *Persian Magi* once,
> Upon their *Mothers*, got their *Sons*,
> That were incapable t'injoy,
> That Empire any other way;
> So *Presbyter* begot the other,
> Upon the *Good Old Cause* his Mother.[13]

There, however, the accusation is corrupt genealogy and incestuous generation, twin problems of the Stuart succession after the execution of Charles and the installation of Commonwealth and Protectorate regimes. Speaking to another moment, Dryden's accusation, as the contrast with Butler makes clear, is a reflection upon private zeal and public access. Dryden charges that the unlearned were coming to see themselves as possessing authority, here authority to interpret the Bible. This is felt as repulsive; the reader is called upon to alter that situation, to defend that precious victim, the 'tender page,' from such a rude assault, rude in its class origins, rude in its mannerless and disgusting corporeality (itching, horny fists, warm devotion), and corrupt in its effects, turning into maggots (putrefied meat) what was before good food.

In *The Hind and the Panther,* with the Fable of the Dog and his Shadow, several Eucharistic cruxes emerge, but one is chief: the willfulness of Anglican interpretation. As the Hind argues with the Panther over the meaning of 'is' in Real Presence, she claims: 'For *real,* as you now the word expound, / From solid substance dwindles to a sound' (3:141, Pt. 3, ll. 46–7). Now comes her reference to Aesop, evoking the rhetorical duplicity of that model of figuration:

> Methinks an *Aesop*'s fable you repeat,
> You know who took the shadow for the meat:
> Your churches substance thus you change at will,
> And yet retain your former figure still.
> (3:141, Pt. 2. 48–51).

The Hind accuses that 'at will' the Anglican Panther changes not simply the Host's substance, but the *Church's* substance. Disloyalty is achieved by the force of desire, with willful capriciousness the emblem of Anglican fickleness and self-interest.

The promises of freedom, of equality of interpretation, of claims to innate authority, and of the rule of conscience are all axioms of bourgeois ideology, including the belief that any one, including Dryden, can read, or change places, or succeed. But these axioms are also the age's chief sources of social anxiety. Dryden's nightmare of biblical access reveals the functional instability of social hierarchy in his time. His condemnation of dispersed authority is at every moment dependent upon the resources of 'literacy,' a form of cultural capital, as John Guillory has called it, which is paradoxically the enabling condition of Dryden's poem.[14] Enough literacy, but not too much, will hold the precarious social order in balance. If education had caused destabilizing social effects, it was education of the wrong sort, as *Religio Laici* makes clear; these are, after all, 'Crouds unlearn'd' for whom 'The *Spirit* gave the *Doctoral Degree.*' If non-institutionalized learning had created opportunities for social mobility, then Dryden synechdocally indicts the wider processes of communication and dissemination of cultural authority in his own time. Those would include a public eager for a non-traditional lay education, such as that provided by coffee-house culture and formal evening lectures by leading Nonconformists; other non-orthodox sites of education were dissenting grammar schools and vocational academies.[15] The wide availability of printed matter was a process from which Dryden himself benefited, but it also created and responded to an uncontrollable audience for that literature. All these are forms against which his defence of the Established Church in *Religio Laici* is meant to brace.

Cultural capital is, of course, acquired, and the disturbing, equalizing logic of acquisition haunts Dryden's religious writing, Protestant or Catholic. Dryden's ambivalence towards the logic of acquisition is nowhere more evident than in his double-edged treatment of conscience. As the Preface darkly registers in *The Hind and the Panther,* conscience is the powerful motor of social conflict. 'All Men are engag'd either on this side or that,' Dryden comments, 'and tho' Conscience is the common *Word,* which is given by both, yet if a Writer fall among Enemies, and cannot give the marks of *Their* Conscience, he is knock'd down before the Reasons of his own are heard' (3:119). Conscience here, as the Bible in the passage I quoted earlier from *Religio Laici,* has become a 'common *Word*': *common* in the sense of its ubiquity in being adopted by different warring factions, but also *common* as low or vulgar, a debased thing of the street.

Conscience in this passage Dryden produces as a private property: it is either 'theirs' or 'his own,' *meum* or *tuum*. At the same time as he notes the socially volatile role of conscience, however, in the Preface to *The Hind and the Panther* he applauds the king's Indulgence to Tender Consciences. Taking note of the thankful Addresses allegedly offered by grateful Dissenters following James's Dispensation of Indulgence, Dryden asserts the supremacy of conscience, but his words may contain more irony than his recent readers admit: 'Some of the Dissenters in their Addresses to His Majesty have said that *He has restor'd God to his Empire over Conscience.*'' Dryden seems to laud this, but he qualifies his praise: 'I Confess I dare not stretch the Figure to so great a boldness: but I may safely say, that Conscience is the Royalty and Prerogative of every Private man. He is absolute in his own Breast, and accountable to no Earthly Power, for that which passes only betwixt God and Him' (3:120). In these words, Dryden casts Nonconformist defences of conscience into a royalist mould, using the language of Royal Prerogative most hated by Whigs. There is a further contradiction in this passage: here conscience is figured as private property, imitative of the social relations of absolute dominion, but also of value only in an unearthly economy, as Dryden voids the material conditions of production and consumption.

The concern that conscience was simply a mask for interest, as instrumental as movable property, pervades Dryden's writing. When in 1688, in *Britannia Rediviva,* Dryden acclaimed the birth of the Stuart Catholic heir, amidst the extraordinary events that would lead to the downfall of that line, he would not hesitate to draw conscience as 'Int'rest ill disguis'd' (3:216, l. 190). Conscience is all too susceptible to market pressures: fetishization, reification, and sale. A quick journey into the concordance shows us Dryden's poetry very often uses conscience simply as a cover for private interest, figured through economic imagery.

Religio Laici offers the word 'conscience' only once, as if Dryden's attempt to defend the Established Church cannot be successful on those grounds. But *The Hind and the Panther* gives an amplified, dark reading of conscience, where it is indistinguishable from private passion. Looking to rewrite the history of the English Reformation, the Hind indicts Henry VIII for his crimes of lust: 'That conscience, conscience wou'd not let him rest, / I mean not till possess'd of her he lov'd, / And old, uncharming *Catherine* was remov'd' (3:167, Pt. 3, ll. 207–9). There, conscience is another word for erotic desire: so fall the lofty aims of Reformation. As the Hind in Part Three impeaches the authority of conscience she catalogues the history of Anglican and dissenting disloyalty and hypocrisy (3:184–5, Pt. 3, ll. 786–824) in an exposé to which the Panther can only assent, albeit in a surly tone, 'Conscience or int'rest be't, or both in one' (3:186, Pt. 3, l. 825). In her final chastisement the Hind banishes conscience from the clutch of legitimate religious justification: 'For shame let Conscience be your Plea no more ... But she's a Bawd to gain, and holds the Door' (3:186, Pt. 3, ll. 857–59).

In a contrast to this prostituted conscience, true freedom of conscience in the Preface to *The Hind and the Panther,* that which is guaranteed by the sovereign's dispensation, cannot then be *common* at all; it must avoid the medium of social relations. It is only ever an object of desire. As Dryden explains his own turn towards the Catholic Church, the language of his autobiography functions symptomatically to register the full force of this problem of propriety or ownership or commodification of conscience in late-seventeenth-century discourse:

> My thoughtless youth was wing'd with vain desires,
> My manhood, long misled by wandring fires,
> Follow'd false lights; and when their glimps was gone,
> My pride struck out new sparkles of her own.
> Such was I, such by nature still I am,
> Be thine the glory, and be mine the shame.
>
> (3:125, Pt. 1, ll. 72–7)

The bourgeois subject is plainly in search of a commodity. In this much remarked-upon passage, there is the structure of desire mapped onto a narcissistic discourse of ownership and self-creation. As his 'vain desires' solicit false guidance, so in the absence of guides, they supply their own: 'My pride struck out new sparkles of her own.' By nature, Dryden admits, humans, beset by longing, are liable to the deceptive pleasures, seduced by the allure of self-fulfilment. As the poem exhorts its God to 'teach me to believe Thee' (3:125, Pt. 1, l. 68), it also marks the central tenet to which the reorganization of the self must adhere: 'Be thine the glory and be mine the shame.' There Dryden asserts the full achievement of selfhood as dependent upon a rough division between Thine and Mine, transcendent and earthly, *meum* and *tuum*, a fundamental division of ownership. To what economy does God's part belong, then, within the structure of desire (Dryden's poem is nothing but the expression of desire for communion), but translated outside the vain economy of self as property?

Economies of Consumption

The Hind and the Panther is an especially fraught case through which to observe the work of theology in relation to that of consumption, since, as many critics past and present have noted, its representational mode is irredeemably fractured, multi-generic, and highly unstable. Even its earliest readers noted the tears in its mimetic fabric, as they mocked the poem for the arbitrariness of its signs. In parody, Charles Montagu and Matthew Prior 'transvers'd' it to 'The Story of the Country and the City Mouse.' Theirs is a brilliant Horatian rewrite of the character of the Hind: 'A milk-white Mouse immortal and unchang'd, / Fed on soft Cheese, and o're the Dairy rang'd.'[16] Dryden, Jayne Lewis has suggested in *The English Fable*, produced his semiologically disorienting effects as a consequence of the age's need for the hybrid and contingent morality of the fable genre. And Dryden's transcending representations are part and parcel of his newly claimed Catholic poetics, as Sanford Budick and Steven Zwicker have shown.[17] If Dryden's poem makes its doctrinal points about the arbitrariness of signs to the eyes of faith it does so through the same means of those arbitrary signs.

Sometimes stability is on offer in the poem: in the representational efficiencies of typology (England as Israel); of allegory (the Baptist boar, etc.); and even of fable (Swallows, Pigeons), all of which strategies ensure visibility in the reading economies of seventeenth-century polemic. But the poem also, however, relies on a central non-iconic representational effect: that of Real, not mediated, Presence. As Donald R. Benson has carefully explained in a very fine essay, the poem defends in theological terms a doctrine of literal interpretation of signs, starting from the Sign of the Host. In Dryden's Eucharistic poetics, goes this reading, the doctrine of Real Presence does indeed exceed all representational claims; but at the same time, it evacuates from representation the possibility of figural meaning to begin with.[18] I would like to extend Benson's findings to suggest that Dryden's experience of the transforming modes of social relations, and with these, of social knowledge, leads him to figures that both imagine and seek to halt the damage caused by this newer logic of fungible exchange. His poem, fixated upon a central theological question, is a productive response and a shaping of the terms of a newer economic logic, as yet unresolved, but aesthetically represented through a poetics of violence. The poem's many figural modes – allegory, fable, type – produce aberrations in stable representation, a dizzying array of effects that emblematize the frail, hungry, human propensity for figural excess. That there should be a struggle, even violence, over the cultural value of a symbolic commodity, such as the Bible, to vernacular literacy is not surprising. That complex negotiation over cultural value was also carried on by means of religious discourse through which that violence could be assimilated or reawakened is equally true. The theological controversy over consumption of the Host helps to *prepare* the meaning of cultural value that it in turn shapes. The figures of Dissenter and Anglican as predatory beasts, then, are no simple icons of terror. Rather, it is precisely because questions of consumption, and those shifts in economic and social entitlement that lay at the heart of England's mid-century struggles, were being registered in the aesthetic motifs of partisan writing, that Dryden's figures of consumption say more than he can know: violence is their excess.

The real violence that erupted in the 1640s was in many ways a sign of another kind of violence which was not completely understood in its own day, that is, the shifts in social relations, results of processes of economic transformation in the early modern period. Changes in the meaning of property, of what was one's own, experienced by ordinary English men and women during the earlier parts of the century, came to justify taking up arms against their king in the revolutionary decades. From the Leveller principle that every man has property in his own person comes a stream of radical redefinitions of property, of which John Locke's conjoining the ideas of self-propriety with natural right culminates in his *Second Treatise*, a work justifying resistance to state authority. In the political movement united by the 1647 Agreement of the People,

Levellers – so called because they were feared to 'level' all social distinction by obliterating the precedence of strictly *landed* claims to authority – proposed a written constitution based on inalienable natural rights, among which were freedom of conscience, the removal of property qualifications for the franchise (indeed, a popular sovereignty), and accountability in government.[19] Whether or not the merchants or the middle class sponsored the Revolution, those in prominent positions in the Commonwealth religious establishment, just as did Dissenters and Whigs after the Restoration, had strong ties to the London merchant community, members of a newer class of citizens who made a commercial revolution the vanguard of revolutionary political transformation.[20]

The distinction between real property, held in land, and movable property, valued through exchange, was increasingly visible in the later seventeenth century; the financial revolution of the 1690s would restate this division as a contest between government patronage and independent virtue in debates erupting over the system of public credit.[21] Historians and historical sociologists such as Joyce Appleby and Albert Hirschmann have tracked how developments in theorizing property and the widespread perception of a capitalist form within political discourse came into being in the 1690s.[22] Renaissance mercantilism, with its emphasis on money, yields a powerful conceptual model for reification. By money, form may be detached from content; the uniquenesses of labour may be diminished, and all the traditional loyalties and obligations required by landed relations may be threatened by its common, equalizing denominations.

Intellectual historians have long disputed the causes and ramifications of the early modern changing conceptions of property.[23] I have no answers to questions they pose regarding the new fungibility of money, or the tension between commodities and land and between public credit and agrarian virtue. Nonetheless, in Dryden we can see a share in this developing struggle. His subtle engagement with the cultural aftershocks of civil war and his complicities in this great social and structural transformation helps me see how theology can mediate such changes in the meaning of property.[24] In my analysis, the theological dispute over transubstantiation may be seen not only as a matter of figuration, or of the materiality of the sign, but also as a gauge of the changing understanding of property and social relations during this explosive moment in history. As economic relations in the later seventeenth century were yielding to newer practices of exchange, so these shifts were registered through the mediating forms of theology, yet to become the mainstream cultural critiques of the newer forms of consumption and luxury.

The Fables

Very real violence ends Dryden's poem, a violence that is withheld until the very last section of his poem. His fantastic tales, the Fable of the Swallows and the Fable of the Pigeons, gory narratives both of them, are positioned well after the initial confession of faith. In juxtaposition to the First Part, which Dryden, in his Preface to *The Hind and the Panther*, proudly describes as his endeavour 'to raise, and give ... the Majestick Turn of Heroick Poesie,' and to the Second Part's 'plain and perspicuous' theological and historical dispute, the Third Part, Dryden admits, has 'more of the Nature of Domestick Conversation' (3:122). But it is here in the realm of the 'Domestick' that the appalling tragedy and violent prophecy are to be found, deeply buried in a poem that is admittedly heterogeneous in its literary aspirations and modes, the realm of the domestic being an all-too-familiar arena for uncivil relations. Is violence a consequence of confession and theological debate? Its only possible 'resolution'? Or is that violence another means of expressing the same?

The two fables interpolated into *The Hind and the Panther* provide what little plot exists in this poem. With the Hind's Tale of the Swallows (3:173–80, Pt. 3, ll. 427–638), roughly two hundred lines of verse, the rash policies of the radical Catholics come to an end in the birds' general slaughter; their political ineptitude leads to their unwise choice and deadly end. Their failure of prudence, specifically, their failure to read the seasons or political timing aright, brings about their destruction. The first cause of their destruction is rendered impersonal – it's merely a wintry storm that causes them to perish – but what comes next shows how impersonal violence can so easily be transformed into social violence:

> The joyless morning late arose, and found
> A dreadfull desolation reign a-round,
> Some buried in the Snow, some frozen to the ground:
> The rest were struggling still with death, and lay
> The *Crows* and *Ravens* rights, an undefended prey;
> Excepting *Martyn*'s race, for they and he
> Had gain'd the shelter of a hollow tree,

But soon discover'd by a sturdy clown,
He headed all the rabble of a town,
And finish'd 'em with bats or poll'd 'em down.
                              (3:179, Pt. 3, ll. 622–31)

If the Panther 'with malice' recounts this after-dinner fable, it is nonetheless a politically topical warning to the hotter sort of Catholics about
their lack of prudence, their weighing hope against common sense. But
Dryden, by giving that not only natural catastrophe but also human cruelty perpetrates this slaughter, warns about the propensity of human
folk to degrade themselves for the purposes of entertainment. These
fragile birds will become victims by 'right' to those scavengers of the
night, and those who had misled them victims of base human malice.
This Great Bird Massacre is meant to frighten the Roman Catholics into
a posture of greater moderation and prudence, but the difference
between the symbolic violence and real violence is unclear: the Panther
issues this story as a threat, a verbal action inciting coercion and terror.

The second interpolated tale is the Hind's, and it foretells a different
violence that is to come. In the Fable of the Pigeons (3:188–200, Pt. 3, ll.
906–1288), Dryden spills close to four hundred lines of ink – twice the
length of the Panther's fable. The Pigeons, who decide they need
greater protection from their feared enemies, bring in a Buzzard, a bird
of prey: 'That desp'rate Cures must be to desp'rate Ills apply'd' (3:194,
Pt. 3, l. 1111). Whether the Buzzard represents Burnet or William is of
less interest here than the way he serves as an unstable sign of predatory
force: the Doves have 'become the Smiths of their own Foolish Fate'
(3:199, Pt. 3, l. 1268), surrendering their own purses and their power to
this strong creature. In Aesop's fable, the Pigeons are devoured by the
Buzzard; Dryden's fable decorously avoids that representation of violence, only to suggest the fate of these birds is still an open question.
The Hind narrates that the Pigeons suffer disempowerment and impoverishment due to their chosen Tyrant, 'Like Snows in warmth that
mildly pass away, / Dissolving in the Silence of Decay' (3:199, Pt. 3, ll.
1271–2). Although they hoped strong leadership would unify them and
protect them from internal divisions, their weakness makes them liable
to subjection and further schism, figured as becoming 'prey' to another.
The hungry oppressor cannot 'long abstain from Food, / Already he
has tasted *Pigeons* Blood' (3:199, Pt. 3, ll. 1279–80). Consumption as eating and consumption as economic loss become figures for each other in
Dryden's poetic imagination.

Unlike the Fable of the Swallows, there is no response by the listener; instead, Dryden's poem closes almost abruptly. The Panther, it appears, heeds not the warning and is merely yawning and sleepy, mouth agape. Dryden's readers, however, are meant to be wide awake.

Dryden's poetry, as the conduit through which were filtered the tremendous currents of violence in the Restoration, reiterated the age's wounds in symbolic form. Here we encounter one writer's attempt to work through the past in an effort to write a future. With his art, Dryden reflects upon the causes of civil violence and revolution, making visible the traces of bloodshed in the social polity, the residue of unresolved aggression. But the trauma of civil war and the remainder of dissent appear not merely in an aftershock of political faction and instability. That conflict was itself a consequence, and also a translation, a surrogacy, of the fact of real social change. Dryden sought through politics and polemical poetry to control and narrate the discontinuities of that unremarked social trauma. I wonder if his late theological turn to Roman Catholicism is yet another, more potent avenue to work through it; was he merely iterating that violence in another form?

Notes

1 *The Works of John Dryden*, ed. E.N. Hooker, H.T. Swedenberg, Jr, et al., 20 vols. (Berkeley: University of California Press 1956–2000), 2:122, l. 450. All subsequent references to Dryden's poems will refer to this edition (hereafter cited as *California Dryden*) and be included within the text of my essay.
2 *The Revolter* (London 1687), 10.
3 George Savile, Marquis of Halifax, *Letter to a Dissenter* (London 1687), 5. Defending the Addresses against this accusation is T.N., *A Modest Censure of the Immodest Letter to a Dissenter, Upon occasion of His majesty's late Gracious Declaration for Liberty of Conscience* (London 1687), 13–4.
4 N.H. Keeble and Geoffrey F. Nuttall, *Calendar of the Correspondence of Richard Baxter*, 2 vols. (Oxford: Clarendon Press 1991), II, 286; in a letter to Sir John Baber, Baxter sets out his reasons. John Howe's diligence against the Dispensing Power is detailed in Edmund Calamy, *Memoirs of the Life of the Late Revd Mr. John Howe* (London: Sam. Chandler 1724), 134–5, where Howe, despite pressure to do so, refused to sign. Douglas R. Lacey summarizes evidence for pressure on Nonconformists to make these Addresses in *Dissent and Parliamentary Politics in England, 1661–1689* (New Brunswick, N.J.: Rutgers University Press 1969), 341 n. 21.

5 In this, I agree with Donald R. Benson, 'Theology and Politics in Dryden's Conversion,' *SEL* 4, 3 (1964), 393–412. Steven Zwicker points out the impossible contradiction of reviling and courting Dissenters in 'The Paradoxes of a Tender Conscience,' *ELH* 63 (1996), 851–69.

6 See Kristen Poole, *Radical Religion from Shakespeare to Milton: Figures of Nonconformity in Early Modern England* (Cambridge: Cambridge University Press 2000), 48–55.

7 Jayne Lewis, *The English Fable: Aesop and Literary Culture, 1651–1740* (Cambridge: Cambridge University Press 1996), 22, and 114, discussing the issue of transubstantiation in relation to this fable.

8 On the Restoration Anglican interpretation of the sacrament, see John Spurr, *The Restoration Church of England, 1646–1689* (New Haven: Yale University Press 1991), 345–9. On the Civil War abolition of the sacrament, see Horton Davies, *Worship and Theology in England from Cranmer to Baxter and Fox, 1534–1690*, 2 vols. (Grand Rapids, Mich.: Erdman Publishing 1996), 2:301; and see 2:286–325.

9 In Renaissance studies, Steven Greenblatt has recently explored what he has called 'Eucharistic anxieties' in his account of the way religion mediated the historical transition from one social formation to another through the great religious upheaval of the Reformation. See Stephen Greenblatt and Catherine Gallagher, *Practicing New Historicism* (Chicago: University of Chicago Press 2000), 151, 154, 160; and his 'Remnants of the Sacred in Early Modern England,' in Maureen Quilligan, Peter Stallybrass, and Margreta DeGrazia, eds, *Subject and Object in Renaissance Culture* (Cambridge: Cambridge University Press 1996), 342. On Eucharistic controversies, see B.A. Gerrish, 'Sign and Reality: The Lord's Supper in the Reformed Confessions,' in *The Old Protestantism and the New: Essays on the Reformation Heritage* (Chicago: University of Chicago Press 1982), 118–30; and on the devaluation of the sacraments in later-seventeenth-century dissent, see Stephen Mayor, *The Lord's Supper in Early English Dissent* (London: Epworth 1972), 74–105

10 John Tillotson, *A Discourse against Transubstantiation* (London 1684), 35. Catholic apologists replied to this charge: J. Gother, *An Answer to a Discourse against Transubstantiation* (London 1687), 75; [Joshua Bassett], *Reason and Authority: Or the Motives of a Late Protestants Reconciliation to the Catholic Church. Together with Remarks upon some late Discourses against Transubstantiation* (London 1687), 90–1.

11 Craig Rose, *England in the 1690s* (Oxford: Blackwell 1999), 183.

12 [Joshua Bassett], *Reason and Authority*, 95–6.

13 John Wilders, ed., Samuel Butler, *Hudibras* (Oxford: Clarendon Press 1967), Pt. 3, ii, 8–18.

14 See John Guillory, *Cultural Capital: The Problem of Literary Canon Formation* (Chicago: University of Chicago Press 1993), 36–42, 60–82.

15 C.E. Whiting, *Studies in English Puritanism from the Restoration to the Revolution, 1660–1688* (New York: Macmillan 1931), 75.

16 [Charles Montagu and Matthew Prior], *The Hind and the Panther Transvers'd To the Story of the Country Mouse and the City-Mouse* (1687), 4; facs. rept. in Drydeniana VIII: *The Hind and the Panther and other Works 1685–1687* (New York: Garland 1974).

17 Lewis, *The English Fable*, 103, 105, 108; Steven B. Zwicker, *Politics and Language in Dryden's Poetry: The Arts of Disguise* (Princeton: Princeton University Press 1984), 126–7, 143; Sanford Budick, *Dryden and the Abyss of Light: A Study of* Religio Laici *and* The Hind and the Panther (New Haven: Yale University Press 1970), 223–37.

18 Donald Benson, 'Dryden's *The Hind and the Panther:* Transubstantiation and Figurative Language,' *JHI* 43:2 (1982), 195–208.

19 David Wootton, 'Leveller Democracy and the Puritan Revolution,' in J.H. Burns and Mark Goldie, eds., *The Cambridge History of Political Thought, 1450–1700* (Cambridge: Cambridge University Press 1991), 412–42. Henry Ireton, arguing at Putney, said that all he was arguing for 'is because I would have an eye to property,' causing a rift in the revolutionary program between the Leveller movement and Cromwell, cited in J.G.A. Pocock, 'Authority and Property: The Question of Liberal Origins,' in *Virtue, Commerce, and History: Essays on Political Thought and History Chiefly in the Eighteenth Century* (Cambridge: Cambridge University Press 1986), 57.

20 J.F. Wilson, *Pulpit in Parliament* (Princeton: Princeton University Press 1969); see also Robert Brenner, *Merchants and Revolution: Commercial Change, Political Conflict, and London's Overseas Traders, 1550–1653* (Princeton: Princeton University Press 1993), esp. 565– 9.

21 Pocock, 'Authority and Property,' 68.

22 See Joyce Appleby, *Economic Thought and Ideology in Seventeenth-Century England* (Princeton: Princeton University Press 1978) for a discussion of how new market relations in the 1690s required new justificatory languages, giving birth to liberal political theory. See also Appleby, 'Political and Economic Liberalism in Seventeenth-Century England,' in her *Liberalism and Republicanism in the Historical Imagination* (Cambridge: Harvard University Press 1992), 34–57.

23 The powerful thesis of C.B. Macpherson's *The Political Theory of Possessive Individualism*, put forward in 1962, offered the hypothesis that seventeenth-century political thought was significantly changing its perception of property as marketable. This new conception of property, based on the writings of

Hobbes and Locke, gave liberal political theory its foundations. See C.B. Macpherson, *The Political Theory of Possessive Individualism: Hobbes to Locke* (Oxford: Clarendon 1962).

24 Jean-Christophe Agnew has suggested that the early modern Puritan attack on players and playgoing may be understood as a response to the market, as an attempt to restrain the 'diminishing transparancy of exchange,' in *Worlds Apart: The Market and the Theatre in Anglo-American Thought, 1550–1750* (Cambridge: Cambridge University Press 1986), 141. See also Joyce Appleby, 'Consumption in Early Modern Social Thought,' in John Brewer and Roy Porter, eds., *Consumption and the World of Goods* (London: Routledge 1993), 162–73.

chapter four

The Politics of Pastoral Retreat: Dryden's Poem to His Cousin

MICHAEL MCKEON

Months before he died, Dryden told a correspondent that his recently published *Fables Ancient and Modern* (1700) was being judged by some readers his best work yet, especially the volume's two original poems. Dryden himself agreed with 'the greater part' that his 'verses to my Cousin Driden were the best of the whole,' and he seems to have agreed as well that 'I never writt better.'[1] 'To My Honour'd Kinsman' is a poem of consummate mastery, its structure densely elegant, its tone exquisitely modulated to meet the shifting needs of its argumentative purpose. Generically the poem draws deeply on a range of forms to fashion something distinct from them all. On the face of it a verse epistle of mixed panegyric and satire, 'To My Honour'd Kinsman' is also a pastoral in the broadest sense of the term – a poem in praise of country life – that's more particularly indebted to the tradition inaugurated by Horace's second Epode and embellished by centuries of imitation. At the same time, however, Dryden's pastoral is quite explicitly a political poem, a poem about contemporary politics.

If only because of its inclusion in *Fables Ancient and Modern*, 'To My Honour'd Kinsman' also asks to be read as a 'fable.' In its broadest usage, Dryden's contemporaries meant by the term 'fable' nothing more specific than a story or a fiction, something that stands for or refers to something else. Dryden's 'Preface' to the *Fables* is somewhat more precise: 'I have endeavour'd to chuse such Fables, both Ancient and Modern, as contain in each of them some instructive Moral, which I could prove by Induction, but the Way is tedious; and they leap foremost into sight, without the Reader's Trouble of looking after them.'[2]

This is still pretty broad, but it may recall the way contemporaries used 'fable' synonymously with terms such as 'parable,' 'allegory,' and 'example' to denote a figure of speech in which a relatively concrete signifier is made to stand for an abstract signified – what Dryden calls here an 'instructive moral.'

At the beginning of the century Francis Bacon, using 'fable,' 'parable,' and 'allegory' interchangeably, had pointed out that 'parables have been used in two ways, and (which is strange) for contrary purposes. For they serve to disguise and veil the meaning, and they serve also to clear and throw light upon it.'[3] The use of fables to obscure meaning is most evident in what we often call 'political' allegories, where the ostensive story alludes to sentiments too controversial to be directly stated.[4] Fables that aim to clarify, on the other hand, usually facilitate semantically difficult ideas, such as spiritual teachings or philosophical precepts. And yet, as Dryden's contemporaries knew, Bacon's 'contrary purposes' were not in practice so easy to disentangle. Andrew Marvell feared that Milton's spiritual pedagogy in *Paradise Lost* (1667) would backfire and 'ruin ... / The sacred Truths to Fable and old Song,'[5] while Aphra Behn's *Love-Letters* (1681–5) conceal the politics of the Exclusion Crisis behind a veil of gossamer. Dryden's own poetry provides comparable complications. *Absalom and Achitophel*'s (1681) scriptural allegory works to obscure, but thereby to disclose, its meaning, whereas the controlling beast fable of *The Hind and the Panther* (1687) does little either to hide or to elucidate its difficult argument. Is it useful to add 'To My Honour'd Kinsman' to this list of Dryden's eclectic fables? If so, what is its work of signification? What is its 'instructive moral'?[6]

Whatever the interest of these questions, we can approach them only by pursuing the poem's undoubted generic standing in the *beatus ille* tradition, named for the opening of Horace's second Epode. Dryden's paraphrase of that poem begins: 'How happy in his low degree / How rich in humble Poverty, is he, / Who leads a quiet country life!'[7] 'To my Honour'd Kinsman' begins: 'How Bless'd is He, who leads a Country Life, / Unvex'd with anxious Cares, and void of Strife!'[8] Despite these similarities, however, Dryden's two poems diverge in fundamental ways, perhaps nowhere more than in the singularity with which 'To My Honour'd Kinsman' deploys its panegyric topics. Alan Roper has acutely described this as a process of 'continuous translation. The values established by one topic of praise are retained in the consideration of subsequent topics because the subsequent topics are introduced as metaphors for the first.'[9] Dryden sufficiently varies the basic pattern captured by this account to maximize its fluidity; the result is a poem that unfolds with the uncanniness of a dream. Vehicles become tenors, means become ends, similarities devolve into differences that somehow retain an aura of the familiar. 'To My Honour'd Kinsman' moves forward in its temporal progression by a process of spatial thickening, repeating motifs and accumulating structure like a sedimented rock or a densely interwoven texture, until it reaches a limit point. Here, halfway through the poem, we feel Dryden's poetic mechanism shift decisively from the private to the public, from rural retreat to political engagement. And yet the work of the second half of the poem seems inescapably to recapitulate, in a higher register, the achievement of the first.

I'd like to spend some time summarizing this singular procedure, and then reflect on what it might tell us about 'politics' in 1700: Dryden's politics at the end of his life, but also the reconception of what 'politics' amounts to now that the old age is out and it's time to begin a new. Dryden told Charles Montague that in 'To My Honour'd Kinsman' he had 'given my Own opinion, of what an Englishman in Parliament oughto [*sic*] be; & deliver it as a Memorial of my own Principles to all Posterity.'[10] Embedded in his meditation on private life, I'll suggest, is a meditation on the public life of the past century – on the wars that brought nothing about, and most of all on the dark lineage of royal absolutism.

I

Dryden's cousin is introduced to us in the character of a Justice of the Peace. What most interests the poet here is his cousin's ability to obviate the *official* system of justice. Cousin Driden decides local disputes with such gratuitous equity that contentious 'Foes' are reconciled to 'Friendship' with speed and finality (l. 9). The poet contrasts these results with those of the legal profession, where bureaucratic delays and 'Expence' only aggravate the terms of conflict that the law exists to resolve (l. 11). Cousin Driden's decisions leave a 'lasting Peace behind'; lawsuits, one instrument of 'Civil Rage,' paradoxically institutionalize a state of war that no one can win: 'he who conquers, is but last undone' (ll. 15, 3, 13). The reconciliation of conflict achieved by Cousin Driden's country justice reflects 'a Pattern of [his] Mind' and provides a link to the poet's second panegyric topic, his cousin's unmarried state (l. 16).

Like the civil law, civil marriage aggravates the condition it's meant to alleviate. True, God himself created the original office of marriage in

Eden. But 'Minds are ... hardly match'd' (l. 21). Adam's integrity lay in the fact that he was made singly, 'to God's Image' (l. 25). By contrast, the conjugal unity of our first parents was 'curs'd' by sin to duplicity: 'For Man and Woman, though in one they grow, / Yet, first or last, return again to Two' (ll. 22–4). Of course, the fault is largely woman's – at worst she's a duplicitous hunter who lays the 'Bait' and the 'Snare'; at best she's simply weak: 'How cou'd He stand, when put to double Pain, / He must a Weaker than himself sustain!' (ll. 33, 27–8). In either case, the result is that both must fall. So civil marriage, bringing duplicity out of unity, recalls the paradoxes of civil law. As 'he who conquers, is but last undone,' so '[t]wo Wrestlers help to pull each other down' (l. 30).

Dryden's third topic of praise, charity, adumbrates the virtues of extra-official integrity and autonomy already praised in his cousin's justice and celibacy. Charity is the quintessential virtue of the country gentleman, rooted in the patriarchal care of the 'feudal' landlord. Like Cousin Driden's justice, his charity is freely given. Both are modelled on divine example; but the poet stresses especially the immediacy of divine *caritas*, whereby Driden's gifts to his neighbours flow directly from God's gifts to Driden himself: 'For God, who gave the Riches, gave the Heart / To sanctifie the Whole, by giving Part' (ll. 38–9). Indeed, the poet imagines Cousin Driden's wealth as an immediate gift of God *rather* than a product of the patriline. Deprived of the 'Father's Share' by his status as 'the Second Son,' Driden, like Jacob, received the divine reward of a maternal inheritance (ll. 41–3).[11] In this way the cousin's charity is reinforced not only by his justice but also by his celibate integrity. For at both ends of the line Cousin Driden is displaced from the paternal lineage, a condition that sharpens his charitable regard by encouraging him to treat his neighbours indiscriminately – both 'the Wealthy' and 'the Poor' – as though they were immediate family. Thus Cousin Driden is 'free to Many,' if also 'to Relations most' (ll. 37, 48), his charitable paternalism paradoxically enhanced by his detachment from strict paternity.

We anticipate the volatility of Dryden's fourth panegyric topic, which envisions his cousin as a hunter, if we recall that the language of the hunt has already been applied to the duplicity of marriage (l. 33). But as the poet affirms, his cousin's hunting is also comparable to the pursuit of common-law justice, for he brings

> the wily Fox
> To suffer for the Firstlings of the Flocks;

> Chas'd ev'n amid the Folds; and made to bleed,
> Like Felons, where they did the murd'rous Deed.   (ll. 54–7)

Here the rough justice of an eye for an eye obliquely echoes the irony of the law courts: as the conqueror is himself at last outdone (l. 13), so the hunter fox at last becomes the hunted fox. But as the simile self-consciously reminds us, foxes are not felons, and the ritual of the hunt is a 'fiery Game' and 'Champian-Sport' rather than a duty of 'serious Hours,' a 'Pleasure' of 'Youth' more than of 'Age' (ll. 51, 58, 60, 61). Foxes are to felons as sport is to justice. Why is it important to distinguish the youthful pleasures of sport from the serious maturity of justice? As though in answer to this question, the poet now offers an ostentatiously exemplary 'Emblem':

> The Hare, in Pastures or in Plains is found,
> Emblem of Humane Life, who runs the Round;
> And, after all his wand'ring Ways are done,
> His Circle fills, and ends where he begun,
> Just as the Setting meets the Rising Sun.   (ll. 62–6)

The poet's care in qualifying the comparison of hunting to justice should make us attentive, in construing this emblem, both to similarity and to difference. And despite the universality implicit in 'Humane Life,' Dryden's terse beast fable would seem to be more pointed than this. After all, the circular plight of the hare – the conflation of ends with beginnings – describes the life not of a man like Cousin Driden, but of one who can't tell the difference between youth and age, sport and justice, more and fewer pleasures. In other words, there are alternatives to this circle, which the poet now associates with a certain *kind* of human life:

> Thus Princes ease their Cares: But happier he,
> Who seeks not Pleasure thro' Necessity,
> Than such as once on slipp'ry Thrones were plac'd;
> And chasing, sigh to think themselves are chas'd.   (ll. 67–70)

Opening a new paragraph, the poet's 'thus' sends us back to several antecedents for the leisured 'ease' of 'Princes': most immediately, to the innocent futility of the circling hare; at one remove, to the circular orbit of the wily fox, who is hunted and murdered in the very place where once

he hunted and murdered. Like him, princes are 'chas'd' – judicially
hunted – from the very thrones they themselves have chased. But if the
royal chase is a way princes 'ease their Cares' by seeking 'Pleasure thro'
Necessity,' princes are not only like foxes; they're also like those who confuse foxes with felons and the 'Pleasures' of youthful sport with the 'serious Hours' of age and necessity (ll. 60–1). The lives of princes – the
mirror for magistrates – reflect a circle because the youthful ambition to
rule with which princes seek to ease their cares returns in their age as the
ambition of others to replace their rule. Against the princes and their
unappeasable 'Cares' the poet sets the example of his cousin, that 'happier he' who, 'Bless'd' with a 'Country Life,' is free of 'anxious Cares' (ll.
1–2), whose 'Age' dependably succeeds his 'Youth' (l. 4), and who is
therefore untempted to seek pleasure through necessity. So although
Dryden's fourth topic, in praise of his cousin as a hunter, begins by inviting us to compare hunting with justice, its main work is rather to warn
against their confusion. As in civil justice, so in civil rule: he who conquers is at last undone. Moreover, as in civil rule, so in civil marriage,
which confuses pleasure with necessity, 'Bait' with 'Snare,' the brevity of
a 'short Delight' with the 'long penitence' of a lifetime (ll. 20, 33).

With each panegyric topic, the layered terms of praise and blame in
'To My Honour'd Kinsman' acquire an increasingly overdetermined
density of meaning. Each succeeding topic is more complex (and simply
longer) than the last, reaching back to implicate and revise earlier ones
within an ever-expanding semantic web. (The exception to this rule is
the topic of charity, which is shorter than those that precede and succeed it.) This process is brought to a head with the poem's fifth topic,
on health, which secretes and reabsorbs all that's come before. And it
may be relevant that the poet's fifth topic, taking us deep into the centre
of his panegyric on his cousin, is also quite devoid of direct reference to
him. It's as though the mechanism of poetic evaluation has attained
such internal momentum and consequence as to outstrip, at least for a
time, the exemplary personality of its subject.

'So liv'd our Sires,' says the poet, alluding back to Cousin Driden, that
happier he who seeks not pleasure through necessity. Against both the
erstwhile example of our sires and the residual anomaly of his cousin,
Dryden now sets the modern institution of medicine: 'So liv'd our Sires,
e'er Doctors learn'd to kill, / And multiply'd with theirs, the weekly Bill'
(ll. 71–2). The doctor's bill stands in direct proportion to the bills of
mortality: medicine only aggravates the condition it was meant to cure.

The culpability of official institutions, a persistent topic of blame in the poem thus far, is now quite decisively linked to the mercenary corruptions of greed. As the 'Expence' of legal suits subverts their ends, so the 'Debauch,' 'Excess,' and 'Sloth' of physicians are pleasures that corrupt the necessity of cure, infecting its single-mindedness with a doubled motive (ll. 74–5). The physicians are bad enough; worse yet are the apothecaries, who 'suck' the 'Blood' of the profession they're meant to serve by selling prescriptions with the 'Random' blindness of the profit motive (ll. 110, 105). The echoing word invites us to see that physicians are to apothecaries as Adam is to Eve: 'So farther from the Fount, the Stream at random stray'd' (l. 26). More darkly than in defending Adam against the 'double Pain' of marriage (l. 27), the poet decries the 'double Bribe' exacted by the medical profession (l. 112): may we at least die at the hands of those with the learning to prescribe!

As the duplicity of marriage begins with the laudable aim of union, so the duplicity of medicine begins in generosity and care (l. 75). Both begin in the Garden of Eden:

> The Tree of Knowledge, once in *Eden* plac'd,
> Was easie found, but was forbid the Taste:
> O, had our Grandsire walk'd without his Wife,
> He first had sought the better Plant of Life!   (ll. 96–9)

Doctors and their 'Humane Science' picked up where our first parents left off, searching 'forbidden Truths; (a Sin to know:)' (ll. 76–7). The Fall brought death out of eternal life; if doctors had their way, divine decree would be suspended: 'The Doom of Death, pronounc'd by God, were vain' (l. 78). In a related fashion, civil lawyers would only postpone and frustrate the equitable 'final Doom' awarded by Cousin Driden as Justice of the Peace (l. 8). Good physicians like Samuel Garth at least avoid aggravating this original duplicity of medical science by that of the doctor's fee (l. 107). Better still is the method of our sires: 'By Chace our long-liv'd Fathers earn'd their Food; / Toil strung the Nerves, and purifi'd the Blood' (ll. 88–9). Unlike those princes who hunt to ease their cares, our ancestors hunted out of necessity, for food and health. And to this day, it's '[b]etter to hunt in Fields, for Health unbought' (l. 92). Indeed, to do otherwise is to dispute the truth that 'God never made his Work, for Man to mend' (l. 95). Rather, '[h]e scapes the best, who Nature to repair, / Draws Phisick from the Fields, in Draughts of Vital Air' (l. 116).

II

The effect of Dryden's procedure in the poem thus far is both centrifugal and centripetal. On the one hand, his cousin is praised in increasingly implicit terms against increasingly explicit negative examples, and he is praised for behaving in capacities that are increasingly detached from his most literal existence: Justice of the Peace, bachelor, charitable landlord, hunter, healer. On the other hand, each of these disparate topics reiterates and reinforces in its own terms the same body of values: the autonomy, integrity, and efficiency of one who stands apart from established institutions and professions (civil law, civil marriage, patrilineal obligation, princely care, medical science) and their paradoxically self-defeating futility. This uncanny accumulation of familiar values out of seemingly unrelated topics is enhanced by the way the poet's various scriptural allusions gradually coalesce around the Garden of Eden, the great prototype for the human tendency to seek pleasure through necessity. The Fall is the source both of our sins and of those civilizing institutions that, meant to alleviate our sins, duplicitously aggravate and reproduce them. Cousin Driden stands apart from these sins as a suppositionally nonlapsarian Adam does, by avoiding the Fall, an avoidance whose real-life approximation is to stay in the Garden by leading a country life.

If we recall for a moment the hypothesis of Dryden's poem as a fable, at the most microscopic level of language use the evidence of signification that both veils and discloses is so rich as to be almost nugatory. But at this point it may be useful to return briefly to the comparison between Dryden's poem and its model, Horace's second Epode. I've already pointed out that 'To My Honour'd Kinsman' differs from Horace's poem (and from Dryden's own paraphrase of it) in pursuing the singular poetic procedure that has been my subject thus far. But there's an even more fundamental difference in voicing. Dryden's paraphrase of Horace closely follows the original in being double-voiced. Most of the poem is an idealizing rumination on the virtues of rural retirement by a city moneylender whose resolve to pursue this ideal is undercut at the end by the ironic intrusion of a speaker who tells us that the moneylender has abruptly decided to abandon his plan. As Dryden's paraphrase puts it:

> He call'd his money in;
> But the prevailing love of pelf

Soon split him on the former shelf,
And put it out again.   (ll. 99–102)

Many contemporary translations of, and allusions to, Horace's poem
pointedly omit this concluding ironic turn, thereby eliminating as
well the tension between idealism and practicality. Nor does 'To My
Honour'd Kinsman' possess such an ending – but, of course, it also
lacks the plot that would make such an ending intelligible. A verse
epistle, Dryden's poem to his cousin speaks in a single voice about the
life of one who already inhabits the countryside, and who therefore
cannot logically abandon his plan to retire to it. And yet the remainder of 'To My Honour'd Kinsman' does take a turn that might be seen
as an ingenious inversion of Horace's. If the second Epode tells the
story of a rustication that surprisingly fails to materialize, Dryden's
poem tells an equally surprising story of rustic bliss that nonetheless
ends up in the city and at court. I left off the interpretation of Dryden's poem with his fifth topic of praise because here, little more than
halfway through the poem, Dryden modulates his rural panegyric to
an urban and official register. But remarkably enough, the poem not
only remains a panegyric; it also praises the urbanized cousin by just
those topics, and for just those virtues, that have dominated the first
half of the poem. In other words, if the procedure of the first half
of 'To My Honour'd Kinsman' consists in the uncanny conflation of
seemingly disparate topics in praise of country life, the second half
of the poem exploits the momentum generated by this mode of argument to cross the threshhold of the rural itself and to conflate those
ultimate disparities of country and city.[12] The site and source of all that
is negative in the first half becomes the repository of all that is positive
in the second, and for the same reasons. In the remainder of this essay
I'll consider how this contradictory strategy works and what its implications might be.

The biographical circumstance on which hangs Dryden's modulation
from country to court and city is the fact that his cousin is not only a Justice of the Peace but also a Member of Parliament. The modulation
itself occurs in the following three couplets:

You hoard not Health, for your own private Use;
But on the Publick spend the rich Produce:
When, often urg'd, unwilling to be Great,
Your Country calls you from your lov'd Retreat,

> And sends to Senates, charg'd with Common Care,
> Which none more shuns; and none can better bear.
>   (ll. 117–22)

The immediately preceding topic, in praise of Cousin Driden as a
health-giver, had been unsupported by any literal or direct connection
to his rural existence. The poet's modulation to the public register now
recapitulates and justifies the role of healer by evoking the figure of the
body politic, which Parliament provides with physic by voting supplies
for the enactment of public policy.

In that fifth topic of praise, the medical profession's insidious tendency to kill where it would cure is bound up with its will to profit where
it would cure – bound up, that is, with its professionalism and with the
duplicity of monetary corruption. Cousin Driden, now an official and
professional legislator, is nonetheless able to appear an effective healer
because the poet conceives his parliamentary role entirely in terms of
giving: as physician to the body politic, Cousin Driden prescribes a cure
that consists precisely in 'spend[ing]' money. His parliamentary function therefore also recapitulates the third topic of praise, his charity.
There in the countryside Cousin Driden, enriched by God's *caritas*,
'sanctifie[s] the Whole, by giving Part'; 'free to Many,' he is unwilling to
choose between the 'Wealthy' and the 'Poor' (ll. 39, 48, 37). Here in the
city Cousin Driden, similarly motivated, is unwilling to

> gratifie whate'er the Great desire,
> Nor grudging give, what Publick Needs require.
> Part must be left, a Fund when Foes invade;
> And Part employ'd to roll the Watry Trade:
> ....
> Good Senators, (and such are you,) so give,
> That Kings may be supply'd, the People thrive.
>   (ll. 129–32, 135–6)

Thus far Dryden has translated his third and fifth topics, in praise of
his cousin's rural charity and health-giving, to the urban and public
realm of parliamentary supply. He now returns to his first and second
topics, in praise of Cousin Driden's justice and celibacy, to elaborate
how rural virtues translate into what he described to Charles Montague
as the principles of 'an Englishman in Parliament.' The terms of this
translation are prefigured by one of the lines I've already quoted: 'Your

Country calls you from your lov'd Retreat' (l. 120). A modern Cincinna-
tus, Cousin Driden is called by his country to leave his country: the pun
that's implicit in the poet's usage lays the ground for a change that both
cancels and preserves what's changed in a higher, more political and
public register. Other seventeenth-century poets in the *beatus ille* tradition already had experimented with the idea that pastoral retreat might
signify a retreat from contemporary political engagement. Maren Sofie-
Rostvig, the exhaustive historian of the form, discusses a number of
poems in which rural retirement takes shape as a royalist response to
the warfare and disruption of the mid-century decades.[13] But if these
poets politicize the *beatus ille* theme as a retreat from politics, Dryden
more inventively politicizes that theme as a politics of retreat.

His aim here is to represent both his own and his cousin's position on
the present crisis. Two years earlier, in 1697, the Peace of Ryswick had
ended the Nine Years War against France, but Europe restlessly awaited
the death of the childless Charles II and the fate of the Spanish succession. William, the Whig ministry, and the House of Lords sought prepa-
rations for renewed war against the bellicose Louis XIV; the House of
Commons favoured peace and opposed the maintenance of a standing
army. In a letter of late 1699, Dryden reported that ''tis thought the
King will endeavour to keep up a standing Army; ... My Cousin Driden,
& the Country Party, I suppose will be against it.'[14] In the poem he had
just completed Dryden advocates peace in his own voice, but in terms
that transform his cousin's country justice into a brief for the country's
foreign policy.

'Contending Neighbours come' to the Justice of the Peace, the poet
had begun, '[a]nd, Foes before, return in Friendship home'; 'The Sanction leaves a lasting Peace behind' (ll. 7, 9, 15). Now we see a similar
blessing on the international level: 'Our Foes, compell'd by Need, have
Peace embrac'd: / The Peace both Parties want, is like to last' (ll. 142–3).
Moreover, the security of rural justice dovetails with the self-sufficiency of
rural celibacy. On the subject of his cousin's bachelorhood, Dryden had
remarked that

> Man and Woman, though in one they grow,
> Yet, first or last, return again to Two.
> ....
> How cou'd He stand, when put to double Pain,
> He must a Weaker than himself sustain!
>
> (ll. 23–4, 27–8)

On the subject of England's alliances, Dryden now praises he

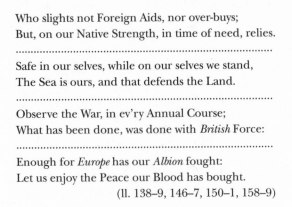

Who slights not Foreign Aids, nor over-buys;
But, on our Native Strength, in time of need, relies.
....
Safe in our selves, while on our selves we stand,
The Sea is ours, and that defends the Land.
....
Observe the War, in ev'ry Annual Course;
What has been done, was done with *British* Force:
....
Enough for *Europe* has our *Albion* fought:
Let us enjoy the Peace our Blood has bought.
                    (ll. 138–9, 146–7, 150–1, 158–9)

Recalling what happens when medicine turns 'Trade' (l. 74), Dryden now remarks that '[w]ho fights for Gain, for greater, makes his Peace' (l. 141). To prosecute a war too far only aggravates the condition it was meant to cure: 'Ev'n Victors are by Victories undone' (l. 164), an irony that also recapitulates the self-defeating paradoxes of civil law and civil marriage: '[H]e who conquers, is but last undone'; 'Two Wrestlers help to pull each other down' (ll. 13, 30). The analogy is subject to different weightings. From one perspective, Cousin Driden's private misogyny dictates xenophobia on the level of international politics; from another, his private prudence dictates a 'retreat' into isolationist foreign policy. But however it's evaluated, the analogy itself has a compelling authority.

Having derived his timely counsel of peace from the example of his cousin's pacific life in the countryside, the poet now turns to broader constitutional issues, for which he is chiefly indebted to his fourth topic of praise, on the hunt. In those earlier passages, Dryden had praised his cousin for knowing how to distinguish pleasure from necessity, the sport of hunting from the serious business of justice. To confuse these is to behave like the prince, whose youthful ambition to rule is its own downfall. Now the poet insists on the importance of a parallel, and related, distinction in the balance of power between prince and people:

Some Overpoise of Sway, by Turns they share;
In Peace the People, and the Prince in War:
....

> Patriots, in Peace, assert the Peoples Right:
> With noble Stubbornness resisting Might:
>   (ll. 180–1, 184–5)

The parallel is fairly precise: as sport is to justice, so peace is to war and the people to the prince. Or again: to hunt beasts as though they were men is like prosecuting peace as though it were war, or like seeking from princes what can only be supplied by the people.

The fact that the distinction between prince and people is also directly related to the earlier caveat against the absolute princely ambition to rule makes the application of this lesson to the present juncture that much easier. As we now find ourselves at peace, the people must resist the might of the potential dictator, who, confusing the body natural with the body politic, the pleasure of personal ambition with the necessity of national policy, would lead us back into war. Of course, Dryden refrains from direct reference to William. Instead he recalls the example of his and his cousin's grandfather, Erasmus Driden, who resisted the might of Charles I when it threatened the balance of power. The crucial issues in the late 1620s bore some similarity to those of the late 1690s. Refusing to grant Charles the supplies needed for pursuing war against Spain and then France, Commons had protested the king's efforts to levy funds without their approval until Charles dissolved Parliament for the final time and began eleven years of unprecedented personal rule. Like his son James, Charles I was one of those absolute princes who, chasing and then chased from their slippery thrones, precipitated a break in the royal succession.

In this way Dryden draws upon his fourth topic of praise, on hunting, to adumbrate the lineage of absolutism. But the question of lineage is raised also by the way he recurs to the third topic of praise, on charity. Earlier the poet had declared Cousin Driden '*Rebecca*'s Heir,' implicating this divine displacement from the paternal line in the generosity of his cousin's charity (l. 43). Now the poet alludes to this heritage by invoking Erasmus Driden, who proved himself a 'Patriot' by retaining 'his Birthright Liberty' (ll. 184, 193). Reminding Cousin Driden that he is the 'true Descendent of a Patriot Line,' the poet stresses the importance not of the royal line of sovereignty, which will break when absolute princes slip from their thrones, but of the patriot line of 'gen'rous' liberty (ll. 195, 188). Like Rebecca's lineage, in other words, the patriot lineage entails a salutary displacement; and as the first transcends the merely historical line through divine gift, the second finds its transcen-

dence in England's immemorial and sempiternal 'Laws' (l. 191).[15]
Where lawful, patriots in Parliament 'in a Body give' generously to their
monarch (l. 187). But their freedom is entailed in the lineage of liberty,
not in subjection to absolute sovereignty. And so they are generously
'free to grant' as Cousin Driden is charitably 'free to Many' not despite
his displacement from the paternal lineage but because of it (ll. 188,
148).

<h2 style="text-align:center">III</h2>

What I've called the uncanny effect that suffuses 'To My Honour'd
Kinsman' at the local level finds its culmination in the way the politics
Dryden propounds for his cousin intricately echoes his virtues as an
explicitly non-political animal. Dryden's pastoral terms of praise, consistently defined against the negativity of 'Civil Rage,' come to fruition precisely in his civil virtues. What are we to make of this? Bacon had
observed that fables can be used 'for contrary purposes,' both to veil
and to clarify meaning. For what purpose is 'To My Honour'd Kinsman'
to be used? A hundred years earlier, George Puttenham had famously
attributed to the pastoral eclogue the first of these fabular purposes,
that is, 'vnder the vaile of homely persons, and in rude speeches to
insinuate and glaunce at greater matters, and such as perchance had
not bene safe to haue beene disclosed in any other sort.'[16] Of course,
Cousin Driden is scarcely the sort of 'homely person' of whom Virgil
writes. But the real problem is that if Dryden intends his cousin's rural
retreat as a 'vaile' for 'greater matters,' he elaborately removes the veil
and reveals its application as soon as it's been set in place. The moral of
a fable is supposed to be disclosed through the process of narration,
and often through a brief concluding discursive tag. Dryden's moral is
disclosed instead through an elaborate retelling of the fable. The
'homely' quality of Dryden's pastoral fable is therefore rendered
uncanny not by extracting its 'greater' meaning in the very process of
reading it, but by the poet's explicit and painstaking translation of the
fable into terms that are both familiar and 'greater,' therefore strange.
Nor does this retelling semantically supersede the first narration as we
expect of the moral to a fable. Rather, the two stories seem to coexist as
a dialectical antithesis of equal parts.

Yet if there is something in Dryden's poem not 'safe to haue beene
disclosed' in any other way, it is surely not just the broadly public implication of private pastoral, but, within that public realm, the specific

implication of a potential absolutism in William's current war policy. This more dangerous meaning, however, veiled by the 'fable''s reference to princes on slippery thrones who seek pleasure through necessity, remains veiled in the 'moral''s substitution of Charles I and Erasmus Driden as foils for his principal characters. In setting the patriot line against the Stuart line, Dryden delicately propounds the problem of the English tradition, now a century old, of royal absolutism. The unstated question that lurks at the heart of 'To My Honour'd Kinsman' concerns the future of England's polity, and it is most directly answered not in the poem itself, but in Dryden's remark about his poem, that he has there 'given my own opinion, of what an Englishman in Parliament ought to be.' To understand Dryden's experiment in fabular form, I think we need to recognize that its prudential motive to veil is inseparable from its heuristic motive to disclose and discover. What the poet seeks to discover is nothing less than the terms of political engagement available to a culture, irreparably scarred by civil war, in which politics (it was becoming apparent) must be changed utterly. And to this end he draws upon a variety of traditional models that had served seventeenth-century English people in their efforts to make sense of their national crisis.

The most celebrated of these models make what feel like no more than guest appearances in the poem. The figure of the body politic implicitly justifies Dryden's discourse on the medical profession, but he shows no interest in establishing the crucial correspondence between the parts of the body and the several estates of the realm. The figure of the ship of state is raised more explicitly ('You steer betwixt the Country and the Court' [l. 128]), but seems most interesting to Dryden on the level of content, as it seeps into his concern with naval affairs and ship-building. Again, the poem's pivotal modulation between country and court, private and public would appear well-suited to a patriarchalist theory of political obligation grounded in the analogy between the family and the state. But the authority of the father, so far from being the norm of 'To My Honour'd Kinsman,' plays no more than an incidental role here, and becomes equivocal when occasionally pushed into the foreground. Or again, in some respects Cousin Driden seems drawn to the lineaments of civic humanism: his disinterested balance is born of material independence (he is '[w]ell-born, and Wealthy; wanting no Support' [l. 127]), he's allergic to profit-taking, and he's at least presumptively opposed to a standing army. But in recent decades the scholarly inflation of civic humanism has made it into something that in explaining everything explains nothing. And although much of Dryden's supportive imagery is drawn from ancient Roman culture, the specific sort of 'republicanism' that Cousin Driden shares with his grandfather is more Anglo-Saxon than Roman, valorizing a 'Birthright Liberty' that's redolent less of civic virtue than of Magna Carta, less a yeoman incorruptibility than a patriotic resistance to royal tyranny (l. 193).

What distinguishes Dryden's language of 'Birthright Liberty' and the 'Patriot Line' from the figures of the ship of state, the body politic, and the state as family is that it doesn't presuppose the sovereignty of the captain, the head, or the father – in a word, the singular leader. Not that these models for thinking about political engagement have no use in the poem. Rather, Dryden uses them opportunistically, borrowing piecemeal from each in the semantically difficult project of approaching a reality for which there appeared to him no precedent. A case in point is the term 'patriot.' In *Absalom and Achitophel* (1681), Dryden's David-Charles had characterized Absalom-Monmouth in the following language: 'Gull'd with a Patriots name, whose Modern sense / Is one that would by Law supplant his Prince' (ll. 965–6).[17] Now, twenty years later, he offers a very different definition:

> A Patriot, both the King and Country serves;
> Prerogative, and Privilege preserves:
> Of Each, our Laws the certain Limit show;
> One must not ebb, nor t'other overflow ...
>   (ll. 171–4)

Of course, the difference registers a significant change in Dryden's own politics over the last two decades of the century. In 1681 he supported the king against unlawful encroachments on royal authority. In 1699 he supports those who would '[n]o Lawless Mandates from the Court receive' (l. 186). But although significant, this change is not in itself fundamental, in so far as both postures seem to coexist within a general commitment to a constitutional theory of mixed, balanced, or coordinate powers. What takes Dryden into unfamiliar, hence fabular, territory is the effort to imagine a model of sovereignty in which governmental balance doesn't require striving to find unity in duplicity – striving, that is, to coordinate the head or captain or father of the state with lesser powers – but is rather an internal and structural feature of governmental power itself.

Dryden has already laid the ground for this sort of model by associating his cousin's parliamentary service with the common interest of the nation itself: 'Your Country calls you from your lov'd Retreat, / And sends to Senates, charg'd with Common Care' (ll. 120–1). Parliament's 'Common Care' is soon identified as national by Dryden's echoing reference to 'the Nation's Care,' and then reidentified as the peculiar charge of Parliament by the poet's echoing reminder that as a parliamentarian, Erasmus Driden was 'tenacious of the Common Cause' – a phrase that itself echoes the earlier avowal that Cousin Driden was in his private capacity 'industrious of the Common Good' (ll. 148, 190, 53). In this way, the poet portrays Parliament as a collective body in two senses of the term: as it *includes* such as the grandfather and the grandson, and as it *represents* both king and people:

> Good Senators, (and such are you,) so give
> That Kings may be supply'd, the People thrive.
>
> ....
>
> Such was your gen'rous Grandsire; free to grant
> In Parliaments ...   (ll. 135–6, 188–9)

At the same time, however, Dryden suggests a crucial difference between the patriotic parliament of the 1620s and its contemporary descendant. Half a century earlier, the patriot Erasmus Driden languished 'in a lothsom Dungeon' (l. 192) for resisting the demands of Charles I, thereby testing the severely strained constitutional balance between Parliament and monarchy. In the 1690s of Dryden's poem, this balance has been internalized within Parliament itself, where the patriot Cousin Driden mediates between 'King' and 'Country,' 'Prerogative' and 'Privilege.' Indeed, as the private focus on the Cousin Driden of the *rural* countryside gives way to the public focus on his service to the *national* country of England, the several forms of the first-person plural pronoun ('we,' 'us,' 'our') proliferate in reference to this *national* collective in a way that makes it hard at times to distinguish from the *parliamentary* collective Cousin Driden metonymically represents: 'Betwixt the Prince and Parliament we stand' (l. 175); 'You steer betwixt the Country and the Court' (l. 128).

For hundreds of years, the maxim 'the King in Parliament' had served as shorthand for the correlative and indivisible legislative authority of monarchy and Parliament.[18] All that changed with Stuart absolutism and the parliamentary response to it. Already in 1610, one parliamentarian was making explicit a potent principle of division: 'The

soveraigne power is agreed to be in the king: but in the king is a two-fold
power, the one in parliament, as he is assisted with the consent of the
whole state; the other out of parliament, as he is sole, and singular,
guided merely by his own will ... [T]he power of the king in parliament
is greater than his power out of parliament.'[19] By the end of the century,
the maxim of 'the King in Parliament' had fallen out of use, to be
replaced in time by the modern notion that the legislative authority of
the monarch is contained within, and articulated by (in Dryden's
phrase), the 'Englishman in Parliament.'

What I'm suggesting is that 'To My Honour'd Kinsman' is an experiment in defining the terms of an emergent system of parliamentary
democracy that will come to organize British political culture in future
years, but that in 1699 is still only nascent. Crucial to its emergence is
the growth of the political party system, in which the danger of direct
contention between prerogative and privilege, absolute monarchy and
headstrong people is contained by conceiving it as a conflict (whether
between Whigs and Tories or between court and country) within a unified and rule-bound arena of conflict resolution. Replicating the terms
of dispute that had proved both irresistible and disastrous over the past
century, the Parliament Dryden's poem imagines would transform the
'lothsom Dungeon' in which their grandfather was involuntarily confined into the voluntary self-confinement of a parliamentary opposition
whose loyalty is guaranteed by the fact of its structural sanction. Henceforth conflicts between monarchy and Parliament will be contained and
detoxified in the form of disputes, within the parliamentary domain,
between the government and the 'opposition.'[20]

It's in imagining the possibility of such a system that Dryden finds
most useful – more than the several models of political engagement
available to him – the literary tradition of classical and Christian pastoral, most of all the *beatus ille* tradition. What that tradition affords the
poet is a multivalent notion of 'retreat' that takes in not just an isolationist foreign policy but an entire ethos of detachment from the official
rule of royal sovereignty. That official rule had authorized a tacit and
duplicitous confusion of the prince's pleasure and his necessity, the
monarch's body natural and his body politic, which 'first or last, return
again to Two' (l. 24). Civil war, the prototype of civil law and civil marriage, only aggravates the condition it was meant to cure, for at its end
'he who conquers is but last undone'; 'Ev'n Victors are by Victories
undone' (ll. 13, 164). Dryden extrapolates from the idea of the retired
country gentleman the notion of a politics freed of this duplicity and

made truly self-sufficient, like a prelapsarian Eden in which the potential terms of conflict are rendered reciprocal and preclude the possibility of a Fall into civil war. As Cousin Driden is legitimated in his several roles through his displacement from the official, professional, and patrilineal corruption of those roles, so the poet imagines Parliament, displaced from the official political scenario, as the institutional 'Body' politic of the future (l. 187). And it's to his own vital contribution – to the way poetic convention offers a proleptic model for politics – that Dryden alludes when he observes to his cousin:

> Nor think the Kindred-Muses thy Disgrace;
> A Poet is not born in ev'ry Race.
> Two of a House, few Ages can afford;
> One to perform, another to record.   (ll. 201–4)

Notes

1 Dryden to Elizabeth Steward, 7 November 1699, 11 April 1700, in *Letters of John Dryden*, ed. Charles E. Ward (Durham: Duke University Press 1942), 123, 135.

2 Preface to *Fables Ancient and Modern* (1700), in *The Poems of John Dryden*, ed. James Kinsley, 4 vols. (Oxford: Clarendon Press 1958) 4:1447.

3 Author's Preface to 'Of the Wisdom of the Ancients' (1609), in *The Philosophical Works of Francis Bacon*, eds. Robert L. Ellis and James Spedding, rev. John M. Robertson (London: Routledge 1905), 823.

4 On the use of Aesopian fables for political purposes see Annabel Patterson, *Fables of Power: Aesopian Writing and Political History* (Durham: Duke University Press 1991) and Jayne Elizabeth Lewis, *The English Fable: Aesop and Literary Culture, 1651–1740* (Cambridge: Cambridge University Press 1996).

5 '*On Mr. Milton's Paradise Lost*,' ll. 7–8, in Andrew Marvell, *The Poems & Letters*, ed. H.M. Margouliouth (Oxford: Clarendon 1927), 1:131.

6 *Poems* 1:43. For a typological reading of the poem see Michael McKeon, *Politics and Poetry in Restoration England: The Case of Dryden's Annus Mirabilis* (Cambridge: Harvard University Press 1975), ch. 5. Compare also Dryden's *Annus Mirabilis* (1667), in which the City of London is figured as 'a great Emblem of the suffering Deity' ('To the Metropolis of Great Britain').

7 First printed in *Sylvae* (1685). *The Works of John Dryden*, ed. E.N. Hooker, H.T. Swedenberg, Jr, et al., 20 vols. (Berkeley: University of California Press 1956–

2000) 3:85, ll. 1–3. Further citations refer to this edition (hereafter cited as *California Dryden*) and appear parenthetically in the text.

8 *Poems of John Dryden*, 4:1529, ll. 1–2. Further citations of 'To My Honour'd Kinsman' refer to this edition and appear parenthetically in the text.

9 Alan Roper, *Dryden's Poetic Kingdoms* (London: Routledge 1965), 124. Other critics have remarked on this singular method. Earl Miner sees the poem as proceeding 'by association,' and Elizabeth Duthie speaks of its 'interconnection of arguments and analogies': Earl Miner, *The Restoration Mode from Milton to Dryden* (Princeton: Princeton University Press 1974), 154; Elizabeth Duthie, '"A Memorial of My Own Principles": Dryden's "To My Honour'd Kinsman,"' *ELH* 47, no. 4 (Winter 1980), 684.

10 Letter of Autumn 1699, in *Letters*, 120.

11 Jay Arnold Levine points out other relevant themes – peacemaking, wrestling, husbandry – implicit in the allusion to Jacob: see 'John Dryden's Epistle to John Driden,' *JEGP* 63, no. 3 (July 1964), 467–9.

12 The poem's basic structural division is well observed by Roper, *Dryden's Poetic Kingdoms*, 125–6, 126–7, and by Levine, 'John Dryden's Epistle,' 455, 457–8; aspects of it also are noted by Duthie, 'A Memorial,' 687, 690, 696, and by James A. Winn, *John Dryden and His World* (New Haven: Yale University Press 1987), 504.

13 Maren-Sofie Rostvig, *The Happy Man: Studies in the Metamorphosis of a Classical Ideal, 1600–1760*, 2 vols. (Oslo: Akademisk Forlag 1954, 1958), 1:22–3, 249.

14 Dryden to Elizabeth Steward, 7 November 1699, in *Letters*, 124.

15 See Christopher Hill, 'The Norman Yoke,' in *Puritanism and Revolution* (London: Panther 1968), 58–125.

16 George Puttenham, *The Arte of English Poesie* (1589), Scolar Press Facsimile (Menston: Scolar Press Limited 1968), 31.

17 *Poems of John Dryden*, 1:241, ll. 965–6.

18 See generally Charles H. McIlwain, *The High Court of Parliament and Its Supremacy* (New Haven: Yale University Press 1910).

19 James Whitelocke, in William Cobbett, *A Complete Collection of State Trials* (London 1809–14), II, 482–3, quoted in Margaret A. Judson, *The Crisis of the Constitution: An Essay in Constitutional and Political Thought in England 1603–1645* (New Brunswick, N.J.: Rutgers University Press [1949] 1988), 86–7.

20 The language, and the institution, of parliamentary opposition coalesced in the three decades following the publication of Dryden's poem: see J.A.W. Gunn, *Beyond Liberty and Property: The Process of Self-Recognition in Eighteenth-Century Political Thought* (Kingston and Montreal: McGill-Queen's University Press 1983), 58–62.

chapter five

Dryden's Emergence as a Political Satirist

DAVID HALEY

John Dryden's first salvo of political satire to hit its mark was casual, yet it nearly cost him his life at the end of 1679 when he was beaten in Rose Alley. To a Tory play called *The Loyal General,* Dryden contributed a Prologue containing some unguarded lines on the City Whigs. The lines compare the anti-Yorkist rally at Guildhall three months earlier to a riot by apprentices, at the same time belittling the Whigs' petitioning drive that would climax on 11 December by calling it a 'libel for the public good.' The Prologue begins as follows:

> If yet there be a few that take delight
> In that which reasonable Men should write;
> To them Alone we Dedicate this Night.
> The Rest may satisfie their curious Itch
> With City Gazets, or some Factious Speech,
> Or what-ere Libel for the Public Good,
> Stirs up the Shrove-tide Crew to Fire and Blood![1]

Assuming that the notorious assault on Dryden was politically motivated, we can date his initial but quite inadvertent sally into partisan satire sometime between 5 November and 19 December 1679.[2]

Before that date, Dryden was not reputed for his comments on the political factionalism that he would soon come to deplore in *Absalom and Achitophel.*[3] He dealt rather in personal satire that ranged from the lampoons written against rival playwrights like Settle and Shadwell to the Horatian detraction calibrated to annoy Rochester and Buckingham. Retorting to a growing number of critics, Dryden had impugned

their judgment and, in the case of Buckingham and Clifford, their religion. But he had never disparaged an enemy's politics or forged so topi-
cally edged a phrase as 'libel for the public good,' nor can he have
weighed the effect his random barb might have on an audience made
violently partisan by events in the fall of 1679. Having drawn blood from
a faceless enemy who brutally retaliated, Dryden wisely laid aside this
lethal weapon and did not take it up again for almost two years. He even
published *Absalom and Achitophel* under a veil of anonymity. Only with
The Medall, early in 1682, did the satirist resume his public persona and
openly commence to flail the now-broken Whigs.

The fullest account of the poet's discovering his new métier of political satire is Phillip Harth's *Pen for a Party.* Harth, too, quotes Dryden's
prologue but he plays down its jibe at the City Whigs as 'comic raillery'
because he thinks that Dryden, at this date, was mainly concerned as
a playwright to avoid partisanship. To illustrate the poet's neutrality,
Harth reviews his choice of patrons during the three years of the Popish
Plot. Early in 1678, Dryden had advertised his personal allegiance by
dedicating *All for Love* to Danby, but when the Plot broke that autumn
he quickly severed any ties to the disgraced minister. He published *Oedipus* without *any* dedication and *Troilus and Cressida* with an address to
the 'Trimmer,' Sunderland. Then came Rose Alley, after which Dryden
published no work of his own for more than a year. Finally, in March of
1681, with the Exclusion crisis approaching its dénouement at Oxford,
he published *The Spanish Fryar.* This play is framed ostentatiously with
a Whig-like dedication to 'a Protestant Patron [whose] Family ... have
been alwaies eminent in the support and favour of our Religion and
Liberties' (14:103). As Harth says, Dryden 'carried his public stance as a
playwright indifferent to party divisions to a point where it must have
raised doubts in some minds about the image of neutrality he was apparently cultivating.'[4]

What brought on this unwonted posturing? Harth demonstrates – to
my mind, conclusively – that before 1682, none of Dryden's contemporaries thought to identify the playwright either with the incipient Tory
party or with the political satire stirred up by the Exclusion crisis. Quite
obviously, Dryden waited until the crisis was over before lending his pen
to a party and producing *Absalom and Achitophel* at the end of 1681. The
satirical prologue of two years before was an aberration. Even without
the dastardly assault to make him wary, Dryden was already practising
the "cautious rhetoric of moderation" that James Winn notes in the dedication of *Troilus and Cressida* written just before the Rose Alley ambush.[5]

The fact is that over the stretch of fifteen years separating his two narrative poems, Dryden was occupied almost exclusively with playwrighting. Between *Annus Mirabilis* and *Absalom and Achitophel* he produced sixteen plays, of which only *Amboyna*, a jingoistic potboiler, bears on contemporary politics. The other fifteen plays entertained the audience by diverting its attention from the current political scene to a counterfactual world of comedy or tragicomedy. From *Secret Love*, the earliest play in the series, to *The Spanish Fryar*, Dryden provides voyeuristic glimpses of the *arcana imperii* without once hinting at their historical relevance to the king or to his government. *Aureng-Zebe*, for example, is ostensibly a study of contemporary tyranny, but it sheds no light on Danby's ministry. One searches this introspective domestic drama in vain for anything like the alarming revelations in Marvell's *An Account of the Growth of Popery*.

Before we can understand, therefore, how Dryden found his way back into politics at the end of the Exclusion crisis, we need to ask when and to what extent he had become alienated from the public life. Twenty years before, at the Restoration, he had embraced the role of public poet with enthusiasm. The eventful years 1665–6 rapidly carried him to the zenith of his civic role, prompting him to inscribe *Annus Mirabilis* 'To the Metropolis of Great Britain' (1:48). But he did not choose – like his rival, Andrew Marvell – to dedicate his talents to serving the civic order. Dryden's greater ambition was to shine in a narrower, genteel society whose ideal portrait he drafted at about the same time that he wrote *Annus Mirabilis*. The brilliantly mimetic *Essay of Dramatick Poesie*, written during his retreat from a plague-ridden London, is the Restoration counterpart of Suckling's *The Wits, or A Session of the Poets*. Emulating Suckling's literary sketch of the contemporary culture that would be erased by the Civil War, Dryden portrays himself among the *Essay*'s four speakers, two of whom – Davenant and Orrery – were Suckling's old friends from the court of Charles I. When Davenant, who is represented in the *Essay* by Eugenius, died in April 1668, his younger admirer succeeded him in the office of Poet Laureate.[6]

After a quarrel with his brother-in-law Sir Robert Howard (who appears in the *Essay* as Crites), the new laureate devoted his genius to entertaining a coterie that, in contrast to an MP like Howard, was out of touch with the broader political nation. Dryden had come of age under Cromwell's strong government and he regarded the monarchy as the legitimate successor of the Protectorate. Unable to foresee divisions between the restored king and his household, Dryden paid court chiefly to the duke of York and to his father-in-law Clarendon – another friend of

Davenant and a survivor, like him, from the Caroline court. From 1662, when Dryden addressed a New Year's poem to the Lord Chancellor, until ten years later, when he dedicated *The Conquest of Granada* to James, the poet seems to have followed the deteriorating political situation from a Yorkist vantage point. That perspective left him vulnerable to the shock of Clarendon's fall in 1667 and to the Test Act, which not only crippled James but destroyed another patron, Clifford, in 1673. One would like to know Dryden's reflections on these events. Although he did glance obliquely in his plays at the issue of religious freedom, as I will show, in the fifteen years before 1678 he steered well clear of contentious political topics that, on the closely censored Restoration stage, were subjects no less taboo than the Civil War and regicide.

Try as he might to gain admittance into the familiar company of wits like Rochester (to whom he dedicated *Marriage A-la-Mode* in 1672) and Sedley (to whom he dedicated *The Assignation* the following year), Dryden found that his Puritan heritage excluded him from the society of born Cavaliers. He frankly acknowledges this historical gap in the *Essay* when Lisideius (who represents Orrery) implies that those like Dryden and himself who served Cromwell need to atone for their part in the Interregnum. For 'since that time, said he, (turning towards *Neander*) we have been so long together bad *Englishmen*, that we had not leisure to be good Poets' (17:33). At the Restoration, Dryden resolved with most of the country to be a good Englishman and to employ his art in the king's service. It took him more than a decade to realize that his loyal behaviour could not expunge the past and that the new generation of Cavaliers and churchmen held him accountable for the historical accident that his family, while they may have balked at the regicide, had nonetheless joined the reformers aligned against Charles I and his bishops.

In 1660 this divisive past could be overlooked. The restored king's Act of Oblivion capped a surge of national unity that lasted until England's defeat by the Dutch and the consequent fall of Clarendon. At the end of 1666, Dryden could still speculate on a year of wonders and read the signs of an even greater unity to come. Yet seventeen months later, at the time of Davenant's death, the unity had collapsed and the continuity that Clarendon had stood for was broken. From the moment he became Poet Laureate, Dryden had to face the realization that the Interregnum's enduring legacy was discontinuity. (It was Clarendon who later fixed on this discontinuity the Tory stamp of rebellion.) After seven years in his new office, Dryden would confess that he felt like a writer 'betwixt two Ages cast, / The first of this, and hindmost of the last'

(12:159, ll. 21–2). This notable turn from an extroverted, epic conception of his public role to an epigone introversion tells us something about Dryden's growing political disillusion.

By 1676 he had begun to lose his trust in the Stuart dynasty. When he dedicated *The Conquest of Granada* to James, Dryden was pleased to recall his twofold office of Poet Laureate and Historiographer Royal. He says that while performing 'the part of a just Historian to my Royal Master ... I have been examining my own forces, and making tryal of myself how I shall be able to transmit you to Posterity. I have form'd a Heroe [Almanzor, for whom] *Homer* and *Tasso* are my precedents' (11:6). Four years later Dryden's epic hopes have been dashed. In the Dedication of *Aureng-Zebe*, he says he has been too necessitous to carry out his design. ''Tis for your Lordship,' he tells Mulgrave, 'to stir up that remembrance in his Majesty, which his many avocations of business have caus'd him, I fear, to lay aside: And, (as himself and his Royal Brother are the Heroes of the Poem) to represent to them the Images of their Warlike Predecessors' (12:155). He blames this neglect of heroic poetry not on the king but on the dullness of courtiers whose only response to heroism is detraction, and he says henceforth he will seek 'True greatness' elsewhere, 'in a private Virtue' (12:153).

The last phrase implies that Dryden has turned his back not just on the court but on the Restoration society he had portrayed so confidently ten years before in *An Essay of Dramatick Poesie*. His discouragement contrasts with Mrs Evelyn's initial response to *The Conquest of Granada*, which she called 'a play so full of ideas ... that one would imagine it designed for an Utopia rather then our stage. I do not quarrel with the poet, but admire one born in the decline of morality should be able to feigne such exact virtue' (11:411n.). At the time, Mrs Evelyn had a quicker eye for the social context of Dryden's success than did the playwright, who declares in a vaunting epilogue that he has conformed his genius to the age. He grounds his boast on a general advance of civilization or manners: 'Our Ladies and our men now speak more wit / In conversation, than those Poets writ' – those poets being 'Shakespeare, Fletcher, and Jonson' (11:201, 204). This view of contemporary mores is diametrically opposed to that of Mrs Evelyn, who thinks Restoration culture shows 'the decline of morality.'

Dryden may have overrated the political significance of his dramatic masterpiece. He envisioned a society far more homogeneous than actual conditions warranted, and in publishing *The Conquest*, he traded upon the Cavalier audience's jaundiced view of Interregnum culture. In his prefatory essay on the origin of heroic plays, he says their prototype, *The Siege of Rhodes,* was invented by Davenant, who was 'forbidden ... in the Rebellious times to act Tragedies and Comedies, because they contain'd some matter of Scandal to those good people, who could more easily dispossess their lawful Sovereign than endure a wanton jeast' (11:9).

In the same measure that he was flattered by the audience's approval, Dryden must have been chagrined at Buckingham's mockery that would soon dampen the éclat of heroic plays. *The Rehearsal* exploits a vulnerability of Bayes that is implicit in Mrs Evelyn's ironical admiration of the poet who can feign a moral knowledge for which his society offers no basis. In 1668, defending *An Essay of Dramatick Poesie,* Dryden had echoed Davenant and Hobbes and had staunchly reaffirmed the objective, political roots of moral art. He told Howard, 'Moral Truth is the Mistress of the Poet as much as of the Philosopher: Poesie must resemble Natural Truth, but it must *be* Ethical' (9:12). By 1672, the social basis of Dryden's moral truth had shrunk to an audience who came to the theatre to escape from reality. In gratifying the elitism and nostalgia of this audience, the poet lost his purchase on the actual, historical politics that fostered its self-indulgence. Bayes conformed his genius to the age all too well.

I shall argue that Dryden recovered his grasp of moral truth only when he turned to political satire ten years after *The Conquest.* What he variously calls 'moral knowledge,' 'moral truth,' and 'moral philosophy' is a main branch of political economy, as it would come to be known. Moral philosophy is much closer to modern sociology than to psychology or religion. When Dryden says that poetry need only resemble truth but must *'be* ethical,' he is not invoking some internal, subjective criterion that allows the poet to ignore the facts, nor is he appealing to a merely private faith or to the poet's sense of poetic justice. Dryden measures the 'ethical' by our collective experience rather than by the individual's intuition. Of the three possible bases of knowledge – namely, reason, faith, and experience – moral truth rests firmly on the last. Hence the quaint phrase, 'moral certainty.' The aim of moral art is not 'representation,' but *mimesis.*[7]

The moral truth with which Dryden was concerned is the truth of mores – manners – and he spent much of his career perfecting his moral art. From his initial Restoration poem to Howard, where he observes that poetry always has been 'Queen' of 'Morall Knowledge,' to his translations of Virgil and the *Fables,* Dryden grounded moral truth in the audience's collective experience (1:18). For a time after 1672, however, his elite audience seemed more fickle in their taste than the Elizabethans, whose manners he deemed less polished. When Rymer published his *Tragedies of the Last Age* in 1677, this crude treatise emphasizing typical characters and probable action came as a revelation to Dryden. He realized that Shakespearean tragedy excelled not by its plot but by virtue of Shakespeare's original moral art. In answering Rymer, Dryden rediscovered the artist's mimetic power of integrating character with history and investing political action with concrete motivation.

The two Shakespearean adaptations of 1677 and 1679 are remarkable, but they make a wobbly bridge from the heroic plays to *Absalom and Achitophel*. Imitating Shakespeare's 'Godlike Romans' did enable Dryden to restore a measure of tragic realism to a theatre long used to providing an avenue of escape from history (12:159). Yet all six of the serious plays he wrote from 1674 to 1680 eschew contemporary politics, exactly as the heroic plays did. The polities we meet in them are increasingly fragmented because the author has lost his integrating vision of a Restoration society unified by its king.

This inference about Dryden's loss of political vision can be substantiated by paralleling the development of his satire to Marvell's. Born a decade later, Dryden emulated the older writer at ten-year intervals. *Astraea Redux* corresponds to Marvell's Cromwell ode, *The Rehearsal Transpros'd* is answered in the preface to *Religio Laici*, and *An Account of the Growth of Popery*, begun in the mid-1670s, has its counterpart in *The History of the League*, which Dryden translated in 1684. Both poets wrote poems on the Protectorate, Marvell on *The First Anniversary of the Government under O.C.* and Dryden upon Cromwell's death four years later. Praising Cromwell allowed either poet to assume the role of civic orator while interchanging the toga with the mantle of the prophet. Both employ historical hermeneutics to explain Cromwell's greatness. Marvell's poem led the way, rendering the Protector's deeds in the light of biblical epic and implying, by the poem's central allusion to Elijah, that Cromwell was a harbinger of the Second Coming. Dryden was particularly responsive to the biblical hermeneutics of *The First Anniversary*. Twenty years later he would invert Marvell's Elijah passage to close *Mac Flecknoe*, just as he opens that satire with a parody of Marvell's anaphoric 'Cromwell alone ... Cromwell alone.'[8]

So sharply do their politics diverge after the Restoration that anybody reading *Annus Mirabilis* alongside the accounts of 1666 in Marvell's 'Advice to a Painter' poems will find it hard to believe the two poets are describing the same events. Dryden had almost finished his work when the Fire broke out in September, and he tried to interpret that catastrophe as an alchemical transformation. In an effort to bring closure to its double action, he calls his work 'An Historical Poem' and dates it 10 November 1666 (1:47, 59). Just two days earlier, on the eighth, the Commons had defeated the court's excise bill, and that is the event Marvell would later describe in his famous *Last Instructions to a Painter*, thereby reopening the history that Dryden sought to close. When Dryden's poem came out late in 1666, Marvell had already expressed his view that courtly history like *Annus Mirabilis* is a pernicious 'lie of state' and that its author deserved to have his tongue bored through, exactly as the Fire punished the bells that pealed a false victory over the Dutch. Here are the lines from Marvell's *Second Advice* of 1666.[9]

> Now joyful fires and the exalted bell
> And court-gazettes our empty triumph tell.
> Alas, the time draws near when overturn'd
> The lying bells shall through the tongue be burn'd;
> Paper shall want to print that lie of state,
> And our false fires true fires shall expiate.

Dryden, writing from the country and before opinion had turned against the war, could still blazon the victory won by the Duke of York off the coast of Suffolk, whence his duchess had seen him embark. Dryden salutes her in the courtly lines he prefixed to *Annus Mirabilis*:

> How pow'rful are chast vows! the wind and tyde
> You brib'd to combat on the *English* side.
> Thus to your much lov'd Lord you did convey
> An unknown succour, sent the nearest way.
> New vigour to his wearied arms you brought;
> (So *Moses* was upheld while *Israel* fought).   (1:57–8)

Marvell, writing from the standpoint of the parliamentary opposition, offers a different perspective on James's consort and her heroic participation:

> O Duchess! If thy nuptial pomp were mean,
> 'Tis paid with int'rest in this naval scene.
> Never did Roman Mark within the Nile
> So feast the fair Egyptian Crocodile,

Nor the Venetian Duke, with such a state,
The Adriatic marry at that rate.

I set Marvell's satire against Dryden's panegyric merely to illustrate
the greater political relevance of the older poet's wit. Marvell's playful
literary allusions are no more adept or wide-ranging than are Dryden's
varied analogies drawn from science as well as from Virgil. Marvell's
advantage lies rather in his political stance. Writing anonymously as a
citizen, he can address the high subject of his verse on an equal footing;
each of his three 'Advice' poems closes with an envoy in which the poet
directly counsels the king. This republican equality seems to have
alarmed the government's supporters. One of them complained that
Marvell 'in soft accents steals the public breast / And kills some noble
fame at every jest.' Dryden, by contrast, casts himself as the deferential
poet sedulous to exalt his patron's heroic status.[10]

Dryden was ready to play the heroic game so long as his audience
took it seriously, and he claimed for it the dignity of Virgilian epic. But
when the natural patrons of the heroic play themselves turned on it and
made a jest of it, Dryden's confidence was shaken. Inventing the spuri-
ous character of Bayes, Buckingham demonstrated the vanity of conforming one's genius to the age. This ridicule stung the laureate, and by
1674, when the second edition of *Paradise Lost* came out with Marvell's
sneer at him as 'the Town-Bayes,' Dryden apparently had abandoned his
usual audience and was re-examining the basis of his moral art. Ignoring the contemporary scene, he reread Milton and Shakespeare and discovered Longinus and Rymer.

His work during the four years from 1674 through 1677 is devoid of
topical political reference. *Aureng-Zebe* plays as if that Mogul emperor
were a fiction, and the 'world' lost by Mark Antony is no more historical,
and politically much less solid, than the kingdoms bandied about in the
heroic plays. The most striking proof of Dryden's political isolation,
however, comes from the greatest personal satire he wrote during these
years. Dryden had the sense not to publish *Mac Flecknoe*; even so, only a
politically insouciant poet could have fashioned a lampoon mocking the
crowning of a successor at the very moment when the Exclusion debate
was brewing in earnest (it dates from late 1673 when James wedded
Mary of Modena). This was to make a jest of monarchy indeed; had Dryden really been noted for commenting on the government – as of
course he was not – *Mac Flecknoe* would undoubtedly have been received
as a satire on the Stuart dynasty.

Another comparison with Marvell will show the bankruptcy of Dryden's moral art at this crisis of his career. *The Rehearsal* spawned a number of satires upon writers who flattered the court and king. The most brilliant of these satires is *The Rehearsal Transpros'd*, Marvell's yeasty retort to the Anglican polemicist Samuel Parker. Parker had violently attacked the Dissenters in a series of treatises, of which the most recent was a remonstrance against the king's Declaration of Indulgence that March of 1672. Skewering the Anglican bully as another Bayes, Marvell identifies Parker with the arrogant faction of Cavaliers and churchmen who presumed to tell the king how to force religious conformity on his subjects. In this witty appeal for toleration of dissent, Marvell strikes the very note of *Areopagitica* and of Milton's warning against Bishop Hall, one of the uprooted Laudians who insidiously petitioned the Long Parliament to assume dictatorial powers. When the Restoration bishops in turn sought to ban Marvell's tract, they were overruled by the king, who ensured the publication of this clever satire because it made him out to be the lone champion of toleration against a tyrannical Anglican clergy and an equally overbearing Cavalier Parliament.[11]

In the sensitive matter of toleration, we would expect Dryden to side with Marvell and the king against the bishops. All three men had cause to resent Anglican intolerance. Marvell, the son of a Congregationalist minister, had always respected Milton's friends among the Independents such as John Owen, whose words on liberty of conscience Marvell quotes against Parker. The king, a libertine who sympathized with the Catholics, before sailing from Breda had promised his subjects liberty of worship at the Restoration and then watched as the intransigent bishops reneged on his promise by enacting the Clarendon Code outlawing dissent. As for Dryden, heir to three generations of Puritan gentry, one can only assume that his outspoken anticlericalism and his marriage into a Catholic family inoculated him against the zeal of Anglican Cavaliers determined to identify crown with church. His respect for the restored monarchy did not extend to the restored bishops or to their neo-Laudian trumpet, Parker. In his politics and his reading of history, Dryden hewed to the Cavalier line as best he might; but his innate spiritual independence prevented his conforming wholeheartedly to the Church the way a born Tory like Danby could. This native insubordination is the root cause of Dryden's growing alienation from politics after 1673, when the Test Act divided the nation and eventually forced the king, in the last years of his reign, to scrap Danby's policy for the still less tolerant regimen of the bishops.

As Dryden would later come to realize, freedom of religion was vital to his moral art. He did not explicitly write about religious freedom until 1682, when he published *Religio Laici.* Two of his heroic plays, however, seem to reflect the king's initial struggle with Parliament over toleration. In the torture scene that Voltaire admired from Act V of *The Indian Emperor,* the church of the conquistadores is exposed as an arrogant monster of intolerance. While Pizarro is racking Montezuma to discover his gold, the Christian priest conducts an inquisition upon the Indian emperor, who becomes a martyr for agnostic freedom. Dryden is solicitous for Montezuma's soul, just as he would later plead for charity to all heathens in his preface to *Religio Laici.* The point here is that Dryden's hatred of dogmatic priests is not Puritan or antipapist, but libertine. His sympathy at this stage lay with the wits, who included Buckingham and Buckhurst. Their society was more tolerant of freethinking than were the Restoration divines and their strong allies among the Cavalier gentry.

Dryden's experience of anarchy when the Protectorate collapsed in 1659 convinced him that republicanism was a fatal delusion. Its 'false freedom,' as he branded the republican ideal in *Astraea Redux,* imposed 'real bonds' in the form of mob tyranny (1:26). For Marvell, as for Milton, Locke, and Shaftesbury, free thought and expression were tolerated as healthy signs; Dryden, on the other hand, worried lest this freedom should tear the community apart as it had in 1659. By the middle of the seventeenth century, heresy had given way to *schism* as the bugbear of the ecclesiastical establishment. Marvell caustically remarks that it was the restored bishops, not the Dissenters, who destroyed the concord of the Church by gratuitously inserting shibboleths into the Book of Common Prayer aimed at stigmatizing Nonconformists. He says, 'I remember one in the Litany, where to False Doctrine and Heresy, they added Schism, though it were to spoil the music and cadence of the period.' In Marvell's view, the bishops were equally responsible with Dissenters for the renewed sectarianism after 1660: orthodoxy produces schism.[12]

The greatest paradox of Dryden's career is his attitude to schism. Believing the 'Universal Church' (2:120) was one and not many, he consistently denounced sectarianism on principle. When eventually he came to look upon the Church of England as just another sect, he converted to Catholicism. In thus separating himself from the Anglican communion, Dryden became a schismatic; and yet only by joining the Universal Church could he finally renounce sectarianism. As he confesses in *The Hind and the Panther,* his wilfulness and his pride of singularity were too strong for him to master unaided (3:125).

He projects something of this wilful singularity in St Catherine, the heroine of *Tyrannick Love*. In this play, one of the very few to defy the Restoration theatre's taboo against king-killing, the tyrannicide is God's response to Catherine's prayers when she is martyred by the insane Emperor. If we read the play in the light of the current political debate, Dryden's 'atheistical' tyrant unexpectedly sounds like the king, whose pleas for toleration in the parliamentary sessions of 1668 and 1669 fell on deaf ears. Maximin, like Montezuma, speaks the lines consonant with the king's libertine wit. 'Zeal is the pious madness of the mind,' he says on being told of the Christians and their 'execrable superstition' (10:121). The intransigent zealots in this play are in fact Catherine and her Christian converts. Politically, they constitute an upstart sect reckless of the 'Common quiet' that should be 'Mankind's concern,' as Dryden insists at the end of *Religio Laici* (2:122). His unflattering dramatization of zealous orthodoxy in *Tyrannick Love* may spring from the same abhorrence of militant Anglicanism that led Marvell to caricature Parker soon after in *The Rehearsal Transpros'd*.

In drawing attention to their shared dislike of intolerance, I am not suggesting that Dryden might have recounted the growth of popery or that Marvell would have relished *The Hind and the Panther*. Except in this vexing matter of Anglican intolerance, their politics were far apart. In the Preface to *Religio Laici*, Dryden shows contempt for his now dead rival when he characterizes Richard Hooker's pseudonymous antagonist, Martin Marprelate, as 'the *Marvel* of those times ... the first Presbyterian Scribbler' (2:106). By imputing his own origins to the deceased Marvell, Dryden preposterously disavows them. The Tory satirist who emerged with *Absalom and Achitophel* now poses as the scourge of sectaries. *Religio Laici* may profess orthodox Anglican doctrine, but its recriminatory preface blaming the Calvinists for king-killing blatantly violates the spirit of charity at the heart of Anglican discipline. In this, Dryden echoes another convert from Presbyterianism, Samuel Parker. And like Marvell's huffing divine, Dryden wields the tyrannical axe of schism that he had already brandished in the Preface to *Absalom and Achitophel*, where he gestures towards an 'Ense rescindendum,' an excrescence to be cut off by the sword (2:5). Both of these prefaces of 1681–2, together with that prefixed to *The Medall*, are polemics by an author who subscribes to the Cavalier axiom and has adopted the belligerent persona of a Tory defending his church.[13]

Dryden has, however, moderated Parker's hectoring style, shifting the political banter much closer to the tone affected by Marvell. The former playwright has dropped his condescension towards inferiors (Shadwell and Settle) and the whining pedantry adopted towards his superiors (Howard, Buckingham, and Rochester) and now assumes a public stance that places him and his foe on an equal footing. Contrast his feeble imitation of *The Rehearsal Transpros'd* back in 1673, when Dryden contributed to the *Notes and Observations on the Empress of Morocco*. He introduced his verse parody of Settle as follows: 'The Poet has not only been so Impudent to expose all this stuff, but so arrogant to defend it with an Epistle; like a sawcy Booth-keeper, that when he had put a Cheat upon the people, would wrangle and fight with any that would not like it, or would offer to discover it; for which arrogance our Poet receives this Correction, and to jerk him a little sharper, I will not Transprose his Verse, but by the help of his own words trans-non-sense sense, that by my stuff the people may judge the better what his is' (17:118).

In his anxiety here to keep Settle at arm's length, Dryden has to forgo the note of familiar mockery with which Marvell addresses an opponent. Nine years later, we hear that note in the 'Epistle to the Whigs': 'A Dissenter in Poetry from Sense and *English*, will make as good a Protestant Rhymer, as a Dissenter from the Church of *England* a Protestant Parson. Besides, if you encourage a young Beginner, who knows but he may elevate his stile a little, above the vulgar Epithets of prophane, and sawcy Jack, and Atheistick Scribler, with which he treats me, when the fit of Enthusiasm is strong upon him: by which well-mannered and charitable Expressions, I was certain of his Sect, before I knew his name' (2:42).

The 1673 squib simply rebukes a despised competitor who has somehow got out of line, diminishing him to an impertinent stall-keeper. The bantering epistle of 1682, drawing upon the full resources of Dryden's moral art, evokes a complete world of social types and interrelations for each of which the poet seems to find just the right place: the analogy between English language/Church and bad poet/Dissenter, the ironic pathos of 'a young beginner' (Oldham, perhaps?), and finally the tempered indignation with which the poet resigns himself to being made a target of the sectarians.

Dryden's new, familiar tone does not mean he endorses republican democracy or that he is reconciled to the rough justice of the Rose Alley beating. His moral art does not evoke a vision of civic participation, as Marvell's satire does. Nonetheless, Dryden has effectively taken over his late rival's satirical persona.

That persona, which Dryden first appropriated in *Absalom and Achitophel*, would undergo further refining, but already in 1681 the playwright has transformed himself into a satirist by modulating the voice of his theatrical prologues and adapting it to Marvell's publicist role. Having long excluded politics from his plays, Dryden now mounts the public stage himself. His partisan drolling replaces Marvell's patriotic buffoonery.

The key to Dryden's new role is its protean character. This marks a significant development in his moral art. A favourite theme of the heroic plays had been *vicissitudo omnium rerum*. While presenting the rise and fall of empire in *The Conquest of Granada*, however, or while analysing revolution in *Aureng-Zebe*, Dryden overlooked the principle of universal change *in himself*. He affected a libertine cynicism and quoted Montaigne while yet clinging proudly to his own intellectual constancy. He treated harshly those he judged 'unfixt in Principles and Place,' from the ambitious Achitophel to the lowly Elkanah Settle. And he probably despised the method behind Marvell's chameleonic effigy of Parker, daubed in with slapdash strokes:

> Truly, Mr. *Bayes*, you have a very notable face, and many men I meet very like you. *Caligula* before ... and now *Julian*, one would almost swear you were spit out of his Mouth. He set up a Nick-name for the Christians, to mark them out to be knock'd o' th' head: So do you give the Non-conformists the name of Fanaticks, as he them of *Galileans*; but the great *Galilean* was too hard for him. Pray Sir, who are these Fanaticks? Most of 'm, I assure you, better men than your self, of truer principles then you are, and more conformable to the Doctrine of the Church of *England*.[14]

Marvell's bequest to Dryden's satirical persona was its protean empathy: in order to mock his subject, Dryden had to impersonate it. This lesson from his enemies did not come easily. Dryden liked to say that Buckingham had portrayed himself in Bayes (4:8). When he caricatured Buckingham as 'the monkey Authour' in *Troilus and Cressida*, Dryden still lacked this insight, and his pusillanimous name-calling is on a par with Thersites' scolding (13:254; compare also the Epilogue). Contrast with this the knowing humour that animates his character of Zimri two years later:

> A man so various that he seem'd to be
> Not one, but all Mankinds Epitome.
> Stiff in Opinions, always in the wrong,
> Was every thing by starts, and nothing long;

But, in the course of one revolving Moon,
Was Chymist, Fidler, States-man, and Buffoon.
(2:21, ll. 545–50)

When Dryden later boasted of this passage, did he remember his rule that the satirist was prone to betray himself? If Bayes was a self-portrait of Buckingham, then the character of Zimri reveals something of the mind of its author.

Dryden emerged as a political satirist in 1681 by taking over a persona created by his wittiest literary rivals. Having Bayes on their side left king and Tories with the dilemma of Odysseus and the Greeks: they could have rejoiced more gladly in the masterful bow of their Philoctetes without the suppurating wound of his dissenting past. Events proved that they had welcomed a dangerous recusant into their midst. Dryden's new persona was not done evolving. Its final form would emerge only when the political satirist discovered in religion the ultimate grounds of his moral art.

Notes

1 *The Works of John Dryden*, ed. E.N. Hooker, H.T. Swedenberg, Jr, et al., 20 vols. (Berkeley: University of California Press 1956–2000), 1:163. Subsequent references to Dryden's writings will be to this edition (hereafter cited as *California Dryden*) and included within my text.

2 Charles Ward, in his *Life of Dryden* (Chapel Hill: University of North Carolina Press 1964), 144, was the first to suggest that the Rose Alley attack was politically motivated. See the discussion in my book, n. 6, below. Some of Dryden's contemporaries, ignorant of his gibing Prologue, speculated that the poet was beaten by one of the persons traduced in 'An Essay on Satire,' published anonymously by Mulgrave.

3 'To the Reader.' *California Dryden*, 2:3.

4 Phillip Harth, *Pen for a Party: Dryden's Tory Propaganda in Its Contexts* (Princeton: Princeton University Press 1993), 296n.101, 60.

5 James Anderson Winn, *John Dryden and His World* (New Haven and London: Yale University Press 1987), 324.

6 For identification of the four speakers, which nobody seems to have attempted in Dryden's lifetime, see chapter 5 in my *Dryden and the Problem of Freedom: The Republican Aftermath 1649–1680* (New Haven: Yale University Press 1997). Towards the end of the *Essay,* Dryden tactfully signals their iden-

tity by dividing the dramatic palm among them according to their seniority: 'No serious Playes written since the Kings return have been more kindly receiv'd by them [Neander is speaking of 'the mix'd audience of the populace and the Noblesse'], then the *Seige of Rhodes*, the *Mustapha*, the *Indian Queen*, and *Indian Emperour*' (17:73–4).

7 On the social epistemology of Dryden's era, see Richard Kroll, *The Material Word: Literate Culture in the Restoration and Early Eighteenth Century* (Baltimore: Johns Hopkins University Press 1991).

8 For a reading of the complex hermeneutics in *The First Anniversary* – the only political poem Marvell published – see Haley, *Dryden and the Problem of Freedom*, chapter 2.

9 Intended to parody Waller's *Instructions to a Painter* (1665), *The Second Advice to a Painter* (backdated 'April 1666') and *The Third Advice to a Painter* (dated '1 October 1666') were both published in 1667. My quotations are from George deForest Lord, ed., *Poems on Affairs of State: Augustan Satirical Verse, 1660–1714*, ed. George deForest Lord, et al. 7 vols. (New Haven and London: Yale University Press 1963), 1:74 and 39. I accept Lord's ascription of *The Third Advice to a Painter* to Marvell. See Lord's bibliographical note (*Poems on Affairs of State*, 1:21) listing the discussions of this ascription.

10 Ibid., 58. For the lines on Marvell, see Christopher Wase, 'Divination,' in *POAS*, 1:58 (ll. 77–8).

11 For the context of Marvell's pamphlet, see D.I.B. Smith, ed., *The Rehearsal Transpros'd and The Rehearsal Transpros'd: The Second Part* (Oxford: Clarendon Press 1971). Parliament, at its next meeting in 1673, retracted the king's Indulgence.

12 Ibid., 136. Against schismatical bishops, Marvell quotes John Hales (79–83). This is the John Hales of Eton who taught Davenant and Suckling to prefer Shakespeare to Johnson, as Neander recalls (17:56).

13 On the 'Cavalier axiom' equating religious dissent with political sedition, see Haley, *Dryden and the Problem of Freedom*, 259n.12 (quoting R.A. Beddard). A similar envy of Dryden's former rival appears in the anonymous pamphlet *His Majesties Declaration Defended*, where the author suggests that Marvell's 'party' gave him a 'Pension of four hundred pounds *per annum*' (17:213). Such a groundless slur would be consistent with Dryden's attacks on Whig 'patriotism.'

14 *The Rehearsal Transpros'd: The Second Part*, ed. Smith, 283.

chapter six

The Political Economy of *All for Love*

RICHARD KROLL

I will begin at what may seem a rather unexpected point in British theatrical history. The reason for this is that the following essay falls into two parts. Like theatre-goers from 1677 until the end of the eighteenth century, I believe that *All for Love* is Dryden's greatest play. A measure of its greatness is that it is not only powerful theatre in its own right, but perfectly expresses a series of decisions by its author, for entirely local political reasons, to shape the play deliberately to mark its departure from the theatrical tradition – less from Shakespeare (despite Dryden's hints to the contrary) than from the Fletcherian and tragicomic tradition that Dryden had inherited from Sir William Davenant, his predecessor as Poet Laureate. I therefore begin by describing both the form and ideological implications of that tradition before proceeding to show what it means for Dryden to have rejected those possibilities in *All for Love*.

Early in Congreve's *The Way of the World*, performed as we know in 1700, there are two highly significant references to William Davenant. Davenant was one of the two holders of theatrical monopolies granted by Charles II at the Restoration proper. He was also the author of *Salmacida Spolia* (1640), the last early Stuart masque performed before the onset of the Civil War, and *Gondibert* (1651), whose Preface, in a famous exchange with Hobbes, initiated many of the standard *topoi* of a distinctly neoclassical criticism, whose greatest exponent is – along with Samuel Johnson – undoubtedly John Dryden. I have argued elsewhere that Davenant's career itself has some considerable bearing on my topic here, but I wish for the time being to stay with the remarkable fact that Davenant remained a distinct memory throughout the entire literary period we now call the Restoration, and Congreve is eulogizing that important founder of the Restoration theatre in his beautifully autumnal farewell to the seventeenth century.[1] Congreve's two allusions to Davenant are fashioned to epitomize the combination of Davenant's institutional and political bequests to later playwrights, for early in Act I, Sir Wilfull Witwoud is, when in his cups, compared to the monster in *The Tempest* (1670, in the Davenant-Dryden version); and only a few lines later, Petulant describes his country cousins as bothersome 'Roxalanas,' an allusion to the Sultana in Davenant's ground-breaking opera performed during the Interregnum, *The Siege of Rhodes* (1656), not coincidentally the first occasion on which an actress played the part of a woman on the English stage.[2]

The significance of the former reference is that *The Tempest* was Dryden and Davenant's one major collaboration before the latter's death, while it also represents one of many revisions of Shakespeare that occurred during the Restoration, as well as – according to Katherine Maus in an important article – supplying a political commentary on contemporary events.[3] For reasons I will describe below, I believe that this version of Shakespeare's play had a considerable imaginative afterlife in the Restoration theatre, since the period seems to have interpreted the plot by asking the following question: what does it mean for an established political economy (in Shakespeare's play, that involving Prospero, Caliban, and Ariel) to be disturbed by figures emerging from the sea – a sea that, in Shakespeare's case, is a watery world ambiguously alternating between the Mediterranean and the Caribbean? Already in Shakespeare's plot, I think it fair to say, our ambivalence about Prospero arises in part from the recognition that the island world is, for all its magical aura, peculiarly static; and inasmuch as Prospero can be imagined as satisfied with his own rule, without intrusion from outside, Miranda will remain perennially virginal, though threatened by Caliban's lust, Caliban will find no greater access to grace, Ariel cannot work his way to freedom, and Prospero's power remains divorced from the compromises and satisfactions of realpolitik, to which he must return in Act V. Thus, in the Restoration, for example, the honour-bound world of the Spanish is upturned by the arrival, in Aphra Behn's *The Rover* – produced in 1677, the same year as Sir Charles Sedley's *Anthony and Cleopatra* and *All for Love* – of Willmore and his associates, always it seems on the move for sex rather than love; significantly for my title, Belville and Willmore on separate occasions speak of the English as 'merchants of love,' while their prince (the exiled Charles II) is continuously afloat aboard his 'little wooden world.'[4] In Wycherley's *The Plain Dealer* (1676–7), Manly arrives from the sea to upset Freeman's, Vernish's, and Olivia's calculations, since he and Fidelia represent an entirely different and unbending epistemological – not to say moral – posture towards the world. And Congreve's first sketch for his own kind of mooncalf, beautifully fleshed out in Sir Wilfull, occurs in the figure of Ben in *Love for Love* (1695), who is described in the *Dramatis Personae* as 'half home-bred and half sea-bred.' Like Sir Wilfull, Ben represents a kind of ongoing benign disruption to the designs of the other characters in the play.

If figures from the sea disturb the lives and expectations of landlubbers, so Congreve's second allusion to Davenant's Roxalana in *The Siege of Rhodes* seeks to remind his audience that Davenant represents a distinct development in the view that seventeenth-century drama has far more than a decorative role in this most political of eras. Martin Butler argues that in the royalist drama of the 1630s the plays themselves served to disrupt and thereby regulate the waywardness of those in power,[5] so that even the court contributed to the antitheatrical sentiment that provoked the closing of the theatres. Davenant renders that view more prescriptive in his Preface to *Gondibert* when he argues that the exemplary force of poetry can assist the magistrate. I believe the intended corollary is that poetry can also serve the king's counsellors, an issue which pervades his addressee's masterpiece, *Leviathan* (1651).[6] Congreve is harnessing this perception by reminding his audience that stage conditions themselves substantially contribute to political applications, so that Davenant's introduction of actresses serves Congreve's subject – what it means for a woman to grow old and so lose her purchase in the sexual marketplace – in the most direct and concrete of ways.[7] It is impossible to imagine Millamant, that is, with all her *douceurs* and *sommeils du matin*, being played by anyone else than an actress like Mrs Bracegirdle.

Put slightly differently, unless we understand what Davenant represented to those who inherited and developed the theatrical culture he revived and moulded, we cannot fully credit the political motives that governed plays in the late seventeenth century. Davenant's role, and his relation also to early Stuart drama, is, for Dryden, axiomatic, so that two running references in numerous critical statements still need proper parsing, namely, his allusions to Davenant and to Fletcher. Of the early-seventeenth-century triumvirate (or quadrumvirate) of dramatic greats, which includes of course Shakespeare and Jonson too, it is Beaumont and Fletcher in their tragicomedies who most clearly anticipate a corrective vision to the potential excesses of Stuart power. Certainly this seems a legitimate view of *Philaster* (1608–10; pub. 1620), *The Maid's Tragedy* (1610–11; pub. 1619), and *A King and No King* (1611; pub. 1619),[8] whose exaggerations and grotesqueries could be read as a highly stylized version of arguments about tyranny and usurpation that were to distinguish many of the pamphlets issued during the English Revolution. I believe that this capacity for debating the conditions of power from different perspectives and through highly artificial kinds of dramatic rhetoric distinguishes Davenant's early career. For example, in contradistinction to what two of the main books about Davenant seem to assume about his early plays, *The Platonick Lovers* (1635) is no mere rehearsal of truisms about the love said to bind Charles I and his court to his people. Davenant remains conscious throughout the play that Platonic epistemology inclines towards a disembodied virtue completely at variance with the basic conditions of drama itself.[9] The implication is that the mere fact of drama supplies a critique of ideology, since it so obviously points to the conditions of its own production, for most early Stuart drama, outside of Shakespeare, the more operatic and stylized the better. What for modern critics, subtly schooled in Coleridgean assumptions about dramatic coherence, creates an aesthetic weakness, supplies precisely these plays' political and rhetorical strength.

Indeed, from as early as Shakespeare's own *Measure for Measure* (1604), we could see seventeenth-century tragicomedy as capable of supplying a kind of experimental space for discussing the nature of political authority and political languages from a critical perspective encouraged by the improbable and highly contestatory conditions under which characters are forced to operate. In that sense, Shakespeare's Duke Vincentio is a kind of postulate opening up a conceptual game whose closest equivalent is the practice of casuistry, where characters wedded to some ideal postulate about what, in the abstract, constitutes virtuous or honourable action, find themselves precipitated into new, surprising, and alien relationships with other characters and, equally importantly, with the languages through which they have hitherto navigated the moral universe. Shakespearean criticism is still sufficiently wedded to psychologistic notions of character to find *Measure for Measure* a puzzling play, but the Duke's behaviour is heuristic for the play's purposes and allows for launching, theatricalizing, and anatomizing competing versions of personal virtue and political *virtu* before he steps in to close the action. His activities in the course of the plot have little to do with his personal development and everything to do with rendering the scenes he observes into something like the early modern laboratory.

Consequently, in the tragicomic tradition represented by *The Platonic Lovers*, characters are constantly arrested in their tracks to descant on the difficulties of reconciling the theatrical conditions that give them life with the axioms – now the official rhetoric of the early Stuart court – that demand to see all things translated into some Platonic never-never land. Even in a pastoral romance like Fletcher's *The Faithful Shepherdess* (1608; pub. 1609–10), the highly seductive pastoral language that all the characters almost seamlessly reproduce strikes violently against changes in fortune represented by sudden and suprising acts of wounding (spearing and stabbing) that occur for example in Act III, so that we are suddenly alerted not only to the artifice but also to the eerie irrelevance of language that increasingly accompanies rather than mediates the action. In this atmosphere, it is as if 'action,' 'character,' and 'language' become hypostatized as distinct conceptual categories competing in a mutually ironic economy. The result is that the texture of the play differentiates the constituent elements of what makes 'drama' possible; the accompanying danger is that the categories of the 'abstract' (here pastoral language) and the 'material' (acts of violence done on bodies) recoil from each other in an almost Manichaean opposition.

Thus, at one point in *The Platonic Lovers*, Theander, a young duke, rebukes his future brother-in-law Phylomont, who wishes to live with his mistress Eurithea only in Platonic harmony since the theatrical framework makes nonsense of such transcendental fictions: 'You two may live and love, become your own best arguments, and so contract all virtue, and all praise: Be ever beauteous, fresh, and young, at least in your belief; for who can lessen or defile th'opinion which your mutual thoughts shall fervently exchange? And then you may beget reflections in each others eyes, so you increase not children, but yourselves a better and more guiltless progeny: those immaterial creatures cannot sin.'[10] Additionally, characters seem aware that this conundrum raises the question of how they even appear as characters in any representational medium – whether in imagined historical accounts or on the stage – so that Davenant's early plays focus on an epistemological problem that also expresses a political ambition.

The epistemological problem is intrinsically dramatic, in the sense that drama, more than any other literary medium, can highlight the extent to which all knowledge is perspectival, an issue which for general cultural reasons is fully alive to Davenant. And this recognition is mainly expressed in two ways. First, it appears in the way characters anticipate the expression of their future reputation, as if, with an eye on the historical record, they permanently inhabit the future perfect tense – they seem curiously apprised of the potential outcome of events, projected as a complete historical tableau, and seem intent on calibrating, if not caressing, their place in that imagined and anticipated scene. Second, the problem of perspective appears within the context of the theatre proper, where the acting space can remind both characters and audience of their various perspectival limitations. And while characters seem so conscious of their place on the stage, they also increasingly define and read their interiority by reference to that very same spatial topography, so that identity is imagined as a version of the three-dimensional space of the proscenium stage.[11] The political corollary for Davenant is explicitly the notion of civility or a civil society, as if in vague but significant outline we can detect the liberal notions that politics must be conducted through the juxtaposition of competing or alternative perspectives, and that those for whom knowledge is self-evident have embarked on the slippery slope to tyranny or delusion, or both.

Famously, Dryden writes in 'Of Heroique Plays: An Essay,' prefaced to *The Conquest of Granada* in 1672, that 'For Heroic Plays ... the first light we had of them on the *English* theatre was from the late *Sir William Davenant*,' who, forbidden to produce tragedy or comedy, 'was forc'd to turn his thoughts another way: and to introduce the examples of moral, virtue writ in verse, and perform'd in Recitative Music.'[12] Though in this version of events, Davenant left plenty for his successors like Dryden to improve, I believe that Dryden here confirms the sense in which, for all their indebtedness to the French (whom he mentions), the English can lay claim to an indigenous heroic tradition, much as Alfred Harbage argues for a continuity between the Cavalier drama of Montague, Suckling, and Carlell, and the serious drama which characterized the decade after the Restoration.[13] And this reading is confirmed by Dryden rightly speaking about *Gondibert* as an heroic poem anticipating the devices of the heroic play,[14] with the result that the poem is almost paralysed by a consciousness of itself as a literary artefact in the process of recording or creating heroic images.

The critical difference between *Gondibert* and *The Siege of Rhodes*, however, is that Davenant's opera instituted a series of theatrical conditions that defined performance for the Restoration, including especially the proscenium, the front and back stages, and scenery, all of which materialized the playwright's ability to discuss the problem of perspective both as a metatheatrical and as a political issue. The introduction of these devices may have also allowed for more spectacular effects, but it does great damage to the intellectual force of Restoration drama to reduce it to such purely sensational aspects of performance.[15] I believe that it is precisely the metatheatrical possibilities of Davenant's reform of the stage that Dryden brilliantly adapted in his serious plays, whether we are talking about *Marriage A-la-Mode* (1671), *All for Love*, or *Don Sebastian* (1689; pub. 1690); and it is for these substantial reasons that Davenant's reputation survived until the end of the century. Moreover, at no point can we argue that though, from Davenant on, this is clearly loyalist drama, it represents anything but a sceptical view of the romance of Stuart kingship. It is as if loyalist playwrights consistently urged their royal audience to examine and so justify rather than merely assert the grounds of their power.

Thus, in the split plot and the on- and offstage business in *Marriage A-la-Mode*, Dryden's use of perspective provided by the proscenium stage urges us to view ironically the machinations of the high plot, in which Leonidas and Palmyra rehearse the romantic delusions that Davenant mocks in *The Platonick Lovers* – also a play set in Sicily – so that the play serves as a meditation on the conditions and limitations of Stuart power. The moral is also rendered comic in Melantha's determination to impress her French credentials on the court. The implication is that power can never operate solely in the belief of its own self-evidence – the attempt to do so is an expression both of epistemological naivety and of the urgency of power itself – but must emerge, Hobbes- or even Burke-like, from within the highly mediated conditions of institutions, in this case represented by the patently material conditions of drama. In *Marriage A-la-Mode*, one of those generic conditions, inherited from the tradition of English tragicomedy, is the double plot, which allows Dryden to reveal the terms of the outcome as the effect of internal competition, and most of the political arrangements at the end as the consequence of détente, as essentially contingent. Similarly, in *Don Sebastian*, Dryden was to return to the double plot as a means both to defend Stuart legitimacy and yet to reveal his dissent from what moderate Catholics saw as James II's abuse of power. Détente and a respect for the mediating force of institutions seem also to be the key to settlements at the end of major comedies from the 1670s: Margery is silenced at the end of *The Country Wife* (1675) to preserve the brittle contingencies of the game enjoyed by Horner and his paramours, as well as to secure the ending of that established institution, the five-act play; and in *The Rover*, Hellena and Willmore engage in an ironical exchange of terms – Robert the Constant for Hellena the Inconstant – that for the time being at least denotes their mutual satisfaction, while, given Willmore's tendencies, we remain aware of the unsettled nature of such agreements.

Because the play engages with the various generic traditions I have described, it is therefore my contention that *All for Love*, probably performed at the end of 1677, and printed the following spring, similarly expresses a scepticism about the self-regarding tendencies of those in power. It does so, however, by calculatedly abjuring the kinds of generic compromises embedded in *Marriage A-la-Mode* and *Don Sebastian*, and by purifying and intensifying its neo-Aristotelian commitments. The play was performed at the height of Danby's pre-eminence as a politician, at which time, the end of 1677, he formed, according to his biographer Andrew Browning, a member of a triumvirate, the other two members of which were the king and the duke of York. The setting of *All for Love*, representing the final dissolution of the most famous political triumvirate in ancient history, already serves to spotlight the difficult balancing act facing Danby. The nature of Danby's success as a politician, the policies he sought to promote, and the parallels between Dryden's literary allegiances and Danby's political allegiances, are all vital to understanding both the argument of *All for Love* as a whole, and the relation it bears to the Dedication included in the printed version of March 1678, at which time Danby's plans for the future and security of the monarchy were already at risk. Dryden's Dedication is full of approving allusions to Danby's significance in the revolutions in British institutional history that mark the entire late Stuart period, and of which Danby's success at the Treasury and creation of party politics constitute a watershed, even though their broader scope and of course their outcome cannot have been visible to any political agent during 1677. Though it is sometimes suspected of being overly Whiggish in the tradition of S.R. Gardiner, David Ogg's splendid, general account of the late Stuart period is germane in dealing with the particular details of Danby's career.[16] In some ways, Ogg's thesis could be reduced to two principles against a common backdrop, namely, that Charles II was naturally inclined to a certain absolutism, both expressed and encouraged by his cousin Louis XIV, with whom he had secret treaties and from whom he was essentially receiving bribes to dissolve Parliament and return the country to the true – that is, Catholic – faith.

These two principles are, first, that the business of government experienced a shift in the economy of scale and complexity, such that the proceedings of the privy council, for example, depended increasingly on the advice of technicians and experts and less on personal allegiances; and second, that in the wake of the Second and Third Dutch Wars, with the application of the Navigation Acts, with Pepys's revolutionary reforms of the Royal Navy, and with the acquisition of the remnants of a vast Portugese trading empire in outposts like Bombay, after 1674, Britain dramatically experienced the results of her de facto control of world trade that followed less from the defeat of the Dutch at sea than their exhaustion through war. In some ways the larger contrasts of Ogg's story are implicit in Figgis's account of the career of divine right theory, since, paradoxically, the theory achieved its most elaborate expression under Charles II (who cured more people of scrofula than any other English monarch) while his personal predilections, his indolence, and his womanizing made him a poor personal exponent of regal sanctity.[17]

Commentators agree that the period between 1660 and 1677 represents a rapid decline in Charles's reputation: the joy of the Restoration was rapidly tempered by plague and fire, and by the Dutch destroying some capital ships of the Royal Navy at their moorings at the close of the Second Dutch War; in 1672 Charles scandalously put a stop on the Exchequer, driving many of his creditors to the brink of bankruptcy, and calling the moral as well as fiscal credit of the government into question. Neither of Charles's most powerful mistresses was popular, and the fact that the second, the duchess of Portsmouth, was French, made more nervous a nation whose Protestant sympathies rightly suspected Charles of improper dealings with Louis. By 1677, moreover, anti-Dutch feeling stimulated by naval rivalry had subsided in favour of the more familiar dislike and distrust of the French – in this case, we now know, well justified. In their different ways, accordingly, Danby's and Dryden's loyalism incorporates an aspect of dissent. Dryden had rarely been properly paid for his post as Poet Laureate and Historiographer Royal; James Winn's biography merely confirms the shoddy treatment Dryden received from his Stuart masters.[18] Meanwhile Danby's pre-eminence in the mid-1670s arose, first, from his highly professional role at the Navy Board, and secondly, from his genius at the Treasury. Dryden's major literary enemies had coincidentally proven to be Danby's political enemies: although Danby owed his start to Buckingham, by 1677 Buckingham had become a faded but still dangerous rival whose final moments at the centres of power eventually undid him; and by an entirely different march of events, Danby, like Dryden, had fallen out with Sir Robert Howard.

When Dryden addresses his Dedication to Danby, therefore, its carefully chosen analogies place a critical distance between Danby, the professional public servant, and his master, such that, while Danby is said to express the virtues of Charles, Dryden's purpose is hortatory, in an attempt, through Danby, to recall Charles to his own best self. The point can be cogently made in Browning's summary of Danby's lifelong political aims, all of which deviate significantly from Charles's inclinations, and all of which, at this point, exactly coincide with Dryden's implicit prescriptions for a healthy polity: 'Protestantism at home and abroad, the maintainance and extension of the Triple Alliance, and observance of rigid honesty and economy in financial matters.'[19]

We can take three moments in Dryden's Dedication to show his appreciation for Danby as a professionally competent politician, his implicit criticism of Charles as something very different, and his elaboration of what we can only call a theory of political economy, in which the power and interests of the state are judged relative to its commercial viability – a commercial viability fundamentally associated with the sea and already recommended many years before in the closing stanzas of *Annus Mirabilis*.[20] Thus, Dryden writes, Danby had first to rescue the Treasury from the wreckage of financial mismanagement: '*All things were in the confusion of a* Chaos, *without Form or Method, if not reduc'd beyond it, even to Annihilation; so that you had not only to separate the Jarring Elements, but (if that boldness of expression might be allow'd me) to Create them.*'[21] Dryden's subtle Lucretianism, for which he pretends to apologize, carefully objectifies and materializes Danby's fiscal reforms in such a way as to prepare us for the next analogy, one opening directly onto political theory proper. Charles's virtue is expressed in his choice of servants, as body expresses soul, but the moderation embodied in Danby then emerges as an obstruction to two opposing forces in the affairs of state. He becomes, in Dryden's vivid metaphor, '*an* Isthmus *betwixt the two encroaching Seas of Arbitrary Power, and Lawless Anarchy*' (13:5), and I think there is enough evidence of Dryden's political sophistication here and elsewhere to argue that he is referring to Danby's management of an embryonic government party in Parliament.[22] Like Clarendon, and like the Dryden of this Dedication, Danby's loyalism was Cavalier and Anglican, and his management of the house, which anticipated – indeed required – the creation of something like a government whip, effectively imagined parliamentary processes themselves as distinct from, on the one hand, the government in the person of the king and his immediate servants, and on the other, the demagoguery of the emerging opposition party led by Buckingham and Shaftesbury. By the end of 1677, Browning writes, 'Not merely had [Danby] obtained for the King one of the largest grants of supply ever accorded him in time of peace, but he had almost contrived to establish a genuine reconciliation between King and Parliament on the basis of a truly national policy.'[23] In passing, Browning also remarks that the failure to develop such a national policy owed much to 'the essential selfishness of Charles' and that in trying to develop it, Danby appeared 'to regard Parliament as a third interest which cannot be identified with either King or People.'[24]

From a theoretical point of view the shifts in political attitude associated with Danby are thus very significant, and their significance was not lost on Dryden, whose final analogy promotes the view of England as a maritime and commercial power whose interests do not include Continental adventurism of the French kind – at this point William of Orange was in a merely defensive position, and was being courted by Danby, with the assistance of Sir William Temple, to marry James's daughter Mary. Having declared his distaste for republican principles, Dryden then writes: '*The Nature of our Government above all others, is exactly suited both to the Situation of our Country, and the Temper of the Natives: An Island being more proper for Commerce and for Defence, than for extending its Dominions on the Continent*' (13:6).

All for Love as a play, by contrast, operates in a world clinically divorced from these values; compromise, political negotiation, concern for the national interest, the political power of commercial sea-borne processes, all are dramatically purged from the main action of the play, but purged in such a way as to make us conscious of their absence, even without the assistance of the printed Dedication. We might begin our analysis of the play by asking how Shakespearean it is.[25] Max Novak's commentary in the *California Dryden* argues that the Shakespearean element emerges only from Dryden's commitment to blank verse[26] and I agree that Dryden's references to Shakespeare are otherwise something of a red herring. In Shakespeare, Caesar appears as the ultimate victor, which is also the point at which Sedley's version of *Antony and Cleopatra*, published in 1677, begins. In his play, Shakespeare posits a language that can legitimate and mediate the world of practical politics, because the Augustan chemistry is able to manufacture contingent fictions out of Antony and Cleopatra's discrete and self-serving metadramatic habits of speech; it is as if the incantatory speech of Richard II encounters in the same plot Henry V's Ciceronian pliability. Taken together, the Shakespearean and Sedleian versions represent Octavius in explicit contrast to the autotoxic world inhabited by the eponymous pair. In Shakespeare, Octavius presents a largely positive assessment of the Augustan enterprise, whereas Sedley's aristocratic libertinism permits him to expose all his chief actors as corrupt: Octavius is clearly a version of Louis XIV, already bent on the expansion of France at virtually any cost to others, including (in Octavius's case) his sister; and Antony is equally clearly, as well as by association, both effeminated by the East and unable to model himself on any image of proper rule, since even Julius Caesar offers no clear precedent for his circumstances.

Especially by contrast to the untidiness of Sedley's play, the action of *All for Love* is essentially Racinian. It is physically isolated from any image of action, whether in Egypt or the Roman Empire. Neither Caesar nor Octavius ever appear in *All for Love*, though the action is marked by the inevitability of Octavius's appproach, and no individual coming from 'outside' approximates a verbal protocal which might signal the nature of rule and speech in the Early Empire under Augustus. Cicero, the figure of rhetoric, has been murdered by the connivance of both Octavius and Antony.[27] Ventidius and Dolabella are extensions of what Antony might be if he were to choose a certain course of action, and that is because they represent features of his past and try to recall him to those forgotten or elided aspects of his personality. Octavia is no stand-in for Octavius – the future Augustus – for she becomes the occasion of a verbal and gestural rhetoric of the sentimental family. She does, however, hint at the possibility of some public world of value, since her proposal of an arrangement with Antony alludes to the public conditions of Restoration comedy – not least *Marriage A-la-Mode* – since it aims less to preserve their putatively private love than the public image of her 'reputation.'

The entire action in any case describes a complete political vacuum. The Battle of Actium has occurred and supplies one boundary; the other is provided by the betrayal by the Egyptian fleet, which acts seemingly autonomously without regard to the action or speeches of the chief characters. And Antony's main action, if it warrants that epithet, is to watch the betrayal occurring from Pharos, and so this itself becomes an emblem of Antony emblematizing knowledge.

The dynamic of the play is brilliantly if inadvertently described by Roland Barthes's *Sur Racine*,[28] and we should notice that Dryden rather backhandedly admits the influence of *Phèdre*, while referring to Shakespeare as, I think, a smokescreen. The action moves obsessively towards the construction of vignettes, emblems, and icons conceived fundamentally in visual terms, so that its vocabulary is more or less saturated with references to the face, to the eyes, to sight. In their exchanges (or what passes for exchanges), characters tend to employ verbal devices that function as discrete visual counters in order to do one of two things: either obsessively search for the self or the other in some visually imagined past, just as Leonidas and Palmyra fantasize about their past through a stylized pastoral haze; or persuade their listeners, as if they were a dramatic audience moved as much by what they see in gesture as what they hear in words. This in turn produces a paradox, since the play's wordiness arises as a result of the degree to which verbal persuasion per se is bankrupt. The situation is exacerbated – in contrast with Shakespeare or Sedley – by the fact that no representative of a functional view of language appears; the closest equivalent is Alexas, whose use of language to persuade is perverse and causes Antony's and Cleopatra's deaths almost directly. Great effort is accordingly expended on the verbal construction of almost reified narratives that tend to leave the speakers stranded in the midst of the putatively dramatic situation.[29]

Shakespearean poetry moves fluently among an enormous range or variety of potential metaphors, any or all of which, as it were, are waiting in the wings at any given moment. Speakers can thus appropriate any metaphor or analogy at will without fixating on the need to complete, caress, or polish any single one. Rather than destabilizing the moment of utterance, the fecundity of Shakespearean metaphor tends to stun the listener with its aptness to the situation – or, if ironic, exactly the reverse. The effect is that of stabilizing representation, such that the plurality of metaphor is, as it were, 'the mind of Shakespeare.'

The marked thinness of Dryden's analogical protocol, by contrast, derives in large part from three causes. First, from the fact that the semantic of the dramatic moment, at any given point, can draw on all the resources of the proscenium stage, with its capacity to create spatial distinctions between the front and back stage, and to materialize the various perspectives that distinguish characters from one another, and the audience from the stage action. These are all possibilities written out of Shakespeare, at least until he began writing consistently for the Blackfriars playhouse, which is yet another reason that the Restoration had such pronounced imaginative sympathies with *The Tempest*. Second, from the clarity of the relations among the chief terms of the governing analogies (for example, the analogy between 'stage' and 'world'), and the degree to which an already selected metaphor of this kind is the methodical key to an entire play. And third, given that in *All for Love* only one side of the analogy is visible – 'play' as opposed to 'world' – figuration appears as a continual repetition of only one side of an analogy whose empirical application or aptness we cannot judge; all we see is people talking, and people constantly conscious that they are talking.

Dryden's play is thus precisely *about* the evacuation of force from the act of speech: the world of words operates at an almost complete remove from the 'business' of the world, whether everyday life, love, or politics. There are several features of the play that expound this concern. First, as with Dolabella and Ventidius commenting on Octavia's possible effect on Antony in Act III, Dryden presents a sequence of hidden or partially hidden viewers who transform the scenes they watch into stylized tableaux of the irrelevance of action in the world. Second, we witness the 'discovery' or stylization of Antony and Cleopatra as one amongst a number of emblems, whether it is Antony surrounded by statuesque Roman soldiers in Act II (Charmion relates, 'I found him, then, / Incompass'd round, I think, with iron Statues; / So mute, so motionless his Soldiers stood, / While awfully he cast his eyes about' [II.i.48–51]), or Cleopatra in her monument. In both cases, the effect is to monumentalize the characters and to suggest that they seek so to monumentalize themselves and each other. Third, in a parody of the living protocols of the Stuart masque, Cleopatra finally monumentalizes Antony by dressing him up in state, so that what was once the theatre of relevance becomes the theatre of irrelevance, for there is no true audience for the image so presented, or at least an audience we must imagine as sentimental rather than political, so that the rhetoric of the image is entirely dissipated in an affective fog. Fourth, in the course of the play each monumentalizes the other by an obsessive relationship to memory – as when Antony recalls first seeing Cleopatra, a passage incidentally from Plutarch, not Shakespeare (III.i.168–87) – which we should not confuse with a genuine relationship to history or the past. Fifth, the tendency to objectify and hypostatize representation migrates into the characters' behaviour towards individual words, which, at the moment they appear in speech, are suddenly held up, as if the word-as-object has transformed into a slightly impenetrable emblem for microscopic and almost physical scrutiny, the word frozen as an anaesthetized patient on the table. That words lose their inner life relative to syntax and context itself describes how fully the atmosphere that Antony and Cleopatra breathe is divorced from historical time and political space. Finally, with the rival queens' entry from opposite doors in the rear of the stage, Act III spatializes a fundamental feature of Ventidius's and Dollabella's roles. Characters try to manoeuvre other characters into assuming postures *within* the syntax of some orchestrated or discrete tableau, just as when Ventidius tries spatially to manoeuvre Antony into a proper spousal relation to Octavia and their children, or when he commits suicide as a predictably ineffective example to Antony. The instant and catastrophic effects of Alexas's lies on what Ventidius tries to effect through such tableaux reveals how completely brittle and superficial they are. The implication is that representation is now worn so thin, that when it fractures, the only option is death or suicide.[30]

I have already been arguing in effect that Dryden contrasts the marmoreal bankruptcy of this world with Danby's success in husbanding England's acknowledged transformation into a commercial power to be reckoned with, with the accompanying view that commerce (an English virtue) rather than glory (a French vice) will strengthen the nation's sinews. The opposition between markets – a fluid system of negotiation and exchange already made imaginatively likely in William Harvey's discovery of the circulation of the blood – and more antique and static systems of honour is suggested by the play itself. As many commentators on the history of economics make clear, mecantilism as a vehicle of thinking about macroeconomics was deeply invested in two aspects of the polity that virtually define Dryden, especially if we remember the conditions of the *Essay of Dramatick Poesie*: 'the discourse of trade' (developed especially in England after about 1620) was centrally a means of adjudicating the relative wealth of European nations, especially with the collapse of Portuguese and Spanish colonial hegemony and the emergence of Holland as the Continental entrepot; and it was, to put it only slightly differently, a means of adjudicating the relative integrity of political bodies that were now distinctively nation states. Both the imaginative transformation of physiology that occurred after *De Motu Cordis*, in which the entire body participates in a single circulatory mechanism, and the net result of the three Dutch Wars, whose consequences in favour of English seaborne trade became increasingly clear after the mid-1670s, move in similar directions which are visible in the dramas of that decade.

Thus, in the Preface to *All for Love*, Dryden expresses resentment against Rochester and the court wits, as well as the French love of ceremony, and contrasts it with a different literary order, one based on merit, and one permitting social mobility based on the market. The world of privilege he associates with Nero, by contrast with which 'the true poets were they who made the best Markets, for they had Wit enough to yield the Prize with good grace, and not contend with him who had thirty Legions' (15). Throughout the play, Octavius is at sea in the Mediterranean, whose commercial possibilities were already obvious to Englishmen in the 1670s, and for that reason Antony dismisses him as a mere usurer and tradesman: 'Nature meant him for an Usurer: / He's fit indeed to buy, not conquer Kingdoms' (III.i.214–15). By contrast, like the Spanish in *The Rover,* Antony and Cleopatra are marooned on the gold standard, a world of intrinsic and transparent value. It is Antony in Act V who most clearly invokes the opposition of his world to a commercial, seaborne economy, for, suddenly convinced of Cleopatra's death by Alexas, he contemplates the alternative:

> She is [fled]: my eyes
> Are open to her falshood; my whole life
> Has been a golden dream, of Love and Friendship.
> But, now I wake, I'm like a Merchant, rows'd
> From soft repose, to see his Vessel sinking,
> And all his Wealth cast o'er.   (V.i.203–8)

A little later, he exhausts that metaphor, resigning the world to Octavius:

> What shou'd I fight for now? My Queen is dead.
> I was but great for her; my Pow'r, my Empire,
> Were but my Merchandise to buy her love;
> And conquer'd Kings, my Factors. Now she's dead,
> Let *Caesar* take the World,———
> An Empty Circle, since the Jewel's gone
> Which made it worth my strife: my being's nauseous;
> For all the bribes of life are gone away.   (V.i.269–76).

Notes

1 See Richard Kroll, 'Davenant and Dryden,' in Sue Owen, ed. *The Blackwell Companion to Restoration Drama* (Oxford: Blackwell, 2002), 311–25.
2 William Congreve, *The Way of the World,* ed. Kathleen M. Lynch (Lincoln: University of Nebraska Press 1965), I:195–6; 355–7.
3 Katherine Eisaman Maus, 'Arcadia Lost: Politics and Revision in the Restoration *Tempest,*' *Renaissance Drama* new series 13 (1982), 189–209.
4 Aphra Behn, *The Rover,* ed. Frederick M. Link (Lincoln: University of Nebraska Press 1967), I.i.787; I.ii.45; V.i.512.

5 Martin Butler, *Theatre and Crisis, 1632–1642* (Cambridge: Cambridge University Press 1984), 280. This is an excellent book that represents a model for linking literature with politics, but I hope that my essay can take issue with Butler's contention that the narrowing of Restoration drama to a court clientele undermined the power of drama to comment critically on high politics. The narrow social basis of Restoration audiences is a view that has been long challenged, and I think Butler mystifies the importance of the division between popular and court theatre in demonstrating the critical power of the former. Part of my argument throughout is that Dryden's royalism is critical and dialectical – true to the Ciceronian grounds of the pedagogy his generation imbibed – and that his attitude to kings was heuristic, not, as Leo Braudy's essay for this volume implies, ontological.

6 For the Davenant-Hobbes exchange, see J.E. Spingarn, ed., *Critical Essays of the Seventeenth Century*, 3 vols. (Bloomington: Indiana University Press 1963), 2:1–67.

7 For a superb article on the ideological implications of the arrival of actresses, see Katherine Eisaman Maus, '"Playhouse Flesh and Blood": Sexual Ideology and the Restoration Actress,' *ELH* 46 (1979), 595–617.

8 I use the approximations supplied by E.K. Chambers, *The Elizabethan Stage*, 4 vols. (Oxford: Clarendon Press 1951).

9 See Mary Edmond, *Rare Sir William Davenant* (Manchester: Manchester University Press 1987), 56–9; Alfred Harbage, *Sir William Davenant: Poet Venturer, 1606–1668* (1935; rpt. New York: Octagon 1971), 235–7.

10 Sir William Davenant, *Works*, 2 vols. (1673; rpt. New York: Blom 1968), 2: 395.

11 This tendency is not typically Shakespearean, though Richard II does precisely this at V.v.1ff. I argue, however, that the feature does become more insistent in the wake of the Harveian revolution in physiology and Davenant's reform of the stage in *The Siege of Rhodes*.

12 'Of Heroique Plays.' *The Works of John Dryden*, ed. E.N. Hooker, H.T. Swedenberg, Jr, et al., 20 vols. (Berkeley: University of California Press 1956–2000), 11:9 (hereafter cited as *California Dryden*).

13 Alfred Harbage, *Cavalier Drama: An Historical and Critical Supplement to the Study of the Elizabethan and Restoration Stage* (1936; rpt. New York: Russell and Russell 1964), 237-8.

14 'Of Heroique Plays.' *California Dryden*, 11:10–11.

15 As they bear on my discussion, there are two different ways in which the purely sensational aspects of performance in the later seventeenth century are not granted the intellectual force I want here to emphasize. Ironically, the most intelligent book on Restoration tragedy, Eric Rothstein's book by

that name, provides a highly intellectualized account of how late-seventeenth-century performance modes provided the rhetorical grounds of the sentimental modes that succeeded it. But the difficulty for me is that an unintended consequence of the argument is that performance conditions become the etiology for something (sentimental experience of the stage) that has less self-conscious *intellectual* validity than the way in which Restoration playwrights approach the performative dimension of drama. See Eric Rothstein, *Restoration Tragedy: Form and the Process of Change* (Madison: University of Wisconsin Press 1967). A cruder privileging of dramatic sensationalism is to be found in Judith Milhous and Robert D. Hume, *Producible Interpretation: Eight English Plays, 1675–1707* (Carbondale: Southern Illinois University Press 1985). Keeping the memory of Davenant alive throughout the entire Restoration period, I would like to suggest, involved a recognizing that in providing new material and operatic possibilities for mounting plays in the wake of *The Siege of Rhodes*, Davenant had also supplied a non-verbal but nevertheless intellectually substantial way to mount dramatic arguments that cannot merely be reduced to some sensationalist view of stage production. The standard account of Davenant's reform of the stage is Richard Southern, *Changeable Scenery: Its Origin and Development in the British Theatre* (London: Faber and Faber 1952), which is more often referred to than cited. Southern argues that the scenery Davenant introduced for Restoration practice was anti-illusionistic and, rather than merely decorating the action, acted as its own form of symbolism in dramatic argument. In his chapter devoted entirely to *The Siege of Rhodes*, Southern writes, 'Davenant as a playwright paid an unprecedented attention to scenery, even regarding it (as his title page suggests) as part of the essential vehicle and medium of his drama – "made a Representation by the Art of Prospective in Scenes ..." Such an attitude had probably existed in no English playwright before' (111).

16 See David Ogg, *England in the Reign of Charles II*, 2nd ed. (Oxford: Oxford University Press 1963).

17 John Neville Figgis, *The Divine Right of Kings*, 2nd ed. (Cambridge: Cambridge University Press 1922).

18 For example, the Stop on the Exchequer had personal consequences for Dryden. See James Anderson Winn, *John Dryden and His World* (New Haven: Yale University Press 1987), 232.

19 Andrew Browning, *Thomas Osborne, Earl of Danby and Duke of Leeds, 1632–1712*, 3 vols. (Glasgow: Jackson and Son 1951), 1:117.

20 See, for example, Blair Hoxby, 'The Government of Trade: Commerce, Politics, and the Courtly Art of the Restoration,' *ELH* 66 (1999), 591–627.

21 John Dryden, *All for Love. California Dryden*, 13:4. All subsequent references

to this work will be to this edition and will appear parenthetically within the text.

22 This intuition is partly confirmed by Michael McKeon's reading of 'To My Honour'd Kinsman' in this volume, though admittedly this poem responds to very different political circumstances. However, though by 1700 Dryden was officially proscribed, I hope that I make it clear that Dryden's loyalism always included a strong impulse to dissent, and a preference for procedure and institutions over personality.

23 Browning, *Danby*, 1:232.

24 Ibid., 227; 227n.

25 An extraordinary recent case of Dryden being unfavourably compared to Shakespeare occurs in Barbara Everett's search for Dryden's *Hamlet* in 'Unwritten Masterpiece,' *London Review of Books* 23 (4 Jan. 2001), 29–32. To Everett's view that Dryden's plays are unperformable, I respond that his dramatic masterpiece was clearly performable for almost 150 years. Everett seems unaware that her notions of performance are themselves the product of nineteenth-century traditions of performing Shakespeare, which incorporated psychologistic assumptions at odds with the Fletcherian tradition Dryden points us to.

26 *California Dryden*, 13:363–89.

27 Given the extent to which I am arguing for a kind of negative dialectics in *All for Love*, it is worth recalling that Dryden co-translated Plutarch. Plutarch's 'parallels' are presented as pairs of ancients, whose values are often juxtaposed in some mutually critical relation. Plutarch does not compare Cicero and Antony directly, but he makes clear that Cicero was often governed by expedient rather than principle, yet that Antony was sordidly implicated in his assassination, so that the implied contrast produces no simple moral allegory of virtue.

27 Roland Barthes, *On Racine* (Berkeley: University of California Press 1992).

28 Many of these formal features of *All for Love* are shared by much Stuart drama as a whole, and are curiously described by Walter Benjamin in *The Origin of German Tragic Drama* (London: Verso 1998), which I would like to take seriously as an essay in seventeenth-century literary history. The combination of these features Benjamin describes by the term 'allegory,' but while I find his linking of formal textual properties to their ideological implications highly productive, I disagree that the self-conscious formalism of English (as opposed to German) seventeenth-century drama is a measure of absolutism. It is, rather, the opposite, on the view that the allegorical mode (if we agree to call it that) serves to lay bare its own machinery, much as Richard Southern argues that scene changes after *The Siege of Rhodes* imported into the

experience of the stage an anti-illusionistic pleasure, especially since those transformations occurred without lowering the front curtain, which only happened at the end of the entire performance. Because dramatic artifice was such an important forum for constitutional debate and political advice, the pleasure in that artifice almost for its own sake served to demystify the magical properties associated with kingship, such that drama as a form of cultural polemic anticipated the eventual reduction of royal power to a contractual model. For a particularly sensitive reading of the 'baroque' forms of representation in Dryden's drama, see Blair Hoxby's essay on *Aureng-Zebe* in this volume.

29 Dryden indeed seems to believe that the health of a language depends on trade and commerce in terms that for him combine poetry and political economy. An important statement to this effect occurs in his 'Dedication of the *Aeneis*,' where he writes, 'If sounding Words are not of our growth and Manufacture, who shall hinder me to Import them from a Foreign Country? I carry not out the Treasure of the Nation, which is never to return: but what I bring from *Italy*, I spend in *England*: Here it remains, and here it circulates; for if the Coyn be good, it will pass from one hand to another. I Trade both with the Living and the Dead, for the enrichment of our Native Language. We have enough in *England* to supply our necessity; but if we will have things of Magnificence and Splendour, we must get them by Commerce' (*California Dryden* 5:336.)

chapter seven

Wit, Politics, and Religion: Dryden and Gibbon

SUSAN STAVES

At the beginning of a new millennium, it is appropriate to consider Dryden's poetry in a broad, world-historical context. Part of what I have always loved about Dryden is his eagerness to engage both large ideas and the exigencies of his own immediate historical situation. Today, I propose to consider Dryden's longest poem, *The Hind and the Panther*, a poem about the grand clashes between church and state, but also a poem very much engaged in the immediate moment of the political crisis caused by James II's efforts to return England to Roman Catholicism. In the interest of suitably millennial contemplation, I want to consider *The Hind and the Panther* together with Gibbon's *Decline and Fall of the Roman Empire*, concentrating on Gibbon's riveting accounts of two great crises in the Western Christian Church: first, the establishment of Christianity as the new state religion of the formerly pagan Roman Empire under the emperor Constantine in the fourth century; and second, what Gibbon enjoys calling 'the conversion of the barbarians' in the fifth and sixth centuries, that is, the conversion of the various Goth, Visigoth, and Vandal inhabitants of what is now the European Union. In considering *The Hind and the Panther* and these sections of *The Decline and Fall*, I want to focus especially on how Dryden and Gibbon treat the great questions of the relation between the state and religion, how they understand a key theological issue that has repeatedly produced schism in the Christian Church – namely, Jesus's divinity – and, last but not least, how they use and think about wit in writing about religion.

Given the startlingly restrictive conventions of our current American public discourse in talking about religion and politics, it may be useful to comment briefly on them and on some different global realities. In

America now, we appear to have arrived at a moment in which major political candidates are required to profess a religion, but simultaneously required to guarantee that their public acts shall not be affected by any tenets of their particular religion that differ from what appears to be a kind of modern American deism, a set of usually unarticulated beliefs supposedly held in common by the overwhelming majority of decent people. It is considered bad form and 'intolerant' to take public political notice of any tenets of a candidate's particular religious beliefs that appear erroneous or even absurd to most Americans, and worse form to ridicule such beliefs. Thus, when the Republicans in Massachusetts not too long ago ran a member of the Church of Jesus Christ of Latter-day Saints for the U.S. Senate, no Democrat publicly asked the electorate: Can you possibly trust the intelligence or judgment of a man who believes that the Angel Moroni led Joseph Smith to gold tablets written in the 'reformed Egyptian language'?[1]

Our logically odd yet politically serviceable American state of affairs is an enlightenment heritage and represents our commitment to the so-called separation of church and state. American law attempts to treat clashes between religious practice, on the one hand, and state law or citizen's rights, on the other hand, as events occurring on the margins of public life. Thus, the state occasionally prosecutes Christian Science parents after their child has died of a medically treatable condition. We tend to hope that the rule John Locke proposed in the *Essay of Toleration* will work: the state should have no authority to suppress or to punish conduct citizens engage in on religious grounds, unless that conduct, in itself, absent religious motivation, would be suppressible or criminal.[2]

The American case, however, is not representative of the condition of humanity in this new millennium. The more typical condition might be described in two quite different ways. One might say, as the American view or the United Nations Charter of Human Rights would suggest, that the inhabitants of China, Russia, Iran, and many other states do not enjoy religious freedom because their states have established either atheism or particular religions and extended limited or no toleration to other religious practices. These states, however, do not see themselves as acting against human rights or prohibiting the free exercise of religion. Instead, they see themselves as exercising their duty to promote civil peace, national unity, and national interest by preventing the growth of religious sects, especially foreign ones, apt to produce civil strife and disunity. After the Chinese Revolution the Chinese government ordered the Roman Catholic Church in China to break with the Vatican, which continues to have diplomatic ties with Taiwan, regarded by China as a rebel province. China permits the Chinese Patriotic Catholic Association, independent of the Vatican, officially recognized in 1957, but suppresses an underground Roman Catholic Church that recognizes the authority of the Vatican.[3]

Modern states like China and Iran also recognize a duty to protect their citizens from religious frauds and impositions, especially foreign ones. How, an Iranian ayatollah might ask, can the United States government accept its duty to protect citizens from wasting money on ineffectual drugs through the Food and Drug Administration, yet deny any duty to protect them from the blandishments of Christian Science practitioners or, worse, soul-destroying false prophets? The current Chinese government has suppressed Falung Gong as a fraudulent cult attempting to prey on citizens; the leader of this group lives in the United States. In China, in 2000, the Li sisters were charged with conducting an illegal business by selling 1.8 million Falung Gong books and tapes. China has treated Falung Gong as the enlightenment English state treated witchcraft (purportedly a survival of paganism and currently recognized as a religion by the Massachusetts Commission Against Discrimination). Blackstone notes that the Renaissance statutes making the practices of witchcraft capital crimes were repealed by 9 Geo. 2, c. 5, which instead treated 'pretending to use witchcraft, tell fortunes, or discover stolen goods by skill in the occult sciences' as a species of fraud punishable as a misdemeanour.[4]

Even in America, there was a time when the government regarded a particular sect as sufficiently threatening to civil order that American Test Acts barred members of that sect not only from holding political office, but even from voting and serving on juries. In the 1880s Mormon officials in the Utah and Idaho territories were refusing to enforce the laws against bigamy, so Congress replied with a series of statutes disqualifying polygamists from office, from voting, and from jury service in the territories.[5] An Idaho Test Act went further to require the taker to swear not only 'that I am not a bigamist or polygamist,' but also 'that I am not a member of an order, organization, or association which teaches, advises, counsels or encourages its members, devotees or any other person to commit the crime of bigamy or polygamy.' Unsurprisingly, the Mormons challenged the constitutionality of this statute on the ground that it disfranchised even Mormons who were not themselves practising plural marriage and was thus a clear violation of Article 6 of the U.S. Constitution: 'No religious test shall ever be required as a qualification to any office of public trust in the United States.' However, the Supreme Court in *Davis* v. *Benson* (1890) found for the government, holding that bigamy was a crime by the laws of the United States and the laws of Idaho and that to advise or counsel bigamy was to facilitate its commission. Hence, 'such teaching and counseling are themselves criminal and proper subjects of punishment, as aiding and abetting crime are in all other cases.'[6] The English Test Acts against which Dryden campaigns in *The Hind and the Panther* were designed for a similar purpose: to prevent the state apparatus from falling into the hands of persons who, motivated by religious principles, were likely to refuse to enforce existing national law. Dryden's earlier work, before his conversion, of course, generally supports the principle that a state has a positive duty to maintain true religion and to protect its citizens from false teachers.

For obvious reasons, we are not accustomed to thinking of Dryden and Gibbon together; admittedly, they do not make so natural a pair as Dryden and Marvell or Richardson and Fielding. Nevertheless, they do have more in common than may at first appear. Dryden, who was, after all, Historiographer Royal, was well read in history and often invokes it, as he invokes the long history of Christianity in the West and of the English Reformation in *The Hind and the Panther*. Dryden in *The Hind and the Panther* expresses a Christian providentialist idea of history; Gibbon in *The Decline and Fall* refers to this providentialist theory only to substitute a narrative of secular causes for the rise of Christianity and the fall of pagan Rome.

Both Dryden and Gibbon began life as members of the Church of England and then converted to Roman Catholicism, Dryden shortly before the composition of *The Hind and the Panther*, Gibbon as a young Oxford student. As has happened many times in the history of Protestantism, both substantially converted themselves by serious biblical, theological, and ecclesiastical study. Gibbon's outraged father sent him to Switzerland to be tutored by a learned Protestant clergyman, who, after an arduous seventeen months, succeeded in inspiring Gibbon's return to the Church of England. Recent Gibbon criticism has, rightly, I think, rejected the earlier notion of Gibbon as simply a religious sceptic, an English version of Voltaire, instead understanding him throughout his life as a man seriously fascinated with religion and retaining complicated sympathy not only for a kind of philosophical deism, but also for the Church of England, which he attended, and even for the Church of Rome.[7] Gibbon's own religious experience, I believe, added depth and imaginative sympathy to his treatment of religion in *The Decline and Fall*.

Because his own feelings on the subject were so complex, the irony and comedy of his writing about religion is especially rich. He never seems to forget that he himself once believed in transubstantiation and was moved by rituals that the Church of England branded idolatrous.

Both Dryden and Gibbon are interested in moments when a sovereign changed his religion from that of the majority of his people and then attempted to use the state apparatus to promote the conversion of his subjects. Despite the argument advanced by liberal thinkers including Milton and Locke that a political sovereign cannot effectively use state power to change the religion of the majority of a people, history seems to demonstrate that whoever controls the state apparatus has considerable, though not absolute, power to effect wholesale conversions. Gibbon studies the conversion of the emperor Constantine from paganism to Christianity, then the conversion of a variety of Goth, Visigoth, and Vandal pagan rulers, and the consequences of these conversions for their various peoples.

Constantine's proclamation of the Edict of Milan, Gibbon shows, prepared the way for the defeat of paganism by Christianity: Dryden's contemporaries feared that James's Declaration of Indulgence would similarly prepare the way for the defeat of Protestantism by Catholicism. The Edict of Milan, proclaimed by Constantine and his colleague Licinius in 313, released the Christians from persecution; indeed, Gibbon says, the emperors proclaimed 'to the world, that they have granted a free and absolute power to the Christians, and to all others, of following the religion which each individual thinks proper to prefer, to which he has addicted his mind, and which he may deem the best adapted to his own use.'[8] Dryden, of course, deals with the new Roman Catholic king, James II, and supports the Declaration of Indulgence he offered in April 1687. The poem presents James as wishing for little beyond full rights of religious practice and political participation for Roman Catholics, and as willing to continue to honour the legally established rights of the Protestant Church of England, only promoting conversion among his Protestant subjects by the gentlest of persuasions. Anne Barbeau Gardiner in her recent book, *Ancient Faith and Modern Freedom*, argues that James was a sincere believer in religious toleration, points out that only about 1 per cent of the population of England was Roman Catholic in 1685, and quotes approvingly James's wonderment that there could be so much Protestant fuss 'of a Kingdom's being enslaved by a few Catholicks, though in imployment, or that a handfull of Papists could endanger the Religion and propertie, which millions of Protestants

were the keepers of.'[9] Gardiner also notes approvingly James's complaints, elaborated by Dryden in the Hind's tale of the Farmer and the
Pigeons, that Test Acts have interfered with the sovereign's legitimate
prerogative of 'employing those best qualified to serve in any employment.'[10]

But many Englishmen rightly doubted that James's brand of religious
toleration would simply secure personal rights for the small minority of
religious dissenters or that he would, as he promised, leave the legally
established Protestant state church alone. From the Protestant point of
view, James's willingness to use his prerogative power to abrogate valid
statutes looked like a use of the dispensing power by a sovereign who
placed his own conception of his religious obligations over his political
obligations to English law. While it is true that a plausible legal argument could be made out to defend James's dispensing individual subjects from statutes as an equitable exercise of the sovereign's prerogative, it is also true that the more he excused whole classes of subjects
from the requirements of statutes, and the more formally he exempted
them by written instruments like the Declaration of Indulgence, the
more it looked like he was attempting to substitute the will of the sovereign for the law of England. Gardiner cites John Miller's *Popery and Politics in England, 1660–1688* at various points in support of her position
that Protestant anxieties were unfounded, but Miller acknowledges that
James's interventions in English political institutions in 1686 and 1687
amounted to 'a revolutionary attack on the existing political order.'[11]

By spring 1687, when Dryden was writing *The Hind and the Panther*, the
determination of James and his increasingly Roman Catholic officials to
substitute Roman Catholics for Protestants in the civil, ecclesiastical,
and military institutions of the nation was evident. Norma Landau has
told the story of how James proceeded to purge Anglican Justices of the
Peace from the bench, substituting Roman Catholic and dissenting justices who would not enforce the recusancy laws or laws against dissenters. In October 1686 a select committee of the Privy Council began
reviewing commissions; it ordered the dismissal of 248 sitting Protestant
JPs who were likely to oppose the admission of Catholics to power and
the admission of 460 new justices, most of whom were Catholics. In
April 1687 all justices were dispensed from the requirements of the Test
Act.[12] James had also indicated his willingness to use his position as
head of the Church of England to promote Roman Catholicism. The
king warned the Archbishops of Canterbury and York to prevent
Church of England clergy from preaching against Roman Catholicism,

then in May 1686 ordered the bishop of London, Henry Compton, to suspend John Sharp for a sermon against Roman Catholicism; when the bishop refused, he was himself suspended.[13] For Ireland, Sunderland had in July 1685 issued an order not to administer the statutorily required oaths to officers and soldiers serving there. By September 1686 Tyrconnel's wholesale purges of Protestant officers and men had already succeeded in remodelling about two-thirds of the Irish army into a Catholic army. Because the new Catholic officers were generally poor, hardly any of the Irish Protestant officers turned out were paid for their commissions, nor did the government compensate them for this loss of their property.[14] One can see why the Catholic Swallows in the Panther's fable were so tempted to hope that James's policies would rapidly provide places and opportunities for almost all Catholics: the birds

> peeping through a broken pane,
> To suck fresh air, survey'd the neighbouring plain,
> And saw (but scarcely cou'd believe their eyes)
> New blossoms flourish, and new flow'rs arise;
> As God had been abroad, and walking there,
> Had left his foot-steps, and reform'd the year:
> The sunny hills from far were seen to glow
> With glittering beams, and in the meads below
> The burnish'd brooks appear'd with liquid gold to flow.[15]

What limited James in putting Catholics in places legally restricted to Protestants was not concern about 'employing the best qualified,' to use Gardiner's phrase, but the short supply of Catholics in England – a state of affairs he devoutly expected to be temporary.

It is a deeply interesting question whether a national sovereign espousing a minority religion will be able to transform the religion of the majority, as Constantine helped make Romans Christians or the Bolsheviks helped make Russians atheists. Rejecting providentialist explanations, Gibbon treats the matter as complex and seeks particular dynamics to explain particular successes or failures. He sometimes refers to 'the enterprise of subduing the minds of a whole people' as 'cruel and absurd' and he recognizes that some people – but not, he thinks, most people – will adamantly resist conversion to the death.[16]

Gibbon attaches considerable weight to material interest and explores how whoever is in control of the state apparatus can incentivize conversions. Thus, once the Edict of Milan has 'removed the temporal

disadvantages which had hitherto retarded the progress of Christianity,'
'the piercing eye of ambition and avarice soon discovered, that the profession of Christianity might contribute to the interest of the present, as
well as of a future, life ... [The] exhortations [of an emperor], his irresistible smiles, diffused conviction among the venal and obsequious
crowds which usually fill the apartments of a palace.' Courtiers' conversions were followed by the conversions of their humbler dependents, cities that had destroyed their pagan temples were rewarded with
municipal privileges, and even the barbarian troops, 'who had dis-
dained an humble and proscribed sect, soon learned to esteem a religion which had been so lately embraced by the greatest monarch and
the most civilized nation of the globe.'[17]

Both the Hind and the Panther recognize that state-shaped material
interests can influence religious affiliation, although each ascribes such
interests to the other. The Hind keeps insisting that Church of England
clergy refuse to acknowledge the Roman Catholic truth because they
seek to maintain material advantages to themselves that come from
their state-sanctioned monopoly. The Panther is jealous even of the
meagre spoils the Catholics have so far acquired. Indeed, the form of
beast fable itself vividly depicts a struggle over material food, as different
beasts are eager to snatch hard-won food out of the mouths of other
beasts. Thus the pampered, greedy Anglican Pigeons malignantly eye
the modest 'Cruise of Water' and the 'Ear of Corn' the farmer gives his
Catholic Chickens: 'Fain would they filch that little Food away,/While
unrestrain'd those happy Gluttons prey' (3:1003–4).

Gibbon is not so cynical as to ascribe the triumph of Christianity
solely to the pursuit of material self-interest; he also explores the less
tangible appeal of Christian ideas and the effect of practices like preaching. There was no preaching in pagan temples, but preaching in the
Christian churches allowed the early bishops and presbyters to inculcate
Christianity, 'without the danger of interruption or reply,' into 'a submissive multitude, whose minds had been prepared and subdued by the
awful ceremonies of religion.'[18] Preaching contributed to making Christianity a popular religion of a new and dangerous kind, one in which
ordinary congregants were drawn into theological disputes and passion-
ately, even violently, took sides. James's understanding of the power of
preaching to affect public opinion made him anxious to muzzle Protestant divines like Sharp and Stillingfleet and contributed to making the
refusal of the Seven Bishops to read his Declaration of Indulgence from
their pulpits a precipitating cause of the Glorious Revolution.

Perhaps the grandest theological dispute within Christianity is one to which both Dryden and Gibbon devote considerable attention: the Arian heresy and its afterlife. From some perspectives, Arianism – the denial that Jesus is of the same substance with God the Father – seemed the quintessential heresy within Christianity. As Gibbon shows, Arianism produced major schisms: first in the reign of Constantine when Constantine banished Arius himself, then in the conversion of the barbarians, then in the break between the Latin and the Greek Churches in 1054.[19] In the Restoration and the eighteenth century, Arianism was a criminal offence.[20] Catholic apologists liked to see Protestantism itself as a reincarnation of Arianism. Thus, giving the genealogy of the fox in *The Hind and the Panther*, Dryden complains that though Athanasius first chased Arius out at the Council of Nicaea,

> His impious race their blasphemy renew'd,
> And natures King through natures opticks view'd.
> Revers'd they view'd him lessen'd to their eye,
> Nor in an Infant could a God descry:
> New swarming Sects to this obliquely tend,
> Hence they began, and here they all will end.   (1:56–61)

In an interesting and provocative book, *The Pillars of Priestcraft Shaken: The Church of England and Its Enemies, 1660–1730*, J.A.I. Champion sees the challenge of Arianism to the Church as 'serious and potentially revolutionary,' and the assault of Arian freethinkers on the power of the clergy and on the 'central relationship of Church and state' as key to the Enlightenment in England.[21]

Gibbon necessarily makes the rise and diffusion of the Arian heresy a principal theme of his history. As he explains, 'from the age of Constantine to that of Clovis and Theodoric, the temporal interests of both the Romans and Barbarians were deeply involved in the theological disputes of Arianism.'[22] Gibbon's richly ironic and amused narrative nevertheless has strong undercurrents of feeling: rueful recognition of the human capacity to mask ego gratification and the sheer pleasure of ratiocination with lofty commitment to spiritual principle, grief at human folly, and outrage at human cruelty. In his view, metaphysical debates tempting to philosophers, and generally at least harmless to them, are apt to become dangerous and destructive when statesmen and the general public pick sides. He traces the early theology of the incarnation from Alexandria, where the Jews, encountering Platonism, 'applied the character of the LOGOS to the Jehovah of Moses and the patriarchs.' Controversy about the character of Christ's incarnation the mature Gibbon regarded as 'derived from the abuse of philosophy': 'We may strive to abstract the notions of time, of space, and of matter, which so closely adhere to all the perceptions of our experimental knowledge. But as soon as we presume to reason of infinite substance, of spiritual generation; as often as we deduce any positive conclusions from a negative idea, we are involved in darkness, perplexity, and inevitable contradiction.' Theological controversialists, Gibbon observes, 'too easily forget the doubt which is recommended by philosophy, and the submission which is enjoined by religion.' When the metaphysical distinctions of Greece and Alexandria made their way into the Latin Church, Latin translations were 'dark and doubtful' and 'the poverty and stubbornness of their native tongue, was not always capable of affording just equivalents for the Greek terms, for the technical terms of the Platonic philosophy.'[23]

The worst mischief was caused by Constantine's convening the Council of Nicaea in 325: 'from the moment that he assembled three hundred bishops within the walls of the same palace ... he extinguished the hope of peace and toleration ... The presence of a monarch swelled the importance of the debate; his attention multiplied the arguments; and he exposed his person with a patient intrepidity, which animated the valor of the combatants.'[24] Constantine endorsed the Nicene Creed, which describes Jesus as 'Begotten of his Father before all worlds, God of God, Light of Light, Very God of Very God; Begotten, not made; Being of one substance with the Father.'[25] The emperor then banished Arius and the Arians, who doubted that Jesus was of the same substance as the Father, and directed capital punishment for anyone found in possession of Arian writings.

In *The Hind and the Panther*, the Hind argues that Protestant heresies are revivals of Arius's denial of the full divinity of Christ. Protestants, she thinks, resist the mystery of Christ's power to be both fully divine and fully present in earthly matter, a power evident both in Christ's incarnation in the form of a man and in Christ's presence in the consecrated bread of the mass according to the doctrine of transubstantiation. As Donald Benson has pointed out, the doctrine of transubstantiation was based on a scholastic conception of substance 'as the determining spiritual or intellectual form imparted to associated material accidents,' a conception that by the end of the seventeenth century was being replaced by a conception 'of an independent material substance – body or undifferentiated matter – defined only by extension and location in space.'[26] The Council of Trent proclaimed a 'marvelous and extraordinary change of the whole substance of the bread into Christ's body and the whole substance of the wine into his blood, so that only the species of bread and wine remain.'[27] Dryden insists that the power of the divine Christ to be fully present in material objects is equally evident in the incarnation and in transubstantiation:

> Could He his god-head veil with flesh and bloud
> And not veil these again to be our food?
> His grace in both is equal in extent,
> The first affords us life, the second nourishment.
>
> (1:134–7)

While Catholics claimed that Protestant denials of transubstantiation were new versions of Arianism, heretical denials of the power of divine substance to be fully present in material substance, Protestants responded by claiming that, because Roman Catholics adored the consecrated bread and wine as themselves divine, the doctrine of transubstantiation was an idolatrous violation of the first commandment, 'Thou shalt have no other Gods before me.' James, as Gardiner points out, construed Protestant claims that the Catholic mass was idolatrous as attacks on himself as an idolator and, consequently, as seditious invitations to rebellion.[28] Protestants ridiculed the doctrine of transubstantiation, in part because they hoped to demystify and diminish priestly power, in part because they thought the doctrine depended on scholastic absurdities that threatened to make religion itself disrespected. Stillingfleet, for example, in *A Discourse Concerning the Idolatry Practised in the Church of Rome*, attacks what he labels the 'unintelligible terms' of a Catholic writer like Bellarmine and offers a grotesque reductio ad absurdum of the idea that the substance of Jesus is present in the substance of the consecrated bread: 'if the bread be converted into that *body* of *Christ*, which is *hypostatically* united with the *divine nature*, then the conversion is not merely into the body, but into the *Person Christ*, and then Christ hath as many bodies *hypostatically* united to him, as there are *Elements* consecrated, and so all the accidents of the *bread* belong to the *body of Christ* which is *hypostatically* united with the divine nature.'[29] Such Protestant characterizations of the Catholic mass as idolatry stand behind Dryden's picture of the kneeling rooster, a comic figure, but one drawn as a monstrous libel that has the ominous power to invite murder:

> There *Chanticleer* was drawn upon his knees
> Adoring Shrines, and Stocks of Sainted Trees,
> And by him, a misshapen, ugly Race;
> The Curse of God was seen on ev'ry Face.
>   (3:1052–5)

There is a long tradition of objecting to the use of wit and humour in discourse about religion. At one level, these objections can be part of a larger objection to the use of wit in any discourse aimed at the establishment of serious truth; the weight of such objections appears in the almost total banishment of wit and humour from modern journal articles in the sciences. But levity, irony, and ridicule have also been more specifically denounced as inappropriate – even blasphemous – in discourse about religion. Consider the high-profile blasphemy trial of Thomas Woolston, learned author of *Six Discourses upon the Miracles of Our Savior* (1727–9), claiming that Jesus' miracles lacked literal historicity and should be read allegorically. The successful prosecution, provoked by Woolston's popularity and his mockery of biblical narrative, contended, 'If Mr. Woolston's intent was to [strengthen Christianity], he would not have turned the Miracles of Our Saviour into Ridicule, and proceed in so Ludicrous a Manner, as he has done, but to have endeavour'd to prove, They were not to be taken as they are Literally Wrote, by a Serious Discourse, and Sound Argument.'[30] Woolston was sentenced on four counts of blasphemy to a fine and a year in jail.

Both Gibbon and Dryden were criticized for using levity in discourse about religion. Upon the publication of the first volumes of *The Decline and Fall* the *Monthly Review* urged readers to consider 'how far it is consistent with the character of good citizens, to endeavour, by sly insinuations, oblique hints, indecent sneer and ridicule, to weaken the influence of so pure and benevolent a system [as Christianity]?'[31] The learned Richard Porson, in many ways an admirer and defender of Gibbon,[32] nevertheless complained that Gibbon used 'improper weapons': 'Such is his eagerness in the cause [of attacking Christianity], that he stoops to the most despicable pun, or to the most awkward perversion of language, for the pleasure of turning the Scripture into ribaldry, or of calling Jesus an imposter.'[33] Dryden in *The Hind and the Panther* exploits the special kind of wit appropriate to the beast fable; many complained that his choice of this form was inappropriate to his solemn subject. Samuel Johnson, for instance, famously objected: 'The scheme of the work is injudicious and incommodious, for what can be more absurd than that one beast should counsel another to rest her faith upon a pope and council?'[34]

In the context of the Restoration and the eighteenth century, objections to Dryden's and Gibbon's using wit in discourse on religion were sharpened by the association between wit and libertine religious scepticism. Thomas B. Gilmore, in his study *The Eighteenth-Century Controversy over Ridicule as a Test of Truth*, observes that 'From a reading of anti-deist literature one would infer that the deists had monopolized ridicule for attacks on Christianity.'[35] It was, of course, true that freethinkers resorted to irony, sarcasm, and ridicule in their attacks on what they considered foolish and dangerous religious superstition. One of the most important freethinkers, Anthony Collins, in a *Discourse Concerning Ridicule and Irony* (1729), rightly claimed that '*want of Liberty to examine into the Truth of Things*' had itself caused freethinkers to resort to the irony of which the pious complained: ''Tis the persecuting Spirit has raised the *bantering* one: And want of Liberty may account for want of a true politeness, and for the Corruption or wrong Use of Pleasantry and Humor.'[36] Yet, using Stillingfleet's ridicule of Dryden as one of his examples, Collins more positively defends ridicule and wit as legitimate and important tools in religious controversy. The 'solemn and grave,' he contends, can bear solemn and grave attack, and such attacks only contribute to sustaining their credibility, 'But *Contempt* is what they ... cannot bear or withstand, as setting them in their true Light, and being the most effectual Method to drive Imposture, the sole Foundation of their Credit, out of the World.'[37] Collins also offers a well-documented argument that while Christian writers complain that their adversaries wrongly use ridicule and irony, the fact is that Christian writers themselves have consistently used ridicule and irony against their adversaries: the early Church fathers ridiculed the pagans, the Protestant Reformers ridiculed the orthodox Catholics, and the orthodox Catholics ridicule the Protestants. Church of England writing against Roman Catholicism during the reign of James II, notably the writing of Stillingfleet and Burnet, abounding in 'Banter, Ridicule, and Irony,' Collins recalls, was 'then very well received and applauded for Learning and strength of Arguing; yet, I believe, it may with more propriety be said, that King *James* II and *Popery* were *laugh'd* or *Lilli-bullero'd*, than that they were *argu'd* out of the kingdom.'[38]

The very incongruity between solemn theology and lowly beasts in *The Hind and the Panther* has caused some critics to complain, while others, including Sir Walter Scott and D.W. Jefferson, have seen it as enjoyable wit. Scott pointed out that in many classic fables animals act 'contrary to their nature' and further suggested that Dryden was following the example of Chaucer's 'Nun's Priest's Tale' and Spenser's 'Mother Hubbard's Tale' to go beyond 'the simplicity of the ancient fable' to 'a species of mixed composition, between that and downright satire.' Thus, if Chaucer had been asked 'why he made his cock an astrologer, and his hen a physician, he would have answered, that his satire might become more ludicrous, by putting these grave speeches into the mouths of such animals.'[39] Dryden's choice of the beast fable as a form effectively yokes together his concerns about religion and the state, underlining how inextricably intertwined they are: he puts the theological discussions in the mouths of animals who have the bodies of predators or prey. As William Meyers observed, the beast fable is 'especially apt' since the poem is significantly 'about power' and about a state of 'suspended violence.'[40] And, as Jayne Lewis has more wittily written in her fine book on the English fable, 'fable is the only literary form in which the principal characters regularly devour one another.'[41]

Dryden matches the Panther's power and rapaciousness as a beast of prey with the image of the Church of England he wants to develop, insisting that despite the Church's loss of the king's support, it still has great power, and that the laws still allow it to wound or even to destroy dissenters. The Panther may be temporarily restrained as the guest of the Hind, but her potential dangerousness is evident:

> [She] civily drew in her sharpn'd paws,
> Not violating hospitable laws,
> And pacify'd her tail, and lick'd her frothy jaws.
>   (2:718–20)

Yet the Anglican Panther becomes a comic character, albeit one with a serious undercurrent of menace. She is a matronly but nervous beast, piquing herself on her respectability, status, reasonableness, and pragmatism, as she parades about in her spotted muff. In the drama of the poem, the Hind undertakes to expose her true savagery, her hypocrisy, and, perhaps, her self-delusion. To the Panther's self-representation of mild reasonableness and toleration, the Hind juxtaposes a frightening image of bitter envy and savage predation. The Hind's rather long-winded Roman Catholic apologetics make the Panther squirm with embarrassment, reducing her to concession, apology, or silence. Occasionally the Panther replies with the sort of feeble, abject questions offered by Socrates' dimmer interlocutors. Thus, when the Hind descants on what she characterizes as the Church of England's inconsistent and garbled invocation of the authority of the Church fathers, the Panther could not 'well enlarge'

> With weak defence against so strong a charge;
> But said, for what did *Christ* his Word provide,
> If still his church must want a living guide?   (2:298–300)

The spectacle of a powerful animal reduced to such tentative helplessness and timidity is a comic one.

Dryden answers Protestant ridicule of transubstantiation by having fun with the Panther's vacillating positions on the real presence of Christ in the Eucharist. The Hind taunts the Panther with having forsaken a true doctrine of the Eucharist for one that is an empty verbal claim, likening her to the dog in the fable who dropped his mutton to snap at its shadow reflected in the water:

> as you the matter state
> Not onely *Jesuits* can equivocate;
> For *real*, as you now the word expound,
> From solid substance dwindles to a sound.
> Methinks an *Aesop's* fable you repeat,
> You know who took the shadow for the meat.   (2:44–9)

Just as Gibbon uses detailed historical narrative of divisions and vacillation in the Councils of the early Church to undermine the notion that they could be authoritative, Dryden's Hind reminds the Panther of the convoluted and often contradictory negotiations of Reformation Church of England convocations. Some of these, conveniently, had recently been carefully reviewed in Gilbert Burnet's *History of the Reformation in England* (1679, 1681) – the Burnet who is the Buzard in Dryden's poem.

The comedy of *The Hind and the Panther* becomes richer when the beasts themselves cite beast fables. It is not clear whether Dryden's talking animals are also reading animals who can make literary references, or whether they are more simply animals living in a world of animals who, consequently, and by experience, know about the nature and conduct of other animals. In any case, when Dryden's animals cite beast fables, one effect seems to be to bolster their arguments by pointing to evidence from the natural world, the facts of which are indisputable. They point outside complex, even scholastic, verbal arguments to a world of primary fact, as Lewis suggests, 'to a mode of representation so simple and sensible as to seem unmediated – almost nonlinguistic.'[42] At the same time, as both Annabel Patterson and Lewis have argued, the Restoration fables depict a treacherous world in which speech often deceives, alliances are unstable, and meanings extremely contested.[43] The Hind, who throughout the poem emphasizes that language is powerless to fix meaning, uses the Fable of the Wolf and the Lamb to mock the Panther's words about the historical dangerousness and crimes against humanity of the Church of Rome and to insist on her own innocence. The Panther, she claims, is like the Wolf in the fable who drank from a stream and then accused a Lamb, drinking downstream from him, of polluting his water (3:123–130). In Ogilby's version of the fable the Wolf indignantly denounces the Lamb:

> The fell *Wolf* grinn'd, his Eyes like Fire-brands glow;
> Oh cursed Race! he said, to mine a Foe,
> Still plotting harmless *Wolves* to overthrow;
>
> Thy Father, Mother, Sacrilegious *Lamb*,
> And all thy bleating Kindred, from the Dam
> Stile themselves Guiltless, but I Guilty am.

He gets maudlin as his accusations become more hyperbolic and ludicrous:

> And none dare say you in *Wolves* Habit come,
> And tear dead Bodies from the New-built Tomb,
> And poor *Wolves* then for your offences doom.
>
> *Dogs*, once our brethren, cursed Curs, you lead
> Against our Race; Who now will hear us plead?
> When you'r the cause of all the Blood is shed.

And finally:

> Thus having said, at the poor *Lamb* he flies,
> His cruel Teeth a purple River dies,
> Whilst warm Blood spurtles in his face and eyes.[44]

The Wolf's accusations of the Lamb are so ludicrous that it is hard to imagine he believes them himself; Dryden's application of the fable thus not only reinforces the alleged savagery of the Church of England and the supposed utter blamelessness of the Catholics, it also associates the Panther with a use of language that is at once utterly shameless and memorably ludicrous.

The creatures who populate Gibbon's history of Christianity are, of course, not animals, but humans: Church fathers, notable heretics and schismatics, pagans, martyrs, and converts in the *Decline and Fall* itself, and secondarily, in the footnotes, Church historians. Gibbon understands the power of religious ideas and he tries to escape from the black and white villains and heroes of earlier Church histories to draw mixed characters. Commenting on some writings of the orthodox Athanasius, Gibbon remarks, 'They are justified by original and authentic documents; but they would inspire more confidence, if he appeared less innocent, and his enemies less absurd.'[45] Recent scholarship has emphasized his use of early modern Roman Catholic scholarship and described him as aiming to produce a work that adjudicated between the earlier, more partisan histories of Catholics and Protestants.[46] There is merit to this view. Yet Gibbon's Christianity is much closer to that of latitudinarian divines like Stillingfleet and Burnet than to Dryden's Catholicism. Like Stillingfleet and Burnet, he finds many of the beliefs of the early Church simply absurd.

Gibbon's account of the conversion of the European barbarians to Christianity in the fourth, fifth, and sixth centuries is dominated by a grand dramatic and comic irony: what he calls the 'unfortunate accident' that the version of Christianity first spread amongst them was Arianism. The military successes of the Goths brought them Roman Christian captives who became 'involuntary missionaries.' The son of one such captive, Ulphilas, apostle to the Goths, 'executed the arduous task of translating the Scriptures into their native tongue, a dialect of the German, or Teutonic language; but he prudently suppressed the four books of Kings, as they might tend to irritate the fierce and sanguinary spirit of the Barbarians.'[47] While individual barbarian leaders were often converted by 'capricious or accidental' events like victory after prayer, Roman Christianity soon began to expand the intellectual hori-

zons of the barbarians, to promote reading and Greek and Latin learning, and to encourage mercy and conscience. Yet, since Ulphilas had
imbibed his Christianity 'during the reign of Arianism,' Arianism was
'adopted as the national faith of the warlike converts'; their conversion
was thus marred 'by the unfortunate accident, which infused a deadly
poison into the cup of Salvation.'[48]

Gibbon's calculated and witty use of the word 'accident' and of
phrases like 'unfortunate accident' inflamed his pious critics. The word
seems to inject a bathetic element into sacred history; instead of the
grand, secure narrative of God's providential plan for mankind inexorably unfolding, we are plunged into a highly contingent sublunary world
where large effects may result from trivial causes. Gibbon does look for
large causes to explain large effects – as, for example, the experience of
Christian priests in the government of the Church as contributing to the
triumph of Christianity over paganism. But he is also alert to the possibility that small, local facts, like the character of an individual or the
sudden death of a leader, may have large consequences. Regarding the
metaphysical distinctions between the Arian and the Athanasian doctrines as in themselves inconsequential scholastic quibbles, Gibbon narrates the early creedal struggles by assuming an orthodox mask partial
to the eventual triumph of the Athanasian view. It is from this perspective that Ulphilas's conversion of the barbarians to Arianism becomes an
'unfortunate accident.' The supposedly inexorable march of orthodoxy
is suddenly interrupted by a small contingency, rather like a coach accident. We are perhaps also invited to smile at this rude importation of a
key term from the very scholastic theology Gibbon elsewhere mocks. An
'accident' in the philosophical sense is a property 'not essential to our
conception of a substance'; in scholastic theology, 'the material qualities
remaining in the sacramental bread and wine after transubstantiation;
the essence alleged to be changed, though the accidents remained the
same.'[49]

Just as, in Gibbon's judgment, the Latin Church had not been
equipped to deal with the metaphysical subtleties of Greece and Egypt,
even more 'the temper and understanding' of the new barbarian converts 'were not adapted to metaphysical subtleties; but they strenuously
maintained, what they had piously received, as the pure and genuine
doctrines of Christianity.'[50] These new Arians were frequently prepared
to tolerate the orthodox Athanasian Catholics, but, Gibbon writes, with
characteristic amused affection for his own northern barbaric ancestors,
the Catholics promptly denounced the new converts as heretics: 'The

heroes of the North, who had submitted, with some reluctance, to believe that all their [pagan] ancestors were in Hell, were astonished and exasperated to learn, that they themselves had only changed the mode of their eternal condemnation.'[51] 'Astonished' and 'exasperated' make a delicious Gibbonian pair: 'astonished' seems in a high enough register to be suitable to talk about the nature of God, yet here it is clearly also comic 'astonishment'; 'exasperated' is a word from a more quotidian register – it would seem appropriate to be 'exasperated' if one's luggage were delayed. 'Exasperation' as a response to having been subjected to a theological whipsawing at once comically deflates theological high seriousness and expresses real sympathy for the barbarians' legitimate annoyance.

Both Dryden and Gibbon use wit to write about religion and politics and clearly relish the exercise of their own wit, yet both also express fear of wit. In *The Hind and the Panther* Dryden presents himself as a man who has, in his earlier life, succumbed to the temptation of relying on his own intelligence and interpretive powers. Now he professes the inadequacy of his own mind to discern the most necessary truths of religion. Heresies in general and Protestantism in particular he figures as abuses of wit, including wit used to ridicule the sacred. Thus, the Hind reflects on the Panther's tale:

> For well she mark'd the malice of the tale:
> Which Ribbald art their church to *Luther* owes,
> In malice it began, by malice grows,
> He sow'd the *Serpent*'s teeth, an iron-harvest rose.
>
> (3:640–3)

Gibbon worries about the results of wit when intellectuals succumb to the self-indulgent, narcissistic pleasures of exercising their own wit, careless of the social and political consequences, and when intellectuals snatch at worldly opportunities for self-advancement, dazzling and befuddling otherwise serviceable political leaders. And though Gibbon is eager enough to display in graphic detail the bloodthirstiness of the Church Fathers, as a man of sensibility he draws back from what he denominates 'affected and unfeeling witticisms.'[52]

Gibbon's history of the Arian heresy is at one level a tragedy in which human wit, excited by the prospects of fame and power, refines metaphysical distinctions, in themselves useless, to inflict suffering on humanity. Gibbon, acutely aware of the pleasure he himself takes in the exercise and display of his own wit, is alert to the temptations of what he calls 'the pride of the professors, and of their disciples.'[53] And he knows how 'in an age of religious controversy' attention becomes a spur to inventiveness and elaboration; indeed, how attempts to oppress a religious idea may serve to add 'new force to the elastic vigor of the mind.'[54] Tragedy comes when men use force, even lurid torture, to coerce agreement.

Given the dangerousness of a politics inflamed by religious ideas – a dangerousness that both Dryden and Gibbon confronted – perhaps the current American decorum that I opened by noticing, the decorum which evades serious consideration of religion and politics and prohibits mixing wit with religion, is a wise one. Dryden and Gibbon remind us of the continuing power of religion and of the profound challenges it has posed, and continues to pose, to states. The idea that rulers are responsible for promoting right religion in their states has an inherent logic and remains powerful. Appeals to religious toleration do not resolve all conflict. At the same time, Dryden and Gibbon remind us of the power of states, or even small religious minorities in control of the state apparatus, to coerce or to incentivize massive religious transformations. I admire the boldness with which Dryden and Gibbon, using history, logic, and pointed wit, inflicted wounds on the faithful. Yet, in deference to the politically prudent anti-intellectualism of our own American moment, perhaps those of us who pick at the scabs that cover those old religious wounds should cease and be silent.

Notes

1 A useful account of the Mormons, from the perspective of the Church, may be found in James B. Allen and Glen M. Leonard, 2nd ed., *The Story of the Latter-day Saints* (Salt Lake City: Desert Book Company 1992). Of the language of the tablets, the authors remark: 'Because Joseph Smith did not know the "reformed Egyptian" language in which the Book of Mormon was written, translation ... was a revelatory process' (44).

2 John Locke, *A Letter Concerning Toleration*, ed. James H. Tully (Indianapolis: Hackett Publishing Company 1983), 41–2.

3 A useful treatment of the modern history of Roman Catholicism in China is offered by Beatrice Leung, *Sino-Vatican Relations: Problems in Conflicting Authority, 1976–1986* (Cambridge: Cambridge University Press 1992). Leung explains the Chinese government's view that it permits freedom of religious

belief and 'normal religious activities,' while resisting hostile religious forces from abroad that attempt to set up illegal organizations. She prints an English translation of the interesting Communist party policy document 'The Basic Policy and Standpoint Our Country Should Have on the Religious Question During the Period of Socialism,' Appendix 2, 348–67. The Pope's canonization on 1 October 2000 of 120 missionaries 'martyred' in China, most of them killed in the Boxer rebellion, was responded to with outrage by both the Chinese government and the Chinese Catholic Patriotic Association, who characterized the missionaries as criminals selling opium and facilitating the division of China among foreign powers. 'China's War on Faith,' *Japan Times* 6 October 2000; 'Catholics across China Join to Slam Vatican,' 4 October 2000, Xinhua General News Service http://web.lexis-nexis.com/um.verse/ (17 November 2000).

4 William Blackstone, *Commentaries on the Laws of England: A Facsimile of the First Edition of 1765–69*, ed. Stanley Katz, 4 vols. (Chicago: University of Chicago Press 1979), 4:61.

5 Allen and Leonard give an account of these clashes between the Mormons and federal authorities in *Story of the Latter-day Saints*, 364–419.

6 *Davis* v. *Benson* (1890), 133 U.S. 333. The anti-Mormon statutes disfranchised, jailed (for bigamy or unlawful cohabitation), or drove underground most of the Mormon leaders and many of their followers. In 1890, divine revelation to the Mormon president produced a manifesto declaring that plural marriage was to be discontinued.

7 For a view of Gibbon as sceptical towards religion in general and as 'hostile' towards Christianity and Judaism, as well as a useful chronicle of contemporary Christian thinkers who attempted to challenge Gibbon, see Shelby T. McCloy, *Gibbon's Antagonism to Christianity and the Discussion that it Has Provoked* (Chapel Hill: University of North Carolina 1933). A good account of the process of Gibbon's conversions is offered in Patricia B. Craddock, *Young Edward Gibbon: Gentleman of Letters* (Baltimore: Johns Hopkins University Press 1982). For considerations of the extent of Gibbon's sympathy towards Christianity, see Paul Turnbull, '"The Supposed Infidelity" of Edward Gibbon,' *Historical Journal* 25 (1982), 23–81, and David Dillon Smith, 'Gibbon in Church,' *Journal of Ecclesiastical History* 35 (1984), 452–63.

8 Edward Gibbon, *The History of the Decline and Fall of the Roman Empire*, ed. David Womersley, 3 vols. (London: Allen Lane, Penguin 1994), 1:729.

9 Anne Barbeau Gardiner, *Ancient Faith and Modern Freedom in John Dryden's Hind and the Panther* (Washington, D.C.: Catholic University Press of America 1998), 163.

10 Gardiner, *Ancient Faith*, 166.

11 John Miller, *Popery and Politics in England, 1660–1688* (Cambridge: Cambridge University Press 1973), 222.

12 Norma Landau, *The Justices of the Peace, 1679–1760* (Berkeley: University of California Press 1984), 76.

13 Hume notes that the bishop was cited before a new Court of Ecclesiastical Commission, 'with inquisitorial powers,' which James had set up despite the parliamentary abolition of the Court of High Commission and the Star Chamber in the reign of Charles I and a parliamentary prohibition against the errection of any such courts in future. Hume comments: 'The king's design to subdue the church was now sufficiently known; and had he been able to establish the authority of this new-erected court, his success was infallible. A more sensible blow could not be given both to national liberty and religion; and happily the contest could not be tried in a cause more iniquitous and unpopular than that against Sharpe and the bishop of London.' David Hume, *The History of England from the Invasion of Julius Caesar to the Revolution in 1688*, 6 vols. (Indianapolis: Liberty Classics 1983), 6:480.

14 John Childs, *The Army, James II, and the Glorious Revolution* (New York: St Martin's Press 1980), chap. 3, 'The Great Purge in Ireland,' 56–82.

15 *The Works of John Dryden*, ed. E.N. Hooker, H.T. Swedenberg, Jr, et al., 20 vols. (Berkeley: University of California Press 1956–2000), 3:177 (3:550–8). All quotations from *The Hind and the Panther* are from this edition (hereafter cited as *California Dryden*); part and line numbers are given in my text.

16 Gibbon, *Decline and Fall*, 2:435.

17 Gibbon, *Decline and Fall*, 1:748–9.

18 Gibbon, *Decline and Fall*, 1:763.

19 On the schism between the Greek and the Latin Churches see Gibbon, *Decline and Fall*, chap. 60.

20 29 Car. 12, c. 9 abolished the writ *de haeretico comburendo*, the writ for burning a heretic. Blackstone comments: 'For in one and the same reign, our lands were delivered from the slavery of military tenures; our bodies from arbitrary imprisonment by the *habeas corpus* act; and our minds from the tyranny of superstitious bigotry, by demolishing this last badge of persecution in the English law.' *Commentaries*, 4:49. To deny 'any one of the persons in the holy trinity to be God' was punishable under 9 & 10 Will. 3, c. 32. For the first offence, a person convicted forfeited all offices; for a second, he was outlawed and imprisoned for three years.

21 J.A.I. Champion, *The Pillars of Priestcraft Shaken: The Church of England and Its Enemies, 1660–1730* (Cambridge: Cambridge University Press 1992), 101, 16.

22 Gibbon, *Decline and Fall*, 1:770–1.

23 Gibbon, *Decline and Fall*, 1:770–88.

24 Gibbon, *Decline and Fall,* 1:790.

25 *The Book of Common Prayer* (New York: Church Pension Fund 1945), 71.

26 Donald R. Benson, 'Dryden's *The Hind and the Panther.* Transubstantiation and Figurative Language,' *JHI* 43 (1982), 196. Benson emphasizes the impact on Dryden of developing '17th-century ontological assumptions' and the seventeenth-century idea of transubstantion as a 'stark paradox – a material presence not materially evident' (206). He argues that 'the greater the independence granted this realm the more anomalous the traditional means of medition between it and the divine power – spirit, reason, language,' and 'the more skeptical and reductive' the treatment of language (206–7).

27 Benson, 'Dryden's *Hind,*' 198, quoting *The New Catholic Encyclopedia.*

28 Gardiner, *Ancient Faith,* 209.

29 Edward Stillingfleet, *A Discourse Concerning the Idolatry practised in the Church of Rome, and the danger of Salvation in the Communion of it: in answer to some papers of a Revolted Protestant. Wherein a particular Account is given of the Fanaticism and Divisions of that Church* (London: printed by R. White 1671).

30 Quoted in James A. Herrick, *The Radical Rhetoric of the English Deists: The Discourse of Skepticism, 1680–1750* (Columbia: University of South Carolina Press 1977), 97–8. Herrick offers an account of Woolston's writings and trial and also of the 1762 blasphemy trial and conviction of Peter Annet, another ridiculer of the miracles of Jesus.

31 Quoted in Patricia Craddock, *Edward Gibbon: Luminous Historian, 1772–1794* (Baltimore: Johns Hopkins University Press 1989), 171.

32 In *Letters to Mr. Archdeacon Travis, in answer to his Defence of the Three heavenly Witnesses, 1 John v. 7.* An extended discussion of Porson and Gibbon is offered in Joseph M. Levine, *The Autonomy of History: Truth and Method from Erasmus to Gibbon* (Chicago: University of Chicago Press 1999), chap. 9.

33 Quoted in McCloy, *Gibbon's Antagonism,* 139.

34 *Johnson's Lives of the Poets: A Selection,* ed. J.P. Hardy (Oxford: Clarendon Press 1971), 183.

35 Thomas B. Gilmore, Jr., *The Eighteenth-Century Controversy over Ridicule as a Test of Truth: A Reconsideration,* Research paper No. 25 (Atlanta: Georgia State University, School of Arts and Sciences Research Papers January 1970), 10.

36 Anthony Collins, *A Discourse Concerning Ridicule and Irony in Writing* (1729; Los Angeles: Augustan Reprint Society 1970), 24.

37 Collins, *Discourse,* 7.

38 Collins, *Discourse,* 5, 35, citing Burnet's *History of his own Times.*

39 *The Works of John Dryden,* ed. Sir Walter Scott, 2nd ed., 18 vols. (Edinburgh: printed for A. Constable & Co. 1821), 10:95.

40 William Myers, *Dryden* (London: Hutchinson 1973), 121.

41 Jayne Elizabeth Lewis, *The English Fable: Aesop and Literary Culture, 1651–1740* (Cambridge: Cambridge University Press 1996), 8.

42 Lewis, *The English Fable*, 20.

43 Patterson discusses *The Hind and the Panther* in her *Fables of Power: Aesopian Writing and Political History* (Durham, N.C.: Duke University Press 1991), 95–105.

44 John Ogilby, *The Fables of Aesop paraphras'd in Verse* (1688; Los Angeles: William Andrews Clark Memorial Library, University of California, Los Angeles 1965), 36–7.

45 Gibbon, *Decline and Fall*, 1:799, n. 105.

46 Owen Chadwick, 'Gibbon and the Church Historians,' in G.W. Bowersock, John Clive, and S.R. Graubard, eds., *Edward Gibbon and the Decline and Fall of the Roman Empire* (Cambridge: Harvard University Press 1976), 223. David P. Jordan has contributed an informative and entertaining essay on Gibbon's use of *Mémoires pour servir a l'histoire ecclésiastique des six premiers siècles* (1706), by the learned Jansenist monk Louis Sébastien le Nain de Tillemont (1637–98): 'LeNain de Tillemont: Gibbon's "sure-footed mule,"' *Church History* 39 (1970), 483–502.

47 Gibbon, *Decline and Fall*, 2:429.

48 Gibbon, *Decline and Fall*, 2:433–4.

49 *Oxford English Dictionary*, s.v. 'accident.'

50 Gibbon, *Decline and Fall*, 2:434.

51 Gibbon, *Decline and Fall*, 2:434.

52 John Clive, 'Gibbon's Humor,' in Bowersock, Clive, and Graubard, *Edward Gibbon*, 185.

53 Gibbon, *Decline and Fall*, 1:775.

54 Gibbon, *Decline and Fall*, 1:778.

chapter eight

How Many Religions Did John Dryden Have?

STEVEN ZWICKER

'My Condition, and my being a Secular Person ... are look'd upon as Circumstances that may advantage an Author that is to write upon such a Subject as I have handled. I need not tell you, that as to Religious Books in general, it has been observ'd, that those penn'd by Lay-men, and especially Gentlemen, have ... been better entertain'd, and more effectual than those of Ecclesiasticks.'[1] If these words seem familiar to students of Dryden's writing, there is a good reason why they should: 'In the first place, if it be objected to me that being a *Layman,* I ought not to have concern'd my self with Speculations, which belong to the Profession of *Divinity*; I cou'd Answer, that perhaps, Laymen, with equal advantages of Parts and Knowledge, are not the most incompetent Judges of Sacred things.'[2] The first sentence is from the Preface to Robert Boyle's *The Excellency of Theology Compared with Natural Philosophy* (1674), the second from the Preface to *Religio Laici* (1682).

Little wonder that Dryden should have borrowed from, or perhaps adapted or echoed, Boyle's language; by the time that Dryden got around to confessing his own faith, Boyle's eminence in natural philosophy and his reputation for Christian piety were very high indeed. As early as 1663 Dryden celebrated the intellectual powers of 'noble Boyle' in the epistle to Walter Charleton;[3] by 1671, when Boyle published *The Excellency of Theology Compared with Natural Philosophy,* he was one of the most distinguished exponents of the new science. Yet for all his distinction in natural philosophy, Boyle rigorously maintained both 'the excellency of theology' against the 'claims of reason, and the importance of revealed truths and consequently of that onely Authentic Repository of them, the Scripture' over and against individual conscience.[4] In *Religio*

Laici Dryden's handling of the inferiority of reason to revelation is strikingly similar, both in idiom and idea, to Boyle's exposition of that theme, and the two texts are very close in their analysis of Epicurean philosophy, what Boyle calls that 'Casual concourse of Atoms.'[5]

My intention is not, however, to catalogue Dryden's debts to Boyle in the exposition of theology, though I suspect that in *Religio Laici* they were substantial, much greater than have been allowed;[6] my aim is rather to argue that at moments of what seem to us deeply personal conviction or in the midst of what we think of as Dryden's characteristic rhetorical gestures we will discover the evidence of other voices – of borrowing, of adaptation, of what Dryden's enemies called his 'plaigery.'[7] So it is with the privileges of a modest layman to discourse of divinity, or with Epicurean atomic theory;[8] and so it is, I suspect, at almost every juncture of spiritual confession in Dryden's masterpiece of Anglican quietism. At one moment it is the language of Robert Boyle, and at another, in his arguments on behalf of charity and toleration, it is the voice, or perhaps the strategic program, of Charles II. At various points in his exposition of spiritual matters it is Hooker or Tillotson, Henry Hammond or Edward Stillingfleet who provide both the idiom and the authority of Dryden's writing. This particular layman could be trusted to judge of 'sacred matters' because he had no spiritual calling, no 'Profession of Divinity.' The penetration of other voices to the heart of *Religio Laici* raises questions about the authenticity of Dryden's spiritual profession, but the issue is not limited to Dryden; it has a broad pertinence to the articulation of belief throughout an age when habits of adaptation and allusion repeatedly complicate the texture of religious expression and when practices of ventriloquism raise methodological problems about the nature and voice of piety.

Dryden himself came to religious confession only in his fifty-first year. *Religio Laici* is the first text in which he expresses anything like personal religious convictions or private devotional experience, and the proximity of this poem to *Absalom and Achitophel* (1681) makes it difficult not to remember Dryden's caustic remarks about religion in the poem he had written a year earlier.[9] Although we should not underestimate the importance of a certain mode of public confession in this age – in writing *Religio Laici* Dryden had before him the example of the *Religio Stoici* (1663) of his friend Sir George Mackenzie, and works like Sir Thomas Browne's *Religio Medici*, which had come into its eighth edition in 1682 – it remains something of a mystery why Dryden himself should have written in this genre, why, that is, he should have produced and published a confession of faith at a time when we have no indication of a spiritual calling, or crisis, or indeed of a reflective pause in his career. The same cannot be said of the circumstances surrounding *The Hind and the Panther*, though many of the same conclusions might be drawn about its spirituality.

Dryden claimed that he was moved to write *Religio Laici* by reading the English translation of Richard Simon's *Histoire Critique du Vieux Testament*, and while he pays a playful tribute to its translator, his comments on the *History* itself make it seem doubtful that Dryden had done more than sampled what he calls its 'crabbed Toil' (l. 235). As H.T. Swedenberg wryly concluded, 'it is unlikely that he gave his days and nights to a study of Father Simon before composing his poem.'[10] The controversy that swirled around the French Oratorian's attack on the verbal integrity of the Old Testament, on vagaries of textual transcription and transmission, and on the relative merits and authority of written and spoken language may well have interested Dryden, but if *Religio Laici* were a response to Father Simon, there is an odd disproportion between the density of Simon's challenge to the textual integrity of the Scriptures and Dryden's casual indifference to religious learning. At one point Dryden calls such learning '*Rabbins* old Sophisticated Ware' (l. 237); at another he gestures dismissively, 'points obscure are of small use to learn' (l. 449). Indeed, Dryden seems wholly to discard the religious, as distinguished from the linguistic, themes and topics of Father Simon's work; for Dryden, the Frenchman's concern with '*Pope*, and *Councils*, and *Traditions* force' (l. 255) is mere fashionable guise, a camouflage that Father Simon wears to obscure the radical implications of *The Critical History*.

Father Simon's work did raise concern in pious Anglican circles, but it is certainly not clear that Dryden, the 'Play-maker,' would have been welcome in such circles, or that his *Religio Laici* would have been seen as a significant defence against the threats of historical philology, fanaticism, or popery. One of Dryden's contemporaries found 'Mr. Dryden's "Religion of a Layman" ... farre below what might have been expected of him on such a subject';[11] another attacked not simply the indifference, but the sordid origins and nature, of Dryden's religious impulse: 'The world is not unacquainted with a certain mercenary Versificator, whose Obscure and Atheistical Sheets (and yet half Stoln too, as this very Preface is from a little Pamphlet of George Cranmers, published about 41.) has done abundantly more shameful mischief than ever Tyndals Translation of the Holy Bible ... 'Tis perhaps necessary that Cromwels Panegyrist and so passionate an Admirer of Pere Simon, should cast a Squint Eye not only on Poor Tyndal, but all English Bibles, and in a word the whole Reformation.'[12]

Such response suggests why Dryden might have seen (and sought) the idioms and authority of Robert Boyle, and as something other than simply a convenient source of quotation, though in coming to terms with the nature of Dryden's writing we ought not underestimate the importance of either convenience or quotation. Boyle provided a useful cover and ally for Dryden's own sudden religiosity of 1682. In the texts of *Religio Laici*, Dryden aimed to strike a posture of balanced and charitable piety, a stance that might allow him to articulate the political quietism for which Charles yearned following the defeat of Whiggery, and the religious toleration that his master had repeatedly sought as a central strategy in his handling of dissent, Roman Catholicism, and the kingdom of conscience. In the articulation of this complex program Dryden covered himself with quiet certitudes; he invoked the name of the 'Reverend Divines of the Church of England'[13] and he prompted identification with Boyle's impeccable spirituality. Not everyone was convinced by these efforts, but the relation of *Religio Laici* to Boyle's *Excellence of Theology* provides an intriguing model for thinking about the ways in which Dryden worked when he entered alien or difficult territory.

And spiritual confession was just such a terrain, both in 1682, when he took up the mantle of religious toleration and political quietism, and in 1687, when he needed to discover a way of advocating conversion and Catholicism while at the same time arguing the case for the toleration of Protestant nonconformity, a case that seems to have cut deeply against, if not his own indifference to spiritual matters, then certainly the prickly intolerance excited by Protestant nonconformity. No one reading the attack on the 'schismatics of the English Church' in the Preface to *Religio Laici*, or the exposition of dissenting zeal in the poem itself, or, for that matter, the little fables of wolves and bears, or the history of English reform in *The Hind and the Panther* would have suspected a deeply spiritual (or, indeed, tolerant) strain in this controversialist's character. They would have detected the power of his ironies, and the force of his scorn; but that these same readers would have discovered within Dryden's vaunted 'talent for satire' either much piety or probity is another matter.[14] And Dryden betrays a certain nervousness on that score when he confesses his 'weakness and want of Learning' in the Preface to *Religio Laici*.[15] Those words cover a different kind of doubt, not I think about lack of learning, but rather about the reputation of his morals as author of *Marriage A-la-Mode*, *The Assignation, or, Love in a Nunnery*, and *The Kind Keeper, or, Mr. Limberham*. The last of these Dryden published in 1680, and it was made quickly and repeatedly a target of opportunity for those who would regret Dryden's morals. One of them remarked that *The Kind Keeper* was 'So bawdy it not only sham'd the Age, / But worse, was ev'n too nauseous for the stage.'[16]

Dryden had a keen sense of occasion, of opportunity and advantage; what drove him to adapt Boyle was in part an appreciation of the uses to which he could put *The Excellency of Theology* and the reputation of its author. Dryden was always on the lookout for useable language. He was a fast worker and he wrote and published a lot over a very long career; he was a learned writer, but learning was not his profession, writing was. What he saw as opportunity, he remembered and adapted. The very rapidity of his writing – and he often wrote under hurried and pressured circumstances – is revealed in Dryden's habits of misremembering and misquotation. He may have done this to cover his tracks, but he also quoted and misquoted out of simpler circumstances, not so much to deceive as to hasten his way. If his readers detected imitation and appropriation, good and well, for what Dryden borrowed from Boyle was not only language but also the splendid reputation that Boyle brought to matters of divinity and belief. How convenient that Boyle offered Dryden at once a language for the expression of his lay spirituality and the prestige, clarity, and strength of his credentials as an exponent of the new science who nevertheless strenuously would combat the irreligion of mere science to profess the 'excellency of theology.'

But the example of Boyle and *Religio Laici* suggests more about Dryden's beliefs and way of writing than the method of one particular text; it suggests the occasional, adventitious, and opportunistic nature of Dryden's beliefs, idioms, and 'spirituality.' When Dryden adapts, plagiarizes, and ventriloquizes, he sets in motion an odd collaboration between his own voice and that of Robert Boyle. Throughout his career, and not only in the territory of religious confession, he keenly mimics, ventriloquizes, and adapts the voices of others, but he is not especially keen on pointing out where his own voice stops and where another begins. Dryden is slippery on echo and adaptation; just when we think we've discovered him lifting from another writer, it might occur to us that he adapts idioms and ideas so that his readers can hear the resonance and recognize the authority of his stance. He had acknowledged in the Preface to *Annus Mirabilis* his dependence on the idioms of others; so that he might not seem a 'plaigery' he adopted a system of marginal annotation indicating where words and ideas belonged to others, and yet to avoid pedantry and punctiliousness, he decided not to note those places too often.[17] The manoeuvre is a shrewdly self-conscious gesture of good faith, a flourish of good manners, and at the same time a posting of notice that the elaborate fabric of *Annus Mirabilis* is woven from fibres of both known and unknown origin, and that we ought not to think the author will tediously track every point at which language belongs to others. The point is minor, but elegantly taken; it surely has larger implications for the originality, the idioms, and the authority of his mature intellectual projects, both religious and political.

And it may point a way to solve the old conundrum of Dryden studies – that misguided project of establishing the continuity, coherence, and integrity of an intellectual and spiritual life that seems to have such glaring contradictions. For that continuity and coherence is a problem only if we are fixed in the opinion that Dryden had one set of organically developing beliefs and convictions. Out of a false notion of coherence and integrity came the desire to discover how *Religio Laici* prepared the way for *The Hind and the Panther*,[18] and while that inquiry has long been discredited,[19] we seem still unwilling to understand the poet's convictions as uneven and opportunistic. Dryden's work was as a writer; and he was quick, often brilliant, and always available for the call of opportunity. He miscalculated more than once, but with a writer whose beliefs were uncertain and uneven and who had the capacity to smooth over or ignore contradiction, I suspect that the drive to discover consistency of belief, even belief itself where we can only be certain of the language of belief, is misguided.

If we are to take seriously Dryden's profession of tolerant Anglican spirituality, of charity, scepticism, and diffidence, what are we to make of his handling of nonconformity? Perhaps there are, in the patchwork text of *Religio Laici*, moments of Dryden's own; but they are not, I think, to be discovered in his 'Profession of Divinity,' but rather in his character of dissent. In the Preface Dryden draws one such picture of his fellow Protestants, who, 'we may see, were born with teeth, foul-mouth'd and scurrilous from their Infancy: and if Spiritual Pride, Venome, Violence, Contempt of Superiours and Slander had been marks of Orthodox Belief; the Presbytery and the rest of our Schismaticks, which are their Spawn, were always the most visible Church in the Christian World.'[20] Dryden claims not to have made himself a 'Judge of Faith, in others, but onely to make a Confession of [his] own,' but that confession strikes its most personal note and takes on its most deeply felt rhythms not in the moments when he adapts the language of his spiritual superiors, or when he whispers of his own humility and ingenuousness, but rather when he turns to those native and reformed hands that had translated the Scriptures into English and aimed directly to read and interpret the word of God:

> The Book thus put in every vulgar hand,
> Which each presum'd he best cou'd understand,
> The *Common Rule* was made the *common Prey*;
> And at the mercy of the *Rabble* lay.
> The tender Page with horney Fists was gaul'd;
> And he was gifted most that loudest baul'd:
> ....
> While Crouds unlearn'd, with rude Devotion warm,
> About the Sacred Viands buz and swarm,
> The *Fly-blown Text* creates a *crawling Brood*;
> And turns to *Maggots* what was meant for *Food*.
> *A Thousand daily Sects rise up, and dye*;
> *A Thousand more the perish'd Race supply*:
> So all we make of Heavens discover'd Will
> Is, not to have it, or to use it ill.
>
> (ll. 400–5, 417–24)

Towards the close of his poem, Dryden argues that spiritual convictions, interests, passions, and professions are best consigned to silence. What this pilgrim's progress turns out to advocate is '*Common quiet*' (l. 450) and something like an indifference to religion of whatever confession – all manner of belief and believers, including those who lived before the incarnation and those who had not heard the gospel, those who were heathens and those who are deists, perhaps even Papists, Turks, and Jews, might aim at salvation.

> Then those who follow'd *Reasons* Dictates right;
> Liv'd up, and lifted high their *Natural Light*;
> With *Socrates* may see their Maker's Face
> While Thousand *Rubrick-Martyrs* want a place.
>
> (ll. 208–11)

Was Narcissus Luttrell wrong to mark the title page of his copy of *Reli-*

gio Laici with the word 'Atheisticall'?[21] Luttrell was a distinguished collector and antiquary, and he had written appreciatively on the title pages of both *Absalom and Achitophel* and *Mac Flecknoe*;[22] there is no reason to think that Luttrell's private (and certainly unpolemical) marking was anything but disinterested reflection on the matter of Dryden's confession of faith.

Dryden wrote *Religio Laici* and *The Hind and the Panther* not, I think, to express his own convictions – these seem hardly spiritual at all; indeed, at a number of points Dryden is openly hostile to the stances and pretensions of spirituality that he detected all around him – but to give the authority of verse and the guise of spirituality to programs of religious toleration that were important to both Stuart kings. In *Religio Laici* Dryden claimed that Father Simon used the idioms of church governance 'for *Fashion-sake*' (l. 254), a guise to cover his 'secret meaning' (l. 252), which cut against the very interests of religion that he claimed to uphold. I suspect that in his *Religio Laici* Dryden is guilty of just such a move, of adopting 'for Fashion-sake' the idioms of spiritual confession, not in this instance to undermine religion but to fashion a program cut to the form of a political and religious quietism that might best suit the policies of Charles II. And political service is exactly what he found himself once again performing, in the guise of spiritual confession following James II's accession to the throne. That guise was now, of course, Roman Catholic, but the spiritual tenor, and certainly the deep satiric vein, of *The Hind and the Panther* seem to me very close to the suspicion of religion and to the deeply ironic address to its instruments that we find throughout Dryden's work. Even, or perhaps especially, after the Glorious Revolution, when Dryden needed to cling to whatever straws of political and spiritual integrity he might grasp, we find the same caustic suspicion leaking out of his address to religion. In the Dedication of the *Aeneis*, Dryden had touched once again, and in his inimitable way, upon the priesthood. Having unveiled the wickedness of Marius and Cinna, and in the midst of targeting the hypocrisy of Sylla, who had 'nothing but liberty and reformation in his mouth,' Dryden remarks, parenthetically, that 'the Cause of Religion is but a Modern Motive for Rebellion, invented by the Christian Priesthood, refining on the Heathen.'[23] Luke Milbourne remarked of the passage, 'This is malicious enough, and would have been an invention becoming Mr. Dryden's wit, had he been unhappily admitted into holy orders; tho for ought I know, his very Christianity may be questionable.'[24]

Late in his life, after the costly conversion to Rome, Dryden may have flirted with a return to the Anglican Church, but he knew that this would be out of the question; he wrote plaintively to his cousin, Mrs Steward, 'I know not what church to go to, if I leave the Catholique.'[25] There is something touching about this confession, but it is not Dryden's spirituality. Gilbert Burnet said of Samuel Parker that 'he seemed to have no other sense of religion but as a political interest and a subject of party and faction.'[26] Parker was Dryden's near contemporary, and like the laureate he had been raised in Northamptonshire nonconformity, migrated to the Church of England, strongly supported the crown, denounced the puritans, and, finally, under James II, become 'an instrument to betray and ruin' the Anglican Church. Perhaps Burnet's words are too harsh to apply to the laureate; at least Dryden had the integrity to sustain his suspicion of and hostility towards nonconformity even in the spring of 1687, when he was being asked to court its members in the interests of the crown.

The Hind and the Panther is unsparing in its portrait of Anglican self-interest, cowardice, and greed, and had the king read and understood his laureate's verse, he would have been pleased with the portrait that there emerged of the Anglican Church. But equally he would have been puzzled and troubled by Dryden's treatment of the sectaries, those unlikely souls whom James II was now caressing in his efforts to achieve a religious toleration that might embrace not only Protestant dissent but also the Roman Catholic confession. What emerges in Dryden's handling of the sectaries is an image not a bit less hostile than the portrait of dissent in *Religio Laici*. In his own defence, and no doubt anticipating the reception that he knew would greet his satiric tactics and his profession of Catholic faith, Dryden wrote of his handling of religion in the Preface to *The Hind and the Panther*, '*I have made use of the Common Places of Satyr, whether true or false, which are urg'd by the Members of the one Church against the other. At which I hope no Reader of either Party will be scandaliz'd; because they are not of my Invention.*'[27] In a career of disingenuous confessions, this surely takes the cake; indeed, so outrageous is the claim of literary and polemical naivety that Dryden could have here intended nothing other than a rubbing of the salt of disingenuousness and false naivety in the wounds that he might hope to have opened with his '*Common Places of Satyr, whether true or false.*' This seems to me a very thin program of spirituality in an age of high religious profession, and I think that it urges us, as does Dryden's whole religious career, to confront directly the problem of quotation and belief.

From the beginning of his religious career even to its end, where he uses Chaucer and Bishop Ken as screens for his own spirituality, Dryden had made a practice of adopting other voices when he entered the territory of belief. Even, or perhaps especially, in *The Hind and the Panther*, where he hit his stride as a religious polemicist, Dryden hides behind the claim of mere commonplaces. I suggest that this claim, disingenuous though it may be in the preface to *The Hind and the Panther*, raises a flag over the entire territory of Dryden's religions. There has, of late, been a revival of interest in Restoration and eighteenth-century English spirituality. J.C.D. Clark's recovery of the continuity of the British confessional state,[28] and Donald Davie's work on the poetry of British dissenting traditions, together with our current interest in recusant communities across the whole of the early modern period have certainly helped to reconfigure relations between religion and what we might think of as the British enlightenment.[29] And no doubt this work has aimed broadly to warn us against the anachronistic imposition of our own unbelief – of our scepticism, materialism, and atheism – on the utterance and integrity of an age that, in certain shades of light, might seem proximate to our own, but that is, in fact, very distant and very unlike our time.

And yet I would urge caution before we sweep all that lies behind us under religion's ample skirt. At least in Dryden's case, I want to warn against the discovery of belief where there is merely its appearance and where opportunity, discretion, and need all advised the wisdom of speaking religion's languages. Whatever our own need to uncover the spirituality of the past, I suggest that we ought not to make it Dryden's need, and more broadly that we should proceed with care as we untangle the voices of Christian profession. Dryden's case seems to me to pose a fascinating problem not only for discussing the relations among authenticity, quotation, and plagiarism, but also for understanding how the voice of belief can best be discerned within a literary culture of allusion, quotation, and innuendo, within the formulaic practices of prayer and institutional piety; and within a spirituality one of whose great callings is for humility and self-denial.

Notes

1 Robert Boyle, *The Excellency of Theology, Compared with Natural Philosophy* (1674), A6r–A6v.
2 Dryden, Preface to *Religio Laici*, quoted from *The Poems of John Dryden*, ed.

James Kinsley, 4 vols. (Oxford: Clarendon Press 1958), 1:302. All references to the text of this poem are to this edition and are cited in my text parenthetically.

3 Dryden, 'To My Honour'd Friend, Dr. Charleton,' *Poems of John Dryden*, 1:33, line 27.

4 Boyle, *Excellency of Theology*, 76.

5 Boyle, *Excellency of Theology*, 74; cf. Dryden's 'To my Honored Friend, Sir Robert Howard,' *Poems of John Dryden* 1:13, lines 31–2, 'No Atoms casually together hurl'd / Could e're produce so beautifull a world.'

6 Philip Harth touches on the precedence of Boyle as a layman writing on religion but does not note the striking congruence of expression; see Harth, *Contexts of Dryden's Thought* (Chicago: University of Chicago Press 1968), 11–13, and passim.

7 See *State Papers Domestic*, 1671? – May 1672, 637–8, 29 May 1672, Martin Clifford to Mr Dryden, 'Refers to the gross scurrility of the last prologue. Will not misemploy his time in exposing all his faults. All the world knows how great a plagiary is Dryden, and his writings are like a Jack-of-all-trades' shop, having variety but nothing of value' (vol. 87, ff. 140–1).

8 See E.N. Hooker, 'Dryden and the Atoms of Epicurus,' *ELH* 24 (1957), 177–90, reprinted in *Essential Articles for the Study of John Dryden*, ed. H.T. Swedenberg, Jr (Hamden, Conn.: Archon Books 1966), 232–44.

9 See *Absalom and Achitophel*, ll. 99–107 in *Poems of John Dryden*, vol. 1.

10 See *The Works of John Dryden*, eds. E.N. Hooker, H.T. Swedenberg, Jr, et al., 20 vols. (Berkeley: University of California Press 1956–2000), 2:343.

11 Gilbert Burnet to Anne Wharton, *The Surviving Works of Anne Wharton*, eds. G. Greer and S. Hastings (Stump Cross: 1997), 349.

12 *The Weekly Pacquet of Advice from Rome*, vol. 21 (12 January 1682–3), 165–6.

13 Dryden, Preface to *Religio Laici. Poems of John Dryden*, 1:302, l. 15.

14 Dryden, Dedication to *Eleonora. Poems of John Dryden*, 2:584, l. 101.

15 *Dryden, Poems of John Dryden*, 1:302, l. 9.

16 And see John Tutchin, *Poems on Several Occasions* (1685), 66, 'Well might the Audience, with their hisses, damn / The Bawdy Sot that late wrote Limberham: / but yet you see, the Stage he will command, / And hold the Laureal in 's polluted Hand.'

17 Dryden, 'An Account of the ensuing Poem, in a letter to the Honorable, Sir Robert Howard.' *Poems of John Dryden*, 1:48, ll. 185–9.

18 The tradition stretches back to Louis Bredvold's *The Intellectual Milieu of John Dryden* (Ann Arbor: University of Michigan Press 1934).

19 Though, see James Winn's biography, which, as late as 1987, seems still to suggest that linkage, 'His sarcastic couplet rejecting those claims – "Such an

Omniscient Church we wish indeed; / 'Twere worth Both Testaments, and cast in the Creed" – may nonetheless record, at some level of consciousness, the appeal of Catholic certainty. Dryden's resistance to that appeal would ultimately prove temporary.' See Winn, *John Dryden and His World* (New Haven, Conn.: Yale University Press 1987), 377–8.

20 Dryden, Preface to *Religio Laici. Poems of John Dryden*, 1:309, ll. 275–80.

21 Folger Library Copy, D2342.

22 Luttrell's copy of *Absalom and Achitophel* is in the Huntington Library with the shelf mark 135868, and his copy of *Mac Flecknoe* is in the Osborn Collection, Beinecke Library, Yale University.

23 Dryden, Dedication of the *Aeneis. Poems of John Dryden*, 3:1012, ll. 376–9.

24 Luke Milbourne, *Notes on Dryden's Virgil* (London 1698), 24.

25 *The Letters of John Dryden*, ed. Charles Ward (Durham, N.C.: Duke University Press 1942), 123.

26 Gilbert Burnet, *An Inquiry into the Reasons for Abrogating the Test Imposed on All Members of Parliament* (London 1688), 4.

27 Dryden, *Poems of John Dryden*, 2:469–70.

28 J.C.D. Clark, *English Society, 1688–1832: Ideology, Social Structure, and Political Practice during the Ancien Regime* (Cambridge: Cambridge University Press 1985).

29 Donald Davie, *The Eighteenth-Century Hymn in England* (Cambridge: Cambridge University Press 1993), and *Essays in Dissent: Church, Chapel, and the Unitarian Conspiracy* (Manchester: Carcanet 1995).

PART II

THE GROUNDS OF ENCHANTMENT

chapter nine

Anxious Comparisons in John Dryden's
Troilus and Cressida

JENNIFER BRADY

During the early spring of 1679, in the febrile atmosphere of the Popish Plot, John Dryden published *Troilus and Cressida, or, Truth Found Too Late*, the third (and last) of his Shakespearean adaptations. Much of the criticism has focused on the question of topical political allusion in Dryden's play, with Michael Dobson's view that Dryden 'smuggle[d] a guarded royalist polemic onto the stage of the Duke's Theatre' under the cover of revising Shakespeare's work being typical of this approach.[1] Over the past decades, Dryden scholars have debated the extent of the political parallels in his *Troilus and Cressida*, with some consensus emerging that the political allegory is, at best, fitful or discontinuous, surfacing in Ulysses' homily on order, the play's famous closing tag, its epilogue, and the vein of reflexive anticlerical satire throughout.[2] Some critical discussion has considered the implications of Dryden's principal revision of Shakespeare's plot – namely, his rehabilitation of Cressida, who dies vindicated, by contrast with Shakespeare's ambiguous heroine – but, of all of Dryden's revisions of Shakespeare, *Troilus and Cressida* has attracted the least attention. It remains an undervalued play.

In deciding to revise Shakespeare's 1602 play, Dryden chose an apprentice work that was, he pointed out, markedly uneven, '*so lamely ... left to us, that it is not divided into Acts*' in the 1623 Folio: '*a more uncorrect Copy I never saw*,' he wrote.[3] Shakespeare's style was '*so pester'd with Figurative expressions, that it is as affected as it is obscure*'; and so Dryden undertook – in provocative phrasing that would resonate elsewhere in his work – to '*remove that heap of Rubbish, under which many excellent thoughts lay wholly bury'd*' (13:225–6). In her valuable study *Authorship and Appropriation* (1998), Paulina Kewes takes Dryden at his word here. She writes: 'The novelty of his adaptation, as it is defined in the preface, amounts primarily to the correction of the imperfections of the Shakespearean source ... His main objective was to show his own plays to be improvements upon largely obsolete or ... structurally flawed originals, and to claim authorship by virtue of the amount of labour involved in the rewriting.'[4] Maximillian E. Novak, in his extensive commentary on Dryden's revision in the California edition, likewise concludes that 'No one would want to replace Shakespeare's genius with Dryden's craft or artistic acumen. Dryden's *Troilus and Cressida* was more of an exercise than a product of his inventiveness and imagination.'[5]

Troilus and Cressida everywhere reflects the sheer professionalism Dryden brought to his work in the theatre, in the ultra-logical reordering of scenes, in the telescoping of Shakespeare's large cast (the cast shrinks by well over a third, from twenty-five to seventeen speaking parts), in the neoclassical coherence of Dryden's act divisions, in the clarity of his editing of individual speeches. But his play does more than demonstrate Dryden's craft. He chose for his adaptation a challenging and in many ways non-representative Shakespearean play, an anomaly in the canon that is more closely allied with the contemporary satire of Jonson or Marston. This interest in Shakespeare's *Troilus and Cressida* coincides with Dryden's burgeoning discovery of his metier as a satirist, with his 1679 play providing a transition between *Mac Flecknoe* (circulating as a manuscript since 1676, but as yet unpublished and unacknowledged by Dryden as his) and his political satire of the early 1680s.

Shakespeare's problem play has a further appeal for Dryden. The protagonists of both Dryden's and Shakespeare's plays are, famously, secondary figures in the Trojan war: Cressida can never compare with Helen of Troy, nor Troilus rival Hector's singular value to the Trojan cause. Dryden's additions to and expansions on Shakespeare's play work to foreground the original work's treatment of anxiety, which repeatedly surfaces in Dryden's *Troilus and Cressida* in the form of anxious comparisons: Ajax's boasts as he measures himself uneasily against Achilles' legendary status, Troilus's helmet, untested in battle, yet said to be 'more hack'd then *Hectors*' (I.ii.217), Cressida's height and waist span, compared by her uncle Pandarus to Helen's. In Dryden's revision, Troilus and Cressida's courtship is farcically interrupted by Pandarus's obtrusive thoughts of Helen; and Troilus's death, following Hector's in the final melee, completes Achilles' revenge in a revealing way: '*Hector*'s dead: / And as a second offring to thy Ghost, / Lyes *Troilus* high upon a heap of slain' (V.ii.309–11). Troilus is the last Trojan to die on stage, but his death is post-climactic since Troy's foundations have already been undermined by the prior death of Hector, as the triumphant Achilles proclaims: 'Our toyls are done, and those aspiring Walls / ... Must crumble into rubbish on the plain' (V.ii.302–4).[6]

Shakespeare's subject matter lent itself to Dryden's own at times highly anxious focus on the pre-war writers, the 'giant race' against whom he measured himself and his generation's achievements over his career. His *Troilus and Cressida* stages its adaptor's fixation on his dramatic precursors, in both displaced and sometimes transparent forms, as Dryden dramatizes, quotes, repositions, augments, and elaborates the idea of coming second. Shakespeare becomes the immediate lightning rod for Dryden's apprehensions in the late 1670s – the Ghost of Shakespeare berates his successors from the stage in the Prologue to *Troilus and Cressida*, inaugurating a spate of ghostly returns to the Restoration stage – but, as the Prologue to *Aureng-Zebe* (1675) and, later, the 1693 Epistle to Congreve make clear, behind Shakespeare's ghost stand at least two other formidable Jacobean playwrights: Ben Jonson (who provides in the figure of 'armed Prologue' to his 1601 satire *Poetaster* the model for Dryden's Ghost of Shakespeare) and Fletcher, who together with Shakespeare comprise 'the greater Dead' against whom Dryden 'dares not strive.'[7] Dryden's stature is diminished by comparison with the Jacobeans, as are his protagonists in *Troilus and Cressida*, who are measured against Troy's icons, Hector and Helen. In the Prologue to *Aureng-Zebe*, which announces the psychological and cultural crisis Troilus and Cressida will revisit, Dryden depicts himself as caught in a kind of no man's land, 'betwixt two Ages cast, / The first of this, and hindmost of the last.'[8] This extraordinary Prologue captures Dryden's sense of dislocation, as he surveys his possible place in a literary history he is simultaneously inventing: if he is the premier writer of his age, he brings up the rear of the 'last' generation, both the last Jacobean and a writer transfixed by his own sense of belatedness.[9] In *Troilus and Cressida*, Dryden's depressive ideation attaches itself repeatedly to the thought of coming in second.

Consider, in this respect, Dryden's praise in his Preface of Shakespeare's depiction of Richard II's entrance onto the stage after Bolingbroke's triumphant entry. Dryden quotes some fourteen lines of Shakespeare's Richard II to 'do justice to that Divine Poet,' confessing that he finds the scene 'so moving, that I have scarce read any thing comparable to it, in any other language.'[10] Here are the opening lines of the passage Dryden selects, from a canon of some thirty-eight plays, to illustrate Shakespeare's capacity to create pathos through a brilliant rendering of Richard's plight:

> As in a Theatre, the eyes of men
> After a well-grac'd Actor leaves the Stage,
> Are idly bent on him that enters next,
> Thinking his prattle to be tedious:
> Even so, or with much more contempt, mens eyes
> Did scowl on *Richard*: no man cry'd *God saue him*.[11]

Dryden's response to this scene is based on his nearly boundariless identification with Richard's ignominious reception on the stage of public life after Bolingbroke's exit. Dryden's investment in the figure of the deposed monarch, revived by the turmoil of the Popish Plot and the Exclusion crisis, supports a political reading of this passage from *Richard II*; but there is a literary application too suggested by the theatrical metaphor. In his 1667 *Essay of Dramatick Poesie*, Dryden envisions the triumvirate of pre-war Jacobean playwrights some forty years earlier as 'just then leaving the world; as if in an Age of so much horror, wit and those milder studies of humanity, had no farther business among us.'[12] Writing in the mode of cavalier nostalgia, Dryden (through Lisideius) represents the Jacobeans' departure from the literary stage as timed and orchestrated, a collective and prescient repudiation on their parts of England's impending civil unrest. These are playwrights whose timing is impeccable, who know how to stage a departure. To re-enter the stage after the 'well-grac'd' principal has exited, as Richard II does, or as Dryden does in following the Jacobean playwrights, invites a comparison that is to the express disadvantage of 'him that enters next.'

Dryden added a scene to the second act of *Troilus and Cressida* that elaborates on his anxious fixation on belated entrances. In this 'wholly New' material,[13] which has no parallel in Shakespeare's play, Andromache petitions Hector on behalf of their young son, Astyanax, who wants to issue a challenge to the Greeks. The mood is initially one of playful banter, as Andromache reports their son's fear that Hector's military prowess will deplete Astyanax's opportunities for establishing his own name, reputation, and valour:

> *Hect.* Welcome *Andromache*: your looks are cheerfull;
> You bring some pleasing news.
> *Andro.* Nothing that's serious.

> Your little Son *Astyanax* has employ'd me
> As his Ambassadresse.
> *Hect.* Upon what errand?
> *Andro.* No less then that his Grandfather this day
> Would make him Knight: he longs to kill a *Grecian*:
> For shou'd he stay to be a man, he thinks
> You'll kill 'em all; and leave no work for him.
> *Priam.* Your own blood, *Hector* ...
> *Hect.* What sparks of honour
> Fly from this child! The God's speak in him sure:
> – It shall be so – I'le do't.   (II.i.78–94)

Hector applauds his son's desire to emulate him, then, prompted by the compulsion to compete, pre-empts Astyanax's initiative by issuing the challenge to the Greek camp. Astyanax's foreboding that his father's conquests will leave him no opportunity to establish his own manhood introduces the element of Oedipal struggle into this domestic scene. Astyanax will, of course, die in Troy's fall, his death made inevitable by Hector's defeat. When Aeneas protests the folly of Hector's challenge, reminding him that '*Troy* has but one, one *Hector*,' Hector replies proudly, 'What will *Astyanax* be?' to which Priam answers: 'An *Hector* one day, / But you must let him live to be a *Hector*. / And who shall make him such when you are gone?' (II.i.117–23). Oedipal struggle coexists with a melancholy premonition of the father's loss in this scene, where fathers and sons lose each other twice over: in Hector's heroic squandering of Astyanax's chances to realize his potential as a warrior and, imminently, in Hector's death at the hands of Achilles' Myrmidons. As Robin Sowerby has recently reminded us, 'Astyanax's very name, meaning "lord of the city," contains irony and pathos, for his fate is at one with the city'; the young child is thrown from Troy's battlements by Ulysses, according to Ovid's *Metamorphoses*.[14]

The psychological dynamics between Hector and Astyanax reproduce on stage the anxiety Dryden himself confessed to in his landmark *Essay of Dramatick Poesie*, published a dozen years earlier, in which he argued that the Jacobean playwrights had virtually exhausted their postwar successors' dramatic resources. 'Our Fathers in wit,' Dryden calls the Jacobeans, his genealogical analogy making the parallel to *Troilus and Cressida*'s added scene in Act II self-evident. He continues, in the voice of the dispossessed child, to complain that the Jacobean fathers have 'ruin'd their Estates themselves before they came to their childrens hands. There is scarce an Humour, a Character, or any kind of Plot, which they have not us'd. All comes sullied or wasted to us: and were they to entertain this Age, they could not now make so plenteous treatments out of such decay'd Fortunes. This therefore will be a good Argument to us either not to write at all, or to attempt some other way. There is no bayes to be expected in their Walks.'[15] The Jacobean precursors have left no laurels for their Restoration heirs to win, just as Hector (in the future Astyanax imagines) has taken all the Trojan honours in the field. Astyanax's projection of a future in which his father's military dominance has left him no Greeks to kill introduces a script that veers away from the tragic momentum of Hector's fate, which makes Dryden's decision to insert this Oedipal crisis into *Troilus and Cressida* all the more revealing of his personal and cultural stake in problematic dynastic successions. The point of identification in both of these passages is with the child's perspective – Astyanax's fear, blithely dismissed by his mother as 'Nothing that's serious,' the heirs' hands' grasping their reduced legacies in *Dramatick Poesie* – and, more specifically, with the children's diminished opportunities. The literary estates of the Jacobeans are 'wasted,' 'used up,' 'ruined,' 'sullied,' 'decayed' before they pass to Dryden's generation;[16] should Astyanax 'stay to be a man,' Hector will have killed all the Trojan foes, leaving him nothing to achieve in battle.

Dryden's fixation on patrilineal legacies has often been remarked, and my emphasis on the Oedipal dimension of this scene has followed that line of thought.[17] I want now to complicate that picture, by considering Priam's appeal to Hector in Act II, scene i. Priam's speech, suffused with a proleptic melancholy, envisions Astyanax's brief life after Hector's death. Over the course of ten lines, Dryden gradually – at first, almost imperceptibly – effects a transformation in the perception of Hector's gender, until Priam compares Hector to 'the Mother tree' and Astyanax to 'the young Sapling' she fosters and protects:

> Who shall instruct his tenderness in arms
> Or give his childhood lessons of the war?
> Who shall defend the promise of his youth
> And make it bear in Manhood? The young Sapling
> Is shrowded long beneath the Mother tree
> Before it be transplanted from its Earth,
> And trust it self for growth.   (II.i.124–30)

Derek Hughes has argued that 'Hector's nomenclature is not only social, but, quite flagrantly, masculine' in a play that focuses on 'the male specialism of war.'[18] Here, however, Dryden represents Hector as 'the Mother tree,' sheltering, nurturant, life-giving. Moments later Andromache will, ironically, subscribe to the hypermasculinity traditionally associated with the figure of Hector when she spurns the designation of Hector's wife, preferring that of masculine soulmate and friend. But Dryden has already brought that posture into question in Priam's brooding speech with its subtle transition in the gender coding of Hector's relationship to his young son. As an ever fuller awareness of the enormity of the parent's imminent loss enters the text, it is the mourned originary attachment to the mother that begins to supersede – or supplant – the Oedipal contest with the father. Suddenly, in Priam's words, what is at stake for Astyanax in his filial relationship to Hector changes.

Astyanax's anxiety focuses on whether the warrior Hector will kill all their enemies; for Priam, the loss encompasses both parents, and while it is couched in a nominal future tense, that future has already been realized in the instant of its prophetic utterance. It may be relevant here that Astyanax is an infant in the *Iliad*, while Dryden presents him as a young child whose age remains unspecified.[19] Dryden's decision to cast Astyanax as a promising youth who will never reach manhood allows him to stage the Oedipal crisis more convincingly. Still, it is at the precise moment when Priam voices his wretched sense of the doom awaiting the unprotected child that the adult protector is identified as maternal, opening the text up to a pre-Oedipal reading: 'when you are gone' turns out to encompass the loss of father and mother, who are embodied in Hector, warrior and 'Mother tree.' There are other such moments in the text, in which Hector is either likened or likens himself to a mother, qualifying significantly Derek Hughes's account of the hero's hypermasculinity.

In adapting Shakespeare's *Troilus and Cressida*, Dryden chose to dramatize his own fears about succession. He does so directly in the Prologue, in which the Ghost of Shakespeare excoriates his Restoration heirs as the '*Weak, short-liv'd issues of a feeble Age*' (l. 19) whose plays are the epitome of dullness, and he does so within the plot, through his protagonists' experiences of living their lives in the shadows of more established luminaries. The Ghost of Shakespeare scoffs: '*Now, where are the Successours to my name? / What bring they to fill out a Poets fame?*' (ll. 17–18).

Dryden's Ghost of Shakespeare owes far more to Jonson's self-portrait of the armed Author dominating and vanquishing his rivals in *Poetaster* than it does to Shakespeare's received reputation.[20] In *Poetaster*'s Prologue, the Author denigrates his rivals as 'that common spawn of ignorance' who threaten to 'beslime his fame,' a hostile characterization that Dryden's Ghost of Shakespeare extends to the Jacobeans' dull and incapable Restoration successors.[21] Troilus, Cressida, and Ajax are confronted with versions of the same dilemma, whether like Ajax they consciously strive to compete with or displace the icon in whose shadow they remain, or whether like Troilus and Cressida that burden of comparison is foisted upon them. These characters are successors in another root sense of the word: they merely 'go after' the inestimable original.

Following Shakespeare's example, Dryden stages the passing of the Trojan troops across the stage as they return from battle. 'I'le tell you all their names as they pass by,' Pandarus tells Cressida, and he at once mistakenly identifies Aeneas as Troilus (I.ii.172). Aeneas, Antenor, Hector, Paris, and Helenus cross the stage before Troilus's undistinguished entry ('What sneaking fellow comes yonder?' [I.ii.210]), and then, to underscore the metaphor being represented on stage, the common soldiers follow Troilus. Pandarus dismisses them, using a word Dryden has used in the Preface in comparing himself to Shakespeare: 'the Lyons are gone; Apes and Monkeys, the fag end of the creation,' Pandarus exclaims, inadvertently implicating Troilus in his withering ridicule (I.ii.226–7). In the Preface Dryden has spoken of himself and his generation as writers who 'ape' Shakespeare's 'sounding words, [but] have nothing of his thought' (13:247). There Dryden impugns his own creativity through a subliminal allusion to Macbeth's despairing words, 'It is a tale / Told by an idiot, full of sound and fury, / Signifying nothing';[22] now, in a further twist of self-disparagement, Dryden's self-quotation implicates him in the satiric devolution Pandarus describes.

As David Hopkins has recently argued, based on his work in editing Dryden for the Longman English Poets edition, scholars need to attend to 'Dryden's self-echoes and self-borrowings, [which] ... reveal the network of larger concerns which run like a set of subterranean passages beneath his work in all genres, surfacing recurrently in sometimes unlikely places.'[23] Dryden's repetition of the word 'apes' matters, because it links his explicit confession of his anxious relation to his principal Jacobean forebears to the parade of Trojans crossing the stage, in decreasing importance. Dryden stages his own fears here in a displaced but traceable form: his self-echo establishes the continuity of his fixation with this kind of freighted comparison, while he seems from a professional standpoint only to be adapting Shakespeare's play for a modern audience.

I want now to turn to Dryden's treatment of anxious comparisons in his protagonists in *Troilus and Cressida*. In the first three acts of the play, before Cressida leaves Troy for the Greeks' camp, she is the subject of many defensive comparisons to Helen of Troy, against whom Cressida can never measure up, a trope that is made literal in her uncle's remarks on her stature in Act I, scene ii. Dryden imitates Shakespeare's play quite closely here in a scene that retains virtually the same number of total lines (roughly eighty) as Shakespeare's Act I, scene i, but which defers Pandarus's and Troilus's exchange of solipsisms to the second scene of the first act. Dryden's revisions of his source include, as many scholars have noted, his further coarsening of Pandarus's character. It is Pandarus who summons up Helen as an overdetermined point of reference, the icon to whom his niece is constantly compared.[24] The first comparison between the two women turns in Shakespeare's play on a conventional Petrarchan contrast between fair- and dark-haired heroines, in Dryden on a matter of inches. Here is Pandarus, extolling Cressida's measurements: 'I measur'd her with my girdle Yesterday, she's not half a yard about the waste, but so taper a shape did I never see; ... And [if] she were a thought taller, – but as she is, she wants not an Inch of *Helen* neither; but there's no more comparison between the Women' (I.ii.37–44). Shakespeare's Pandarus also defends Cressida's beauty through making an explicit comparison to Helen: 'An her hair were not somewhat darker than Helen's – well, go to – there were no more comparison between the women.'[25]

Dryden draws attention through his close quotation of Shakespeare to a dimension of the 1602 play that he will emulate and develop further in his adaptation. In both plays, Pandarus's speech inaugurates a pattern of fixated comparisons between Helen and Cressida, interrupted by disclaimers that any such comparison is being lodged. Dryden, however, foregrounds anxieties centring on stature. Within some sixty lines, Cressida's subordinate status is driven home to her when Helen and Hecuba pass (her) by, ostensibly offstage. 'Whither go they?' she asks, to which Aeneas responds, pointedly, 'Up to the Western Tower, / Whose height commands as subject, all the vale,' a vantage point Cressida will never gain in a world in which she remains a nominal heroine and Helen will always be not only the commanding subject, but 'a thought taller' (I.ii.98–100). It is not only Cressida whose stature is being measured in Dryden's *Troilus and Cressida*. Some two years earlier, in 1677, Dryden had ended his Preface to *All for Love* on a comparatively confident note: 'Yet I hope I may affirm, and without vanity, that by imitating him [Shakespeare], I have excell'd my self throughout the Play.[26] Now, reconsidering his relation to Shakespeare, Dryden resorts to a self-denigrating comparison that implicates him in the crises faced by his Trojan protagonists. The remarks follow immediately on Dryden's extensive quotation of Shakespeare in his Preface to *Troilus and Cressida* and are spurred by his abashed tribute to the 'height of thought'[27] realized in Shakespeare's *Richard II:* 'but I fear (at least, let me fear it for myself) that we who Ape his sounding words, have nothing of his thought, but are all out-side; there is not so much as a dwarf within our Giants cloaths.'[28]

James Winn has called attention to Dryden's precipitous loss of self-confidence over the late 1670s, arguing that 'the relative dullness of its [*Troilus and Cressida*'s] ... figurative language' suggests Dryden had apparently 'lost his literary nerve.'[29] Dryden's self-punishing stance in this passage, highlighted by the shift within the parenthesis to the first-person singular, invites a psychological reading. Freud's portrait of the melancholic in his clinical study 'Mourning and Melancholia' (1917) illuminates Dryden's state of mind as he compares his literary stature to Shakespeare's: 'The melancholic,' Freud writes, 'displays ... an extraordinary diminution in his self-regard, an impoverishment of his ego on a grand scale ... [He] represents his ego to us as worthless, incapable of any achievement and morally despicable ... He abases himself before everyone ... He is not of the opinion that a change has taken place in him, but extends his self-criticism over the past; he declares that he was never any better.'[30] And, as Freud goes on to argue, it is the 'capable, conscientious' person, not the 'worthless,' who is especially prone to melancholia: the rhetoric of his own essay, *Civilization and Its Discontents*, in which Freud abases himself repeatedly before his reader, and even the compositor and printer, offers an exemplary instance of Freud's clinical portrait being exhibited in his own work.[31]

Dryden too exhibits a penchant for self-exposure in his Preface to *Troilus and Cressida*. A short man, Dryden turns his own stature against himself with the same merciless accuracy he mustered against Thomas Shadwell's Jonsonian corpulence in *Mac Flecknoe*, turned outward, against a rival playwright, that formidable critical capacity unleashes the energy that produces satire; interiorized, as self-criticism, it targets the ego itself. In *Troilus and Cressida*, this diminished ego strength translates into Dryden's protagonists' inevitable sense of their shortcomings when they compare themselves or are compared by others to Troy's legends. It is mirrored too in the language Dryden uses to expose his fears that his work written in emulation of Shakespeare is insubstantial: Dryden is a dwarf swamped by a literary giant's hand-me-downs.

Dryden decided to remove Helen of Troy as a speaking character from his adaptation of Shakespeare's *Troilus and Cressida*. Why, we might wonder, is Helen's name so continually invoked in a play from which she is simultaneously absent? Dryden emphasizes the principle of dramatic economy in his prefatory remarks: 'I new model'd the Plot; threw out many unnecessary persons,' he writes, in explaining the kind of 'rubbish' he removed from Shakespeare's play.[32] The removal of Helen as a speaking character is nevertheless a brilliant tactic, as canny as Dryden's removal of Octavius Caesar from *All for Love*.[33] Helen is an object of intense speculative fascination in Dryden's *Troilus and Cressida*. If Shakespeare's Helen is vain, shallow, trivial, a travesty of her legend, Dryden's Helen is reimagined to a different end. She is literally incomparable, because utterly removed from the action. She has the perfect inaccessibility Freud observed in beautiful women, who, he wrote in *On Narcissism* (1914), 'compel our interest by the narcissistic consistency with which they manage to keep away from their ego anything that would diminish it. It is as if we envied them for maintaining a blissful state of mind – an unassailable libidinal position which we ourselves have since abandoned.'[34] Helen's iconic status is unassailable in Dryden's play; Cressida, by contrast, cannot fend off the comparisons that diminish her stature in the play. She is a secondary heroine who is displaced for three acts from the play that bears her name by a woman whose power to enthral is a function of her inaccessibility, as both character and icon.

In Act I, scene i, Pandarus lingers over the thought of Helen's 'marvellous white hand,' then awkwardly corrects himself before Cressida: 'But let that pass, for I know who has a whiter' (I.ii.161–3). He returns to his erotic fixation with Helen's hand in Act II, scene ii, in which Pandarus's fantasies delay – and upstage – the consummation of Troilus and Cressida's affair. As Pandarus describes a scene of marital foreplay between Paris and Helen for his nervous listener, Troilus, Troilus repeatedly asks, 'What's this to *Cressida*?' (II.ii.125). It is Helen's white hand, slipping beneath the bedclothes, not Cressida's, that absorbs Pandarus's attention, making Troilus and Cressida's first night as lovers secondary to Helen's foreplay with Paris. Pandarus is ravished by that recollected spectacle of the married lovers, and in particular by 't'other hand ... under the bed-cloaths' whose unseen movements he imagines, because – like Helen in the play itself – that hand is provocatively absent:

> *Pand.* And she lay with one white arm underneath the whorsons neck: oh such a white, lilly white, round, plump arm it was – and you must know it was stript up to th' elbows: and she did so kisse him, and so huggle him: – as who shou'd say –
> *Troil.* But still thou stay'st: what's this to *Cressida?*
> *Pand.* Why I made your excuse to your Brother *Paris*, that I think's to *Cressida*; – but such an arm, such a hand, such taper fingers! t'other hand was under the bed-cloaths; that I saw not, I confess; that hand I saw not.
> *Troil.* Again thou tortur'st me.
> *Pand.* Nay I was tortur'd too; old as I am, I was tortur'd too: but for all that, I cou'd make a shift, to make him, to make your excuse, to make your father; – by *Jove* when I think of that hand, I am so ravish'd, that I know not what I say. (II.ii.120–34)

In Shakespeare's Act III, scene ii of *Troilus and Cressida*, the focus is on Troilus's 'imaginary relish' of the act, and the interval between Pandarus's promise to bring Cressida to Troilus and their return is compressed into the space of Troilus's monologue.[35] Dryden, who has claimed to be cutting superfluous characters and speeches in his Preface, adds some fifty-five lines between Pandarus's 'Walk here a moment more: I'le bring her straight' (l. 83) and Troilus's monologue (ll. 138–47). The effect is to divert the focus of attention from Troilus and Cressida's courtship, underscoring Cressida's secondary status as the heroine of her own play. Like Shakespeare's Ghost in the Prologue dominating his weak successors, Helen's erotic allure readily eclipses Cressida. Cressida's Act V suicide briefly elevates her from second to principal in the play – 'Oh, thou purest, whitest innocence,' Troilus protests (V.ii.268), quite as if his use of the superlative degree could rewrite the comparatives with which Cressida has been encumbered for the play's previous acts, or Helen's enticing lily-white arm be dislodged from memory. When Dryden tries belatedly to make Cressida into a figure of singular tragic pathos he fails, because the groundwork has so successfully been laid for another script in which she plays a secondary role by contrast with Helen of Troy.

Troilus's relation to the singular icon Hector follows a similar pattern. Even Agamemnon's welcome of Troilus to the Greek camp is an afterthought ('My well fam'd Lord of *Troy*, no less to you' Agamemnon says to Troilus [IV.ii.115]); he, not Paris, is the brother expected to relinquish his lover in the exchange for Antenor; he is the 'hindmost' knight in the procession filing past Cressida. If Hector is Troy's 'base and pillar' (IV.ii.129), Troilus is untested, inexperienced. He is openly in awe of Hector, and Hector in turn views Troilus as a child, as virtually his child, to be protected and ordered about. The older brother will break the news of the decision about Cressida to Troilus with 'terms so mild, / So tender, and so fearful to offend / As Mothers use to sooth their froward Babes," (III.ii.255–7), but then expect his immediate compliance with the Trojan council's edict.

In the scene Dryden thought his best writing in the play, Hector invokes Priam's authority to enforce Troilus's submission, and the brothers immediately begin to wrangle over who has the larger share of the father's soul. The scene translates the sibling feud of *Mac Flecknoe*, which had pitted Shadwell against Dryden into a contest over their respective shares in Ben Jonson's soul, into the sibling rivalry of Troilus and Hector, with its '*tu quoque*' exchanges, its Jonsonian ring of narcissistic, childish self-absorption on both their parts:

> *Hect.* Go to, you are a boy.
> *Troil.* A Boy! I'me glad I am not such a Man,
> Not such as thou; a traytor to thy Brother:
> Nay more, thy friend: ...
> *Hect.* Well, young Man,
> Since I'me no friend (and oh that ere I was
> To one so far unworthy) bring her out,
> Or by our Fathers Soul, of which no part
> Did ere descend to thee, I'le force her hence.
> *Troil.* I laugh at thee.
> *Hect.* Thou dar'st not.
> *Troil.* I dare more,
> If urg'd beyond my temper: prove my daring,
> And see which of us has the larger share
> Of our great Fathers Soul.   (III.ii.338–52)

The psychological stakes are very real here, and resonate in much of Dryden's work. What stands out in this scene, which Dryden added to Shakespeare's play, is Hector's categorical demands of renunciation, and the childish escalating rage and possessiveness on both his and Troilus's parts as they contest which of them can claim the larger portion of the father's soul. Dryden returns to this issue over and over in his career as he fixates on his relation to his Jacobean 'Fathers in Wit.' His response to his English forefathers fluctuates; *Troilus and Cressida* can be considered one of the nadir points in Dryden's ego strength in a career far more various than this play reflects. The marked childishness of Hector and Troilus's quarrel, with its odd debt to Jonsonian humours comedy, once again displays the Drydenian preoccupation with children fearful of being dispossessed of someone or something vital to their well-being, something they identify as their father's soul. Dryden has dramatized his insecurities in and through these projections of fathers and sons: Astyanax and Hector, Troilus (who is at once Hector's brother and son), Hector and Priam, Dryden and the Ghosts of his Jacobean literary fathers. These fathers are experienced as at once overwhelming and unavailable for attachment, figures who are mourned with a peculiar intensity.

In describing the unresolved mourning typical of melancholia, Freud observed one of the puzzling features of the condition for the analyst: 'In yet other cases one feels justified in maintaining the belief that a loss [of a more ideal kind] ... has occurred, but one cannot see clearly what it is that has been lost, and it is all the more reasonable to suppose that the patient cannot consciously perceive what he has lost either. This, indeed, might be so even if the patient is aware of the loss which has given rise to his melancholia, but only in the sense that he knows whom he has lost but not what he has lost in him. This would suggest that melancholia is in some way related to an object-loss which is withdrawn from consciousness, in contradistinction to mourning, in which there is nothing about the loss that is unconscious.'[36] I have often felt that this puzzled description of the patient who knows whom but not what he has lost speaks to Dryden's reception of his Jacobean predecessors. He can readily summon up their names, which he invokes in his elaborately constructed literary genealogies, or subject them to the kind of comparative judgment that he wields against himself, or his contemporaries, at other moments; but he never quite articulates what this object-loss means to him. In *Troilus and Cressida* the idealized parent being mourned is both the warrior-hero and the nurturing mother. These two figures coexist in an uneasy juxtaposition in a few speeches, unintegrated into the masculinist vision of Hector predominating in the play. As Hector wavers about going to the battle in which he will die, Troilus presents him with this stirring, poignant sight:

> The Matrons to the turrets tops ascend
> Holding their helplesse children in their arms,

> To make you early known to their young eyes;
> And Hector is the universal shout.   (V.i.105–8)

It is a prevision of his son Astyanax's fate disguised as the irrefutable proof of Hector's celebrification. It is the final image of Troy's children before the holocaust. Hector, like the Jacobeans apotheosized in so much of Dryden's work, is assured of his ultimate place in the pantheon of the demigods. He tells his wife Andromache of his vision:

> Last night I dreamt *Jove* sate on *Ida*'s top
> And beckning with his hand divine from far,
> He pointed to a quire of Demi-gods,
>   *Bacchus*, and *Hercules*, and all the rest
> Who free from humane toils had gain'd the pitch
> Of blest eternity: *Lo there*, he sayd;
> *Lo there's a place for* Hector.   (V.i.43–9)

There is a triumvirate of heroes here, Hector, Bacchus, and Hercules, whose literary analogues are the Jacobeans. 'Lo there's a place for Hector' applies with equal force to Shakespeare, Jonson, and Fletcher, each of whom is assured honour and renown in English literary history, while Dryden wonders uneasily about his own place in that history. If literary history is the byproduct of Dryden's anxious, unstable, and moving attachment to these figures, born out of an object-loss he can attach names and cultural memories to but can never adequately define in his obsessive genealogies of influence, then *Troilus and Cressida* captures a particular moment of that history of reception, in which Dryden focuses those anxieties on Shakespeare, the Titan among Titans, adapting a play of Shakespeare's that allows him to give particularly transparent voice to those concerns.

Notes

1 Michael Dobson, *The Making of the National Poet: Shakespeare, Adaptation and Authorship, 1660–1769* (Oxford: Clarendon Press 1992), 73.

2 See James Anderson Winn, *John Dryden and His World* (New Haven and London: Yale University Press 1987), 316–7, who argues Dryden's caution in introducing political parallels in this turbulent time.

3 John Dryden, Preface to *Troilus and Cressida. The Works of John Dryden*, ed.

E.N. Hooker, H.T. Swedenberg, Jr, et al., 20 vols. (Berkeley: University of California Press 1956–2000), 13:226. Future citations to the play are to this edition (hereafter cited as *California Dryden*) and will appear in the text parenthetically.

4 Paulina Kewes, *Authorship and Appropriation: Writing for the Stage in England, 1660–1710* (Oxford: Clarendon Press 1998), 59–60.

5 Maximillian E. Novak, Commentary. *California Dryden* 13:522. These notes have been an invaluable aid in working on Dryden's play.

6 Dryden's use of the word 'rubbish' in the final scene recalls his phrasing in the Preface, where he claims that his adaptation of *Troilus and Cressida* seeks to recover or reconstitute the genius of its author, now buried 'under a heap of Rubbish' (13:226). His labour is, in other words, a kind of excavation; he uncovers and in a sense rebuilds the edifice of Shakespeare's play. The end of the play envisions another fate for Troy, whose 'aspiring Walls / (The work of Gods' (V.ii.303–4) are toppling.

7 Dryden, *Essay of Dramatick Poesie. California Dryden* 17:34

8 *California Dryden* 12:159.

9 See further on this subject, Paul Hammond, *Dryden and the Traces of Classical Rome* (Oxford: Oxford University Press 1999).

10 *California Dryden* 13:246.

11 Shakespeare, *Richard II*, ed. Stanley Wells (London: Penguin 1969), V.ii.22–8, quoted by Dryden. *California Dryden* 13:246.

12 *Dramatick Poesie*, 17:33–4

13 Preface to *Troilus and Cressida*, 13:227.

14 Robin Sowerby, 'The Last Parting of Hector and Andromache,' in Paul Hammond and David Hopkins, eds., *John Dryden: Tercentenary Essays* (Oxford: Oxford University Press 2000), 242.

15 *Dramatick Poesie*, 17:73.

16 Ibid.

17 The most influential treatment of this Oedipal crisis as it repeats itself in the reception of one generation of writers by their successors is Harold Bloom's *The Anxiety of Influence: A Theory of Poetry* (London: Oxford University Press 1973), which focuses principally on Romantic and modernist writers. Bloom's emphasis on Oedipal competition tends to minimize the counter-longing to attach oneself to the precursor. In Dryden's career, this longing to affirm the continuity of influence is particularly acute because the traumatic rupture of the English Civil War has obviated the need to declare his separation from his chosen precursors.

18 Derek Hughes, *English Drama, 1660–1700* (Oxford: Clarendon Press 1996), 267.

19 Hector refers to 'my Sons green years' (II.i.4).

20 Shakespeare promptly parodied Jonson's belligerent Author in the armed Prologue to *Poetaster* in his Prologue to *Troilus and Cressida*. See further on the reception of Jonson and Shakespeare by their contemporaries, Ian Donaldson, *Jonson's Magic Houses: Essays in Interpretation* (Oxford: Clarendon Press 1997), 180–97.

21 Jonson, *Poetaster*, ed. Tom Cain (Manchester: Manchester University Press 1995), Prol. 79–80.

22 Shakespeare, *Macbeth*, ed. G.K. Hunter (London: Penguin 1967), V.v.26–8.

23 David Hopkins, 'Editing, Authenticity, and Translation: Re-Presenting Dryden's Poetry in 2000,' in *John Dryden: Tercentenary Essays*, eds. Hammond and Hopkins, 353.

24 See further on Helen of Troy as a constant point of comparison in Shakespeare's *Troilus and Cressida*, René Girard, 'The Politics of Desire in *Troilus and Cressida*,' eds. Patricia Parker and Geoffrey Hartman (New York: Methuen 1985), 188–209, which explores the issue of mimetic desire in the play, and Janet Adelman, '"This Is and Is Not Cressid": The Characterization of Cressida,' in *The (M)other Tongue: Essays in Feminist Psychoanalytic Interpretation*, eds. Shirley Nelson Garner et al. (Ithaca: Cornell University Press 1985), 119–41, especially note 24, in which Adelman notices that the protagonists' 'first two meetings are symbolically mediated by Helen' (137).

25 Shakespeare, *Troilus and Cressida*, I.1.41–3.

26 Dryden, Preface to *All for Love. California Dryden* 13:18–9.

27 Preface to *Troilus and Cressida*, 13:246.

28 Ibid, 13:247. See further on the implications of Dryden's frequent allusions to giants for his theories of translation, Paul Davis, '"But slaves we are": Dryden and Virgil, Translation and the "Gyant Race,"' in *John Dryden: Classicist and Translator*, ed. Stuart Gillespie (Edinburgh: Edinburgh University Press 2001), 110–127.

29 Winn, *John Dryden and His World*, 320.

30 Sigmund Freud, 'Mourning and Melancholia,' in *The Standard Edition of the Complete Psychological Works of Sigmund Freud*, trans. James Strachey, 24 vols. (London: Hogarth Press 1953–74), 14:246.

31 Ibid, 14:247. See further Freud, *Civilization and Its Discontents*, 21:64–145, including the self- depreciation by Freud of his own work-in-progress, as, for example, in his introductory remarks to chapter 6: 'In none of my previous writings have I had so strong a feeling as now that what I am describing is common knowledge and that I am using up paper and ink and, in due course, the compositor's and printer's work and material in order to expound things which are, in fact, self-evident' (117).

32 Preface to *Troilus and Cressida*, 13:226.
33 I am influenced on this point by R.J. Kaufmann, 'On the Poetics of Terminal Tragedy: Dryden's *All for Love*,' in Bernard N. Schilling, ed., *Dryden: A Collection of Critical Essays* (Englewood Cliffs, N.J.: Prentice-Hall 1963), 86–94.
34 Freud, 'On Narcissism: An Introduction,' 14:89.
35 Shakespeare, *Troilus and Cressida*, III.ii.16.
36 Freud, 'Mourning and Melancholia,' 14:245.

chapter ten

Dryden and the Canon: Absorbing and Rejecting the Burden of the Past

CEDRIC D. REVERAND II

Dryden's last major poetic work, *Fables Ancient and Modern* (1700), opens with a poem addressed to his patron's wife, the duchess of Ormond. Since the first fable to follow will be a translation of 'The Knight's Tale,' Dryden, naturally, begins by praising Chaucer. For now, I would like to call your attention to the name-dropping:

> The Bard who first adorn'd our Native Tongue
> Tun'd to his *British* Lyre this ancient Song:
> Which *Homer* might without a Blush reherse,
> And leaves a doubtful Palm in *Virgil's* Verse:
> He match'd their Beauties, where thy most excell;
> Of Love sung better, and of Arms as well.
> (20:48, ll. 1–6)[1]

This is a familiar routine, with Dryden linking Chaucer to the ancients so as to enrich the English literary tradition. From here, Dryden goes on to connect himself to Chaucer, claiming he is capable of understanding his predecessor's inspiration because 'Poets can divine each others Thought' (20:48, l. 12), a claim that, presumably, gives him the right to translate a kindred spirit. Thus, the great literary tradition that begins with Homer and Virgil does not just culminate in Chaucer, but continues to live in Chaucer's heir, Dryden. What I find intriguing about this tradition building is that Dryden is not merely putting Chaucer alongside Homer and Virgil, but is suggesting that Chaucer has improved upon these noble authors – he 'Of Love sung *better*, and of Arms as well.' And the act of improvement occurs because Chaucer, instead of merely borrowing from the ancients, adjusted his sources to the needs of the English. To use Dryden's own phrase, he '*Tun'd* to his *British* Lyre this ancient Song.' If, in his translation of Virgil, Dryden 'endeavour'd to make *Virgil* speak such *English*, as he wou'd himself have spoken, if he had been born in *England*, and in this present Age,' Dryden praises Chaucer for achieving basically the same thing, for Englishing the classical epic tradition.[2]

As this example implies, Dryden's attitude towards the literary past, both the distant past and the immediate English past, is complex. He is obviously relying upon older traditions to bolster his own authority, but even as he leans upon the past, he also seems to push it aside. I do not think we have fully appreciated this give-and-take, or rather take-and-leave, attitude. Instead, we have acknowledged either his appropriation of previous authors, or his radical departure from them. Although this habit of ennobling his own poetic enterprise by linking himself to great writers is a common strategy, it is seldom so explicitly argued. Spenser uses it when he echoes Homer, Virgil, Ovid, Horace, Tasso, Ariosto, and Chaucer; Pope does it more insistently when he translates Horace and includes the Latin original on the page facing his own translation so that we can see for ourselves that the brilliance on one side of the page matches that on the other; Milton, of course, does it relentlessly. But Dryden employs this same strategy with exceptional self-consciousness. He does so particularly in his self-justifying critical essays, such as his Preface to *The Conquest of Granada* (1672), where he attempts to defend his rhymed heroic plays by arguing that the genre and apparatus descend from Homer, Virgil, Statius, Ariosto, Tasso, Spenser, and Davenant, a list that covers the ground from ancient worthies, through the Renaissance, and then moves from Europe across the channel to his immediate English antecedents. And Dryden uses the strategy as well in his poetry, especially when the subject is poetry itself: Shadwell's failure is established partially by Dryden's making him heir to a lineage of dullards – Flecknoe, Heywood, Shirley, and Ogilby, to be specific. By implication, Dryden is aligned with the great dramatists, with whom Shadwell is urged to have no part, namely, Jonson and Fletcher of the previous generation, and Etherege and Sedley of the current age.

While Dryden's attempts to connect himself to the literary past may be obvious, his radical departures from his predecessors have received less critical attention, until recently, thanks to Howard Weinbrot's forceful arguments against considering Dryden and his successors as Augustans, either humbly worshipping the ancients, or beset by Bloomsian anxiety of influence and cringing deferentially. On the contrary, Dryden 'indicts classical culture as an inadequate model for a modern nation seeking its own civilization,'[3] and instead forges a new tradition that is ultimately self sufficient and distinctly British. As Weinbrot describes it, for Dryden, the basic pattern for dealing with classical culture in this progress towards a national poetic is 'discovery of the past, absorption of what is of value for a different modern culture, and rejection of what is useless or pernicious.'[4] While I agree that there is both absorption and rejection, I do not think the progress from the one to the other is quite as straightforward as Weinbrot implies. Instead, I think Dryden is doing both of these contrary activities at the same time, boldly relinquishing the past while simultaneously dragging it along with him. In part, this is because of his own ambivalence, not merely about the past, which he both admired and questioned, but also about his own culture, which, just as he began his career in all earnestness, was scraping itself off the ground after the less than sparkling Interregnum years. I do not think Dryden would have been all that confident about the literary world around him, although he certainly would have been hopeful about its future.

If we acknowledge that there is a simultaneous pull from the past and push against it, I think we may discover that some of the oddities, and the apparent inconsistencies, in Dryden's critical positions start making more sense; they are signs of an ongoing struggle to adjust to the past, or, returning to Dryden's own metaphor, to *tune* the ancient songs to his British lyre. We can detect this in his first critical essay, the *Essay of Dramatick Poesie* (written in 1665, published in 1667), where the very first topic addressed is the influence of the past, with Crites opening the discussion by proclaiming that the ancients are the foundation on which all is built. Since in his view of the modern scene 'Vertuous Emulation' has given way to sloppiness, he proposes to remind the company of 'all the Rules by which we practise the *Drama* at this day,' so 'that you may know how much you are indebted to those your Masters,' which he does by explaining and justifying the unities of time, place, and action, citing Aristotle as his source (17:16–17).[5] But no sooner does Dryden establish a rigorous neoclassicism, with Crites lamenting the nation's habit of straying from the rules, than he has Eugenius reject the argument, and along the way criticize classical plays as deficient – the plots are hackneyed and predictable, the characters limited in scope, the playwrights narrowly confined by the three unities, and so on. Eugenius ends his commentary by indicating that superior plays can be found in English literature by authors like Shakespeare and Fletcher, which means that by the end of the first dialogue we have moved away from the past towards the national poetic Weinbrot discusses.[6]

The second dialogue moves on to the comparative merits of French and English drama, but since one of the features that distinguishes the two is the regularity and correctness of the French, we find ourselves immediately back in another discussion of the unities, in the same sequence as before, first pro, and then con. Lisideius demonstrates the supposed superiority of the French over the English by praising their scrupulous adherence to the unity of time, their skill at limiting their plays to 'that very spot of ground where the Play is suppos'd to begin,' and their 'yet more conspicuous' concern for the 'unity of Action,' whereby they focus on a single plot and 'do not burden' their plays 'with under-plots, as the *English* do' (17:34). This sets up Neander's long defence of English drama. Against the single, direct French plot with its inevitable focus on one major character, he presents the multiple plots and many characters of the English plays, and against the unvarying mood entailed in having one unified action in a tragedy, which he refers to as 'a continued gravity' that 'keeps the spirit too much bent' (17:46), he places the happy mixture of tragedy and comedy that provides English drama with good pacing. In fact, English drama succeeds precisely because the English are indifferent to the rules; they achieve 'variety and copiousness' (17:46), while the French, 'by their servile observations of the unities of time and place ... have brought on themselves that dearth of Plot, and narrowness of Imagination, which may be observ'd in all their Playes' (17:51–2). Throughout the discussion, we get the sense that the unities are restrictive; Eugenius refers to the 'straight ... compass' in which the French 'have bounded their Plots and Characters' (17:25), and Lisideius praises French plays that are 'reduc'd' into the 'compass' (17:34) of twenty-four hours for the sake of the unity of time.

Neander emphasizes the constrictive nature of the rules all the more when he translates Corneille, cleverly relying upon a major French author to endorse the English side of the case: ''Tis easie for speculative persons to judge severely [says Corneille]; but if they would produce to publick view ten or twelve pieces of this nature, they would perhaps give more latitude to the Rules than I have done, when by experience they had known how much we are limited and constrain'd by them, and how many beauties of the Stage they banish'd from it' (17:51).[7] English drama is superior because it is free from such constraints, and this becomes not merely an aesthetic advantage, but a political one as well. The English are free from the rules because they are freeborn Englishmen, by temper and character unlikely to accept the limitations one would encounter in autocratic France, where the unities were not only a matter of style, but were also made mandatory by Cardinal Richelieu around 1636, a point that keeps surfacing in the *Essay.* Furthermore, Neander dares to claim that English drama is so clearly in the ascendance, that now the French can follow the example of the English: 'But of late years, *Moliere,* the younger *Corneille, Quinault,* and some others [Neander explains], have been imitating afar off the quick turns and graces of the *English* stage. They have mix'd their serious Playes with mirth, like our Tragicomedies, since the death of Cardinal *Richelieu,* which *Lisideius* and many others not observing, have commended that in them for a virtue which they themselves no longer practice' (17:45). Thanks to the English, it is now possible for future Corneilles to ignore the constraining rules that Corneille himself was obliged to obey. England's dramatists, by freeing French playwrights from the need to observe the unities, have brought English liberty to France, which, as I have suggested elsewhere, is one of the reasons that Dryden ends the *Essay* with the image of '*French* people ... merrily dancing in the open air' (17:80).[8] They are ostensibly celebrating the English naval victory, but in a way, they are also celebrating the cultural liberation of France that, according to Neander, great English playwrights have made possible.

The conclusion about the irrelevance of the unities seems to me inescapable. But then comes the oddity. Having demonstrated that English drama excels over the French because it ignores the dramatic unities, having made the unities restrictive, narrowing, obsolete, and above all, un-English, why then does Dryden's Neander select as his model play Ben Jonson's *Silent Woman,* instead of a play by Shakespeare, who 'of all Modern, and perhaps Ancient Poets, had the largest and most comprehensive soul' (17:55)? And what is it Neander chooses to praise first in this exemplary English play? 'To begin first with the length of the Action, it is so far from exceeding the compass of a Natural day, that it takes not up an Artificial one. 'Tis all included in the limits of three hours and a half, which is no more than is requir'd for the presentment of the Stage' (17:58).

After the unity of time comes the unity of place – 'the latitude of place is almost as little as you can imagine' – and then 'the continuity of Scenes' (17:58–9), that is, the unity of action. In fact, Jonson's ability to sustain a central action is better than what Corneille accomplishes in two of his best plays, and Jonson achieves the 'most noble of any pure unmix'd Comedy in any Language' (17:59), which runs contrary to Neander's earlier praise of the English for cleverly mixing tragedy with comedy. Jonson appears to be an exemplary English playwright because of his strict observation of all the virtues of drama that the English have successfully rejected and transcended.

I do not think this is a matter of confusion, but rather Dryden's attempt to have his cake and eat it too. Not only are the English happily free from the constraint of these artificial classical precepts to which the unfortunate French have been captive, not only have they helped, by their example, enrich drama and liberate the French from these narrowing rules, but they also can, if they desire, follow the rules even more regularly than the best of the French. Even though he has shaken off these alien rules, Dryden keeps returning to them, and he seems to have done this throughout his career. A decade later, for instance, when he decided to turn Shakespeare's *Antony and Cleopatra* into *All for Love*, an act that in itself is a celebration of his native heritage, he took pains to make his version as classical as possible. Having insisted that one of the advantages of the multi-plotted play is its great variety of characters, he now eliminated all sub-plots and reduced the number of characters to make the play tidier. Having demonstrated the inadequacy of the unities to meet the needs of the English stage, he now claimed that in his adaptation of Shakespeare 'the Unities of Time, Place and Action [are] more exactly observ'd, than, perhaps, the *English* Theater requires.'[9] Notice, even as he proudly announces the correctness he has achieved, he implies that it is both un-English and unnecessary. Notice also to whom Dryden turns as an authority for maintaining classical propriety: 'I have endeavoured in this Play to follow the practise of the Ancients, who, as Mr. *Rymer* has judiciously observ'd, are and ought to be our Masters' (13:18). Thomas Rymer? Next to Rymer, Crites looks hesitant and flexible.[10]

Another oddity in the *Essay* is the argument in favour of rhyme in serious drama with which it concludes, although I may be one of the few people to regard this as an oddity. Given the historical and biographical circumstances, advocating the use of rhyme makes perfect sense. Since King Charles was fond of rhymed plays, and since rhymed plays were now in possession of the stage, Dryden, ever the practical-minded author, was eager to acquiesce to popular tastes. When rhyme went out of fashion, he acquiesced just as readily. More specifically, the defence of rhyme is also a piece of self-promotion, since Dryden had just written two serious plays in rhyme: *The Indian Queen* (1664), a collaboration with Robert Howard, and its sequel, the much more popular *The Indian Emperour* (1665). Moreover, Neander's argument on behalf of rhyme is clever. Against the charge that rhyme is artificial, and thus contravenes the principle of imitating nature – Aristotle again serves as a standard – Neander argues that a serious play is more than just natural: it is 'Nature wrought up to an higher pitch' (17:74). Its characters are not 'common persons' who indulge in 'ordinary speaking' – presumably we ordinary mortals generally speak in blank verse – but rather elevated figures, who are 'exalted above the level of common converse' (17:74). Ordinary discourse would be inappropriate for noble persons; for them, 'Heroick Rhime is nearest Nature, as being the noblest kind of modern verse' (17:74). Thus, a verse form that is admittedly unnatural, by being natural for heroes, can be construed to satisfy Aristotle's requirement that tragedy be an imitation of nature. This amounts to another example of Dryden being non-classical and classical at the same time, endorsing the non-mimetic in practice as basically mimetic in spirit. What I find odd, however, is that the defence of rhyme runs counter to the thrust of the essay, which praises the English for escaping the binding, narrowing, restrictive unities that have so limited the French. Would not rhyme, like the unities, impose constraints rather than produce the freedom the essay endorses as part of England's accomplishment? Instead of adhering to rhyme, the English dramatist should, logically, 'dis-incumber' himself from rhyme, to use the word Dryden himself was to use later (1677), when he decided to employ blank verse in writing *All for Love* (13:18).

We become so accustomed to Neander having the last word (and in this case Neander's last word is more than three times the length of Crites's brief case against the use of rhyme) that we may not consider Crites's points all that carefully, knowing that he is a straw man. Let me revisit his statements for a moment. In criticizing the use of rhyme, Crites not only states that it is unnatural, but also that it is 'the most constrain'd' 'way of speaking,' and that rhyme in general exerts a 'great confinement to the imagination' (17:66–7). And what examples does he supply? 'To prove this, I might satisfie my self to tell you, how much in vain it is for you to strive against the stream of the peoples inclination; the greatest part of which are prepossess'd so much with those excellent Playes of *Shakespeare, Fletcher,* and *Ben. Johnson,* (which have been written out of Rhyme)' (17:65). I do not believe anybody has commented on this, but in this dialogue, Crites, with his objections to constraint and

confinement, and his reliance on the example of excellent English playwrights – Shakespeare, Fletcher, and Jonson, no less – sounds more like
Neander than Neander.

Aside from his practical concerns, which entail him justifying the
rhymed plays he is now writing, I think there is another factor at work
that nudges Dryden into allowing his final argument to run counter to
the guiding principles of the essay, and again it has to do with his
attempts to deal with the past, this time, the more immediate past. When
Neander makes the case for the English dramatists, he not only discusses
their specific qualities, but aligns them into a progression. He starts with
Shakespeare, 'the man who of all Modern, and perhaps Ancient Poets,
had the largest and most comprehensive soul,' to which he adds that the
Bard 'wanted learning,' but this does not count because he was 'naturally
learn'd.' He is also 'many times flat, insipid; his Comic wit degenerating
into clenches, his serious swelling into Bombast,' which again is of little
significance, since he is 'always great, when some great occasion is presented to him' (17:55). Next come Beaumont and Fletcher, and they
move things forward, because they 'had with the advantage of *Shakespeare*'s wit, which was their precedent, great natural gifts, improved by
study.' We learn that 'their Plots were generally more regular than *Shakespeare*'s,' that in their plays 'the *English* Language arriv'd to its highest per-
fection,' and that they are now more popular than Shakespeare because
of a certain 'gayety in their Comedies' and because of their lively representation of 'all the passions ... above all, Love' (17:56–7). Along with
Beaumont and Fletcher is Ben Jonson, 'the most learned and judicious
Writer which any Theater ever had,' who borrowed heavily from Roman
authors, resulting in weighty, serious tragedies, who gave us 'the most
correct Playes,' and whose 'proper Sphere' was 'Humour' (17:57–8),
which eventually leads to a discussion of how Jonsonian humour characters differ from Shakespearean comic characters. For Neander, English
drama evolves, moving from Shakespeare, the native genius, untutored,
clumsy in his construction, now obsolete in his diction, occasionally bom-
bastic and contrived, but unquestionably great, to authors who, following
Shakespeare as 'their precedent,' improved the theatre, smoothing the
language, adding learning, borrowing profitably from the ancients,
achieving regularity. If we take Shakespeare's greatness, Beaumont and
Fletcher's ease, gaiety, and quick wit, Jonson's strength, judiciousness,
and correctness, then we seem to have a polished, full, accomplished tradition, a tradition that also seems to have covered most of the available
genres, from tragedy, to comedy, to tragicomedy, to comedy of humours.

This raises a reasonable and fairly obvious question: what is left to be done by Dryden's generation?

Advocating rhymed heroic plays, then, can be seen as not just an appeal to popular taste, but rather as a deliberate departure from a well-established tradition into an unexplored genre, as Dryden's attempt to clear a little space for himself, to find a new territory, the larger ground of drama having already been covered by the last generation. The geographical metaphor is not mine, but Neander's, in a passage that has been too little emphasized: 'We acknowledge them our Fathers in wit, but they have ruin'd their Estates themselves before they came to their childrens hands. There is scarce an Humour, a Character, or any kind of Plot, which they have not us'd. All comes sullied or wasted to us ... This therefore will be a good Argument to us either not to write at all, or to attempt some other way' (17:73).

He admits that it would be 'presumptuous' of the living dramatists 'to contend' with the dead, and then defensively concludes that 'this way of writing in Verse, they have onely left free to us' (17:72–3).[11] I think it fair to say that at this point Neander sounds anxious about the past and worried about how modern playwrights are to proceed. Yet it was only a few pages ago that this same Neander praised the drama of this new age extravagantly. After the Civil War, and after the 'barbarous race of men' who 'buried the Muses' during the Interregnum, came 'the restoration of our happiness, [wherein] we see reviv'd Poesie lifting up its head, & already shaking off the rubbish which lay so heavy on it. We have seen since His Majesties return, many Dramatick Poems which yield not to those of any forreign Nation' (17:63).

Neander even states that, admitting some blemishes in the plays 'made within these seven years' (17:64), we can nonetheless 'be thus equal to ourselves,' that is, that modern dramatists can be every bit as great as those of the last generation. He expands on the subject: 'I think it may be permitted me to say, that as it is no less'ning to us to yield to some Playes, and those not many of our own Nation in the last Age, so can it be no addition to pronounce of our present Poets that they have far surpass'd all the Ancients, and the Modern Writers of other Countreys' (17:64). Now the match between past and present appears to be a tie. What we have, then, is an apparently anxious Neander, overwhelmed by the burden of his immediate antecedents, hesitant about how modern dramatists are 'to write at all' in the wake of the oppressively successful tradition that has preceded them, as well as a confident Neander proclaiming that this new generation, if it does not outreach the plays of the previous generation, at least equals them, while surpassing all non-English drama, stretching back to the ancients.[12]

  · Like his carefully elaborated rejection of the alien dramatic unities, along with his endorsement of those unities when convenient, this reluctance about how the present age is to proceed, together with his unbridled enthusiasm for its grand accomplishments, can perhaps be better understood as another reflection of his complex, give-and-take attitude towards the past. It seems to me that Dryden is contradictory because he is blurring the distinction between past and present, although our hindsight may initially obscure this from us. We know how Restoration drama is going to turn out, and when we hear Neander affirm the superiority of 'our present poets,' we can sympathize with his rallying cry for this emerging national poetic. But if we ask ourselves just exactly who were these brilliant new dramatists in those early years – this would be 1660–5 – we discover a long list of the eminently forgettable, including Thomas Jordan, John Tatham, Thomas Porter, Sir Samuel Tuke, Richard Rhodes, and George Digby.[13] Are these the luminaries who have 'revived poesy' and who 'have far surpassed all the Ancients, and the modern writers of other countries'?

  Hardly. The new generation of good dramatists has not yet arrived. However, there *is* a thriving English stage 'since his Majesty's return,' a stage filled primarily with plays from the past. When the theatres reopened in May 1660, they depended primarily on revivals, a good way of luring back audiences, since the old plays were a known commodity, like modern reruns of television sitcoms. The 1660–1 season, for example, included eight performances of Shakespeare, thirteen of Beaumont and Fletcher, fifteen of Fletcher alone, two more Fletcher collaborations, one with William Rowley, the other with Philip Massinger, and ten performances of Ben Jonson. There were five performances of James Shirley, twenty-one of Davenant, most of them the two-part *Siege of Rhodes*, Shirley and Davenant being holdovers from the last age who were still alive but at the ends of their careers. For the 1660–1 and 1661–2 seasons, the ratio of revivals to original plays was about eight to one. By the next season, 1662–3, the balance of new plays to revivals was about even, remaining that way in 1663–4, with the moderns beginning to pull ahead slightly in the 1664–5 season, at which point the playhouses were closed because of the plague. If we look at the rough frequency of productions during the period from 1660 to the closing of the playhouses in 1665, we discover that the leading playwrights were Fletcher, followed by Shakespeare, then by the collaboration of Beaumont and Fletcher, then Ben

Jonson, which explains why these are the very playwrights under discussion in the *Essay*.[14] Dryden is not recalling an earlier time, and with critical detachment calmly reflecting on its merits; rather, he is surveying the current theatrical scene. Little wonder Neander sounds apprehensive; although these authors are long dead, they are nonetheless active and are the ones against whom fledgling playwrights, like Dryden, are competing. And we might note that from the 1662–3 through the 1664–5 seasons, the two leading playwrights, tied with a total of fifteen productions each, are Shakespeare and Dryden. If elsewhere in the *Essay* Dryden shows a capacity for relinquishing the past while at the same time dragging it along behind him, the historical circumstances surrounding the early Restoration stage have done this for him by importing so much of the past into the present. In effect, the past *is* the present, which means that living dramatists can be apprehensive about how to compete with their fathers, and at the same time be proud that their fellow moderns, Shakespeare, Beaumont, Fletcher, and Jonson, have enriched the stage and helped the English triumph over the French, over all nations, and over the ancients. Little wonder that these modern poets can be said to equal those greats of the last generation; they *are* the last generation.[15]

If we move ahead a few years, to 1672 and Dryden's 'Defence of the Epilogue,' which is included in the published version of *The Conquest of Granada*, we can detect an interesting shift in attitude. The essay's subtitle, 'Or *An Essay on the* Dramatique Poetry *of the last Age*,' suggests we are going to revisit some of the issues raised in the *Essay of Dramatick Poesie*, only this time the topic is not just the state of drama, but, in particular, the relationship of the current age to the last one. As Dryden states at the outset, he feels 'oblig'd by many reasons to write somewhat concerning our present Playes, and those of our predecessors on the *English* stage' (11:203), and one of the many reasons may be that he has not satisfactorily come to grips with the problems he had raised earlier and now wants to try again. This time, we notice two things immediately: first, by 'the present age,' Dryden means the present age, not the one that includes Shakespeare and company; second, the present age is unambiguously better than the past. It is better because things progress, and what he sees now is '*An improvement of our Wit, Language, and Conversation: or, an alteration in them for the better*' (11:204) – an improvement *and* an alteration for the better as well (Dryden even italicizes this phrase for further emphasis). Since language has improved, plays have improved also, and he places this in the broader context of improvement across a whole culture: 'I profess,' he says, 'to have no other ambition in this Essay, than that Poetry may not go backward, when all other Arts and Sciences are advancing' (11:203).

With progress as his theme, Dryden examines authors of the last age, when poetry was 'if not in its infancy among us, at least not arriv'd to its vigor and maturity' (11:206), discussing their shortcomings not only in wit, language, and conversation, but also in sense, plotting, credibility, and consistency. He pays special attention to 'manners' (falling under the heading of conversation), which is something like propriety and courtliness, associated with the gallantry that Charles II brought back to England, a marked improvement over the 'ill-bred and Clownish' wit employed by poets who, because they were 'bred in an unpolish'd Age,' never had the opportunity to frequent the court and converse with gentlemen (11:215–16). Dryden's review of the ignorant generation includes remarks on Shakespeare's false wit and low expressions, Fletcher's weak plotting and awkward mixture of humour and pathos, Jonson's unfortunate 'meanness of expression' (11:210) and indulgence in wordplay. All of them are consistently guilty of lapses in decorum, and 'in every page' of Shakespeare and Fletcher one finds 'either some Solecism of Speech, or some notorious flaw in Sence' (11:205). The criticism sounds like a replay of some of the remarks in the *Essay of Dramatick Poesie*, only now, because of his notion about progress, Dryden can offer a historical explanation for the faults of the last generation: 'these absurdities, which those Poets committed, may more properly be call'd the Ages fault than theirs' (11:207).

Having set up this contrast between the more primitive times and the 'improv'd and refin'd' (11:204) present, Dryden seems to be leaving the great masters behind and moving unabashedly forward. However, when he gets beyond his survey of cultural progress, and beyond the individual criticisms, when he touches upon the question of comparative quality and accomplishment, Dryden is not quite so complete the progressive as we might expect. Consider this comment, towards the end of the essay: 'But, to conclude with what brevity I can; I will only add this in defence of our present Writers, that if they reach not some excellencies of *Ben. Jonson*; (which no Age, I am confident, ever shall) yet, at least, they are above that meanness of thought which I have tax'd, and which is frequent in him' (11:215). Dryden is having it both ways again: the moderns do not reach the excellencies of Ben Jonson, and yet they are all superior to him at the same time. The same with Shakespeare: '*Shakespear*, who many times has written better than any Poet, in any Language, is yet so far from writing Wit always, or expressing that Wit according to the Dignity of the

Subject, that he writes in many places, below the dullest Writer of ours, or of any precedent Age' (11: 212–13).

Because of the superior modern culture, the dullest of moderns will never commit the lapses that abound in Shakespeare, and yet Shakespeare remains 'better than any Poet, in any Language.' We end up with a superior present that has its share of dull writers, and an inferior past that can claim unbeatable geniuses. Even though the main argument in the 'Defence' is for '*an improvement ... or, an alternation ... for the better*' in drama of the present over that of the past, Dryden cannot relinquish the inferior past with its superior poets.[16] The fact that his ringing defence of the present does not so much as mention a single modern play tends to mitigate his central argument, and one could reasonably conclude that if defending the present depends upon attacking the past, this may not be so much a move forward as another effort at ground clearing.[17]

While the apparent step forward towards confidence in the modern tradition may not have been quite so far forward as we anticipated, a few years later, Dryden boldly stepped backwards. Thomas Rymer had published *Tragedies of the Last Age* in 1677, an uncompromising insistence on the necessity of the supposedly classical rules, together with a castigation of English playwrights for straying from the straight and narrow, and Dryden, apparently taken aback by the force of Rymer's argument, responded in 'The Grounds of Criticism in Tragedy,' published as part of the Preface to *Troilus and Cressida* in 1679.[18] There are no claims for the superiority of the present age here, no boasts about the variety, copiousness, or liveliness that characterize the vibrant English tradition. Instead, Dryden marches through an orderly summary of Aristotle, beginning with the definition of tragedy as imitation of an action, and that would be a single action – that is, no 'double action[s]' as one finds in 'all *Shakespears* Historical Plays.' The events in the play, he says, should be probable and the plot consequential, with 'a natural beginning, a middle, and an end,' rather than 'accident ... heap'd upon accident' (13:230). The hero should be primarily virtuous rather than wicked, but he should not be perfect. The play should invoke pity and fear. And so it goes, strictly by the book, with Dryden sounding much more like Crites than Neander. The essay even ends with Dryden translating Rapin praising the classical rules because they 'reduce Nature into Method' and help regulate the potentially dangerous fancy (13:248). Not only are reduction and regulation virtues now, but they are to be all the more respected because they are recommended by a French critic.

The weight of the classical tradition, which we thought Neander had tossed aside, is once more bearing down on Dryden. One could say he responds to Rymer by employing a flanking manoeuvre rather than a head-on approach: he will endorse Rymer's classical precepts, and yet reject his conclusions about the English stage; and he will again blur the past and the present. As he proceeds to discuss Aristotle, Dryden fleshes out his summary with illustrations, and when he talks about specific authors, we can see him mingling past and present, covering Sophocles, Euripides, Fletcher, Shakespeare, and Jonson, going back and forth, criticizing and praising. In the process, Dryden rescues the moderns from Rymer's dismissal by putting them on the same plane as the ancients. But there is more to this blurring. We might also notice that, with respect to classical principles, the ancients sometimes behave surprisingly like moderns. For instance, Dryden explains Aristotle's idea that a play should have '*but one single action*,' immediately pointing out that this principle '*condemns all* Shakespears *Historical Plays*,' to which he adds his own *Marriage A-la-Mode* as another example of an incorrect 'two action' play (13:229–30).[19] This is what we would expect of the unclassical English. But then, Dryden says that 'Terence *made an innovation*' in his Roman plays: '*all his Plays have double Actions*' (13:230), which he sometimes achieved by translating and then weaving together two Greek comedies. Thus, the classical principle that condemns Shakespeare and Dryden turns out to be ignored by a classical dramatist, who instead relies upon double actions, which is a deliberate innovation rather than a failing. Multiplicity of plot, a feature associated with the English stage, since it appears in the works of an ancient Roman playwright, has just become a classical practice.

Dryden is equally adept at blurring things from the other direction; in addition to making the ancient authors look like modern practitioners, he can make contemporary authors seem classical. In discussing the unities, under the heading of '*the mechanic beauties of the Plot*,' Dryden repeats the observations from the *Essay of Dramatick Poesie* about how Shakespeare was deficient in observing the unities, while 'Ben. Jonson *reform'd those errors*' (13:233–4). But then, he reverses field, immediately adding that Shakespeare achieved classical regularity in *The Merry Wives of Windsor* before Jonson, and furthermore, that '*amongst all the Tragedies of* Sophocles, *there is but one*, Oedipus,' that is regular (13:234). It would appear, then, that even those who do not observe the unities, like Shakespeare, sometimes do, and those who do observe the unities, like Sophocles, usually don't. This is ludicrous, since the English theatre, as Neander was once proud to proclaim, is enriched by a multiplicity of characters and intertwining plots, and it takes considerable stretching to find a play by Shakespeare that observes the unities. (*Merry Wives*, by the way, does not: it has numerous scene changes and the events of the play take place over three days, not one.) Dryden is hedging his bets, endorsing classical principles while making them both optional and non-classical. Along the way, he has, in effect, made the moderns seem like ancients, and the ancients like moderns; this is not so much discarding the past as it is fusing with it.

As we see Dryden returning time and again to discussions of classical principles and of the faults and merits of the last generation of poets, I think it becomes clear that he is struggling with the past, while it is equally clear that he is trying to endorse the modern tradition, to distinguish it both from the classical world and from the more immediate last age. But of course, all this is in the early part of Dryden's career (1665–79); most of his significant works still lie ahead of him. One can reasonably expect Dryden to be more confident in the emergent tradition once both he and the poetic tradition had more fully emerged. And once his career was in full stride, from the 1680s forward, we notice him turning increasingly to translations, daring to rewrite, adjust, adapt, and correct the hallowed worthies, whether the author be Chaucer, with his 'obsolete' language and unequal numbers, which make him 'a rough Diamond' that 'must first be polish'd e're he shines,' or the unwieldy and uneven Shakespeare, or Juvenal, or Persius, Horace, Ovid, Boccaccio, or Virgil.[20] Surely the man who translated Virgil had to be confident in his ability to match the epic author, as well as confident in the medium of English poetry and the couplet to sustain a major classical epic. It would appear that the literary estate no longer seemed to have been ruined by the fathers before the sons could take possession; now it looked more like a country lying open, without defence, ready for the enterprising poet to make some landscaping improvements.

By the end of his career, when there was little reason for him to feel anxious and plenty of reason to feel confident, we would expect Dryden to deal with the past differently, and in fact he does ... and he doesn't. I would argue that he still uses the past in the same way, not merely rejecting it, but departing from it while pulling it along behind him, but his purpose has changed. In a manner of speaking, instead of being on the defensive, he goes on the offensive, using the strategy primarily to promote himself and the native tradition he is in the process of defining. In looking at Dryden's 1693 poem 'To Congreve' (published in 1694), I cannot help but be struck by the return of this topic, present age versus past, in the opening couplet, and it quickly becomes clear that this new, self-sufficient literary tradition has finally triumphed: 'Well then; the promis'd hour is come at last; / The present Age of Wit obscures the past' (4:432, ll. 1–2).

We seem to be picking up the argument about the superiority of the present age just where we left it in 'Defence of the Epilogue' twenty-one years earlier, although if the arrival of the present age is also 'the pro-mis'd hour,' the implication is that Congreve's appearance, as the embodiment of modern dramatic accomplishments, is like the Second Coming. This is more than an improvement, or even an alteration for the better; it is complete fulfilment. As Dryden proceeds, he gives a brief survey of the English stage, beginning with the 'Strong ... Syres' before the Interregnum, the 'Gyant Race, before the Flood' (4:432, ll. 3–5), moving quickly to the Restoration and, using an agricultural meta-phor, giving Charles II credit for cultivating the arts in the wake of the devastating Puritan 'Flood':

> And thus, when *Charles* Return'd, our Empire stood.
> Like *Janus* he the stubborn Soil manur'd,
> With Rules of Husbandry the rankness cur'd:
> Tam'd us to manners, when the Stage was rude;
> And boistrous *English* Wit, with Art indu'd.
> Our Age was cultivated thus at length.
>   (4:432, ll. 6–11)

There is no quibbling with authors from the past, nor are there apolo-gies for the underachieving present with its occasional dull writers. It appears that the past is actually past, and the present is, as we can see, nourished, cured, tamed, endowed with art, 'cultivated ... at length.'

But wait. The promised hour has not yet arrived; it will arrive only when Congreve appears, later in the poem. Dryden has to back up:

> Our Age was cultivated thus at length;
> But what we gain'd in skill we lost in strength.
> Our Builders were, with want of Genius, curst;
> The second Temple was not like the first:
> Till You, the best *Vitruvius*, come at length;
> Our Beauties equal; but excel our strength.
>   (4:432, ll. 11–16)

There we are again: the all-important 'but.' After opening the poem with unequivocal praise of the perfected present, a present that obscures the past, Dryden establishes a balance whereby not only is the present better than the past, but the past is also better than the present. While the previous age was superior 'in strength,' the present is superior in 'skill,' and one is reminded of Dryden's commentary in the 'Defence of the Epilogue' on the increase in courtliness, the refinement of language, and the improvement of wit that occurred when Charles returned and brought with him a habit of gallantry and 'excellency of manners' (11:216). This division of qualities between generations sets up the introduction of Congreve, who, as we see, combines the distinctive strengths of both past and present. In terms of the architectural metaphor, after being likened to Vitruvius, he is then likened to a properly designed Vitruvian building, 'Firm *Dorique* Pillars' forming the base, with 'Fair *Corinthian*' columns above: 'Thus all below is Strength,' the accomplishment of the last age, 'and all above is Grace' (4:432, ll. 17–19), the achievement of the present.

Dryden now turns to a specific account of how Congreve is to combine strength and grace, leaving the architectural metaphor behind, and instead naming names to give us a sense of what these features mean in literary terms:

> In easie Dialogue is *Fletcher*'s Praise:
> He mov'd the mind, but had not power to raise.
> Great *Johnson* did by strength of Judgment please:
> Yet doubling *Fletcher*'s Force, he wants his Ease.
> ....
> But both to *Congreve* justly shall submit,
> One match'd in Judgment, both o-er match'd in Wit.
>
> (4:432, ll. 20–3, 26–7)

Dryden supports his claim for Congreve's accomplishments by making him the combination of his predecessors' virtues, with the strength of Jonson, the ease of Fletcher, and, a little later on, the genius of Shakespeare (4:433, ll. 61–3), the very authors who figured so prominently in the *Essay of Dramatick Poesie*, when the speakers were considering the comparative merits of the earlier authors and the moderns. Here, the authors of the last age are not assessed, judged, or criticized, because they are not regarded as having used up literary possibilities, thereby inhibiting their would-be successors; instead, they are an enabling force, a justification. What makes Congreve so complete is that he is the sum of the best from the past.

Nor is Dryden finished naming names:

> In Him [Congreve] all Beauties of this Age we see;
> *Etherege* his Courtship, *Southern*'s Purity;
> The Satire, Wit, and Strength of Manly *Witcherly*.
> All this in blooming Youth you have Atchiev'd.
>
> (4:432–3, ll. 28–31)

As we would expect, Congreve is also the sum of the best from the moderns. Dryden is essentially assembling his own personal canon, not with a new tradition distinct from the old, but rather combining the best from the old with the best from the new, a tradition in which Dryden plays a leading role, which becomes clear in the next verse paragraph. Now that he has been deposed as Poet Laureate, he wishes that he could bequeath his wreath to Congreve:

> Oh that your Brows my Lawrel had sustain'd,
> Well had I been Depos'd, if You had reign'd!
> The Father had descended for the Son;
> For only You are lineal to the Throne.
>
> (4:433, ll. 41–4)

The laureateship having gone to Shadwell, Dryden in a way compensates by bestowing the true laurel wreath, his laurel, upon Congreve, assuming that the young playwright will value Dryden's approval more than a shallow official honour. Thus, the listing of names is ultimately a piece of self-promotion, for the 'Native Store' (4:433, l. 61) that Congreve embodies contains Fletcher, Johnson, Shakespeare, Etherege, Southerne, Wycherley, and Dryden – it also explicitly excludes Shadwell – with past and present combined into a continuity. No longer is this a matter of fathers exhausting the estate and leaving their rightful heirs empty-handed, but of Dryden acting as 'The Father' receiving the heritage from the past and passing it on intact to 'the Son' who is 'lineal to the Throne.'

The poem to Congreve can serve as a representative example of Dryden's attitude towards the past late in his career. The past no longer serves as an inhibiting force, but now as a resource, and Dryden no longer struggles to wrench free from it. He assumes that the present is distinct and superior, but the promised hour that obscures the past happens to have subsumed the past in the process. The final major works in his career, which are much too long to discuss here, exhibit the same pattern, now on a grand scale. I am referring to his translation of Virgil in 1697 – not just the *Aeneid*, but also the *Eclogues* and the *Georgics*, that is, all of Virgil – followed by his great collection primarily of translations, *Fables Ancient and Modern*. In effect, these serve as a final statement by the great poet, and I think it significant that in the late works Dryden should turn to translations. The present now, with Dryden in command, has not merely broken away from the past, but has appropriated the past, with Dryden first Englishing Virgil, making Virgil speak as if he were alive now, or, making Virgil Dryden, which is the same thing. And *Fables*, which contains eight translations from Ovid, three from Boccaccio, and five from Chaucer, is Dryden's *Metamorphoses*, and Dryden's *Decameron*, and Dryden's *Canterbury Tales*. I am among those who regard these as deeply original works, not merely adaptations, and I believe scholars are beginning to study them as something more than unimaginative exercises; and if they are original works, part of the distinctly English tradition that has matured during the Restoration, it is worth noting that they do not so much break forth from the past as they absorb it and renew it.

Notes

1 The text used for quotations from all of Dryden's poetry and prose is that of *The Works of John Dryden*, ed. E.N. Hooker, H.P. Swedenberg, Jr, et al., 20 vols. (Berkeley: University of California Press 1956–2000) (hereafter cited as *California Dryden*). Parenthetical citations throughout the essay allude to this text.

2 Dryden, Preface to the *Aeneis. California Dryden*, 5:330–1.

3 Howard D. Weinbrot, *Britannia's Issue* (Cambridge: Cambridge University Press 1993), 6. Since Weinbrot is trying to dislodge a tenacious commonplace about Dryden and Pope being devotees of the original Augustan age, dutifully echoing classical accomplishments, he has to emphasize the breaking away, the innovation, and not dwell on the acts of relying on the past. He is careful to acknowledge that these authors borrowed from the past as well, but this is regarded as an inevitable inheritance, of less significance than the innovations. I am arguing that Dryden uses the past as a resource, not just

borrowing from it, but strategically, and at times cagily, incorporating elements from earlier traditions even as he seems to be moving off independently into new directions.

4 Weinbrot, *Britannia's Issue*, 331. Weinbrot is speaking specifically of the development of the English ode, but the pattern is equally applicable in general to the development of the national tradition.

5 Eugenius's argument about the unities not originating in Aristotle is based on Corneille's third *Discours*, as George Watson points out in his Everyman Library edition of *John Dryden: Of Dramatic Poesy and Other Critical Essays*, 2 vols. (London: E.P. Dent 1962), 1:36n. In a footnote that has long puzzled me, Watson observes that Crites's 'extraction of the three dramatic unities from Aristotle' is erroneous, but that this misreading, 'though blatant, was current for some two centuries, until Johnson in his preface to Shakespeare (1765) dismissed it as a logical absurdity in a few vigorous paragraphs' (27n). Thus, Dryden's spokesman is held accountable for successfully importing and then imposing this classical artificiality on an entire culture for the next hundred years. Watson seems not to have noticed that far from lasting for a century, this blatant misreading lasts for about two pages, since Dryden's next speaker, Eugenius, just like Watson, immediately explains that the unities are not in Aristotle, and that they are, instead, imposed by inventive Renaissance commentators, especially the French.

6 For the sake of clarity, let me reinforce what Phillip Harth persuasively argued back in 1968, and that Howard Weinbrot felt necessary to reargue as recently as 1995, namely, that this essay is not a waffling discussion of different critical positions with the issues left unresolved, but rather an essay sceptical in its procedure, but clear in its conclusions. Dryden prefers the moderns to the ancients, insists on the superiority of English dramatists to the French, and advocates the use of rhyme in tragedy. By the end of the essay, when the disputants bump into the stairs at Somerset House, they have won a victory for England and its dramatic tradition, parallel to the military victory that the English navy has achieved over the Dutch. See Harth, *Contexts of Dryden's Thought* (Chicago: University of Chicago Press 1968), 34, and Weinbrot, *Britannia's Issue*, 150–92.

7 The *California Dryden* text of the *Essay of Dramatick Poesie* used here is based on the second edition (1684); where this text reads 'limited and constrain'd,' the first edition (published in 1667, although dated 1668), somewhat more graphically, has 'bound up and constrain'd.'

8 In 'Dryden's "Essay of Dramatick Poesie": The Poet and the World of Affairs,' *SEL* 22 (1982), 375–93.

9 Dryden, Preface to *All for Love. California Dryden* 13:10.

10 As late as 1697, Dryden was still endorsing and rejecting the unities simultaneously; in his Dedication to his translation of the *Aeneid*, he noted that Aristotle derived the 'many Rules of imitating Nature' from Homer's epics; he then advocated a flexible application of the rules, again citing Corneille, who thought it 'better a Mechanick Rule were stretch'd or broken, than a great Beauty were omitted' (*California Dryden* 5:268–70), which in essence repeats Neander's argument from thirty years earlier.

11 Weinbrot, who argues insistently against the anxiety of influence in *Britannia's Issue*, does not deal with this passage where Neander worries about the dramatic estate being exhausted. Weinbrot does, however, quote passages before and after what I have quoted above (*Britannia*, 189–90), where Neander claims that every age is different, and that, although we cannot equal Jonson, Fletcher, and Shakespeare, were they alive now, 'they could never equal themselves' either (17:72–3). For Weinbrot, Neander confidently regards the current age as superior, as 'improved in its opportunities' (189), but Dryden's remarks about an estate that has been used up, making it difficult for the would-be heirs to 'write at all,' suggest to me something less than confidence.

12 Weinbrot, who cites these very passages while discussing Dryden's endorsement of the present age, happily describes Neander's outburst in favour of the moderns as 'an enthusiastic fit' (*Britannia's Issue*, 189).

13 In talking about the newly revived stage, Dryden refers to the period as 'these seven years,' which he does to cover the time from the Restoration itself until the 1667 publication of the *Essay*, but in fact the period under discussion would have to have been five years, from the reopening of the playhouses in May 1660 to their closing, because of the plague, on 5 June 1665. When the theatres closed, Dryden, like many of his compatriots, retreated to the countryside, and it was there, somewhere 'between the summer of 1665 and the late autumn of 1666,' that he wrote the *Essay of Dramatick Poesie*, according to James Anderson Winn, in *John Dryden and His World* (New Haven and London: Yale University Press 1987), 159. By 1684, when the second edition of the *Essay* was published, this passage praising modern playwrights would have had a different impact, since by that time numerous talents had obviously emerged. However, the passage praising the Restoration stage appears in the first edition of 1667, when there was barely anything we would now regard as a thriving new dramatic tradition. The information in this and the next paragraph about authors and the frequency of play production is based on the calendars in *The London Stage: 1660–1800*, Part 1: *1660–1700*, ed. William Van Lennep (Carbondale: Southern Illinois University Press 1965).

14 William Davenant is next in frequency after Ben Jonson, if we count each
   production of *The Siege of Rhodes*, which is in two parts, as one performance,
   not two.

15 Earl Miner, in his 'Introduction: Borrowed Plumage, Varied Umbrage,' from
   Literary Transmission and Authority (Cambridge: Cambridge University Press
   1993), 1–26, regards Harold Bloom's 'anxiety of influence' as an inappropriate and 'monolithic' (10) modern imposition on the past, and with respect
   to Dryden prefers to consider the issue more flexibly, as a complex and varie-
   gated interrelationship with past authors that can be benign, neutral, com-
   petitive, or negative, with Dryden receiving as well as rejecting and
   sometimes ignoring. Miner also claims that authors are generally much
   more concerned with living rivals than dead antecedents. I agree with Miner
   on both points. Dryden's 'anxiety' – and it is generally both more, and less,
   than just anxiety – occurs when he considers rivals, not when he confronts
   the long dead. However, this distinction becomes problematic in the 1660s,
   when the leading 'contemporary' playwrights competing against Dryden
   happen to be dead authors.

16 Similarly, Jennifer Brady, in 'Dryden and Negotiations of Literary Succession
   and Precession,' from *Literary Transmission and Authority*, 27–54, takes issue
   with the notion of anxiety of influence and instead emphasizes the give and
   take involved in what she calls 'the distinctly unBloomsian ideal of affirming
   influence' (51). Speaking of Dryden's critical prose of the 1660s through
   1670s, she remarks: 'At no point does Dryden endorse the accomplishments
   of his own age without qualifying contemporary claims to superiority. In the
   early essays and prefaces, his most optimistic stances are couched in condi-
   tionals and concessives. By the late 1670s, even these tempered expressions
   of high self-regard undergo a significant retrenchment, when he confronts
   his fear that the fathers have not been restored in the sons ... Dryden's
   approach to his fathers typically veers between a mutually affirmative filial
   devotion and an abashed sense of their achieved greatness' (34–5).

17 We get a further hint of Dryden's defensiveness from a comment he makes
   to justify his criticizing Ben Jonson: 'And I once more beg the Readers par-
   don, for accusing him of them [i.e., errors]. Onely let him consider that I
   live in an age where my least faults are severely censur'd: and that I have no
   way left to extenuate my failings but by showing as great in those whom we
   admire' (11:207). This is good-humoured and self-deprecating, to be sure,
   but within the remark is a hint of self-consciousness. Dryden criticizes
   because he is being criticized, and he can compensate for this inconvenience
   by passing it along to others, not so much to reduce recognized authors to

his level as to raise himself to theirs by making them all fellow-travellers on the literary journey, subject to similar hazards.

18 Dryden's more immediate response to Rymer was in the form of sketchy notes written in the margin of his own copy of *Tragedies of the Last Age*, published posthumously as 'Heads of An Answer to Rymer' (1711). The notes reveal Dryden attempting to rebut Rymer's inflexible classicism, experimenting with different lines of attack, none of which seems to work, which may explain why the essay was never finished. Much as he wanted to play Neander and defeat Crites again, he could not quite muster up arguments sufficient to the task. One could consider 'The Grounds of Criticism' as a second attempt in the battle against Rymer, using a different approach.

19 To make matters all the more complicated, Dryden no sooner admits to committing a grievous Shakespearean sin of double plots than he adds that his version of *Oedipus* (written with Nathaniel Lee) is a proper example of unified design; it has plot and sub-plot, but it 'cannot properly be said to be two Actions,' because of a 'necessary dependence' of one plot on the other (13:230). In other words, he follows the superior English practice of double plots, and strains to explain that this is really a unified, single action, and thus classical in spirit.

20 Dryden, Preface to *Fables Ancient and Modern. California Dryden*, 7:41, 34, 39–40.

chapter eleven

'Betwixt two Ages cast': Theatrical Dryden

DEBORAH PAYNE FISK

It is easy to forget amidst postmodern incarnations of Dryden that he was, to use that shopworn but nonetheless apt phrase, the consummate 'man of the theatre,' and his ease with performance put him in a singular position among Restoration dramatists. No other playwright in the period is so closely associated with every aspect of production, from scene design, to casting, to rehearsal. In part, Dryden's affinity for collaboration can be explained by his good nature: he enjoyed the camaraderie of the theatre, as well as the company of men and women who knew their craft.[1] The collaborative impulse in Dryden can also be explained by his unique position in the marketplace of late-seventeenth-century theatre: he married Restoration authorship to a residual model of playwriting derived from the pre–Civil War theatre. Like most unions of opposing natures, the result was tempestuous, exciting, and ultimately doomed. Dryden clearly revelled in the theatre, embracing with gusto the unprecedented opportunity of making the drama anew after an eighteen-year closure. As youthful passion faded, he increasingly voiced reservations about his profession, this marriage of the old and the new. For several years in the late 1680s, Dryden effected something of a separation from the stage, returning briefly until death in 1700 released him from a relationship that for some time, to indulge an anachronistic expression, 'had not served his needs.'

From the beginning, Dryden's age predestined him to a singular model of dramatic authorship. Born in 1631, Dryden was far closer in years to the gentlemen dramatists who dominated the first decade of the Restoration theatre, men like Roger Boyle, the earl of Orrery (1621), Sir Rob-

ert Howard (1626), or George Villiers, duke of Buckingham (1628), than
he was to the professional dramatists who wrote in the 1670s and 1680s.
He did not, of course, share the social standing of the gentlemen amateurs.[2] Dryden also got an early start, being the sole professional playwright in the 1660s, with the exception of Thomas Shadwell (who
produced his first play five years after Dryden's initial effort). Dryden was
the only professional dramatist privileged to work alongside older theatre practitioners who knew the Caroline stage and could relate stories
about Shakespeare, Jonson, Fletcher, and other members of 'the Gyant
Race, before the Flood,' as Dryden styled them in the 1694 epistle to
Congreve.[3] At the King's Company, where Dryden was a shareholder
until 1678, he worked with Michael Mohun, Robert Shatterell, and Theophilus Bird. All of these men trained as boy actors under Christopher
Beeston at the Cockpit Theatre and collectively constituted an important
link to the drama of the 1630s.

Thomas Killigrew, who managed the King's Company until 1676, provided another important connection to the early English stage. The
author of two lacklustre plays for the commercial theatre, *The Parson's
Wedding* (1640?) and *The Prisoners* (1641), Killigrew continued to write
closet dramas for the queen's entourage while they were wandering the
Continent during the Interregnum. Despite this meagre professional
experience, Killigrew was, as we know from Pepys's *Diary*, given to reminiscences about the 'old days'; and he was sharply observant of the differences between the Caroline stage and the new Restoration theatre.
On one occasion he stressed to Pepys the differences between now and
then: wax, not tallow, candles; 'all things civil, no rudeness anywhere;
then, as in a bear-garden'; now, ten fiddlers rather than a paltry two or
three musicians. Best of all, Killigrew stressed, now the king and all 'civil
people' attend the theatre.[4] On another occasion he boasted of plans to
stage four operas a year at a nursery in Moorfields 'where we shall have
the best Scenes and Machines, the best Musique, and everything as Magnificent as is in Christendome.'[5]

Beyond the King's Company, Dryden met other men who knew the
pre-war theatre well. William Cavendish, duke of Newcastle, with whom
Dryden co-authored *Sir Martin Mar-all* (1667), self-consciously modelled
his plays after the 'humours' comedies of his former client, Ben Jonson.
The most munificent literary patron in the 1630s, Newcastle supported
dramatists such as Brome and Shirley, in addition to a host of non-theat-
rical writers. Newcastle tried his hand at penning several dramas, as did
his wife, Margaret Cavendish, who wrote several closet dramas during

the Interregnum. Like Killigrew, Newcastle was another keen observer of the pre-war stage. He was also, unlike the manager of the King's Company, hopelessly nostalgic for the old days. In an advice book written for Charles II on the eve of the Restoration, Newcastle recommended appropriate 'devertisements' for the people, which he modelled after his youthful memories of the Caroline stage, what had been current 'in my time': Paris Garden 'for the meaner People'; 'five or Six playe houses,' which he thought 'Enough, for all Sortes of peoples'; puppet plays; ropes and jugglers; 'besides strange Sightes of Beastes, birdes, monsters, & many other things.'[6]

By far the strongest link was in the person of William Davenant, the manager of the rival Duke's Company. Davenant had far more experience of the Caroline theatre than did Killigrew: he had written court masques, such as the platonic *Temple of Love* (1634), for Queen Henrietta Maria and tragicomedies, such as *The Unfortunate Lovers* (1638), for the commercial stage. He acquired – through fairly backhanded means – a patent for an acting company just before the outbreak of the Civil War, and he staged opera in London just prior to the Restoration. Davenant, who liked innovation, is customarily credited with introducing moveable scenery to the commercial stage. Dryden and Davenant collaborated together on their redaction of *The Tempest* (1667); and it was from Davenant that Dryden professed to have acquired an enduring love of Shakespeare, '*a Poet for whom he had particularly a high veneration, and whom he first taught me to admire.*'[7] Through this process of literary transmission, Davenant ensured the perpetuity of Shakespeare's reputation – as well as his own. Indeed, so keenly did Davenant want identification with Shakespeare that, in his cups, he 'seemed contented enough to be thought his Son ... in which way his mother had a very light report, whereby she was called a Whore.'[8] Dryden, in turn, embraced the Shakespearean mantle passed on by Davenant; and by the mid-1670s, he had become the main advocate among Restoration playwrights for Shakespeare's worth. In the Preface to *The Tempest*, Dryden not only emphasizes his indebtedness to Davenant but also his eagerness to join a line of apostolic succession that originates, of course, with Shakespeare:

> It had perhaps been easie enough for me to have arrogated more to my self than was my due in the writing of this Play, and to have pass'd by his name with silence in the publication of it, with the same ingratitude which others have us'd to him, whose Writings he hath not only corrected, as he has done this, but has had a greater inspection over them, and sometimes added whole Scenes together, which may as eas-

ily be distinguish'd from the rest, as true Gold from counterfeit by the weight. But
besides the unworthiness of the action which deterred me from it (there being nothing
so base as to rob the dead of his reputation) I am satisfi'd I could never have receiv'd
so much honour in being thought the Author of any Poem how excellent soever, as I
shall from joining my imperfections with the merit and name of Shakespear *and Sir*
William D'avenant.[9]

By dint of age and access, Dryden truly was 'betwixt two ages cast,' straddling the divide between the Restoration and the Caroline stage. It should not surprise that he is the only Restoration dramatist who was also a shareholder in an acting company, an arrangement, of course, enjoyed by his revered Shakespeare. Judith Milhous maintains that at the Restoration most professional dramatists 'were evidently given a salary in addition to the customary third night profits,' and the bit of fragmentary evidence that exists bears out her assertion.[10] Thomas Shadwell in the dedication to *The Virtuoso* (1676) mentions his pension – in seventeenth-century usage, a salary or stipend – from the Duke's Company.[11] The lawsuit the King's Company brought against Dryden in 1678, when he decamped to the rival Duke's Company, also names Nathaniel Lee, 'who was in Pension with us to the last day of our Playing, & shall continue,' as well as John Crowne 'being under the like agremt with the Dukes house.'[12] That same lawsuit hints at the sort of annual salary a professional dramatist might expect in the 1670s. After the Duke's Company rejected Crowne's play *The Destruction of Jerusalem,* he offered it to the King's Company, which not only accepted the play but quickly put it into rehearsal. In retaliation, the Duke's Company demanded 'all the pension he had received from them Amounting to one hundred & twelve pounds paid by the Kings Company, Besides neare forty pound he the said Mr Crowne paid out of his owne Pocket.'[13] Since *The Destruction of Jerusalem* premiered early in 1677, it stands to reason that if 'pensions' were paid annually, the joint reimbursement of £152 represents Crowne's wage from the Duke's Company for 1676. If salaries were paid according to the theatre season – which ran from September until June – then the £152 represents the work Crowne did for the company the preceding fall season, hardly paltry wages by seventeenth-century standards. Dryden's arrangement was unique in so far as it not only sheltered him from the whims of audience taste – he did not receive the third-night benefit – but it also protected him from the company.[14] Someone with a yearly 'pension' can be fired should he fail to please; a shareholder can hardly fire himself. As long as the company did well

(which the King's Company did in the early years), a dramatist holding
a one and one-quarter share would see a tidy profit. According to James
Winn, Dryden 'often realized a yearly income of over £300 from this
contract.'[15]

More important were the psychological benefits of such an arrangement. I am not suggesting that shareholding somehow liberated Dryden
from socio-economic constraints: obviously, no writer operates outside
of social forces. Any shareholder wants to realize his profit and therefore will contribute to the overall financial well-being of the company,
but he also knows that individual failures are amortized over the course
of the season. One's own play might fail at the box office, but the shareholder will invariably work to ensure the success of the next production,
even if written by someone else. Perhaps, then, not sufficiently appreciated is the extent to which Dryden's status as a shareholder between
1668 and 1678 allowed him some degree of experimentation. It is during this period that Dryden writes such curiosities as the heroic drama
Tyrannick Love (1669) about the martyrdom of St Catherine, hardly the
stuff of typical Restoration fare; or the blank-verse domestic tragedy
Amboyna (1673); or, strangest of all given Dryden's High Church and
royalist inclinations, *The State of Innocence* (1677), a drama in couplets
based on *Paradise Lost* that never made it to the stage. The shareholding
contract also sheltered Dryden from the *immediate* pressures of the audience, a long-standing irritant to the dramatist. Indeed, even prior to the
contract, Dryden defiantly rattled the manacles of popular taste, making
clear his resentment of audiences. In the 'Defence of an *Essay of Dramatique Poesie*' appended to *The Indian Emperour*, published just four years
after his theatrical debut, Dryden wrestles with the notion of aesthetic
value, arguing ultimately that even though 'the liking or disliking of the
people gives the Play the denomination of good or bad, [it] does not
really make, or constitute it such.' Dryden further qualifies his reservations about permitting audiences to confer value on the author's dramatic output: 'To please the people ought to be the Poets aim, because
Plays are made for their delight; but it does not follow that they are
always pleas'd with good Plays, or that the Plays which please them are
always good. The humour of the people is now for *Comedy*, therefore in
hope to please them, I write *Comedies* rather than serious Plays: and so
far their taste prescribes to me: but it does not follow from that reason,
that *Comedy* is to be prefer'd before *Tragedy* in its own nature.'[16]

Dryden's misgivings about the power of the audience become far
more pronounced after he leaves the King's Company – and the refuge

shareholding afforded him. He was now in the position of other professional dramatists who depended upon the author's third-night benefit
and perhaps, if they were lucky, a company pension for a hundred
pounds or so. What originally began as the occasional grumbling about
the popularity of comedy – a genre Dryden disliked both for its low status and, for him, its inherent difficulty – swells after 1678 to denuncia-
tions about audiences in general, the very audiences upon whom
Dryden now depended directly for his livelihood. The Prefaces to both
The Spanish Fryar (1680) and *Don Sebastian* (1690) contain heartfelt,
almost elegiac musings about the futility of authorial effort in the face
of stupid, inconsiderate, or even downright hostile audiences. By 1690
Dryden, nearly thirty years after his career began, would confess that '*all
these discouragements had not only wean'd me from the Stage, but had also given
me a loathing of it.*'[17] Evidence suggests that even popular dramatists were
reduced to the status of free agents by this time; with only one company
in place from 1682 to 1695, there was little need to dispense contracts
to playwrights to prevent them from writing for rivals.[18] Moreover, as
actor-dramatists and manager-dramatists increasingly replaced the professional company writers of the 1670s and early 1680s, opportunities
were even scarcer.

The very atavistic ideal that eventually fuelled Dryden's flight from the
market conditions of the 1690s permitted him earlier in the period to
fashion a singular authorial self that, on the one hand, distinguished
him from the gentlemen amateurs of the 1660s and, on the other, from
the professional writers of the 1670s and '80s. Simply put, no other dramatist of the period goes to such lengths to represent himself as a working member of a company, someone who collaborates eagerly with
actors, managers, musicians, even scene painters. Revealingly, Dryden
reserves his ire for rival dramatists and, later on in his career, for audiences; never does he bestow upon actors the sort of blame common in
the mouths of other dramatists: dropped lines, besotted performances,
too hasty rehearsals. Typically, Dryden credits actors with whatever success the production has enjoyed. Of *Secret Love* (1667), he says 'the chief
parts of it both serious and comick, being performed to that height of
excellence, that nothing but a command which I could not handsomely
disobey, could have given me the courage to have made it publick.'[19] He
attributes the success of *Amphitryon* (1690) again to the cast: 'if it has
pleas'd in Representation, let the Actors share the Praise amongst themselves,'[20] a note he sounds again in the Preface to *Cleomenes* (1692): 'A

great part of my good Fortune, I must confess, is owing to the Justice
which was done me in the Performance: I can scarcely refrain from giving every one of the Actors their particular Commendations; but none
of them will be offended, if I say what the Town has generally granted,
That Mrs. *Barry*, always Excellent, has, in this Tragedy, excell'd Herself,
and gain'd a Reputation beyond any Woman whom I have ever seen on
the Theatre.'[21]

Thrice Dryden credits Thomas Betterton, the great Restoration actor
and stage manager, with improvements to his plays, the first time in
regard to the script of *Troilus and Cressida* (1679): 'But I cannot omit the
last Scene in it [the third act], which is almost half the Act, betwixt
Troilus and Hector. The occasion of raising it was hinted to me by Mr.
Betterton: the contrivance and working of it was my own.'[22] Six years
later Dryden again acknowledges Betterton, this time in regard to scenic innovation in *Albion and Albanius* (1685): 'The descriptions of the
Scenes, and other decorations of the Stage, I had from Mr. *Betterton*, who
has spar'd neither for industry, nor cost, to make this Entertainment
perfect, nor for Invention of the Ornaments to beautify it.'[23] And he
attributes to Betterton the success of *Don Sebastian* (1689). Dryden saw
at the first performance that the play was too long to work on the stage,
but it was Betterton, as he notes in the Preface, who 'so judiciously lopt'
1200 lines and to 'whose care and excellent action, I am equally oblig'd,
that the connexion of the story was not lost.'[24] Composers too come in
for their share of credit. Henry Purcell, who scored the music for *King
Arthur* (1692) 'with so great a Genius,' is praised for his 'Artful Hands.'
In the midst of writing *The Spanish Fryar* – he has at this point finished
two acts – Dryden summons the comic actor Thomas Doggett to his
home 'to consult with him concerning his own Character: & truly I
thinke he has the best Understanding of any man in the Playhouse.'[25]

Colley Cibber's memorable account of Dryden reading *Amphytrion* to
the assembled cast for the first rehearsal provides a glimpse of a dramatist who is generous in other respects towards his actors. While Dryden,
according to Cibber, 'deliver'd the plain Sense of every Period,' nonetheless, 'the whole was in so cold, so flat, and unaffecting a manner, that
I am afraid of not being believ'd when I affirm it.'[26] Cibber contrasts
Dryden's manner of reading with Nathaniel Lee, who 'was so pathetick
a Reader of his own Senses, that I have been inform'd by an Actor, who
was present, that while *Lee* was reading to Major *Mohun* at a Rehearsal,
Mohun, in the Warmth of his Admiration, threw down his Part, and said,
Unless I were able to *play* it, as well as you *read* it, to what purpose should

I undertake it?'[27] Although Cibber marvels that Lee, in his words, 'the inferior poet,' reads more dramatically, his anecdote inadvertently reveals Dryden's regard for the actors' art. Lee, less sensitive to rehearsal, interprets the role for Mohun, leaving the actor nothing to do. As Mohun declares impatiently, 'to what purpose should I undertake it?' Dryden, by contrast, conveys the 'plain Sense' of each period to the cast, but he refrains from acting out the parts. His 'cold, flat, and unaffecting manner' opens a space for delivery, just as his use of dramatic language gives the actors clearly defined performative goals while leaving them room to develop characterization. Samuel Chappuzeau, an invaluable source of information for the late-seventeenth-century theatre, noted that the response of actors to a new play often depended on how well the playwright read to the assembled cast. Interestingly, Chappuzeau regards the best readings as the least emotionally demonstrative; those playwrights 'qui ont le récit pitoyable' injured their prospects with the company.[28]

On rare occasions, one finds a freelance writer praising some aspect of the performance. William Joyner, for instance, commends Elizabeth Boutell as Aurelia in *The Roman Empress* ('which, though a great, various, and difficult part, was excellently performed'), his sole effort for the stage.[29] The major professional playwrights remain obdurately silent or, even worse, irritably vocal on the subject of the production. Gentlemen professionals, such as Sir George Etherege or William Wycherley, say nothing. Thomas Otway's views on the theatre are expressed in sufficiently bitter terms in that endless lamentation, *The Poet's Complaint of His Muse*. Complain he does; never does he have a good word to say about anyone. Nathaniel Lee, despite two writing partnerships with Dryden, never took inspiration from the senior man's generosity towards the acting company. Like Otway, he remains silent about the productions of his plays and shifts his efforts into petitioning patrons through clenched teeth, grumbling about critical factions while shovelling praise. The sole occasion on which Lee admits the success of a production – in this instance, *Sophonisba* (1676) – he attributes it to his patron the duchess of Portsmouth, not the efforts of the company. Thomas Shadwell, although married to an actress, is similarly tight-lipped except to complain in the Dedication to *The Virtuoso* (1676) that the theatre 'is either unwilling or unable to reward a Man sufficiently for so much pains as correct Comedies require.'[30]

Aphra Behn similarly desists from acknowledging the company except to blame them for lapses. In the Epistle prefacing *The Dutch Lover,*

she announces '*that this Play was hugely injur'd in the Acting*,' especially by
the actor playing the title role: '*My Dutch Lover spoke but little of what I
intended for him, but supplied it with a great deal of idle stuff, which I was
wholly unacquainted with until I had heard it first from him.*' Behn admits she
knew of the actor's reputation for improvising lines, but '*I gave him yet
the part, because I knew him so acceptable to most o' th' lighter Periwigs about the
Town, and he indeed did vex me so, I could almost be angry.*'[31] Effectively,
Behn made a strategic misjudgment when casting the play. Hoping for a
full house, she gambled on a questionable choice and lost. In the Preface to *The Lucky Chance* Behn faults the superb comedian Anthony
Leigh for the allegations of indecency women in the audience have lev-
elled against the play. Leigh in the character of Sir Feeble Fainwould
evidently opened his nightgown – how much he revealed is anyone's
guess – upon entering the bedchamber of Leticia, played by Sarah
Cooke. It was, Behn assures the reader, 'a Jest of his own making, and
which I never saw.'[32] That Behn admired Leigh is evident from her pattern of casting – six leading roles in ten years – but she lets him take the
fall in this particular instance.

Given this climate, Dryden's embrace of theatrical culture is all the
more startling. We know that Restoration dramatists, like their predecessors in the Renaissance, cast plays and sometimes explained roles to
actors. Although theatre historians to date have taken the portrait of
Bayes in Buckingham's *The Rehearsal* as typifying company practice that
Restoration dramatists were fully involved in rehearsal, Tiffany Stern has
recently argued otherwise:

> The Restoration theatre, which had started by producing plays without
> authorial help, speedily learnt that it did not generally need authors – with
> the exception of the useful contractually attached professionals. The idea
> that the playwright was in charge of production was adhered to in form,
> but not in fact. With the institution of theatrical managers who wanted an
> active role in the production of all plays (like William Davenant, and after
> him, Thomas Betterton), and with the growth in the importance and
> power of the actor – leading first to the rise of the actor-manager, and sec-
> ondly, to a large number of actor-triumvirates (Betterton, Barry, and Brace-
> girdle in 1695; Cibber, Wilks, and Doggett in 1710) – the playwright's active
> presence became a hindrance instead of a help.[33]

While Stern maintains that Buckingham satirizes an amateur playwright in a French, not English, rehearsal – she notes, for instance, the

play's indebtedness to Molière's *L'Impromtu de Versailles* – her discussion never addresses what contemporaries took to be its true target: John Dryden.[34] Arguably, Buckingham went after Dryden for his inordinate concern with the details of rehearsal, a preoccupation the aristocratic Buckingham considered somewhat common. Perhaps this explains Buckingham's decision to set a lousy play within a rehearsal; he could, after all, have simply parodied the form itself if his central target was the heroic drama, as most modern critics aver. Instead, Buckingham encloses the generic excess and repetitiveness of heroic drama within repetition of another sort, implicitly comparing both endeavours. Buckingham's satiric response frames Dryden's avidity for rehearsal as a tasteless anomaly, an aberration akin to heroic drama, that generic anomaly. Given the hostility of his contemporaries to actors and production, Dryden's enthusiasm for all things theatrical undoubtedly seemed peculiar. Stern maintains that actors, not dramatists, were responsible for overseeing revivals.[35] Again, Dryden proves exceptional. In a letter written to Jacob Tonson around August 1684, Dryden rattles off a list of concerns: Is the United Company 'making cloaths & putting things in a readiness for the singing opera'? If Sarah Cooke is not available for the role of Octavia in a revival of *All for Love*, will Charlotte Butler do? And how will Sue Percival (later Mrs Verbruggen), a comedienne, manage the serious part of Benzayda in the revival of *The Conquest of Granada*?[36] Comments from Restoration actors suggest a range of authorial participation in the rehearsal and production process. Thomas Betterton claimed that he and Elizabeth Barry never embarked upon the study of a role without first consulting 'even the most indifferent poet in any part we have thought fit to accept of,' a custom, he laments, overlooked by the new generation of actors.[37] Betterton's remark suggests that actors, not dramatists, initiated most discussions over roles, further securing Stern's point that by the Restoration most authors faded away after the initial reading of the play and casting of roles – unless they had reason to fear that a poor production might result in the loss of their third-night benefit.

Collaboration of another sort figures in Dryden's career. Among professional writers, Dryden is the only dramatist until the 1690s to hazard a series of writing partnerships: first with Newcastle, then with his brother-in-law Sir Robert Howard, next with William Davenant, and finally with Nathaniel Lee, who, like Dryden, decamped to the rival Duke's Company in 1678. Dryden's penchant for collaboration is at odds with Restoration authorial practice. In the 1660s there are two

exceptions to this rule: the 1664 edition of Pierre Corneille's *Pompey* –
'*Translated out of French by Certain* Persons of Honour' – and a couple of
joint ventures undertaken by the duke of Newcastle and Sir Robert
Howard, both, of course, with Dryden.[38] Authorial collaboration in this
period of solitary authorship is a markedly Renaissance gesture; as Jeffrey Masten observes, playwrights in the early modern period frequently
'wrote with another playwright, or with several others, or revised or aug-
mented scripts initially produced by others.'[39] Gerald Eades Bentley
points out that more than two-thirds 'of the 282 plays mentioned in
Henslowe's diary' are the result of collaborative efforts.[40] And many
early modern dramatists, as recent scholarship has stressed, did not
share our post-Enlightenment notions of possessive individualism and
therefore seemingly cared little about authorial attribution.

In Dryden one sees both models of authorship. His Renaissance self
not only undertakes collaboration but also minimizes the visible signs of
authorial legitimation common to the Restoration. In the two partnerships with Nathaniel Lee, Dryden refrains from using his customary
title 'Servant to His Majesty'; instead, the title page reads simply 'The
Authors Mr. Dryden and Mr. Lee,' as if he did not want to overshadow
the lesser writer. In his collaborations with titled dramatists, Dryden van-
ishes altogether: no authorial attribution exists on the title pages to *The
Indian Queen, Sir Martin Mar-all,* or *The Tempest.* But Dryden's Restoration self cannot at points resist making apparent the ownership of language, especially when it comes to collaboration with another
professional writer; in both *Oedipus* and *The Duke of Guise,* Dryden is
careful to explain who wrote which bit. Angry at murmurings that he
unfairly received credit for *The Duke of Guise,* Dryden appeals to the acting company for corroboration of the 'facts': 'First, That I *assum'd* any
part of it to *my self,* which I had not *written*; wherein I appeal, not only to
my particular *Acquaintance,* but to the whole Company of *Actors,* who will
witness for me, that in all the *Rehearsals,* I never pretended to any *one
Scene* of Mr. *Lee*'s, but did him all imaginable Right, in his title to the
greater part of it.'[40]

Dryden's theatrical interests ranged well beyond acting and authorship. As we know from an extant lawsuit, it is Dryden, not the company
manager, who goes to the painter Isaac Fuller to consult about scene
designs for *Tyrannick Love.* While the editors of the superb California
edition of *The Works of John Dryden* have carefully considered Dryden's
casting of parts, or how the availability of certain actors may have
affected dramatic choices, they perhaps have not fully appreciated the

extent to which Dryden responded to changes in theatre technology over the course of his career. In part, their hesitation is well-founded: much of our evidence remains speculative. Nonetheless, it is striking that whenever Dryden moves to a new playhouse, he writes a script that exploits its technical capabilities. For instance, Dryden's first play, *The Wild Gallant* (1663), is often described in old-fashioned terms. Critics have noted its indebtedness to Caroline and Jacobean playwrights, such as Brome, Shirley, and Jonson, in its mixture of 'humours' comedy and romantic intrigue. The play premiered circa 5 February 1663 at the Vere Street Theatre, a playhouse hastily constructed from Gibbons's Tennis Court. The editors of volume 8 of the *California Dryden* speculate that the Vere Street Theatre had shutter-and-groove technology, a conclusion overturned by more recent theatre historians. It appears to have been an old-fashioned playhouse modelled loosely on the private theatres of the earlier seventeenth century. When Dryden reworked the play for a later revival, it was staged in the Bridges Street Theatre, which did indeed have the capacity for scene discoveries and changes. The first edition of 1669 has the ghostly imprint of both playhouses: characters enter rapidly from side doors, and the plot does not require abrupt shifts in locale or quick discoveries. The two discoveries that appear in the script, extraneous to the plot, may very well have been part of Dryden's attempt to restage the play for the better-equipped Bridges Street Theatre.

In several instances, Dryden uses stage technology, if not to shape form, then at least to suggest metaphoric possibilities about the form itself. It is suggestive that Dryden's experiments in tragicomedy coincide with the move to the Bridges Street Theatre. The first edition of *The Rival Ladies* (1664) includes detailed descriptions of scene changes and descents; and these visual alterations mirror divisions in the script, as Dryden oscillates from rhyme to prose, from comedy to tragedy. When Dryden moves to Dorset Garden, the superior technology, which allowed for sound and lighting effects, makes possible his experiments in opera, as several scholars have noted. One might go farther. Dryden's willingness to collaborate with Nathaniel Lee on *Oedipus* (1679) may have resulted from his move. Their styles differed wildly; as Alan Roper observes, 'terms like "passionate" for Lee, "argumentative" for Dryden, come unbidden to mind. Perhaps the best distinction is between the "naive" style of Lee and the "knowing" style of Dryden.'[42] Briefly put, the technical capabilities of Dorset Garden tempers the incongruity of the respective styles, balancing language with spectacle. Not only does the playhouse literally echo Lee's bombast, answering the swelling tones in Act II with thunder and lightning, but also it harmonizes their very different voices by providing a continuity of visual display. Dryden also thinks metaphorically here. Incest saturates the play; the sub-plot involving Creon and his niece, which, as Roper notes, Dryden probably borrowed from Corneille, mirrors the well-known tale of the main plot. Excessive scenic effects run alongside these excesses of plot, materializing the horror and dread expressed throughout by the characters. It stands to reason that Dryden, so very much the 'man of the theatre,' would think through the metaphorical possibilities of playhouse space.

This very thoughtfulness, so habitual to Dryden, eventually precipitated his reservations about spectacle overpowering language. The much-maligned Richard Flecknoe observed astutely in 1664 that 'that which makes our Stage the better, makes our Playes the worse perhaps, they striving now to make them more for sight, then hearing; whence that solid joy of the interior is lost, and that benefit which men formerly receiv'd from Playes.'[43] Stephen Orgel has warned of the 'easy antithesis between verbal and spectacular theaters,' arguing that 'the court theatre, with its scenes and machines, did not diminish the oratorical aspects of the drama, but rather intensified them.'[44] This certainly was not the perception of Restoration dramatists who, enmeshed in a theatre of special effects, cast a longing glance backwards at the theatre of Jonson and Shakespeare. Restoration drama is drenched in Elizabethan nostalgia, especially by the mid-1670s, when professional dramatists have come to dominate the market. Elizabethan nostalgia also coincides with the advent of the semi-opera, those multimedia spectaculars, as Judith Milhous calls them, that increasingly consumed the resources of both companies.[45] During this period, Nathaniel Lee invokes Jonson and Shakespeare in the Dedications to four of his tragedies. Aphra Behn defends her lack of learning in the Preface to *The Dutch Lover* by observing Shakespeare and Jonson's modest share of knowledge ('Benjamin *was no such Rabbi either*').[46] The title page and advertisement for Dryden's *All for Love* announces it is written 'in the stile of Shakespeare.' Thomas Otway models blank verse tragedies after Shakespeare; and John Banks turns to the stories of Elizabeth and the earl of Essex, Anne Boleyn, and Mary, Queen of Scots, for his rhymed heroic plays.

As Dryden's career progressed, he faced down another troubling aspect of the theatre: its evanescent nature. Like others before him, Dryden turns to print for immortality. He very well may have praised Betterton for his skill in having 'lopt' 1200 lines from *Don Sebastian* and making the play more performable, but Dryden quickly reinserted the lines when the play was printed. Dryden took unusual care with correcting plays; for instance, he revised the first three editions of *The Indian Emperour* (1665), and he makes apparent in the Dedication to *The Kind Keeper* (1678) his desire for close authorial oversight of the printed script. The Folio edition of *Troilus and Cressida* horrifies him: '*so lamely is it left to us, that it is not divided into Acts: which fault I ascribe to the Actors, who Printed it after* Shakespear's *death; and that too, so carelessly, that a more uncorrect Copy I never saw.*'[47] By the time of *The Spanish Fryar* (1680), Dryden's disenchantment goes far beyond issues of evanescence; increasingly he worries that the theatre deceives spectators, lulling them into believing these 'false Beauties of the Stage':

> And a judicious Reader will discover in his Closet that trashy stuffe, whose glittering deceiv'd him in the action. I have often heard the Stationer sighing in his shop, and wishing for those hands to take off his melancholy bargain which clapp'd its Performance on the Stage. In a Play-house every thing contributes to impose upon the Judgment; the Lights, the Scenes, the Habits, and, above all, the Grace of Action, which is commonly the best where there is the most need of it, surprize the Audience, and cast a mist upon their Understandings; not unlike the cunning of a Juggler, who is always staring us in the face, and overwhelming us with gibberish, onely that he may gain the opportunity of making the cleaner conveyance of his Trick. But these false Beauties of the Stage are no more lasting than a Rainbow; when the Actor ceases to shine upon them, when he guilds them no longer with his reflection, they vanish in a twinkling.[48]

There is, as Dryden observes in this Preface, a great difference between a public entertainment in the theatre, and private reading, and the subsequent lines make apparent his shifting preference for print by the 1680s. It is during this decade that Dryden embarks upon various translations and miscellanies, channelling his erstwhile interest in theatrical collaboration into large-scale publication projects with other writers. Dryden acts as editor on behalf of the publisher Jacob Tonson for the four parts of the *Miscellany Poems*, which includes translations of Virgil's *Eclogues*, Ovid's *Elegies*, and some Horatian odes, among other pieces (1684–94). He similarly oversees for Tonson the translation of *Plutarch's Lives* 'By Several Hands' (1683–6). And during the same period Dryden translates Maimbourg's *The History of the League* (1684) and Fr Bonhours' *The Life of St. Francis Xavier* (1688), both also for Tonson. By the time Dryden leaves the theatre for good, in 1694, he rejects collaboration utterly. While poetry had always for Dryden been a solitary endeavour, he now took up translation as a lone occupation, embarking upon the edition of Virgil that he would market – a good thirty years before Pope – through subscription, yet another indication of his increasing desire for authorial control.

Clearly, one can read Dryden's shift away from the theatre as a sane response to changing market conditions: with only one theatre in place until 1695, there was not the sort of competition between companies that necessitated an outpouring of scripts. The establishment of Lincoln's Inn Fields in 1695 did not assuage the situation but merely instituted a triumvirate of actor-managers who increasingly wrote and adapted plays, further shutting writers out of the marketplace of letters. Dryden's residual ideal of himself as a Restoration Shakespeare, the consummate man of the theatre who holds shares in a company, scribbles plays, directs actors, and fusses over scenery, did not answer the harsh requirements of the theatrical economy of the 1690s. He no longer fit. 'No body can imagine,' Dryden remarked in the Preface to *Cleomenes* (1692), 'that in my declining Age I write willingly, or that I am desirous of exposing, at this time of day, the small Reputation which I have gotten on the Theatre. The Subsistence which I had from the former Government, is lost; and the Reward I have from the Stage is so little, that it is not worth my Labour.'[49] Queen Mary banned *Cleomenes*, worrying that it might encourage the supporters of her ousted father, James II. Characteristically, Dryden worries more about the effect of the ban on the fortunes of the company, not himself: 'had it not been on consideration of the Actors, who were to suffer on my account, I should not have been at all sollicitous, whether it were play'd, or no.'[50] Even in the twilight of his fortunes, Dryden cannot entirely divorce himself from the community of the theatre.

Notes

1 Dryden's good nature was legend. In 1704 the sixteen-year-old Alexander Pope remarked to William Wycherley of Dryden that 'Had I been born early enough, I must have known and lov'd him: For I have been assur'd, not only by your self, but by Mr. *Congreve* and Sir *William Trumbul*, that his personal Qualities were as amiable as his Poetical, notwithstanding the many libelous

Misrepresentations of them.' Alexander Pope, *The Correspondence of Alexander Pope*, ed. George Sherburn, 5 vols. (Oxford: Clarendon Press 1956), 2.

2 While Dryden's social credentials were sufficient to justify marriage to Lady Elizabeth Howard, the sister to Sir Robert Howard, he was something of a poor cousin within the Berkshire clan, a somewhat ironic position given their own impecunious straits.

3 *The Works of John Dryden*, ed. E.N. Hooker, H.T. Swedenberg, Jr, et al., 20 vols. (Berkeley: University of California Press 1956–2000), 4:432, l. 5 (hereafter cited as *California Dryden*).

4 Samuel Pepys, *The Diary of Samuel Pepys*, ed. Robert Latham and William Matthews, 11 vols. (Berkeley: University of California Press 1970), 8:55–6.

5 Ibid., 5:230.

6 Thomas P. Slaughter, ed., *Ideology and Politics on the Eve of Restoration: Newcastle's Advice to Charles II* (Philadelphia: American Philosophical Society 1984), 63.

7 *California Dryden* 10:3.

8 Oliver Lawson Dick, *Aubrey's Brief Lives* (London: Secker and Warburg 1949), 85.

9 *California Dryden* 10:4–5.

10 Judith Milhous, *Thomas Betterton and the Management of Lincoln's Inn Fields, 1695–1708* (Carbondale: Southern Illinois University Press 1979), 23.

11 Thomas Shadwell, *The Virtuoso*, ed. Marjorie Hope Nicolson and David Stuart Rodes (Lincoln: University of Nebraska Press 1966), 5.

12 James M. Osborn, *John Dryden: Some Biographical Facts and Problems* (New York: Columbia University Press 1940), 188.

13 Ibid., 189.

14 Again, the language of the lawsuit reveals that Dryden did not typically receive the author's third-night benefit. The company alleges that Dryden complained about his lack of profit because of the new playhouse – they had incurred great debts – and the company 'was so kind to him, that they not onely did not presse him for the Playes which he so engag'd to write for 'em (and for which he was paid before [ )] But they did also at his earnest request, give him a third day for his last new Play, call'd All for Love.' Clearly, receiving the benefit for *All for Love* was an extraordinary occurrence. See Osborn, *John Dryden*, 188.

15 James Anderson Winn, *John Dryden and His World* (New Haven: Yale University Press 1987), 191.

16 *California Dryden* 9:11–12.

17 *California Dryden* 15:66.

18 For instance, a lawsuit between the actress Elizabeth Leigh and Elkanah Set-

tle indicates that, despite his popularity, by 1687 he was operating independently. So eager for income was Settle by this period that he contracted with Leigh to produce what we would now call a 'treatment' (or a plot outline) based on her idea. Settle had trouble persuading the United Company to purchase or produce the play and therefore was unable to pay Leigh for her idea. See Leslie Hotson, *The Commonwealth and Restoration Stage* (Cambridge: Harvard University Press 1928), 274–6.

19 Dryden, Preface to *Secret Love. California Dryden* 9:118.

20 Dryden, Preface to *Amphitryon. California Dryden* 15:225.

21 *California Dryden* 16:77.

22 Dryden, Preface to *Troilus and Cressida. California Dryden* 13:227.

23 Dryden, Preface to *Albion and Albanius. California Dryden* 15:11.

24 Dryden, Preface to *Don Sebastian. California Dryden* 15:66.

25 John Dryden, *The Letters of John Dryden*, ed. Charles E. Ward (Durham: Duke University Press 1942), 54.

26 Colley Cibber, ed., *An Apology for the Life of Colley Cibber* (Ann Arbor: University of Michigan Press 1968), 67.

27 Ibid., 67–8.

28 Samuel Chappuzeau, *Le Théâtre François* (Paris: Jules Bonnassies 1875), 66.

29 William Joyner, *The Roman Empress*, (London: printed for T.N. for Henry Herringman 1671), A2v.

30 Shadwell, *The Virtuoso*, 5.

31 Aphra Behn. Preface to *The Dutch Lover. The Works of Aphra Behn*, ed. Janet Todd, 7 vols. (Columbus: Ohio University Press 1992–6), 5:163.

32 Behn, *Works*, 7:216.

33 Tiffany Stern, *Rehearsal from Shakespeare to Sheridan* (Oxford: Clarendon Press 2000), 125–6.

34 See the Epistle to the Reader prefacing *The Rehearsal ... with A Key & Remarks* (London 1710): 'Mr. *Dryden* a new *Laureat* appear'd on the Stage, much admir'd and highly Applauded; which mov'd the Duke to change the name of his Poet from *Bilboa*, to *Bayes*, whose Works you will find often mention'd in the following *Key*,' A7r–v.

35 Stern, *Rehearsal from Shakespeare to Sheridan*, 150.

36 Dryden, *Letters*, 24.

37 William Oldys, *The History of the English Stage* (Boston: William S. & Henry Spear 1814), 29.

38 The editors of *The London Stage* attribute the play to Edmund Waller, Sir Charles Sedley, Edward Filmer, Sidney Godolphin, and Charles Sackville. See William Van Lennep, *The London Stage 1660–1800*, 5 vols. (Carbondale: Southern Illinois University Press 1965), 1:73.

39 Jeffrey Masten, 'Playwrighting: Authorship and Collaboration,' in *A New History of Early English Drama*, ed. John D. Cox and David Scott Kastan (New York: Columbia University Press 1997), 357.

40 Gerald Eades Bentley, *The Profession of Dramatist in Shakespeare's Time 1590–1642* (Princeton: Princeton University Press 1971), 199.

41 Dryden, Preface to *The Duke of Guise. California Dryden* 14:311.

42 Alan Roper, Commentary on *Oedipus. California Dryden* 13:449.

43 Richard Flecknoe, *Love's Kingdom with a Short Treatise of the English Stage*, ed. Arthur Freeman (New York: Garland Publishing 1973), G8v.

44 Stephen Orgel, *The Illusion of Power: Political Theater in the English Renaissance* (Berkeley: University of California Press 1975), 20.

45 See Judith Milhous, 'The Multimedia Spectacular on the Restoration Stage,' in *British Theatre and the Other Arts, 1660–1800*, ed. Shirley Strum Kenny (Washington, D.C.: Folger Shakespeare Library 1984).

46 Behn, Preface to *The Dutch Lover. Works* 5:162.

47 Dryden, Preface to *Troilus and Cressida. California Dryden* 13:226.

48 Dryden, Preface to *The Spanish Fryar. California Dryden* 14:99–100.

49 Dryden, Preface to *Cleomenes. California Dryden* 16:79.

50 Ibid., 78–9.

chapter twelve

Dryden's Baroque Dramaturgy: The Case of *Aureng-Zebe*

BLAIR HOXBY

I suspect that *Aureng-Zebe*'s critical reputation has never fully recovered from Harley Granville-Barker's charge that 'a true dramatist would not have attempted the thing at all,' for its actions are 'mechanical from beginning to end,' its characters possessed of 'little dramatic life,' and the considerable 'virtues' of its writing undramatic, even anti-dramatic.'[1] To be sure, critics have published more generous and insightful appraisals since, but many of these have applauded the play's virtues (particularly as a species of heroic literature) while leaving unanswered the question of whether those virtues are antidramatic.[2] My aim is to demonstrate that *Aureng-Zebe* is every inch a piece of theatre, one that is interested in its own dramatic processes and in the meaning of performance both on-stage and in culture. To object that the play fails as realistic drama is to miss the point that it succeeds brilliantly as baroque theatre.

As I employ the term, baroque theatre originates with Bernardo Buontalenti's intermezzi for the Medeci wedding of 1589, for which the scenographer worked in tandem with a costumer, machinest, and composer to present a series of neoplatonic allegories and classical scenes illustrating the power of music to sway the human soul.[3] By 1618, Ranuccio I, the Farnese duke of Parma and Piacenza, had constructed a theatre that, with more than 135 feet reserved for a prosceniuim arch, sliding flats, machines, and tiring rooms, was the first permanent structure designed to meet the requirements of the new dramaturgy.[4] Theatres designed in the style of the Teatro Farnese, and suitable for mounting sung dramas with moveable scenery, were soon constructed in Spain, France, Germany, and England.[5] Although the princely courts and Jesuit college that lent crucial support to the new dramaturgy often favoured tragicomic plots, the baroque theatre also produced numerous tragedies that draw their inspiration less often from Sophocles than from Euripides, Seneca, the Old Testament, saints' lives, classical epyllions, and history. They are less concerned to chart the fall of tragic heroes than to display their passion and suffering. They are thickly populated by tyrants and martyrs, but suffering women – like the abandoned Dido, who lamented in song and died for the inauguration of the Teatro Farnese – are perhaps their most characteristic subject.[6] They display an almost paradoxical ability to combine passion with detachment, illusionism with self-consciousness. By baroque tragedy, then, I mean a form of tragic dramaturgy – or a whole field of inter-related forms – that flourished in Europe from about 1628, when the Teatro Farnese was inaugurated, to about the 1760s, when Jean-Philippe Rameau staged the last of his *tragedies en musique*. I mean what René Wellek calls 'not an ideal type or an abstract pattern ... but a time section, dominated by a whole system of norms, which no work of art will ever realize in its entirety.'[7]

I contend that we can best understand *Aureng-Zebe* when we interpret it in the context of this system of norms. I therefore examine the staging conditions of the Restoration theatre and Dryden's theories of dramaturgy in order to suggest the terms on which we should take *Aureng-Zebe*. I then offer a reading that focuses not on the play's dramatic action, but on its management of the passions as it stages a series of revelatory transitions that are punctuated by scenic tableaux. My aim in doing so is not simply to enhance the critical reputation of one of Dryden's finest plays by refining our sense of the theories that motivated its writing and of the theatrical conditions that inflected its performance; it is to offer a thick description of one specimen of a style of dramaturgy that flourished in the princely courts, Jesuit colleges, and public theatres of Europe for more than a century.

I

Sir William Davenant, who had written masques for Charles I and witnessed operas staged in the new baroque theatres of the Continent during the Civil War, did not open a new theatre after the Restoration until it could be equipped with scenes and machines.[8] At least one foreign visitor in 1667 claimed that even Davenant's theatre at Lincoln's Inn Fields, opened in a converted tennis court, was equal to the Italians' for its scene changing, lighting, machines, and music.[9] But Lincoln's Inn

Fields was a modest affair in comparison to the two theatres that
were built to the designs of Sir Christopher Wren in 1671 and 1674. The
Drury Lane Theatre, where *Aureng-Zebe* was played in November of
1675, possessed a deep stage with perspective scenes that could shift
before the eyes of playgoers. We can imagine how these moveable
scenes contributed to what Eugenius identifies in the *Essay of Dramatick
Poesie* as the objects of tragedy: 'to stir up a pleasing admiration and concernment.'[10] For each time the shutters were opened, an unfamiliar
scene of uncertain significance was revealed – precisely the circumstances that should, according to Descartes, produce the first of all
the passions, *l'admiration*, or wonder.[11] As subsequent sets of shutters
opened, they drew the audience's focal point closer to the rear of the
stage in a progress that not only altered their visual perspective but
deepened their moral involvement with the action that was represented
on stage. The poet was justified in making use of such spectacle, music,
and sound effects, said Dryden, because they 'are no more than necessary to produce the effects of an Heroick Play; that is, to raise the imagination of the Audience, and to perswade them, for the time, that what
they behold on the Theatre is really perform'd. The Poet is, then, to
endeavour an absolute dominion over the minds of the Spectators.'[12]

Dryden's emphasis on creating a convincing illusion on stage should
not be taken to mean that he prized the realistic depiction of action.
The representation of action does not figure at all in the definition that
Lisideius contributes to the *Essay of Dramatick Poesie*. As Dean T. Mace
has stressed, Lisideius calls a play '*A just and lively Image of Humane
Nature, representing its Passions and Humours, and the Changes of Fortune to
which it is subject; for the Delight and Instruction of Mankind.*'[13] In Dryden's
dramatic theory – as, indeed, in the opinion of seventeenth-century theorists of all the arts – the representation of the passions was a central
part of art's mimetic ambition. Because, according to Descartes, the passions were activities of the soul that might be sources of either good or
ill, happiness or pleasure, and because their reality was immediately felt
in the soul and was in that sense indubitable, actions, and particularly
changes of fortune, assumed meaning only as they produced feeling in
those whom they affected.[14] Davenant averred that 'Wise poets think it
more worthy to seeke out truth in the passions, then to record the truth
of actions,' and Dryden concurred.[15] Playgoers, says Eugenius, 'watch
the movements of [the characters'] minds [onstage], as much as the
changes of their fortunes. For the imaging of the first is properly the
work of a Poet, the latter he borrows from the Historian.'[16] 'The Stage,'

confirmed the actor Thomas Betterton, 'ought to be the *Seat* of *Passion.*'[17]

It was the actor's business to *embody* passions on stage. 'Every *Passion* or *Emotion* of the *Mind* ... has from Nature its peculiar and proper Countenance, Sound, and Gesture,' said Betterton, relying on a Jesuit writer, 'and the whole Body of Man, all his Looks, and every Tone of his Voice, like Strings on an Instrument, receive their Sounds from the various Impulses of the Passions.' That is why, said Betterton, the representation of movement and action in paintings 'strikes the Passions, and makes Impressions on our Minds more strong and vivid, than all the Force of Words.'[18] In his late essay 'Parallel of Poetry and Painting' (1695), Dryden likewise showed himself to be a shrewd student of expression, gesture, and posture in painting and poetry.[19] An actor who could either *feel* what his characters did, or who understood the bodily language of the passions well enough to express a state of soul unfelt, could make effective use of the Drury Lane Theatre's forestage, which permitted actors to move in front of the proscenium arch. There, said Colley Cibber, the minutest 'Motion of a Feature (properly changing with the Passion, or Humour it suited)' was visible and 'a Voice scarce rais'd above the Tone of a Whisper' could be heard.[20] Ideally, even actors who were not advancing the action on stage should be so concerned with it that their aspects would betray their inner states. That was truly 'to express the Passions in the Countenance and Gesture.'[21]

Baroque artists and theorists made many attempts to formulate systematic languages of the passions for their respective art forms. In a book that was owned by Betterton, John Bulwer tried to establish a 'natural language of the hand' (fig. 12.1).[22] In a series of studies known to both Dryden and Betterton, Charles Le Brun applied Descartes's theory of the passions to the depiction of facial expressions (fig. 12.2).[23] Literary critics like Jules de la Mesnardière, whose writings seem to have influenced Dryden, sought to establish correspondences between particular passions and the tempos, metres, and forms most appropriate to them.[24] Claudio Monteverdi, who made his own attempts to theorize about such matters, also left performance notes that are just as telling: one part of his *Lamento della ninfa* (1638), for instance, is to be performed in 'tempo dell'affetto del animo e non quello de la mano,' or in time with the feelings of the heart, and not in time with the hand.[25] Marin Mersenne tried to establish even more systematic correspondences between the passions and musical symbols in his *Harmonie universelle* (Paris, 1636–7). Theatre, and particularly *dramma per musica*, proved to be the ultimate baroque

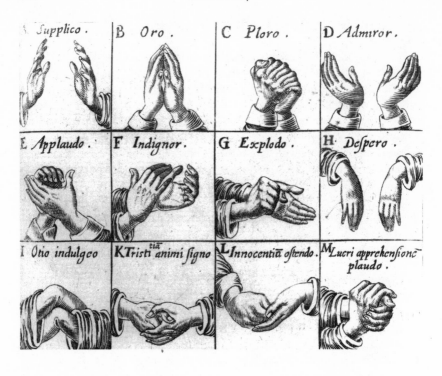

Fig. 12.1. John Bulwer, *Chirologia: or the Natvrall Langvage of the Hand* (1644). The chirograms illustrate the hand gestures appropriate to various passions, such as admiration (D), despair (H), and sorrow (K), and different speech acts, such as supplication (A) and prayer (B). By permission of Beinecke Rare Book and Manuscript Library, Yale University.

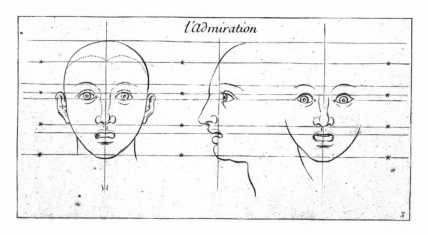

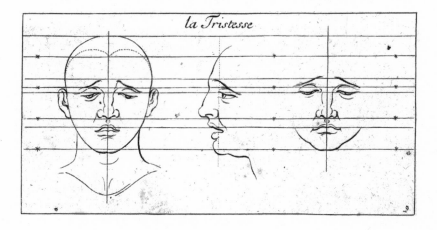

Fig. 12.2. Charles Le Brun, *Conférence sur l'expression des passions* (presented publicly in 1668, published in 1696), illustrating the facial expressions appropriate to various passions: wonder, sadness, reverence, rapture, physical pain, pure love, dejection, and desire. Typ 615.06.514, Department of Printing and Graphic Arts, Houghton Library of the Harvard College Library.

art form because it could bring all these languages to bear on the audience.

Although the representation of the mind and heart lay at the centre of baroque dramaturgy, dramatists were perhaps less interested in revealing the passions than in stirring them up. When the Epilogue to *Aureng-Zebe* refers to '*The Passions rais'd and calm'd by just Degrees, / As Tides are swell'd, and then retire to Seas,*'[26] we may at first assume that Dryden is writing about the representation of his characters' passions, but the reference is unclear, and he may just as easily be referring to the experience of the audience. In practical terms, the tides on stage *had* to coincide with those in the audience. For as Dryden warned in his 'Grounds of Criticism of Tragedy' (1679): '*He who would raise the passion of a judicious Audience, says a Learned Critic, must be sure to take his hearers along with him; if they be in a Calm, 'tis in vain for him to be in a huff: he must move them by degrees, and kindle with 'em ... 'Tis necessary therefore for a Poet, who would concern an Audience by describing of a Passion, first to prepare it, and not to rush upon it all at once.*'[27] Dryden's language suggests that we should judge his plays (and arguably those of a good number of his near contemporaries, from John Fletcher to Thomas Otway) less as continuous representations of actions than as audience-centred works meant to raise and calm the passions by just degrees – in other words, to deliver scripted affective experiences. This impression is reinforced by Dryden's comparison of dramatic techniques to medicines, whose efficacy should not be judged by whether they are offered by the mountebanks at the Red Bull or by physicians like himself.[28] Like drugs in a pharmacopoeia, the effects of the theatre – spectacle, music, action, speech – can be administered as needed to manipulate the passions and bodies of the audience.

It may not be too much to say that Dryden, who traced the ancestry of his own heroic drama back through Davenant's *Siege of Rhodes* to the example of '*Italian* Opera's,' was striving for an effect somewhat akin to *dramma per musica*.[29] In that dramatic form, recitative advanced the dramatic action rather perfunctorily until a passion had been raised that could be represented by an aria. As he sang, an accomplished Italian *musico* like Nicolino 'gestured deliberately and majestically until a strong accent or climax in the score required him to stand motionless for a moment in an exceptionally expressive pose, and he held this attitude until he had made his *point*.'[30] 'There is scarce a beautiful posture in an old statue which he does not plant himself in,' said Richard Steele appreciatively.[31] The changeable scenery of *dramma per musica* repeated at a slower tempo this dynamic rhythm of metamorphosis and fixity. The acting of Nicolino would not have been so admired by observers like Steele if it had not brought something *new* to the English stage, yet the difference was, I think, one of training, refinement, and execution as much as it was of intention. For new theories of cognition were already, in the mid-seventeenth century, attributing special force and clarity to images instead of words and were thus promoting an emblematic mode of representation on stage.[32] As we shall see, *Aureng-Zebe* requires its actors and actresses to freeze themselves momentarily into works of visual art just as surely as Nicolino's training did.

Dryden need not have looked to contemporary *dramma per musica*, however, to discover the affective power of metamorphoses that end in fixity. Dryden's critics have perhaps paid too little attention to Eugenius's claim in the *Essay of Dramatick Poesie* that it was Ovid who had 'a Genius most proper for the Stage,' for 'he had a way of writing so fit to stir up a pleasing admiration and concernment, which are the objects of a Tragedy, and to show the various movements of a Soul combating betwixt two different Passions, that, had he liv'd in our age, or in his own could have writ with our advantages, no man but must have yielded to him.' We can see what Eugenius means when he points to the stories of Myrrha and of Byblis as particularly near 'the *Drama*,' for as stories of incest, they certainly cause wonder, and as stories of the destructive power of youthful passion, they also elicit our compassion.[33] In their *suasoria*, Ovid's heroines argue *in utrumque partem*, or both in defence of and in condemnation of their illicit passions. Ovid thus transforms a rhetorical exercise into a vehicle for representing passionate indecision, a vehicle that must be counted among the formal models for the sort of externalized inner dialogues that baroque dramatists, including Dryden, use to represent the movements of a soul swayed by its passions. As they labour under the burden of their passions, Ovid's heroines grow pale, lower their eyes, and weep. Some of them, like Byblis, entertain the notion of turning their bodily signs of grief into a theatrical spectacle calculated to move compassion as mere words cannot.[34] Eventually their passion is so perfect, so permanent, so reified, that they are transformed into emblems of their own grief. The weeping Byblis becomes a fountain under a dark ilex, and Myrrha becomes a tearful tree: 'Though she has lost her old time feeling with her body, still she weeps, and the warm drops trickle down from the tree. Even her tears have honour: and the myrrh which distills from the bark preserves the name of its mistress.'[35] Like *dramma per musica*, Ovid's *Metamorphoses* periodically suspends its action in order to make its point.

Eugenius values Ovid's stories in part because, as Aristotle says any tragedy should, they make us wonder.[36] Dryden strives for the same effect in *Aureng-Zebe* with his heroic couplets, which surprise us repeatedly with the implied relationship between words that rhyme. This sequence of tiny revelations is punctuated at longer intervals by jarring changes of tone in the midst of scenes. At the opening of Act IV, for example, Aureng-Zebe contemplates his own mortality as '*Soft Music*' plays:

> Distrust, and darkness, of a future state,
> Make poor Mankind so fearful of their Fate.
> Death, in it self, is nothing; but we fear
> To be we know not what, we know not where.
> This is the Ceremony of my Fate:
> A parting Treat; and I'm to die in State.   (IV.i.1–6)

The quiet mood of his soliloquy is suddenly disturbed by his stepmother, Nourmahal, who, far from bringing him news of his imminent death, professes her love for him. If Nourmahal's incestuous proposition is chilling, it is also disconcertingly funny, for she, a hardened virago, incongruously speaks lines that she borrows from Ovid's young and pathetic Myrrha.[37] Dryden could offer respectable justifications for such shameless attempts to make us wonder. For according to Descartes, wonder is an aid to memory. More importantly, it is rarely unaccompanied. So where wonder comes, can other passions be far behind?[38]

The possibility that wonder might serve as a lure to other passions would have appealed to Dryden, for he was moving towards a new interest, expressed in his 'Grounds of Criticism in Tragedy' (1679), in pity and fear. These, he says, are the passions that are most likely to win our concernment, one of our chief sources of '*pleasure*': '*when the Soul becomes agitated with fear for one character, or hope for another; then it is that we are pleas'd in Tragedy, by the interest which we take in their adventures.*' Not only the pleasure of tragedy but its instructional value depends on our passions being stirred, for '*to purge the passions by Example, is ... the particular instruction which belongs to Tragedy.*' In what sense can feeling teach? Our vicarious terror abates our pride and our pity tempers our natural want of commiseration, making us instead '*tender over the distress'd, which is the noblest and most God-like of moral virtues.*'[39] This is an insensible lesson of the heart that cannot be inculcated by any precept.

But were Restoration theatres really suited to teaching such lessons, particularly if they depended on the audience's intense identification with the action onstage? Seating arrangements made it possible for some audience members to sit onstage, while others were placed along each side of the auditorium, opera-house style. Because the entire house remained lit during performance and because the audience was permitted to move about, playgoers were cast, and were aware of each other, in multiple roles – as observers, performers, and objects of observation. The stage was an open and permeable space, and even the backstage might be penetrated by the curious: royal proclamations enjoined the audience not to interfere with the operation of the stage machinery, and visits to the tiring rooms to speak with the actors and actresses, who might enjoy celebrity status, were not unusual for the well-connected. The practice of having actors and actresses speak the prologues and epilogues of plays out of character must further have encouraged playgoers to see them even when *in* character as just that: persons inhabiting the places of others, rehearsing prior events, acting as surrogates. Thus, in *Aureng-Zebe*, when Indamora announces, 'I know / My Beauty's pow'r', and what my charms can do' (II.i.91–2), and when Nourmahal maintains that 'each glance, each grace / Keep their first lustre, and maintain their place; / Not second yet to any other face' (II.i.209–11), we are meant to enjoy the rivalry not only between two characters but between two actresses: Elizabeth Cox, a newcomer to the stage, and Rebecca Marshall, an actress who had been impressing Samuel Pepys since 1666 with her interpretations of determined and unscrupulous women like the Evadne of *The Maid's Tragedy* and the Lyndaraxa of *The Conquest of Granada*.[40] If the theatre for which Dryden wrote was dedicated to illusion and concernment, then it was also intensely conscious of its own processes, of its status *as* theatre.

It would be a mistake to think that we can or should even wish to filter out this quality of the Restoration stage, for even taken singly, the baroque arts aspired to this condition of self-conscious theatricality. Let me point to just one well-known example, an example that Dryden himself could not have seen: Gian Lorenzo Bernini's Cornaro Chapel (fig. 12.3).[41] Drawing on his experience as a scenographer, theatre architect, and opera composer, Bernini presents the ecstasy of St Teresa as if it were transpiring on a proscenium stage, with the chapel's patrons seated in boxes like the audience of an opera and the machinery of heaven above. In mystical writings known to Dryden, Teresa reported that an angel had pierced her heart several times with a spear, causing her an intense but sweet pain that induced in her a great love of God.[42] It was a spiritual

Fig. 12.3. Gian Lorenzo Bernini, *The Ecstasy of St Teresa* (1642–52), Cornaro Chapel, Santa Maria della Vittoria. Nimatallah / Art Resource, NY.

pain, she said, 'though the body has some share in it – even a considerable share.'[43] As some of the Cornaro cardinals are shown reading or in contemplation, the chapel even suggests the possibility that what we are seeing is *their* vision of her ecstasy, an artistic re-evocation of an actual event. The Cornaro Chapel not only stages an encounter between viewer and sculpted figure that may be said to make the affect and embodied passion of each, conceived in theatrical terms, its ultimate object, it makes the viewer conscious of that relationship by staging another between Teresa and the cardinals. The chapel thus seems capable of promoting a perfect identification between figure and viewer even as it admits that it is attempting to promote it. The Cornaro Chapel does not succeed artistically despite its theatrical quality; it succeeds because of it.[44] What happens, I wish to ask in the remainder of this essay, if we read *Aureng-Zebe* as Dryden's attempt to stage a similar affective experience, part of whose method is to reveal its very status as theatre?

II

For his 'Tragedy; the Characters of which are the nearest to those of an Heroick Poem,' Dryden turned to contemporary Agra, where the succession of Aureng-Zebe in 1660, the year of the Stuart Restoration, had brought an end to civil war.[45] The action opens with two of the younger sons of the Mogul Emperor in revolt. Faced with the prospect of being executed upon the succession of their eldest brother, they prefer to fight. It is left to the youngest son, Aureng-Zebe, to uphold the 'sinking State' like '*Atlas*' (I.i.104). He does so out of loyalty to his ruler and father, with the prospect of scant reward except for the hand of the beautiful Indamora. The Emperor recognizes Aureng-Zebe's merits by trying to steal his bride. That puts Aureng-Zebe in the tough position of remaining loyal to his sovereign and father while staying true to the woman he loves. The play's next acts introduce permutations on this tragic situation. First the honourable governor Arimant finds his loyalty to the Emperor tested by his admiration for Indamora, then the ambitious younger son Morat betrays his father, his brother, and his wife, Melesinda, for her. Abandoned by her husband the Emperor, Nourmahal becomes a rival to Indamora, not for the Emperor but for the love of her own stepson, Aureng-Zebe. The play's intrigue thus satisfies Aristotle's preference for tragic action in which 'suffering is inflicted upon each other by people whose relationship implies affection,' a preference that Corneille endorsed: 'The oppositions of the feelings of nature to the transports of passion, or to the severity of duty, create powerful excitement, which is received by the audience with pleasure.'[46] Although the Emperor tries to give his empire to Morat and keep Indamora for himself, Morat is determined to win both her and India, and the struggle that ensues is a costly one. By the play's end, only the Emperor, Aureng-Zebe, and Indamora are left standing. The father comes to his senses, reconciles with his son, and blesses Aureng-Zebe's union with Indamora and his figurative marriage, as ruler, to the land.

Rather than analyse *Aureng-Zebe* as a poem whose philosophical ideas, topical allusions, or even dramatic action and poetic imagery will reveal its significance, I propose to treat it as a theatrical piece that is intended to generate a scripted affective experience in spectators.[47] Our knowledge of how *Aureng-Zebe* was staged is, of course, limited. Every performance and the experience of every spectator must have differed. But unless we are willing to imagine and describe the experience of ideal spectators – by which I mean astute and educated men and women of the Restoration, vulnerable to all the distractions and excitement of the public theatre but attentive to the stage itself – we will remain but poorly attuned to the virtues of baroque tragedy.

Watching *Aureng-Zebe* bears an important resemblance, I submit, to the experience of walking into and later exiting the Cornaro Chapel. Spectators take in the design in the first scene of the play. They then behold, and become increasingly concerned with, theatrical presentations of the passions. As these scenes of passion affect the audience, they also enact onstage a transition from the dramaturgy of Dryden's earlier heroic dramas, with their rhetoric of the passions, to that of his subsequent pathetic tragedies, *All for Love* and *Troilus and Cressida,* with their reliance on scenic tableaux of grief that employ gesture and posture to make their point.[48] In a process of reciprocal reconstruction, the play and the spectators renovate themselves. As the audience's passions are purged, the spectators become increasingly aware of *Aureng-Zebe*'s self-consciousness about its status as theatre, about the theatrical construction of the passions, and about the role of performance in the perpetuation of culture. They can therefore appreciate the study in contrasts presented in the final scene as the logical conclusion to an intrigue designed in terms of binary oppositions. Their pleasure, by the end of the play, is as much intellectual as emotional. Now let us consider in greater detail how *Aureng-Zebe* scripts this experience for an audience.

Performing the function of a chorus, Arimant opens the action of *Aureng-Zebe* by announcing that 'Heav'n seems the Empire of the East to lay / On the success of this important day' (I.i.1–2). At stake is 'What e'r can urge ambitious Youth to fight,' with 'Laws, Empire, All permitted to the Sword' (I.i.7, 9). As a classical *protasis* should, this scene 'gives light onely to the Characters of the persons, and proceeds very little into any part of the action.'[49] But the characters are described with such bracing clarity – Darah 'Too openly does Love and hatred show' (I.i.92), Sujah is 'a Bigot of the *Persian* Sect' (I.i.95), Morat is brave but insolent and envious (I.i.98–101), and Aureng-Zebe is temperate in all his passions 'Except his Love,' 'sums' the 'Virtues' of his other brothers in himself, and adds to them the loyalty of a son (I.i.102–9) – that not only the bloody struggle for power among the sons, but even the grounds for Aureng-Zebe's impending conflict with his father, are foreseeable. It is here in the opening scene that Dryden most clearly shows that he is undertaking '*to please by Rule*' (Epilogue, l. 2), for he signals that he will respect the unities of time, place, and action.

The inner turmoil of the state – reported rather than depicted onstage – is soon mirrored in the soul of the Emperor himself. *Aureng-Zebe*'s language implies that the play's incisive analysis of the heart and mind is as painful as are the battles being fought offstage: 'No more; you search too deep my wounded mind,' says the Emperor to Arimant, only to complain shortly thereafter, 'Thou shouldst have pull'd the secret from my breast, / Torn out the bearded Steel to give me rest' (I.i.229, 247–8). Among the many precedents for the Emperor's description of his secret passion as a wound is Ovid's story of Byblis (*Met.* 9.585), and we may fairly say that as he describes the cross-currents of his soul ('Thou seest me much distemper'd in my mind: / Pull'd back, and then push'd forward to be kind' [I.i.327–8]), as he admits the illicit nature of his desire ('my crime I sadly view, / Acknowledge, am asham'd, and yet pursue' [II.i.460–1]), and as he describes his unsuccessful struggle to be virtuous with a verb proper to legal argument ('I *represented* to my self the shame / Of perjur'd Faith, and violated Fame. / Your great deserts, how ill they were repay'd' [II.i.454–6; my emphasis]), he is, more often than not, speaking in the mode of one of Ovid's heroines. I say 'heroines' because classical decorum dictated that Ovid reserve for women the *suasoria* that baroque writers, no longer so reserved about depicting the passionate lives of men, turned into such good theatre.

Much as Ovid turns from the internal debates of his heroines to their physical symptoms of decline – pale cheeks, sighs, and tears – *Aureng-Zebe* begins with Act II to give dramatic prominence to the embodiment of the passions onstage. 'These alter'd looks some inward motion show,' says the

Emperor to Arimant and Indamora when he interrupts the governor's attempted courtship, 'His cheeks are pale, and yours with blushes glow' (II.i.120–1). Indamora, Melesinda, and even the hero Aureng-Zebe weep on stage. Rather than say what he is feeling, Aureng-Zebe has a tendency to report the physical effects of his passion. Remorse is proved by some symptoms: 'Behold these dying eyes, see their submissive awe; / These tears, which fear of death could never draw: / Heard you that sigh?' (IV.ii.140–2). Other sensations attest to his love: 'Love mounts, and rowls about my stormy mind, / Like Fire, that's born by a tempestuous Wind' (IV.ii.144–6). The bliss of imagined – or should we say premature? – consummation feels different again: 'my conscious Limbs presage / Torrents of joy, which all their banks o'erflow!' (IV.ii.151–2). And astonishment, which, according to Descartes, 'makes the entire body immobile like a statue,'[50] does just that: 'I grow a Statue, Stiff, and motionless' (V.i.415). This theatrical mode presupposes that the body is a more reliable indicator of the soul's passions than are mere words. But it also presents an opportunity for an actor like Charles Hart, who played Aureng-Zebe, to show that the body can be *tuned* as surely as the voice. As each physical symptom is announced like a visiting dignitary, we perceive 'the reciprocal construction of nature (passion and mortality) and second nature (manners and ceremony).'[51]

At its mid-point, *Aureng-Zebe* begins to freeze the passions momentarily in tableaux that, like many of Ovid's metamorphoses, seem to concentrate the meaning of the story in a gesture or pose that resembles a work of visual art. Take, for instance, Indamora's comment on the weeping Melesinda:

> When graceful sorrow in her pomp appears,
> Sure she is dress'd in *Melesinda*'s tears.
> Your head reclin'd, (as hiding grief from view,)
> Droops, like a Rose surcharg'd with morning Dew.   (III.i.72–5)

Melesinda weeps and bows her head because, as Betterton tells us, 'the *Demission* or *hanging down of the Head* is the Consequence of *Grief* and *Sorrow*.'[52] But Indamora turns Melesinda into an emblem of grief whose pathetic appearance is reinforced by a poetic line that, after its initial caesura, seems itself to proceed with bowed head: 'Droops, [ll] like a Rose surcharged with morning Dew.' *Aureng-Zebe* repeatedly dramatizes the capacity for such theatrical presentations of piety to affect spectators, to renovate them, and to transform their habits.

Grateful for Indamora's compassion, Melesinda determines to return the favour, something that she is in a position to do once her husband, Morat, has the (temporary) upper hand in the state's civil war. She implores Morat to interview Indamora. He agrees to 'view this Captive Queen' only to prove that 'Pray'rs and complaints are lost on such as me' (III.i.439–40). As he stands upright, Indamora kneels before him. He asks her to rise and she does, only to prostrate herself before him as she begs for Aureng-Zebe's life: 'An humble Suppliant at your feet I lie' (III.i.447).[53] Not her arguments but her form and voice begin to soften Morat: 'All Reasons for his safety urg'd, are weak: / And yet, me-thinks, 'tis Heav'n to hear you speak' (III.i.483–4). Acting as director of the spectacle, and reminding us of the uses of wonder as a lure to the other passions, Melesinda asks, 'Can Beauty wonder, and not pity raise?' (III.i.494). Morat's initial reaction is nearer sexual arousal than pity, but the play insists, as does so much baroque art, that profane and sacred desire, passion and pious suffering, are near things, and the effects of this dramatic spectacle seem to work insensibly on Morat through Acts IV and V, for by the time of his death scene – the last of the play's great pathetic tableaux – he has become a new, if still flawed, man. 'You show me somewhat I ne'er learnt before,' he confesses to Indamora, 'But 'tis the distant prospect of a Shore, / Doubtful in mists; which, like inchanted ground, / Flies from my sight, before 'tis fully found' (V.i.100–3). But he is closer to the shore than he realizes. For at least he can feel the pain of others now: 'Your grief, in me such sympathy has bred, / I mourn' (V.i.149–50).

As he dies, Morat catches hold of Indamora's gown and falls by her. She then sits beside him. He says,

> I can no more; yet, ev'n in death, I find
> My fainting body byass'd by my mind:
> I fall toward you; still my contending Soul
> Points to your breast, and trembles to its Pole.
>
> (V.i.333–6)

The word 'trembles' recalls Nourmahal's description of her own sympathetic response to the brow of Aureng-Zebe as he was berated by his father: 'My Virtue, like a String wound up by Art, / To the same sound, when yours was touch'd, took part, / At distance shook, and *trembled* at my heart' (IV.i.76–8; my emphasis). It is typical of *Aureng-Zebe*'s complex tone, and of its knowing attitude towards its own theatrical processes, that

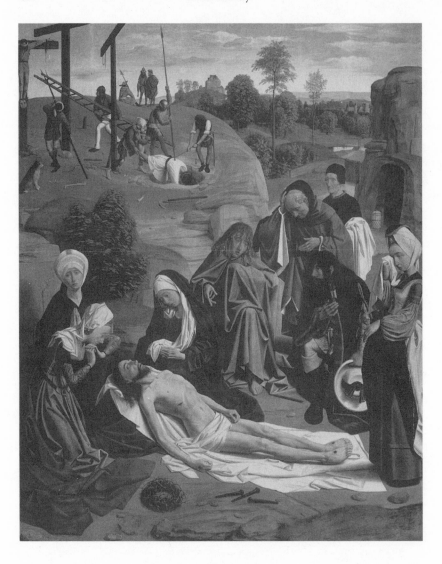

Fig. 12.4. Geertgen tot Sint Jans, *The Lamentation* (1485–90). Formerly in the
collection of Charles I. Kunsthistorisches Museum, Vienna.
Erich Lessing / Art Resource, NY.

Fig. 12.5. Jacob Jordaens, *The Lamentation* (c. 1650). Formerly in the collection
of the Duke of Marlborough. Copyright: Hamburgher Kunsthalle.
Photographer: Elke Walford, Hamburg.

it should, on the one hand, place the most definitive description of how
'kindness to desert ... / by Secret Sympathy is ty'd' in the mouth of Nourmahal (IV.i.71–2) and, on the other, expect us to recall that description
in all seriousness and to recognize Morat's fall as his own theatrical
answer to the spectacle that Indamora earlier made of herself. No naif in
such matters, Melesinda hurries to cast herself on the other side of Morat.
She is anxious for him to behold the countenance of patient grief that
she can present: 'Ah turn your sight to me, my dearest Lord! / Can you
not one, one parting look afford?' (V.i.374–5). From the viewpoint of the
play's audience, a recumbent male flanked by grieving women and identified as 'my dearest Lord' recalls the arrangement of the figures in a *Lamentation* like that of Geertgen tot Sint Jans, formerly in the collection of
Charles I (fig. 12.4), or that of Jacob Jordaens, formerly in the collection
of the duke of Marlborough, where Betterton appreciated it as a study in
the varied expressions of sorrow (fig. 12.5). Morat's death thus alludes to
the tableau of grief, the lamentation for Our Lord, who, in the ultimate
act of theatrical surrogacy, died for all mankind.[54]

Much as the Cornaro Chapel invites us to see St Teresa's ecstasy as
theatre, *Aureng-Zebe* asks us to admit that culture perpetuates itself only
because it remembers, substitutes, and performs, so that far from being
a thing apart from the realities of political force and sexual desire, theatre, with its roles and rehearsals, its borrowed desires and reflected
power, is the very stuff of culture. Aureng-Zebe sees himself as trying to
'fulfil the parts' that being a son and lover 'require' (I.i.466). After the
Emperor recalls his own feats in battle, the prince responds, 'Those fair
Idea's to my aid I'll call, / And emulate my great Original' (II.i.406–7).
In a play whose political intrigue is dramatized as a contest to see which
of four understudies will get the part of playing one of the gods' 'Images
below' (V.i.346), Aureng-Zebe's succession depends on yet another act
of surrogacy, when the loyal Arimant, unable to fill Aureng-Zebe's role
as the lover of Indamora, dons the young man's armour, identifies himself in battle as the prince, and, by drawing death on himself, permits
the young man to infiltrate the fortified city without being identified
(V.i.489–506).

But it is the language of surrogacy running through Nourmahal's professions of desire and rivalry in Acts IV and V that makes us most acutely
aware of how often the play represents one character filling the shoes of
another. No longer willing to sustain the Emperor's 'cold long-labouring
age' (II.i.234), she seeks a replacement in his son, Aureng-Zebe:

> I am not chang'd; I love my Husband still;
> But love him as he was, when youthful grace,
> And the first down began to shade his face:
> That Image does my Virgin-flames renew,
> And all your Father shines more bright in you.
>
> (IV.i.148–152)

That Nourmahal is here repeating the lines of Seneca's Phaedra to her stepson, Hippolytus, only reinforces our sense that, far from being a peculiar expression of vice, Nourmahal's wish to find a surrogate for her aging husband obeys a more general law of human desire.[55] Aware that she herself is not among those who will 'accept no substitute,' Nourmahal is ready to assume that the Emperor may be as content to find a surrogate. Of Indamora she therefore says,

> This wondrous Master-piece I fain would see;
> This fatal *Helen*, who can Wars inspire,
> Make Kings her Slaves, and set the World on fire.
> My Husband lock'd his Jewel from my view,
> Or durst not set the false one by the true.
>
> (V.i.256–60)

The false one by the true: this is an allusion to a lesser-known variant of the Helen story, recounted in the *Palinode* of Stesichorus, in which Paris carries off not Helen herself but a phantom substitute for Helen. When Nourmahal actually beholds Indamora, she exclaims, 'Some Angel copi'd, while I slept, each grace, / And molded ev'ry feature from my face' (V.i.265–6). From her outward form, Nourmahal shifts to a consideration of Indamora's inward being:

> The Palace is, without, too well design'd;
> Conduct me in, for I will view thy mind. [*To her.*
> Speak, if thou hast a Soul, that I may see,
> If Heav'n can make throughout another Me.
>
> (V.i.270–3)

Indamora kneels but remains almost dumb in what may be a deliberate attempt to stage a spectacle of pathos for the benefit of Nourmahal: 'My tears and miseries must plead my cause; / My words, the terror of

your presence awes' (V.i.274–5). 'Heav'n did, by me, the outward model
build,' says Nourmahal,

> Its inward work, the Soul, with rubbish fill'd.
> Yet, Oh! th'imperfect Piece moves more delight;
> 'Tis gilded o'r with Youth, to catch the sight.
> The Gods have poorly robb'd my Virgin bloom,
> And what I am, by what I was, o'rcome.
> Traitress, restore my Beauty and my Charms,
> Nor steal my Conquests with my proper Arms.
>
> (V.i.280–7)

For Nourmahal, this is a recognition scene, for the sight of Indamora is
enough to make her realize that this is the woman to whom she will lose
her husband *and* her stepson. Nourmahal's demand that Indamora
deliver a speech that will reveal her soul is in keeping with her consistent preference for action – and dramaturgy – befitting an heroic
drama. But the play implicitly condemns her for her taste. Characters
like Morat, who harbour at least some sparks of virtue, may believe they
are proof to such silent pictures of grief and misery, that they are
immune to tears, but their hearts are not so hardened, and it is their
very susceptibility to the methods of pathetic tragedy that redeems them
according to the moral terms of the play.

For *Aureng-Zebe*, surrogacy is a fact of culture and of life: we must
learn how to resist its unlawful temptations and how to use it well. Its
proper use is demonstrated in the death scene of Morat. Indamora
falsely believes that Aureng-Zebe is dead and that his body lies somewhere outside the walls where she cannot retrieve it. 'Oh stay,' she says
to the dying Morat, 'or take me with you when you go: / There's nothing now worth living for below' (V.i.432–3). Upon Morat's death, she
exclaims, 'Oh dismal day! / Fate, thou hast ravish'd my last hope away'
(V.i.438–9). Aureng-Zebe inconveniently witnesses this affecting scene
and is deeply moved, repeating back Indamora's words verbatim, and
doubtless in a mocking falsetto, as the prelude to a denunciation of
women (V.i.469–70). Most critics have assumed that the prince is on
solid ground when he concludes that Indamora was a little in love with
Morat and that he is right, when she offers as her excuse that 'He di'd
my Convert,' to cap it: 'But your Lover too: / I heard his words, and did
your actions view; / You seem'd to mourn another Lover dead' (V.i.511–
13). I think it is more important, however, to recognize in watching this

scene that Indamora is shedding tears *for* Aureng-Zebe *over* Morat, who serves as an effigy of her missing beloved. 'My sighs you gave him, and my tears you shed,' says Aureng-Zebe, and he is more right than he knows (V.i.514). Similarly, if the play's spectators are moved to weep *over* the effigies on stage, they do not weep *for* them. They weep *for* the missing bodies in their own lives. Such are the ways of pathetic tragedy.

The end of the play is a study in contrasts that spells out the several fates of the major characters. The lovelorn Melesinda exits to seek the breast of her dead husband, Morat, so that, 'kindling by his side' on his funeral pile, she might 'mount a glorious Bride' (V.i.634–5). Nourmahal then enters, raving and poisoned by her own hand: 'I burn, I more than burn; I am all fire: / See how my mouth and nostrils flame expire' (V.i.641–2). Whereas Melesinda had declared that her unconditional love for Morat could burn even though, as a faithless husband, he 'suppli'd no fuel' (V.i.629), Nourmahal attempts to feed her own flames with her husband and her stepson. 'Pull, pull that reverend piece of Timber near,' she says of the Emperor, 'Throw't on – 'tis dry – 'twill burn' (V.i.646–7). She then catches at Aureng-Zebe. Aureng-Zebe's cry, 'Alas, what fury's this?' (V.i.659) – which might refer to his stepmother's state of mind or to her person – reinforces our sense that we are witnessing an eruption from hell. Nourmahal confirms as much. Having already described herself as a 'burning Lake' (V.i.644) in a recollection of Milton's hell (*Paradise Lost* I.210), she exclaims, 'poor helpless I / See all; and have my Hell before I die!' (V.i. 666–7). What she sees are her stepson and rival huddled in each other's arms. For Aureng-Zebe, this embrace is that long-anticipated 'promis'd Paradice: / An Ages tumult of continu'd bliss' (I.i.380–1). But Dryden's play, with its ability to sustain multiple perspectives, never lets us forget that one man's paradise may be another woman's hell.

Harold Brooks is right to hear echoes of Seneca's Hercules in the ravings of Nourmahal.[56] Because we have earlier heard the Emperor compare himself to Hercules and wives like Nourmahal to 'invenom'd Shirts we wear; / And cleaving mischiefs' (II.i.312–13), it is poetically just that Nourmahal should, in turn, be dealt the role of Hercules. The reversal has some of the rough and giddy humour about it that marks the couple's domestic squabbles. But we should also remember that Nourmahal 'generously did life disdain!' (V.i.637). The word 'generously' imports from Corneille's drama the rich significance of *généreusement* – an action done capaciously and nobly in the spirit of the great-souled. Nourmahal remains true to her ideal of generosity precisely by warming to the role of Hercules. As 'Th'invenom'd Body does the Soul attack,' as 'Th'invenom'd Soul works its own poison back,' she dies standing up in a gesture of defiance worthy of a Stoic hero (V.i.639–40). For a theatrical moment, the uncertain connection between body and soul, gesture and passion is firmly established.

Nourmahal's last stand asks us to compare her ideal of generosity to the virtue that Morat learns from Indamora. Not disdain for his own life, but respect for another's, motivates his great act, when he raises himself from the ground just enough to prevent Nourmahal from killing Indamora. As he lies dying, he tells Indamora,

> I leave you not; for my expanded mind
> Grows up to Heav'n, while it to you is joyned:
> Not quitting, but enlarg'd! A blazing Fire,
> Fed from the Brand.   (V.i.434–7)

In a play that invests gesture and movement with a tremendous weight of meaning, Morat and Indamora perform two of their most memorable acts of generosity while lying prone, and Melesinda, Indamora, and Aureng-Zebe all must learn the art of kneeling and weeping. 'When she exacts it, can I stoop so low?' asks the reluctant hero before he kneels to effect a lasting reconciliation with his beloved (V.i.568).

In the last of his heroic plays, Dryden hit upon that rich theatrical – and ethical – vein, pathetic tragedy. It is no accident that the Antony of Dryden's next tragedy, *All for Love*, has scarcely walked upon the stage before he throws himself down and speaks of tears (I.i.203–27). By the time Dryden wrote *Troilus and Cressida*, he held that the heroes of tragedies must be virtuous not so much so that they might set examples, but so that they might be sure of eliciting pity.[57]

Notes

1 Harley Granville-Barker, *On Dramatic Method: Being the Clark Lectures for 1930* (London: Sidgwick and Jackson 1931), 143–5, 150.
2 For readings of *Aureng-Zebe* that stress its debt to heroic literature from the epic to seventeenth-century French romances, see Michael W. Alssid, 'The Design of Dryden's *Aureng-Zebe*,' *JEGP* 64 (1965), 452–69; Richard Law, 'The Heroic Ethos in John Dryden's Heroic Plays,' *SEL* 23 (1983), 389–98; and

Derek Hughes, *Dryden's Heroic Plays* (Lincoln: University of Nebraska Press 1981), ch. 6. For readings that stress the parodic, ironic, or campy aspects of the play, see D.W. Jefferson, 'The Significance of Dryden's Heroic Plays,' *Restoration Drama*, ed. John Loftis (New York: Oxford University Press 1966), 161–79; Bruce King, *Dryden's Major Plays* (Edinburgh: Oliver & Boyd 1966), 116–32; and Robert S. Newman, 'Irony and the Problem of Tone in Dryden's *Aureng-Zebe*,' *SEL* 10 (1970), 439–58. For two readings that treat *Aureng-Zebe* first and foremost as a play, see Harold F. Brooks, 'Dryden's *Aureng-Zebe*: Debts to Corneille and Racine,' *Revue de Littérature Comparée* 46 (1972), 5–34; and Arthur C. Kirsch, *Dryden's Heroic Drama* (Princeton: Princeton University Press 1965), ch. 4. My own reading is closest to that of Kirsch, who sees in *Aureng-Zebe* a movement towards the representation of domestic piety and compassion that characterizes much drama of the late 1670s and 1680s, including Dryden's.

3 See Aby Warburg, 'The Theatrical Costumes for the Intermedi of 1589,' in *The Renewal of Pagan Antiquity*, intro. Kurt W. Forster, trans. David Britt (Los Angeles: Getty Research Institute for the History of Art and the Humanities 1999).

4 Irene Mamczarz, *Le Théâtre Farnese de Parme et le drame musical italien (1618–1732)* (Florence: L.S. Olschki 1988), 31.

5 On baroque theatres, see Margarete Baur-Heinhold, *The Baroque Theatre: A Cultural History of the 17th and 18th Centuries*, trans. Mary Whittall (New York: McGraw-Hill 1967), chap. 6.

6 Although an inauguration of the Teatro Farnese was initially planned for 1618, it was cancelled because of the illness of Cosimo de Medeci II. *Dido and Aeneas* was performed as a sung intermezzo in 1628, when the theatre was inaugurated by Ranuccio I's son, Odoardo I. See Mamczarz, *Le Théâtre Farnese*, 128.

7 René Wellek and Austin Warren, *Theory of Literature* (New York: Harcourt Brace 1949), 278. Heinrich Wölfflin is largely responsible for the introduction of the word 'baroque' into modern scholarly accounts of the fine arts; see his *Renaissance and Baroque* (1888), intro. Peter Murray, trans. Kathrin Simon (Ithaca: Cornell University Press 1964). The term was a victim of its own success among literary critics in the first half of the twentieth century, for it was used so profligately that it lost precision; see René Wellek, 'The Concept of Baroque in Literary Scholarship,' *The Journal of Aesthetics and Art Criticism* 5.2 (1946): 77–109. Perhaps the most influential attempt to describe a peculiarly baroque form of tragedy is Walter Benjamin's *The Origin of German Tragic Drama* (1963), intro. George Steiner, trans. John Osborne (Lon-

don: NLB 1977). I subscribe to many of Benjamin's views but see the German *Trauerspiel* as a local variant of a European-wide form, one that is less important to English baroque tragedy than are its French, Italian, and Spanish variants. While Benjamin believes that from the point of view of the *Trauerspiel* 'opera must seem unmistakably to be a product of decadence' (212), I see the moveable scenes and *stilo rappresentivo* of seventeenth-century opera as answers to the original and legitimate requirements of baroque tragedy. For an application of the term 'baroque' to Dryden's drama, see Landrum Banks, 'Dryden's Baroque Drama,' in *Essays in Honor of Esmond Linsworth Marilla*, ed. Thomas Austin Kirby and William John Olive (Baton Rouge: Louisiana State University Press 1970), 188–200. Jocelyn Powell occasionally invokes the term 'baroque' in her readings of Restoration plays other than *Aureng-Zebe*; see her *Restoration Theatre Production* (London: Routledge & Kegan Paul 1984).

 8 On the history of changeable scenery, see especially Richard Southern, *Changeable Scenery: Its Origin and Development in the British Theatre* (London: Faber and Faber 1952). Also see Sybil Rosenfeld, *A Short History of Scene Design in Great Britain* (Totowa, N.J.: Rowman and Littlefield 1973); Powell, *Restoration Theatre Production*; and Edward A. Langhans, 'The Theatre,' in *English Restoration Theatre*, ed. Deborah Payne Fisk (Cambridge: Cambridge University Press 2000), 1–18.

 9 Samuel Chappuzeau, *L'Europe vivante* (Paris 1667), 214–15.

10 John Dryden, *An Essay of Dramatick Poesie. The Works of John Dryden*, ed. E.N. Hooker, H.T. Swedenberg Jr, et al., 20 vols. (Berkeley: University of California Press 1956–2000),17:30 (hereafter cited as *California Dryden*).

11 René Descartes, *The Passions of the Soul*, trans. Stephen Voss (1649; Indianapolis: Hackett Publishing Co. 1989), Article 53.

12 Dryden, 'Of Heroique Plays.' *California Dryden* 11:14.

13 See Dean T. Mace, 'Dryden's Dialogue on Drama,' *Journal of the Warburg and Courtauld Institute* 25 (1962): 87–112; Dryden, *Essay of Dramatick Poesie. California Dryden* 17:15.

14 Mace, 'Dryden's Dialogue,' 91.

15 Sir William Davenant, Authors Preface, *Gondibert*, ed. David F. Gladish (Oxford: Clarendon Press 1971), 5. Davenant's Preface first appeared by itself in 1650; the first three of *Gondibert*'s five projected books appeared in 1651.

16 Dryden, *Essay of Dramatick Poesie. California Dryden* 17:32.

17 [Thomas Betterton,] *The History of the English Stage* (London: Printed for E. Curll 1741), 54.

18 [Betterton,] *History*, 64, 72.

19 Dryden, 'Parallel of Poetry and Painting.' *California Dryden* esp. 20:64.
20 Colley Cibber, *An Apology for the Life of Mr. Colley Cibber*, ed. B.R.S. Fone (1740; reprint, Ann Arbor: University of Michigan Press 1968), 225.
21 [Betterton,] *History*, 53.
22 John Bulwer, *Chirologia: or the Natvrall Langvage of the Hand* (London: printed by Tho. Harper 1644). For the books in Betterton's library, see Jacob Hooke, *Pinacotecha Bettertonaeana* (1710). For a discussion of Betterton's holdings, see Joseph Roach, *Cities of the Dead: Circum-Atlantic Performance* (New York: Columbia University Press 1996), 106–9.
23 Charles Le Brun, *Conférence sur l'expression des passions.* Le Brun presented his work to the Royal Academy of Painting and Sculpture in 1668, but it was not published until 1696.
24 Jules de la Mesnardière, *La Poétique* (Paris: chez Antoine de Sommaville 1640). On La Mesnardière and Dryden, see Mace, 'Dryden's Dialogue,' 95–6, 100–4.
25 For an example of Monteverdi's thought on the passions, poetic form, and musical tempo, see 'Claudio Monteverde a' chi legge,' in *Madrigali guerrieri et amorosi* (1638; reprint New York: Dover Publications 1991), xv. For the note on performance, see 304.
26 *California Dryden*, 12:249, ll. 7–8. All subsequent references are to this edition and are cited parenethically in the text.
27 Dryden, 'A Grounds of Criticism in Tragedy.' *California Dryden* 13:241–2.
28 Dryden, 'Of Heroique Plays.' *California Dryden* 11:14.
29 Dryden, 'Of Heroique Plays,' 11:9.
30 Joseph Roach, *The Player's Passion: Studies in the Science of Acting* (Newark: University of Delaware Press 1985), 69.
31 Richard Steele, *Tatler*, no. 115, 3 January 1709/10, quoted in Roach, *Player's Passion*, 69.
32 See Richard Kroll, 'Emblem and Empiricism in Davenant's *Macbeth*,' *ELH* 57 (1990), 835–64.
33 Dryden, *Essay of Dramatick Poesie. California Dryden* 17:30–1.
34 See, for example, Ovid, *Metamorphoses*, trans. Frank Justus Miller, Loeb Classical Library, 2nd ed. (Cambridge: Harvard University Press 1984), 9.603–7, where Byblis regrets professing her desire to her brother in written tablets:

> vidisset lacrimas, vultum vidisset amantis;
> plura loqui poteram, quam quae cepere tabellae.
> invito putui circumdare bracchia collo,

> et, si reicerer, potui moritura videri
> amplectique pedes, adfusaque poscere vitam.

[He should have seen my tears, he should have seen his lover's face; I could have spoken more than any tablet could hold; I could have thrown my arms about his unwilling neck and, if I were rejected, I could have seemed at the point of death, could have embraced his feet and, lying prostrate there, have begged for life.] All references to the *Metamorphoses* are to this edition and are cited parenthetically in the text.

35 For the metamorphosis of Byblis, see *Met.* 9.649–65. The Latin of Myrrha's metamorphosis reads,

> quae quamquam amisit veteres cum corpore sensus
> flet tamen, et tepidae manant ex arbore guttae.
> est honor et lacrimis, stillataque cortice murra
> nomen erile tenet nulloque tacebitur aevo.
> (10.499–502)

36 Aristotle, *On Poetry and Style*, trans. G.M.A. Grube (Indianapolis: Bobbs-Merrill Educational Publishing 1958), 1460a.

37 Nourmahal says,

> Custom our Native Royalty does awe;
> Promiscuous Love is Nature's general Law.
> For whosoever the first Lovers were,
> Brothers and sisters made the second Pair,
> And doubled, by their love, their piety
> (IV.i.131–5).

Compare Myrrha's similar arguments, which also turn on natural law, human laws, and piety (*Met.* 10.323–35).

38 Descartes, *Passions of the Soul*, Articles 72 and 75.

39 Dryden, 'Grounds of Criticism in Tragedy.' *California Dryden* 13:232, 231.

40 See Elizabeth Howe, *The First English Actresses: Women and Drama, 1660–1700* (Cambridge: Cambridge University Press 1992), esp. 110, 147–8, 153.

41 My description of the Cornaro Chapel draws heavily on Howard Hibbard, *Bernini* (London: Penguin 1965), 128–41.

42 Dryden echoes St Teresa's language in 'To Her Royal Highness, the Dutchess,' Preface to *The State of Innocence* (1677). *California Dryden* 12:83. Montague Summers cites the parallel passages in his edition of *John Dryden: The Dramatic Works* (London: Nonesuch Press 1931–2), 3:580. Also see James Anderson Winn, *John Dryden and His World* (New Haven: Yale University Press 1987), 296.

43 *Life of St Teresa*, ed. J.M. Cohen (London: Penguin Books 1957), 210.

44 As Hibbard notes, Bernini's detractors have often applied the adjective 'theatrical' to the Cornaro Chapel in an opporobrious sense (*Bernini*, 135). Bernini's more sympathetic interpreters, such as Hibbard and Rudolf Wittkower, are, predictably, at ease with the theatrical aspects of Bernini's sculpture. See Rudolf Wittkower, *Gian Lorenzo Bernini: The Sculptor of the Roman Baroque*, 2nd ed. (London: Phaidon Press 1966). In a fascinating moment of candour, Sir Herbert Read, a staunch detractor of Bernini, admits that he is 'subdued by the wonderful dramatic effects of Bernini's St. Teresa group ... but only by forgetting (or not noticing) that I am looking at sculpture,' an art form that should more properly reject everything for which Bernini stands – 'for a pictorial conception of the art of sculpture ..., for emotional involvement rather than timeless contemplation; for tumult rather than peace; for conscious conceit rather than naivity' ('Michelangelo and Bernini,' *The Listener* [24 Nov. 1955]): 888.

45 Dryden, 'To the Right Honourable John, Earl of Mulgrave.' *California Dryden* 12:155.

46 Aristotle, *On Poetry and Style*, 1453b; Pierre Corneille, 'Discours de la tragédie et des moyens de la traiter selon le vraisemblable ou le nécessaire,' in *Théâtre complet*, ed. Alain Niderst, 3 vols. (Rouen: Publications de l'Université de Rouen 1984), 1.1:72; my translation. Corneille's French reads, 'Les oppositions des sentiments de la nature aux emportements de la passion ou à la sévérité du devoir, forment de puissantes agitations, qui sont reçues de l'auditeur avec plaisir.'

47 For the argument that Dryden's plays are dramas of ideas, see Anne T. Barbeau, *The Intellectual Design of John Dryden's Heroic Plays* (New Haven: Yale University Press 1970); for the argument that they were meant to be applied (however complexly) to contemporary events, see John M. Wallace, '"Examples Are Best Precepts": Readers and Meanings in Seventeenth-Century Poetry,' *Critical Inquiry* 1 (1974), 273–90; for the best reading of *Aureng-Zebe*'s action and imagery, see Alssid, 'The Design of Dryden's *Aureng-Zebe*.'

48 My reading thus reaffirms, in some respects, Kirsch's interpretation of the play; see his *Dryden's Heroic Drama*, 118–28.

49 Dryden, *Essay of Dramatick Poesie. California Dryden*, 17:23.

50 Descartes, *The Passions of the Soul*, Art. 73.

51 Joseph Roach, 'The Performance,' in *The Cambridge Companion to English Restoration Theatre*, ed. Deborah Payne Fisk (Cambridge: Cambridge University Press, 2001), 23

52 [Betterton,] *History*, 65.

53 There is no explicit stage direction saying that Indamora prostrates herself.
    Alternatively, she may speak the line while standing erect before Morat, as if
    already aware that the power of her outward form has placed her on an
    equal footing with the man she is ostensibly suing for mercy.
54 On surrogacy as a notion of performance and cultural perpetuation, see
    Roach, *Cities of the Dead*, 2. Also see Richard Schechner, *Between Theater and
    Anthropology* (Philadelphia: University of Pennsylvania Press 1985), 36–7.
55 Brooks, 'Dryden's *Aureng-Zebe*,' 19.
56 Brooks, 'Dryden's *Aureng-Zebe*,' 22.
57 Dryden, 'Grounds of Criticism in Tragedy.' *California Dryden* 13:232.

chapter thirteen

'The ~~Rationall~~ Spirituall Part': Dryden and Purcell's Baroque *King Arthur*

DIANNE DUGAW

In early winter of 1691 the poet John Dryden (then old and famous, though out of favour) 'ghost-wrote' for the young composer Henry Purcell a prose dedication for the latter's published score, *The Vocal and Instrumental Musick of THE PROPHETESS, OR THE HISTORY OF DIOCLESIAN.* Existing in a manuscript in Dryden's hand and in the shorter version that was printed (presumably later), the essay reveals conceptual affinities between the two artists, including a view of the collaboration of poetry and music. The two arts are 'acknowledgd Sisters': 'As poetry is the harmony of words, so musick is that of notes ... Both of them may excell apart, but sure they are most excellent when they are joind ... for thus they appear like wit & beauty in the same person.'[1] The final, published version of the Dedication omits nearly thirty lines that, in the original manuscript, add painting to the aesthetic sorority of poetry and music.[2]

The longer, manuscript essay – thought to be Dryden's creation[3] – introduces my discussion of his mixings of music and poetry for two reasons. First, this text reflects the poet's late-career attention to multimedia collaborations both practically, in his own dramatic and lyric poetry, and theoretically, in his critical and aesthetic discussions. Second, the manuscript accords music and poetry 'precedence' over painting, 'a confind, & solitary Art.' By contrast, music and poetry exist 'in consort, & diffus'd through the world; partakeing somewhat of the Nature of the deity, which at once is in all places' (17:324–5). Music and poetry 'are of nearer kindred to the soule; have less of the matter, & more of the forme; less of the manuall operation, & more of the spirituall part, in humane nature' (17:325).

This last statement reaches us in pentimento in the manuscript. Dryden changed his wording – that music and poetry have 'more of the spirituall part' – from an original formulation: they have 'more of the rationall part.' What precisely comes to us of his thinking in the document is that music and poetry convey for us 'more of the ~~rationall~~ spirituall part in our humane nature.' 'Rational' becomes 'spiritual.'

This shift in conception encapsulates a development in intellectual and artistic sensibility that marks Dryden's late poetry and drama. From the 1680s Dryden's art increasingly takes on a pansensory, multimedia aspect, in which words are not enough. Multiple arts, ceremony, synaesthetic and synergistic imagery, and symbology are summoned up in songs and odes that make reference to, and theatrical works that incorporate, visually spectacular dramatic scenes, usually with music and dance as well. In other, strictly poetic texts, Dryden points beyond linguistic limits by evoking multisensory and awe-inspiring expressions of paradox. Even his translations, which work as tradition-citing recreations, acquire an almost typological new textual life. However much they echo and invoke their originals, they pointedly 'reincarnate' their models – Virgil, Ovid, Chaucer, Boccaccio. The texts of earlier poets work with resonance as analogical figures applied to the modes and circumstances of Dryden's own day.

Late works that develop a theoretical preoccupation with the arts as arts, especially interrelations of poetry and painting, include the odes to Anne Killigrew (1686) and Sir Godfrey Kneller (1694) as well as the 'Parallel of Poetry and Painting,' prefaced to the translation of Charles Dufresnoy's *De Arte Graphica*.[4] At the same time, Dryden, in conjunction with musicians, created numerous mixed-media works: the St Cecilia's Day odes, and theatrical works with developed scenes of music and dance.

All these strategies point beyond the 'rationall' to the 'more spirituall part' of readers and audiences. Their use coincides with Dryden's conversion to Catholicism and continuing loyalty to the ousted Stuart king, James II. Dryden's late works counter the rational, textual emphasis of Anglo-Protestantism and, it would seem, of Milton in particular. As Jean Hagstrum has observed, 'No account of Dryden can be satisfactory that does not consider both the classical-Renaissance and the Counter-Reformation–baroque in his poetic genius.'[5] It is the latter I wish to invoke here.

Dryden's late works set up sense-engaging dramatic and poetic figures that situate us not allegorically within the text, but outside it in the typological mode accessible through the connective mirrorings of allusion and analogy. Images, narrative events, or persons stand in historical relation to other images, events, or persons as types and antitypes, that is, as echoing prefigurations and fulfilments.[6] Dryden's multimedia works especially direct us beyond their texts to consider relations of prefiguring 'shadows' and fulfilling 'images' because they evoke and insist upon suprarational responses that lift characters in the works and, if successful, audiences of the works to a spiritual dimension. This notably sensual engagement resonates with the incarnational approach to typology of baroque Catholicism, particularly in the arts.[7] From our point of view, this Anglo-Catholicism can seem retrospective and conservative. In the baroque world of Dryden's time and from his perspective, it was innovative and synthesizing. Articulating a newly self-conscious artistry of sensory experience, *King Arthur,* for example, offers a new representation of a gendered humanity in a reimagined sacramental and suprarational world.

These music dramas, odes, and translations, far from being accidents of a disgruntled and financially desperate old age, pointedly 'English' the baroque spiritual aesthetic of Catholic Europe. Dryden's much-puzzled-over conversion to Catholicism, interpreted variously as a moment of political expediency or a cover for radical scepticism, fits coherently within a developing aesthetic of a collaboration of the arts traceable after *Absalom and Achitophel* on through such works as *King Arthur* and *Alexander's Feast.* Dryden's remarks in the Purcell dedication about the enspiriting 'forme' of music and poetry implicitly cite Aristotle in a recognizably Aquinian mode as the aesthetically accessible Word Incarnate of the Catholic baroque, in keeping with Counter-Reformation theories of the arts. As the Spanish painter Francisco Pacheco said in 1649 of his art: 'It would be hard to overstate the good that holy images do: they perfect our understanding, move our will, refresh our memory of divine things. They heighten our spirits ... and show to our eyes and hearts the heroic and magnanimous acts of patience, of justice, chastity, meekness, charity, and contempt for worldly things in such a way that they instantly cause us to seek virtue and to shun vice, and thus put us on the roads that lead to blessedness.'[8] Art, thus, points beyond the materials and limits of its making to move minds and spirits by means of its material experience through the senses, to a greater 'blessedness' in a world in which the divine is present.

The collaborative combinings of music and words (often together with staged visual scenes) disclose most clearly the 'memory of divine things,' the enspiriting embodiment for which Dryden's later works reach. Throughout his dramas, Dryden made use of music in songs and lavishly staged masque scenes. However, in his last decade he fashioned pointedly ambitious collaborations with composers, including the through-composed political masque of *Albion and Albanius* (1685), the 'Song for St. Cecelia's Day' (1687), the farcical *Amphitryon* (1690), the lavishly musicked semi-opera *King Arthur* (1691), *Alexander's Feast* (1697), and the *Secular Masque* (1700). Dryden's undertaking of these works can be seen as a practical decision, prompted by financial necessity and the requests of patrons. Nonetheless, considering them together illuminates their coherent ontological and theological sensibility, especially in the context of the poet's conversion and the theology and baroque aesthetic of Catholicism. *King Arthur* demonstrates this sensual dimensionality and spiritual 'lift.' While the work's form suggests that the collaboration of text, music, and spectacle reaches beyond the limitations of language alone, thematic elements underscore this message as well. Discernment and power require more than textual acuity and the empirical reason it yields.

Dryden's *King Arthur* originated in an early form in 1684, when it was intended to celebrate the twenty-fifth anniversary of the restoration of the Stuart monarchy in 1685. However, Charles II died, and the libretto was shelved, to be taken up again in 1690, when Dryden and the young Henry Purcell refashioned it as a dramatic opera or semi-opera (that is, a spoken play with interpolated musical sections) for production at Dorset Gardens in June of 1691. Dryden's text appeared in print in early June. The music, with a range of textual variations, exists in a complicated and incomplete array of manuscript and printed versions.[9] We cannot reconstruct exactly what Purcell and Dryden created and oversaw, though *King Arthur* has been revived many times in diverse arrangements of the libretto and scores.

The story imagines a conflict for the rule of Britain between 'Heathen' Saxons under the leadership of Oswald, King of Kent, and the Christian Britons under the rule of Arthur.[10] Filled with magic and supernatural interventions, the play pits the powers of the Britons' 'famous Inchanter,' Merlin, against those of the Saxons' devilish Osmond, whose 'Earthy Spirit,' the bass-singing Grimbald, has a counterpart on the Briton side in the Ariel-like 'Airy Spirit,' Philidel. A soprano, Philidel has converted from the ranks of the fallen angels 'to shun the *Saxon* Wizard's dire Commands' and aid Arthur and the Britons.[11]

After an initial battle in which the Britons prevail, the play takes up the competition between the Briton Arthur and the Saxon Oswald for the hand of the blind Emmeline, daughter of the duke of Cornwall, whose sight is miraculously restored midway in the action. Although she loves Arthur, Emmeline is courted and kidnapped by Oswald. Osmond, his lusting sorcerer, holds her captive among the Saxons and accosts her unsuccessfully through magical schemes meant to induce her betrayal. When Arthur nears, Osmond and Grimbald, his demon, turn their sorcery on him, tempting him with the lure of sexy sirens and finally an apparition of Emmeline, whose form the evil Grimbald assumes. Aided by Philidel, Arthur withstands these tests, whose devilishness is disclosed and disempowered amid a peal of thunder. Arthur and Oswald then meet in hand-to-hand combat for the crown and Emmeline. After both are wounded, Arthur disarms Oswald, and the two forge a peace in which '*Britains* and *Saxons* shall be once one People; / One Common Tongue, one Common Faith shall bind / [Their] Jarring Bands, in a perpetual Peace' (V.ii.87–9).

A wave of Merlin's wand calls up a final, multifaceted musical masque that envisions Britannia in a unified prosperity and peace. Against the political backdrop of the Dutch William's displacement of James II, the play, as critics note, continually brings to mind the national predicament, albeit ambiguously. Concluding with a dream of hoped-for resolution between Saxons and Britons, *King Arthur* subtly yet insistently invokes through text, music, and allusion the Jacobite cause and the aesthetic and moral sensibility of the Catholic baroque that it represents.[12]

Music, dance, and visual design shape songs and episodes that, beyond dialogue alone, supply models and mappings for human decision making. We witness a human experience that is both rational and sensory, and that not only benefits from but also requires priestly and supernatural help. Music, words, dance, and spectacle construct a scene in the baroque rhetoric that assumes a world that manifests itself in the parallel realities of matter and spirit. Musical scenes show how, on the one hand, guidance is available, and on the other, deception and temptation, as appearances are channelled from the supernatural realm to this world and the experiences we mortals either plunge into or ponder.

An example supplies a figurative representation for this mapping of decision making. In Act II, following their initial victory, the Britons seek a safe passage through a dark swampland. Merlin's powers, delegated through the music of Philidel, supply a needed guidance. Imagery in Dryden's text and a telling allusion offer Arthur and his Britons the means to navigate their predicament safely. Telltale sounds in Purcell's music make recognition of the right way possible.[13]

Even as Merlin sends Philidel with his 'Band of Spirits' to aid the wandering Britons in their pursuit of the fleeing Saxons, Grimbald, '*Osmond*'s fierce Fiend,' enters '*in the Habit of a Shepherd*' to mislead Arthur and his aides (II.i.43, 54). 'Here, this way, *Britons*, follow *Oswald*'s flight' (II.i.55) the disguised Grimbald beckons. 'Lead on, we follow thee' (II.i.63), the duped Arthur replies, as he misses a revealing precedent to the masquerade. Grimbald's ruse echoes that of Milton's Comus, who, in a masque focused on music's power and sway, disguises himself as a shepherd to confound and seduce a lady.[14] In contrast to the treatment of Milton and Henry Lawes, however, a pointedly sensual music here provides guidance rather than delusion. Dryden and Purcell pose the dilemma of Arthur and his men: whether to follow the tangible-seeming shepherd or the unseen spirit voices.

Reasoning alone offers no guarantee against deception. When Arthur and his men prepare to follow the masquerading Grimbald, Philidel and her chorus warn them of the '*Malicious Fiend*' (II.i.65) and his '*false deluding Lights*' (II.i.66): 'Name but Heav'n, and he'll avoid ye' (II.i.75). The devil and demons shy from the mention of God. The Britons thus face a task familiar to Counter-Reformation spirituality: the discernment of spirits – distinguishing authentic, divinely granted spiritual experience from delusion caused by devils or self-interest:

> *Hither this way, this way bend,*
> *Trust not that Malicious Fiend:*
> *Those are false deluding Lights,*
> *Wafted far and near by Sprights.*
> *Trust 'em not, for they'll deceive ye;*
> *And in Bogs and Marshes leave ye*
> ....
> *If you step, no Danger thinking,*
> *Down you fall, a Furlong sinking:*
> *'Tis a Fiend who has annoy'd ye;*
> *Name but Heav'n, and he'll avoid ye.*
> (II.i.64–6, 72–5)

Purcell's setting here creates a harmonic pull in the opening phrase that engages the listener in an experience of 'bending' as the melody moves from the tonic chord of D minor to the dominant A major. In addition, the melodic chromaticism of the C-sharp on the word 'bend' sharpens the experience. This initial chromaticism is itself heightened

Fig. 13.1 *'Trust not ... the malicious fiend'*

by contrast as the C-sharp quickly moves to a C-natural, and the text goes from a physical directive – 'bend' – to a moral and spiritual one – *'Trust not ... the malicious fiend'* (fig. 13.1).

Significant also is the tumbling on 'malicious,' certainly another warning in the sensual realm, an auditory and experiential 'descent' that will be echoed and articulated even more elaborately in the melodic setting for the word *'down'* in the song's second stanza. These warning signs are carefully carried out in the sensory realm as melody and harmony move the listener, both within the play and without, to 'bend' with the music and to be alerted to warning and 'descent.'[15]

Among the Britons, Conon suspects deception in the supposed-shepherd Grimbald's recommendations: 'Some wicked Phantom, / Foe to Human kind, / Misguides our Steps' (II.i.81–2). 'I'll follow him no farther,' announces his colleague Albanact. In an aside, the chagrined Grimbald curses the success of Philidel's cautionary art. Identifying himself in Miltonian terms as one of the fallen angels, Grimbald attempts to regain his singing voice, lost at the time of his fall from grace. 'By Hell,' he groans, 'she sings 'em back, in my despight. / I had a Voice in Heav'n, ere Sulph'rous Steams / Had damp'd it to a hoarseness; but I'll try' (II.i.83–5). Grimbald then sings a song. This relatively unadorned strophic piece admonishes its listeners to apply reason to the dilemma of their disorientation. The singing Grimbald urges the Britons to appraise the evidence of Oswald's *'Footsteps plain appearing'* (II.i.92) and to proceed with him after thus rationally and empirically assessing the firmness of turf that looks steady.

The song itself, however, is notably awkward in the execution, as the fiend attempts to negotiate, Philidel-like, a piece whose singing is beyond him. However reasonable the content of his suggestions, Grimbald cannot manage the form: he cannot sing. His unmusical utterance should guide neither his listeners onstage nor his audience in the theatre, but it should tip us off. Further, for any attentive Briton, the first verse raises a menacing image of flames followed by a breathless exhortation that tumbles precariously down a full octave: *'Hurry, hurry, hurry, hurry on'* (II.i.91). The engaged responses of passion and the senses must complement, rather than be replaced by, reason. The sensual experience of this tuneless tune's unsteady rhythms (——) and gapping and graceless intervals (– – – –) alerts us to a clumsiness that is not to be trusted (fig. 13.2).

The temptation to engage only in rationality's dispassionate analysis of sensory experience at the expense of other kinds of evidence sways the confused Britons, who interrupt their responsiveness to aesthetic persuasion to take up the content of Grimbald's message. Doing so, they fail to appreciate the warnings recognizable in the form of the badly sung song. ''Tis true, he says,' observes Aurelius, 'the Footsteps yet are fresh / Upon the Sod, no falling Dew-Drops have / Disturb'd the Print' (II.i.98–100). They succumb to the enticements of reliance on this limited and detached sensory plane of visual experience alone – an empiricism typical of Whig Protestantism – and nearly lose their way in fatal fashion. *'All are going to follow* Grimbald' prompts the stage direction (II.i.100).[16]

At this point Philidel and her Chorus resume their admonition – *'Hither this way, this way bend'* (II.i.102) – whose persuasiveness brings the listeners to *'incline to* Philidel' (II.i.106). Hereupon Grimbald breaks from his cover with a telltale curse: 'Curse on her Voice, I must my Prey

Fig. 13.2 '*Hurry, hurry, hurry, hurry on*'

forego.' He is revealed as he '*sinks with a Flash*' (II.i.107–8). 'At last the
Cheat is plain,' cries Arthur, 'The Cloven-footed Fiend is Vanish'd from
us; / Good Angels be our Guides, and bring us back' (II.i.109–11).

The music in English drama of the seventeenth century articulates
aesthetically a view of human experience within a complex world of
planed realities. This is particularly true with regard to dramatic operas
like *King Arthur*, in which spectacular scenes of music and dance are
interpolated within plots that unfold in spoken dialogue. Musical scenes
are 'critical instants' performed by spirits, priests, rustics, or other figures from a caste apart, often a mediating caste. These episodes stop the
plot for the contemplation of the dilemmas in the dramatic action, pos-
ing analogues and prototypes to disclose their meaning; their deeper
spiritual or psychological implications; or their further consequences or
possible resolutions.[17]

Interpolated musical scenes function within the drama as a whole in
emblematic or typological ways. They intersect the strictly textual plane
of the play's present tense with its merely human actors to offer the
echoing of literary and historical precedence in one dimension, of the
interior and psychological experience of the individual in another, and
of the presence of forces from supernatural realms in a third. These
dimensions, the latter two especially, require the suprarational rhetorics

of music and spectacle to articulate fully that 'spirituall part of our nature' that functions beyond the rational plane of merely human action and dialogue.

The resonant interlacing of the voices, images, and presences of masque scenes in the fabric of music dramas is of a piece with the dynamic and complex aesthetic of baroque art. One finds counterparts in the emblematic paintings of Rubens or the portraits by El Greco that bring earthly patrons and their bishops together on a canvas alongside assemblies of heavenly saints and angels. Certainly Bernini's suspended sculpture 'The Ecstacy of St Teresa' engages its viewers in the Roman Church of Santa Maria della Vittoria in exactly this manner. Virtually all the musical episodes in *King Arthur* likewise stitch the actors at the dramatic level into a multiplaned world whose voices and movements present an aesthetic comment upon or a foreshadowing of predicaments that they (and we) are being guided to undergo and understand.

The masque scenes in *King Arthur*, with enhancements of music and dance, prompt a suprarational response in characters and audience. Reasoning in the plane of the material world of quotidian experience must be guided by supernatural presences to resolve conflicts of discernment and right action. The masquing thus becomes a central, even a chief component, of *King Arthur*.

Dryden sought to represent a gendered human nature whose spirit is expressed in the reasonings of thought and yet, for both men and women, reaches beyond the bounds of words. In musically encoded scenes, Emmeline and Arthur are by turns subjected to gender-differentiated trials that evoke both chivalric conventions and Christian models of spiritual temptation. At the play's centre is a complex masque to 'thaw' the captive Emmeline to the sexual demands of Osmond, whose aggressive virility is underscored. 'My Name is *Osmond*, and my Business Love,' the Saxon greets her. 'Thou hast a griezly look,' she replies, 'forbidding what thou ask'st, / If I durst tell thee so.' 'My Pent-House Eye-Brows, and my Shaggy Beard / Offend your Sight, but these are Manly Signs,' he insists. 'Be Woman; know your Sex, and Love full Pleasures ... Come you must Love, or you must suffer Love; / No Coyness, None, for I am Master here' (III.ii.238–47). 'I Freeze,' the metaphorizing Emmeline declares, 'as if his impious Art had fix'd / My Feet to Earth.' 'But Love shall thaw ye,' Osmond predicts as he prepares a stark, then sensuous anti-masque of 'impious Art' (III.ii.265–7) to sway Emmeline's resolve. Striking the ground, he brings on '*a Prospect of Winter in Frozen Countries*' (III.ii.276).

'Cupid' descends and arouses for Emmeline's persuasion a '*Genius of the Clime ... asleep beneath those Hills of Snow*' (III.ii.277–8). Purcell's music raises a frosty baritone from a laboured and trembling chromaticism to the warm tunefulness of song.[18] '*Let me, let me, Freeze again to Death*' (III.ii.287), the Genius poignantly pleads. Cupid replies with a trivializing rebuke sung to a phrase that tumbles precipitously downward: '*Thou Doting Fool, forbear, forbear; / What, Dost thou Dream of Freezing here?*' (III.ii. 288–9). Persuaded by promises of '*Spring*' and warming '*Beams*' (and overlooking Cupid's troubling dismissiveness), the Genius responds:

> *Great Love, I know thee now;*
> *Eldest of the Gods art Thou:*
> *Heav'n and Earth, by Thee were made.*
> *Humane Nature,*
> *Is thy Creature,*
> *Every where Thou art obey'd*   (III.ii.292, 293, 296–301)[19]

However sensually persuasive, the Frost Scene is, as the right-thinking Emmeline discerns, 'impious Art.' The Genius's adoration of Cupid reveals his faulty, not to say blasphemous, understanding. Should the idolatry of the text escape her, the clumsy, gapped melody of his singing – as with Grimbald's in the earlier example – should alert her to the baritone's misallegiance as the fitful melody lurches throughout in downward octave jumps.

Cupid then conjures complicit singers and dancers whose antics echo the tempting call to surrender to love. The spectacle ends with a command consonant with Osmond's abusive threat to Emmeline. '*Sound a Parley, ye Fair, and surrender,*' demands Cupid,

> *Set your selves, and your Lovers at ease,*
> *He's a Grateful Offender*
> *Who Pleasure dare seize:*
> *But the Whining Pretender*
> *Is sure to displease.*   (318–23)

The menacing intrusion of G-minor harmonies into this ostensible song of triumph undermines any careful listener's assent to the text's assurances.[20]

This masque alternately tempts and threatens Emmeline to betray her love for Arthur. However, the discerning heroine will not be deceived

and recognizes this Frost Scene – a justly famous and periodically
revived set piece from the play – for the 'impious Art' (III.ii.265; her
phrase) that it is. 'I cou'd be pleas'd with any one but thee, / Who entertain'd my sight with such Gay Shows,' she declares to the lusting
Osmond (III.ii.330–1). 'From my sight' (III.ii.337) she cries after witnessing the scene's spectacular music and dancing. Hers is the conventional language of Catholic hagiographies for casting out demons:
'Thou all thy devils in one, thou dar'st not force me' (337–8). But
Osmond will not be dissuaded except by forces beyond him. At this
point Emmeline prays for deliverance, and the supernaturally aided
Arthur arrives to intervene.

Arthur too undergoes trials instigated by the spell-casting Osmond
and Grimbald; like Emmeline he must withstand the seductive idea that
'*No Joys are above, / The Pleasures of Love*,' as the sinuously harmonic trio
of Nymphs and Sylvans sing and dance before him (IV.ii.73–4). However, his third and most dangerous temptation is not a musical entice-
ment, but a challenge to his reason, appealing to a notably manly and
post-Reformation aspiration. Only supernatural intervention prevents
disaster.

Grimbald takes on the appearance of Emmeline to misdirect Arthur,
who thus again faces a dilemma of discernment. 'Break up, ye thickning
Foggs, and filmy Mists,' he implores, 'All that be-lye my Sight, and cheat
my Sense. / For Reason still pronounces, 'tis not she' (IV.ii.107–9). But
Grimbald's false 'Emmeline' persuades him in lines whose fallacious
appeal to self-will he fails to recognize. 'Believe thy Self, thy Youth, thy
Love, and me,' the phantom advises ominously, 'They only, they, who
please themselves are Wise: / Disarm thy Hand, that mine may meet it
bare' (IV.ii.123–5). 'By thy leave, Reason, here I throw thee off, / Thou
load of Life (IV.ii.126–7),' Arthur replies. Then, in a parody of reasoning, he postulates his self-justification in burlesque Neoplatonic syllo-
gisms. 'If thou wert made for Souls,' he declares to Reason, 'Then Souls
shou'd have been made without their Bodies' (IV.ii.127–8). He proceeds to forgive Adam's sin with an assertion of his own intention to
repeat it: 'If, falling for the first Created Fair, / Was *Adam*'s Fault, great
Grandsire I forgive thee, / *Eden* was lost, as all thy Sons wou'd loose it'
(129–31). However, Philidel intervenes, revealing the supposed Emmeline to be the 'ugliest Fiend in Hell' (IV.ii.139). The rescued Arthur ventures on to meet the Saxons for final victory over Oswald. Purified in
companionate trials of discernment, Emmeline and Arthur stand ready
to preside over a restored and unified Britain.

Their paring presents a gendered ideal. In *King Arthur,* a deliberately sensuous and bi-gendered sensibility counters the manly, text-based rationalism of Anglo-Protestantism in which a 'manly' subject – a category that subsumes women as well as men – deciphers divine intention through a circumscribed reason. In the sacramentalized spirituality of baroque Catholicism, by contrast, women and men alike proceed with a more obligatory engagement of a passionate sensory experience together with reason. Both are required for a faith and discernment open to the active presence of supernatural guidance and aid. The feminized and restrained courtliness of Arthur, who requires divine help, contrasts with the boorish masculinity of the Saxons, implicitly represented as demonic.

Evidence suggests that, despite the careful ambiguities and unresolved ironies of *King Arthur,* contemporaries suspected, even if they could not prove, its Jacobite and Catholic sway. The play was staged in 1691 with no censorship or overt complaint of its political and religious tenor. But the play's Stuart leanings, however ambivalent and couched in ironic subversions, were discernible. In a short time, Dryden's detractors voiced objections to the poet's blasphemies in terms that suggest a link between his collaborations with Purcell and a noticeably 'Popish' reach beyond the rational.

In 1695 there appeared Richard Blackmore's *Prince Arthur,* an ambitious and pointedly unambiguous recasting of Arthur as an arriving Williamite conqueror who likewise battles for his fair Ethelina and the union and peace of Britain.[21] Blackmore's Preface to his ten-book epic opens with an attack on the licentiousness of the stage – certainly pointing to the Dryden-Purcell play. The Preface goes on to declare the superiority of Blackmore's own rendering of the story in the unmystifying truths of an unadorned text. 'The Action,' he says, 'must be related in an *Allegorical* manner; and this Rule is best observ'd, when as *Divines* Speak; there is both a *literal* Sence obvious to every Reader, and that gives him satisfaction enough if he sees no farther; and besides another *Mystical* or *Typical* Sense, not hard to be discover'd by those Readers that penetrate the matter deeper.'[22]

A second edition of *Prince Arthur* in the first year of publication clarifies both the rationality and the politics of Blackmore's recommended allegory. An elaborate index identifies the fancifully mythic names of the poem ('Dornavaria,' 'Vendogladia,' 'Durotriges,' and so on) with the towns and counties of southwestern England (Dorset, Winburn, the river Stoure), and with various allies and enemies that featured in the progress of William of Orange and his army in 1688 from their landing in Torbay to his assumption of the crown. Blackmore's heroic couplets thus rebut both the content and the form of the Dryden-Purcell *King Arthur* in an unabashedly Williamite celebration.[23]

In the same year, 1695, appeared *Urania's Temple: or, a SATYR upon the Silent-Poets*, an anonymous verse condemnation of those poets who pointedly did *not* offer panegyrics at the crowning of William and Mary.[24] Dryden, a '*Senior Delphick* 'mongst the *minor Wits*,' of course, headed the list as 'A Magisterial *Belweather* Tupe / The Lordly *Leader* of his *Bleating Troop*.'[25] Amidst sixty lines of ill-natured excoriation, the poem's characterization of Dryden's 'strange bigotted Muse' suggests the link between the poet's Catholicism and his musical masques.[26] Observing that he had 'Tun'd to the late great *Court-Tarantula*' – in Samuel Johnson's definition, 'an insect whose bite is only cured by music'[27] – the scornful satirist scoffs that Dryden '*lured* to *Bread*, and *maskt* into *Religion*.'[28] This line, bringing together 'bread,' 'masques,' and 'religion,' thus proposes the link between such musical drama and the much contested idea of transubstantiation that marked doctrinal and devotional difference between Catholic and Protestant. The belittling *SATYR* underscores the Catholic resonance to the musical masquing in *King Arthur* and other works of Dryden.

The death of the young Henry Purcell in 1695 put an end to whatever further collaborations the two may have had in mind. Dryden's elegiac ode for his young friend provoked an attack that, like *Urania's Temple*, clarifies the meaning of the poet's change of emphasis from the 'rationall' to the 'spirituall part.' Dryden's elegy was published in 1696 with a musical setting by John Blow.[29] The poem laments the loss of this 'God-like Man,' who 'Alas, too soon retir'd, / As He too late began.'[30] Blow's published setting changes Dryden's 'God-like Man' to a 'matchless Man.'[31] Whatever Blow's reasons for the rewording, Arthur Bedford, in a treatise of 1711 entitled *The Great Abuse of Musick*, castigates Dryden for the original '*blasphemous Epithet*.' Bedford's remarks suggest the deeper implications of Dryden's conversion in his art and indicate contemporary reception of the Catholic elements in his work. Bedford commends Blow for replacing 'one *blasphemous Epithet*' with 'another less offensive,' where 'instead thereof the *Poet* had twice call'd him the *Godlike Man*.'[32] As Bedford complains, Dryden 'goes on according to the usual Fancy, in comparing of every thing with *God*, and the Joys of *Heaven*, that the Hearer may entertain mean Thoughts of both.'[33] As I suggest here, Bedford is right. But this presence of the supernatural in the lines is not blasphemy for Dryden. On the contrary, it is for the poet the necessary appeal to and articulation of 'the spirituall part of our humane nature.' This 'Englishing' in Dryden's art of the incarnational sensibility of the Catholic baroque remains almost invisible to an English literary history profoundly shaped by the dominant assumptions and modes of Anglo-Protestantism.

Notes

1 John Dryden, Dedication to *The Prophetess. The Works of John Dryden*, ed. E.N. Hooker, H.T. Swedenberg, Jr, et al., 20 vols. (Berkeley: University of California Press, 1956–2000), 17:324–6 and 482–4. All references are to this edition (hereafter cited as *California Dryden*) and will be cited parenthetically in the text.

2 See Roswell Ham, 'Dryden's Dedication for *The Music of THE PROPHET-ESSE, 1691*,' *PMLA*, 50 (1935), 1065–75. In addition to what is apparently the printer's copy in Dryden's hand, the longer text exists as well in a second manuscript in an unidentified hand. With regard to the discussion of painting, it is not hard to imagine Purcell insisting on the removal of these digressive remarks from the dedication.

3 On the attribution, see Ham, 'Dryden's Dedication,' 1065–68 and *California Dryden* 17:482–4.

4 See A.E. Wallace Maurer's discussion in the *California Dryden* 20:337–52. For discussion of the importance of painting in general to Dryden's work, see especially 345–9. See also Jean Hagstrum, *The Sister Arts: The Tradition of Literary Pictorialism and English Poetry from Dryden to Gray* (Chicago: University of Chicago Press 1958), 173–209.

5 Hagstrum, *The Sister Arts*, 178

6 For important standard works on 'typology,' see Paul Korshin, *Typologies in England, 1650–1820* (Princeton: Princeton University Press 1982) and Earl Miner, *Literary Uses of Typology* (Princeton: Princeton University Press 1977).

7 In *Typology and Seventeenth-Century Literature* (The Hague and Paris: Mouton 1975), Joseph Galdon, S.J., stresses the 'spiritual' and supratextual nature of typology and the distinction between it and allegory, which concerns 'words themselves.' See esp. 19–53.

8 Francisco Pacheco, *The Art of the Painter* (Seville 1649), in R. Enggass and J. Brown, *Italy and Spain, 1600–1700, Sources and Documents in the History of Art* (Englewood Cliffs, N.J.: Prentice-Hall 1970), 163–4.

 9 *Works of Henry Purcell,* Vol. 26, revised edition (London: Novello 1971),
    vii–xiv.

10 Dryden's heroic Arthur, known to have originated in the 1680s as a tribute to
    a triumphant Stuart monarchy, may have from the start been conceived in
    relation to Milton. The latter wrote a number of Latin poems on Arthur in
    his youth and seems to have planned an epic on the hero. These poems were
    published in the 1670s and would have been known to Dryden.

11 *California Dryden,* 16:22, II.i.23. All subsequent references are to this edition
    and will be cited parenthetically in the text.

12 On the Jacobite tenor of the play that persuasively argues from the musical
    scenes and settings, see Curtis Price, *Henry Purcell and the London Stage* (Cam-
    bridge: Cambridge University Press 1984), 289–319. As Price concludes:
    'Only the politically naive could have heard it as a celebration of the British
    monarchy. *King Arthur* is an audacious study in irony' (319). See also Howard
    Erskine-Hill, *Poetry of Opposition and Revolution: Dryden to Wordsworth* (Oxford:
    Clarendon Press 1996), 21–4.

13 For a detailed analysis of this scene, see Rodney Farnsworth, '"Hither, this
    Way": A Rhetorical-Musical Analysis of a Scene from Purcell's *King Arthur,*'
    Musical Quarterly 74 (1990), 83–97.

14 Dearing notes a number of parallels between the two works at this point in
    the *California Dryden,* 16:322. For an apt analysis of Milton's *Comus* as a voice
    for the Puritan sensibility regarding the senses and the dangers of artistic
    forms, see Leah Marcus, 'Milton's Anti-Laudian Masque,' in *The Politics of
    Mirth: Jonson, Herrick, Milton, Marvell, and the Defense of Old Holiday Pastimes*
    (Chicago: University of Chicago Press 1986), 169–212.

15 This contrasts to the notably theoretical appeal to rationality in Henry
    Lawes's musical settings for Milton's *Comus.* Chromaticism and sensual
    arousal in these settings signifies and effects waywardness and danger.

16 Farnsworth notes 'Dryden's distrust of what we today would call "hard evi-
    dence"' ('Hither, this Way,' 95).

17 See Dianne Dugaw, '"Critical Instants": Theatre Songs in the Age of Dryden
    and Purcell' *18th-Century Studies* 23 (1989), 157–81.

18 Curtis Price observes of this aria: 'The carefully calculated, occasionally
    abstract harmonies are profoundly moving, as they twist a feeling of awe into
    a vision of agonizing death' (*Henry Purcell,* 305).

19 Price rightly recognizes this scene's mockery and telling evocation of previ-
    ous musical episodes (*Henry Purcell,* 306–7).

20 Price, *Henry Purcell,* 290–5 and 319.

21 Richard Blackmore, *Prince Arthur. An Heroick Poem. In Ten Books* (London:
    Printed for Awnsham and John Churchil 1695).

22 Ibid., b2r.

23 Brean Hammond, commenting on the poem as failed epic poetry, notes the transparency of this move in *Professional Imaginative Writing in England, 1670–1740* (Oxford: Clarendon Press 1997), 129.

24 *Urania's Temple: or, A SATYR upon the Silent-Poets* (London 1695).

25 Ibid., 5.

26 Ibid., 6.

27 Samuel Johnson, *A Dictionary of the English Language*, 2 vols. (London 1755).

28 *Urania's Temple*, p. 6.

29 *An Ode, on the Death of Mr. Henry Purcell; Late Servant to his Majesty, and Organist of the Chapel Royal, and of St Peter's Westminster. The words by Mr Dryden, and sett to Musick by Dr Blow* (London 1696).

30 Ibid., Av.

31 Ibid., 16.

32 Arthur Bedford, *The Great Abuse of Musick* (London: J.H. for John Wyatt 1711), 164.

33 Ibid.

chapter fourteen

Dryden's Songs

JAMES A. WINN

'No man hath written in our Language so much, and so various Matter, and in so various Manners, so well,' wrote William Congreve of his friend John Dryden. 'If he had written nothing but his Prefaces, or nothing but his Songs, or his Prologues, each of them would have intituled him to the Preference and Distinction of excelling in his Kind.'[1] That Congreve, writing in 1717, should have remembered Dryden's excellence as a writer of songs is a striking fact – and a sad contrast to the neglect in which the songs languish today. Dryden used songs in twenty-three of his twenty-eight plays, working with composers including John Banister, Nicholas Staggins, Robert Smith, Pelham Humfrey, Louis Grabu, Giovanni Baptista Draghi, John Blow, and Henry Purcell. The songs call forth some of his most intense expressions of erotic feeling, and demonstrate his skill in verse forms unlike his characteristic couplet. Attentive to vowel colour and metrical variety, he made his lyrics musical before he passed them along to the composer. Yet the distinguished editors of the California edition have chosen not to print any of the surviving music from the plays; Dianne Dugaw's article on the music for the Dryden-Davenant *Tempest* appears to be the only essay touching on the subject in the last fifty years;[2] and Cyrus Day's edition of 1932 remains the only volume devoted to the songs.

Day's book will strike anyone who uses it now as a quaint piece of work. He prints fuzzy facsimiles of the surviving music, now happily superseded by the more readable versions in Ian Spink's edition of John Playford's songbooks,[3] but he never comments analytically on the music, and his commentary on the text is rarely helpful. Here, for example, is his embarrassed account of the eroticism many modern readers might find the most attractive feature of Dryden's songs: 'His most characteristic love-songs are marred by a recurrent note of cynicism and sensuality, by an unpleasant insistence upon the physical aspects of love amounting almost to morbidity (so it seems to me), and only imperfectly concealed by the conventional euphemistic disguise in which his immodest conceptions are garbed.'[4]

Yet even Dryden's eroticism, so troubling to the prudish Professor Day, has not attracted much attention in recent years, despite considerable scholarship devoted to sexual matters in Rochester, Behn, and others of his period. I suspect this neglect has to do with form: pure lyric, whether or not a musical setting survives, does not provide obvious opportunities for critics eager to display theoretical sophistication. Still, the tercentenary of the death of a great poet is not necessarily an occasion for criticism rooted only in the fashion of the here and now, and no collection of essays on Dryden and the arts would be complete without some consideration of the songs.

I

Although Dryden never claimed professional expertise as a musician, and even glanced satirically at Shadwell's pride in his skills as a lutenist, circumstantial evidence suggests that he was well informed about music. When his enemy George Villiers, second duke of Buckingham, brought a version of Dryden onstage in *The Rehearsal* (1671), he cluttered the speeches of 'Mr. Bayes' with technical terms related to music and dance. Bayes keeps referring to his dance in '*Effaut flat*,'[5] and this detail, like other aspects of Buckingham's caricature, may well be based on reality. Although he often spoke slightingly of songwriting, Dryden evidently took pride in his musical ear and his talent for lyrics. When he discusses the poet's 'nicety of hearing' in the Preface to his opera *Albion and Albanius*, he identifies the 'necessity of double Rhymes, and ordering of the Words and Numbers for the sweetness of the Voice' as 'the main hinges, on which an *Opera* must move.' 'Both of these,' he explains, 'are without the compass of any Art to teach another to perform; unless Nature in the first place has done her part, by enduing the Poet with that nicety of hearing, that the discord of sounds in Words shall as much offend him, as a Seventh in Musick wou'd a good Composer.'[6] This easy and correct analogy with a musical interval is typical, but at least one of the compos-

Figure 14.1 'Why should a foolish Marriage Vow'[7]

ers who set Dryden's works employed a shocking seventh in a prominent position. The song that opens *Marriage A-la-Mode*, in the original
setting by Robert Smith, is shown in fig. 14.1.

The drop from a high B-flat to a low B-natural at 'long ago' is an
extreme example of the kind of dissonance called 'cross-relation,' of
which Restoration composers were especially fond. History does not
record what Dryden thought of this setting, or whether the original

singer found it difficult. Still, in identifying 'a Seventh in Music' as an analogy to a 'discord of Sounds in Words,' Dryden was on reasonably solid ground. The seventh *was* a dissonance, and the normal expectation for song tunes, as for song lyrics, was that they be smoothly consonant.

As in so many other aspects of the culture, the Restoration marked a change in the accepted style of English song. Dryden doubtless heard ballads as a child: country singers in his native Northamptonshire knew the old favourites, and city singers in London were producing new words to old tunes daily in order to comment on the dizzying political events of his schoolboy years. The Preface to *Albion and Albanius* glances at this practice when Dryden compares his task as librettist to being a 'bound 'Prentice to some doggrel Rhymer, who makes Songs to Tunes, and sings them for a lively-hood' (15:10). As his scorn for such 'drudgery' suggests, neither the old ballads nor the newly minted versions were a model for Restoration theatrical practice, which sought from the outset an urbane and Continental sophistication; both the words and the music of our first example suggest a conscious striving for courtly refinement. Nor could Dryden and his contemporaries easily recover earlier courtly modes. The rich tradition of the English lutenist-songwriters of the Elizabethan era had been largely forgotten; John Dowland died in 1628, and the last publication of works in his style took place in 1622. No English songbooks of any kind were published between 1622 and 1652, when Playford's first collection appeared; these years of political tension and open war were not happy times for the printing of music. Although Dryden was familiar with lyrics by Shakespeare and Donne, he probably never heard anyone sing them to their original tunes. Nonetheless, the texts alone would have taught him that in English as in Italian, the genre required short lines and discouraged complexities of syntax or imagery.

Dryden's first songs, performed in *The Indian Queen* in 1664, reflect both his awareness of the past and his desire to satisfy current fashions. With Sir William Davenant's musical productions drawing crowds to the rival Duke's Theatre at Lincoln's Inn Fields, Dryden and his collaborator Robert Howard needed music for *The Indian Queen* at the King's Theatre, and the court signalled its support by a grant of silk to costume the orchestra.[8] The play includes the first of many scenes in which Dryden used music to lend atmosphere to a scene of prophecy and incantation. One incentive was the success of Davenant's version of *Macbeth* (1663), with new music by Matthew Locke, including a dance for the witches. At least since Elizabethan times, chanted charms had typically

fallen into trochaic tetrameter, a heavy, hypnotic verse form; a familiar
example is the witches' spell in *Macbeth*: 'Round about the cauldron
go; / In the poisoned entrails throw' (IV.i.4–5). In the first song in *The
Indian Queen*, which may have been chanted, Dryden follows the convention: the conjuror Ismeron invokes the God of Dreams in a tetrameter charm that begins and ends iambically, with a sustained trochaic
section in the middle:[9]

> *You twice Ten Hundred Deities,*
> *To whom we daily Sacrifice;*
> *You **Powers** that dwell with Fate **below**,*
> *And see what men are doom'd to do;*
> *Where Elements in discord dwell;*
> *Thou God of Sleep **arise** and tell*
> *Great* Zempoalla *what strange Fate*
> *Must on her dismal Vision wait.*
> (18:III.ii.64–71; emphasis mine)

After an impatient interruption by Zempoalla, the charm shifts to
trochees:

> *By the croaking of the Toad,*
> *In their Caves that make aboad,*
> *Earthy* Dun *that pants for **breath**,*
> *With her swell'd sides full of **death**;*
> *By the Crested Adders Pride*
> *That along the Clifts do glide;*
> *By thy visage fierce and black;*
> *By the Deaths-head on thy back;*
> *By the twisted Serpents plac'd*
> *For a Girdle round thy Waste;*
> *By the Hearts of Gold that deck*
> *Thy Brest, thy Shoulders, and thy Neck:*
> *From thy sleepy Mansion **rise**,*
> *And open thy **unwilling** Eyes,*
> *While bubling Springs their Musick keep,*
> *That use to lull thee in thy sleep.*
> (III.ii.79–94; emphasis mine)

Especially in the middle section, this song owes much to *Macbeth*, but
Dryden and Howard's conjuring scene, with its exoticism, special ef-

fects, and atmospheric music, led to theatrical episodes quite different from anything in *Macbeth*. Dryden's sequel, *The Indian Emperour* (1665), includes a more sophisticated version using the same basic elements, which recur in Dryden's *Tyrannick Love* (1669), Charles Davenant's *Circe* (1677), the Dryden-Nathaniel Lee *Oedipus* (1678), Betterton's *The Prophetess* (1690), Dryden's *King Arthur* (1691), Granville's *The British Enchanters* (1706), and Handel's *Rinaldo* (1711). In all these productions, a prophet or prophetess calls up visions in the form of singing spirits, stage machinery brings the spirits up from trap doors or down on wires, and music contributes crucially to the magical atmosphere. One indication of the continuity between these scenes is the fact that Dryden repeated a number of the words he had used in this first song in the Frost Scene in *King Arthur* (16:1–69), performed almost thirty years later. The Cold Genius, rising from below the stage, complains:

> *What **Power** art thou, who from **below**,*
> *Hast made me **Rise**, **unwillingly**, and slow.*
> ....
> *I can scarcely move, or draw my **Breath**;*
> *Let me, let me, Freeze again to **Death**.*
> (III.ii.281–2; 286–7; emphasis mine)

If Dryden crafted Ismeron's charm with one eye aimed at *Macbeth*, the rest of the scene reflects more recent influences. Abraham Cowley's enormously popular collection *The Mistress* (1647), published when Dryden was a student at the same Westminster School that Cowley had earlier attended, provided models for the intensely lyrical, metrically varied verses he was learning to write; songs from that collection were set by many contemporary composers.[10] We can also be certain that Dryden had seen Davenant's opera *The Siege of Rhodes* (1656), an attempt to produce in English the kind of musical play that had been common on the Continent for fifty years; as Davenant explains in his Preface, 'frequent alterations of measure are necessary to *Recitative* Musick for variation of *Ayres*.'[11] More remarkably, Dryden had also been reading the French texts of the *ballets de cour* that the newly restored king was known to admire.[12] All of these models involved irregular metres designed for recitative, as opposed to the strictly strophic forms of ballads and the normally strophic forms of Elizabethan lute songs. Although the music is lost, the form of the second song in the conjuring scene in *The Indian Queen* reveals Dryden's attention to these models. The 'Aerial-Spirits,' invisible and sexless, celebrate their freedom from earthly passions:

> *Poor Mortals that are clog'd with Earth below*
> *Sink under Love and Care,*
> *While we that dwell in air*
> *Such heavy Passions never know.*
> *Why then shou'd Mortals be*
> *Unwilling to be free*
> *From Blood, that sullen Cloud,*
> *Which shining Souls does shroud?*
> *Then they'l shew bright,*
> *And like us light,*
> *When leaving Bodies with their Care,*
> *They slide to us and Air.*   (III. ii. 119–30)

This song is the prototype for some of Dryden's most richly lyrical songs; the experience he gained in controlling shifting meters in these irregular verses helped assure the metrical virtuosity of his great pindarics of the 1680s.

The content of the scene reveals much about Dryden's attitudes towards music. Ismeron appeals to the 'Spirits that inhabit in the Air' in the hope that their 'powerful Charms of Musick' may bring Queen Zempoalla's 'Soul back to its harmony' (III.ii.116–18). The idea of music as healing comes from the Pythagorean tradition; the contrast between earth and air depends upon the basic Pythagorean association between music and the elements; and the highly Platonic message of the 'Aerial-Spirits' urges lovers to forget their bodily cares and 'slide' into the air, leaving 'heavy Passions' and 'Blood' behind. Although he employed similar aerial spirits in *The Tempest, Tyrannick Love,* and *King Arthur,* this was the only time Dryden made his spirits truly sexless; in later plays, even the airy sprites express love for others of their kind and compassion for humans. Here, the empty freedom offered by the singing spirits is unappealing; as Zempoalla's angry dismissal suggests, they can provide neither rest nor requited love:

> *Zempoalla.* Death on these Trifles: Cannot your Art find
> Some means to ease the Passions of the Mind?
> Or if you cannot give a Lover rest,
> Can you force Love into a Scornful Brest?
> *Ismeron.* 'Tis Reason only can make Passions less;
> Art gives not new, but may the old encrease;
> Nor can it alter Love in any Brest

That is with other flames before possess'd.
(III.ii.131–8)

Dryden's first dramatic scene involving singing thus dramatizes the *limitations* of music. Zempoalla rejects the songs as 'Trifles'; Ismeron explains that 'Art' can only increase the pains of love, praising 'Reason' as the only way to gain control over the passions. Bending the elements of Pythagoreanism to his own purposes, Dryden, even at this early stage of his career, exhibits his characteristic unwillingness to grant deep meaning or moral power to music.

In this and many later musical sequences in Dryden's plays, music proves untrustworthy. Scenes of unreliable prophecy, here and in later plays, were a way of satisfying the audience's appetite for music while still claiming primacy for poetry; scenes of musical and sexual temptation were another way of accomplishing the same goal. Dryden's next rhyming play, *The Indian Emperour* (9:1–112), includes the first of these: a beautiful song forms the centrepiece of an episode in which the Indian women tempt the Spanish explorers.

A pleasant Grotto discover'd: in it a Fountain spouting; round about it Vasquez, Pizarro, *and other* Spaniards *lying carelessly un-arm'd, and by them many* Indian Women, *one of which Sings the following Song.*

SONG.
Ah fading joy, how quickly art thou past?
Yet we thy ruine haste:
As if the cares of Humane Life were few
We seek out new:
And follow Fate which would too fast pursue.

See how on every bough the Birds express
In their sweet notes their happiness.
They all enjoy and nothing spare;
But on their Mother Nature lay their care:
Why then should Man, the Lord of all below,
Such troubles chuse to know
As none of all his Subjects undergo?

Hark, hark, the Waters fall, fall, fall;
And with a Murmuring sound

> *Dash, dash upon the ground,*
> *To gentle slumbers call.*

After the Song two Spaniards *arise and Dance a Saraband with Castanieta's: at the end of which,* Guyomar *and his* Indians *enter, and e're the* Spaniards *can recover their Swords, seize them.* (IV.iii.1–16)

Languishing in the grotto, listening to the ravishing music of the women, the Spaniards abandon their phallic weapons in favour of dancing with castanets and are unable to 'recover their Swords' when the Indians attack.[13] The song seductively advocates such carelessness, suggesting that 'Man, the Lord of all' should live as thoughtlessly as the birds, trusting to 'Mother Nature' and choosing not to know or confront his troubles. This supple text shows how much Dryden had learned from Cowley, Davenant, and French models. In the final verse, carefully writing out repetitions of the words 'hark,' 'fall,' and 'Dash,' he pushes the composer towards a metrically regular, lyrical idiom that would lead easily into a dance.

Although we do not know whether it was used in the original production, we possess a setting by Pelham Humfrey,[14] who had the talent and training to respond to the challenge of this stylish verse: he had studied in France and been strongly influenced by Lully. When he returned to England, Pepys sneered at him as 'an absolute Monsieur,'[15] but Humfrey had learned more in Paris than affected dress and manner. The alternation between recitative and vocal trio, which he would use again in one of his songs for the operatic version of the Dryden-Davenant *Tempest,* is quite effective, especially in the lovely appoggiaturas on the repeated and ominous word 'fall' (see fig. 14.2).

Humfrey may have fancied himself a poet: his setting adds several lines of verse designed to facilitate the alternation between metres in the recitative section. This unwelcome editing may have been one of Dryden's first experiences with the uneasy relations between poet and composer, of which he complains so memorably in the Prefaces to *Albion and Albanius* and *King Arthur,* but at least one of Humfrey's alterations is a distinct improvement: 'Dash, dash against the ground' is a far more felicitous phrase for singing than 'Dash, dash upon the ground.'

Twenty-seven years later, in *King Arthur,* Dryden was still working with the same elements: the Frost Scene is a false vision conjured up by the evil magician Osmond to tempt the virginal Emmeline, and the naked 'Daughters of this Aged Stream,' who offer Arthur their bodies and

Figure 14.2. 'Ah, fading Joy!'[16]

their harmonies in Act IV, are lineal descendants of the Indian singer. In a section for which no music survives, one of them urges Arthur to

> waste the Joyous Day
> With us in gentle Play:
> Unbend to Love, unbend thee:
> O lay thy Sword aside,
>   And other Arms provide;
> For other Wars attend thee,
> And sweeter to be try'd.
>   (IV.ii.29–35)[17]

Here the connection between the sword and the phallus, implicit in

The Indian Emperour, is entirely explicit, just as the naked singers are more overtly tempting than the Indian women. The second song, for which we do have Purcell's music, links sexual pleasure with music and water – again, more directly than in the earlier prototype. Here is Dryden's text:

> *Two daughters of this Aged Stream are we;*
> *And both our Sea-green Locks have comb'd for thee;*
> *Come Bathe with us an Hour or two,*
> *Come Naked in, for we are so;*
> *What Danger from a Naked Foe?*
> *Come Bathe with us, come Bathe, and share,*
> *What Pleasures in the Floods appear;*
> *We'll beat the Waters till they bound,*
> *And Circle, round, around, around,*
> *And Circle round, around.*
>
> (IV.ii.37–46)

In his setting, Purcell respects the natural accent of English words and the flow of the poetic phrase, but some of his finest effects come in moments that hesitate, repeat phrases, and even alter the text. Where Dryden had written 'Come Bathe with us an Hour or two,' with the stress falling on 'Bathe,' Purcell places the important and explicitly sexual verb Come in a much more prominent position by accenting and repeating it, with an enticing series of overlapping slurs (see fig. 14.3).[18]

The music here closely resembles Humfrey's similarly shaped and harmonized repetitions of the word 'fall.' The two pieces have in common the key of G minor and a similar texture; both composers capture the temptation to yield to the liquid pleasure of music with falling slurs harmonized in smooth thirds over a slower moving bass line. As Dryden indicates by a stage direction identifying the singers in the stream as 'Syrens,' both these episodes are variants of the story of the Sirens in the *Odyssey,* an archetypal instance of the linking of musical beauty with sexual temptation and the abandonment of manly virtue.[20] The island of the Sirens in Homer is littered with the bones of sailors; it takes little effort to see in this myth the male terror of female sexual voracity, presented as cannibalism. The close association between music and water is also negative: by describing music as a liquid element, Dryden denies its structure, its architecture, its status as a made thing; instead, he makes it fluid, formless, and dangerous. Whatever moral or allegorical meaning these scenes had for the audience, I believe they played out for Dryden

Fig. 14.3. Excerpt from 'Two Daughters of this Aged Stream'[19]

an allegory of the relations between the arts, with poetry as the stern male hero who must try to resist the seductive appeal of music, here represented as a false siren.

II

There are similar musical temptation scenes in *Tyrannick Love,* for which the music is lost, and in the unproduced *State of Innocence,* for which no music was ever composed, though in both these cases the tempted party is female. In his comedies and tragicomedies, however, Dryden typically used simpler strophic songs to express and celebrate erotic feeling. His first such song appears in *Secret Love* (January 1667; 9:113–203). The singer, Asteria, is one of the attendants of the 'maiden Queen' of the subtitle, but the queen herself is supposed to have written the song; this awkwardness, like many similar moments in other plays, stems from the fact that few of the actors in either company were professional singers. The text includes Dryden's first use of the Petrarchan trope of pleasing pain, to which he would often return:

> *I feed a flame within which so torments me*
> *That it both pains my heart, and yet contents me:*
> *'Tis such a pleasing smart, and I so love it,*
> *That I had rather die, then once remove it.*
>
> *Yet he for whom I grieve shall never know it,*
> *My tongue does not betray, nor my eyes show it:*
> *Not a sigh nor a tear my pain discloses,*
> *But they fall silently like dew on Roses.*
>   (IV.ii.23–30)

The eroticism here is subtle, understated; the song actually dramatizes a refusal to speak the words of desire. Although the music is lost, the text itself is a particularly fine instance of Dryden's attention to 'the necessity of double Rhymes, and ordering of the Words and Numbers for the sweetness of the Voice.' I especially admire the double rhyme between 'discloses' and 'roses' and the internal modulation from 'eyes' to 'sigh' to 'silently,' true instances of verbal music.

The lyricism of this song deserves the praise that Rochester lavished on Sedley and denied to Dryden in his 'Allusion to Horace':

> For Songs, and Verses, Mannerly Obscene,
> That can stirr Nature up, by Springs unseene,
> And without forceing blushes, warme the Queene:
> Sidley, has that prevailing gentle Art,
> That can with a resistlesse Charme impart,
> The loosest wishes to the Chastest Heart,
> Raise such a Conflict, kindle such a ffire
> Betwixt declineing Virtue, and desire,
> Till the poor Vanquisht Maid, dissolves away,
> In Dreames all Night, in Sighs, and Teares, all Day.[21]

Rochester is celebrating the capacity of 'Songs and Verses' to serve the ends of a male hoping to seduce a female, but much of his imagery – stirring up Nature, unseen springs, kindling fires, dissolving virtue – will remind us of Dryden's language in the songs we have been examining, in which female singers attempt to seduce males. In light of Dryden's talent for lyric, it is surprising to find Rochester alleging that he was incapable of this kind of writing:

> Dryden, in vaine, try'd this nice way of Witt,
> For he, to be a tearing Blade thought fit,
> But when he wou'd be sharp, he still was blunt,
> To friske his frollique fancy, hed cry Cunt.[22]

Although Shadwell would also accuse Dryden of vulgar speech in polite company, there is no real pretext for Rochester's criticism in Dryden's published songs. In *An Evening's Love* (1668), produced just one year after *Secret Love,* he included four songs that were much more explicitly erotic than any of his previous lyrics, songs that probably reflect the tastes of Rochester and the other Court Wits. But even here the obscenity is 'mannerly.' In the first song, the male singer expresses a libertine delight in seeking a partner who belongs to another man:

> *You charm'd me not with that fair face*
> *Though it was all divine:*
> *To be anothers is the Grace,*
> *That makes me wish you mine.*

Part of the fun here is the irreverent use of such religious terms as 'divine' and 'Grace.' Invoking pagan gods and aggressive kings, the speaker goes on to praise bold lovers:

> *The Gods and Fortune take their part*
> *Who like young Monarchs fight;*
> *And boldly dare invade that heart*
> *Which is anothers right.*
> *First mad with hope we undertake*
> *To pull up every barr;*
> *But once possess'd, we faintly make*
> *A dull defensive warr.*
> *Now every friend is turn'd a foe*
> *In hope to get our store:*
> *And passion makes us Cowards grow,*
> *Which made us brave before.*
> (10: II.i.129–44)

The use of military imagery to describe courtship was at least as old as Petrarch, and was especially popular among Restoration libertines, as the familiar example of Rochester's 'Disabled Debauchee' will suggest. Dryden had done the same thing in reverse in *Annus Mirabilis*, where he described the Dutch sailors trying to retain their shiploads of spices as fighting 'like Husbands' and the English as fighting 'like Lovers' (1:64, l. 109). In the Prologue to *Tyrannick Love* (X:114), which was on stage one season later, he even applied similar imagery to the act of poetic creativity:

> *Poets, like Lovers, should be bold and dare,*
> *They spoil their business with an over-care.*
> *And he who servilely creeps after sence,*
> *Is safe, but ne're will reach an Excellence.*
> (ll. 12–15)

Here the poet, seeking Longinian sublimity, must act like a bold lover demanding the favours of a coy maiden. Perhaps such a poet is even a 'tearing blade.' But there is still a vast distance between these lines and Rochester's crude caricature of Dryden crying 'cunt.'

The second song in *An Evening's Love* dramatizes the joy of a lover who achieves his goal, but even here the delight is mutual – sensual, but not vulgar:

> *After the pangs of a desperate Lover,*
> *When day and night I have sigh'd all in vain,*
> *Ah what a pleasure it is to discover*
> *In her eyes pity, who causes my pain!*
>
> *When with unkindness our love at a stand is,*
> *And both have punish'd our selves with the pain,*
> *Ah what a pleasure the touch of her hand is,*
> *Ah what a pleasure to press it again!*
>
> *When the denyal comes fainter and fainter,*
> *And her eyes give what her tongue does deny,*
> *Ah what a trembling I feel when I venture,*
> *Ah what a trembling does usher my joy!*
>
> *When, with a Sigh, she accords me the blessing,*
> *And her eyes twinkle 'twixt pleasure and pain;*

> *Ah what a joy 'tis beyond all expressing,*
> *Ah what a joy to hear,* Shall we again?
>   (II.i.499–514)

As the repeated rhymes suggest, the solution to 'the pangs of a desperate lover' is not only sex, but repeated sex. Unlike the lovers in 'imperfect enjoyment' poems by Rochester, Behn, and others, Dryden's imagined lovers do not experience the male's orgasm as an occasion for embarrassment or anger; they appear more than content to seek better timing in the next round. A song from *Marriage A-la-Mode* (11.221–316) is entirely devoted to developing this idea:

> *Whil'st* Alexis *lay prest*
> *In her Arms he lov'd best,*
> *With his hands round her neck,*
> *And his head on her breast,*
> *He found the fierce pleasure too hasty to stay,*
> *And his soul in the tempest just flying away.*
>
> *When* Coelia *saw this,*
> *With a sigh, and a kiss,*
> *She cry'd, Oh my dear, I am robb'd of my bliss;*
> *'Tis unkind to your Love, and unfaithfully done,*
> *To leave me behind you, and die all alone.*
>
> *The Youth, though in haste,*
> *And breathing his last,*
> *In pity dy'd slowly, while she dy'd more fast;*
> *Till at length she cry'd, Now, my dear, now let us go,*
> *Now die, my* Alexis, *and I will die too.*
>
> *Thus intranc'd they did lie,*
> *Till* Alexis *did try*
> *To recover new breath, that again he might die:*
> *Then often they di'd; but the more they did so,*
> *The Nymph di'd more quick, and the Shepherd more slow.*
>   (IV.ii.47–67)

Although this song falls within the orbit of court libertinism, the contrast with the priapic lyrics of Etherege, Dorset, and especially Rochester is telling. Dryden's knowing narrator lets us hear the voice of the woman; neither he nor the silent Alexis appears to resent her taking control of the pace of their lovemaking. Unlike the truly obscene verses of the Court Wits, which often reduce the woman to one or more of her orifices, these erotic songs describe not only physical coupling but also emotional sympathy.

A more developed and comic version of this interest in the dynamics of couples comes at the end of *An Evening's Love,* where Dryden lets a sung duet between Jacinta and Wildblood do the work of concluding the main romantic plot, framing the song with a witty dialogue in which both speakers boast of their incompetence at singing – almost as a way of claiming competence at lovemaking.

> *Maskall.* You have quarrell'd twice to night without bloodshed, 'ware the third time.
>
> *Jacinta. A propos!* I have been retrieving an old Song of a Lover that was ever quarreling with his Mistress: I think it will fit our amour so well, that if you please I'll give it you for an Epithalamium: and you shall sing it.
>
> Gives him a Paper.
>
> *Wildblood.* I never sung in all my life; nor ever durst trie when I was alone, for fear of braying.
>
> *Jac.* Just me, up and down; but for a frolick let's sing together: for I am sure if we cannot sing now, we shall never have cause when we are married.
>
> *Wild.* Begin then; give me my Key, and I'll set my voice to't.
>
> *Jac.* Fa la, fa la, fa la.
>
> *Wild.* Fala, fala, fala. Is this your best, upon the faith of a Virgin?
>
> *Jac.* I, by the Muses, I am at my pitch.
>
> *Wild.* Then do your worst: and let the company be judge who sings worst.
>
> *Jac.* Upon condition the best singer shall wear the breeches: prepare to strip Sir; I shall put you into your drawers presently.
>
> *Wild.* I shall be reveng'd with putting you into your smock anon; *St. George* for me.
>
> *Jac. St. James* for me: come start Sir.

SONG.

Damon.   Celimena, *of my heart,*
    None shall e're bereave you:
    If, with your good leave, I may
    Quarrel with you once a day,
    I will never leave you.

> Celimena. *Passion's but an empty name*
> *Where respect is wanting:*
> Damon *you mistake your ayme;*
> *Hang your heart, and burn your flame,*
> *If you must be ranting.*
>
> Damon. *Love as dull and muddy is,*
> *As decaying liquor:*
> *Anger sets it on the lees,*
> *And refines it by degrees*
> *Till it workes it quicker.*
>
> Celimena. *Love by quarrels to beget*
> *Wisely you endeavour;*
> *With a grave Physician's wit*
> *Who to cure an Ague fit*
> *Put me in a Feavor.*
>
> Damon. *Anger rouzes love to fight,*
> *And his only bayt is,*
> *'Tis the spurre to dull delight,*
> *And is but an eager bite,*
> *When desire at height is.*
>
> Celimena. *If such drops of heat can fall*
> *In our wooing weather;*
> *If such drops of heat can fall,*
> *We shall have the Devil and all*
> *When we come together.*
>
> *Wild.* Your judgement Gentlemen: a Man or a Maid?
> *Bellamy.* And you make no better harmony after you are married then you
>   have before, you are the miserablest couple in *Christendome.*
> *Wild.* 'Tis no great matter; if I had had a good voice she would have spoil'd
>   it before to morrow. (V.i.480–539)

In the text of the song, the notion of anger as a 'spurre to dull de-light' may remind us of the earlier song in the same play, in which the bold invasion of a charmer belonging to another stimulates passion. Here, however, both parties are active, and passion and violence are linked not only in metaphor but in bed. I believe that is the only way to read the astonishing reference to 'an eager bite,' though Dryden does not tell us which lover bites the other. In verbal terms, Jacinta has the last word: her closing stanza, with its repeated references to 'drops of heat,' links the flames of desire and the liquid of fountains and streams that feature in other songs; one of the many meanings should be clear in her reference to the wished-for moment 'when we come together.'

The framing dialogue also shows how well the lovers are matched. Jacinta's stipulation that 'the best singer shall wear the breeches' is an assertion of power and independence, but it finally points not towards the ultimate disguise of cross-dressing, but towards the ultimate honesty of nakedness. On this wedding night, both characters must 'prepare to strip'; the brilliant masquerades with which they have amused one another are at an end. As practical theatre, the jokes about braying voices reflect the fact that Charles Hart and Nell Gwyn, the talented actors who played Wildblood and Jacinta, were not professional singers. At another level, however, we may again detect Dryden's characteristic need to assign music to a subsidiary role: if he was willing to use a song to conclude a play, he was careful to frame that song with dialogue discounting the quality of the performance, and thus by extension the power of the music.

III

The musical dream of temptation in *The State of Innocence,* Dryden's unproduced opera based on *Paradise Lost,* actually conflates the conventions of the temptation scenes from the rhymed heroic plays, typically involving elaborate scenery and recitative music, with the conventions of the erotic songs in the comedies. As the actress playing Eve sleeps, the stage directions call for '*A Vision, where a Tree rises loaden with Fruit; four Spirits rise with it, and draw a canopie out of the tree, other Spirits dance about the Tree in deform'd shapes, after the Dance an Angel enters, with a Woman, habited like* Eve.' Dryden then imagines a series of contrasting musical pieces, carefully dictating a rhythmic setting to the composer. First comes a dialogue in recitative:

> *Angel, singing.* Look up, look up, and see
> What Heav'n prepares for thee;
> Look up, and this fair fruit behold,
> Ruddy it smiles, and rich with streaks of gold.
>
> The loaded branches downward bend,
> Willing they stoop, and thy fair hand attend.
> Fair Mother of Mankind, make haste,

And bless, and bless thy senses with the taste.
    Woman. No; 'tis forbidden, I
In tasting it shall dye.
    Angel. Say who injoyn'd this harsh command.
    Woman. 'Twas Heav'n; and who can Heav'n withstand?
    Angel. Why was it made so fair, why plac'd in sight?
Heav'n is too good to envy man's delight.
See, we before thy face will try,
What thou so fear'st and will not dye.
    [*The Angel takes the fruit and gives to the Spirits
    who danc'd, they immediately put off their deform'd
    shapes, and appear Angels.*   (12:III.iii.13–28)

As we have seen, composers in this period freely rearranged or altered texts, often repeating short phrases for the sake of musical expression. Dryden attempts to control even that part of the composer's art by
writing out the repetitions ('Look up, look up ... And bless, and bless'),
assuring that the important imperative verbs in the tempter's appeal will
receive emphasis.

At a larger level, he makes sure that the transformation of the 'deform'd' dancers into angels will correspond with a pronounced change
in musical style. Singing words designed for a rollicking dance tune in
triple time, rhythmically similar to 'After the pangs of a desperate lover,'
the tempter persuades Eve to join in the eating of the fruit.

    Angel, singing. Behold what a change on a sudden is here!
    How glorious in beauty, how bright they appear!
    From spirits deform'd they are Deities made
    Their pinions at pleasure, the clouds can invade,
    [*The Angel gives to the Woman who eats.*
    Till equal in honor they rise
    With him who commands in the skies:
    Then taste without fear, and be happy and wise.
    Woman. Ah, now I believe; such a pleasure I find
    As enlightens my eyes, and enlivens my mind.
    [*The spirits who are turn'd Angels fly up, when they have tasted.*
    I only repent
    I deferr'd my content.
    Angel. Now wiser experience has taught you to prove

What a folly it is,
Out of fear to shun bliss.
To the joy that's forbidden we eagerly move;
It inhances the price, and increases the love.
Chorus of both. To the joy, &c. (III.iii.29–45)

Like the lovers in the earlier song from *An Evening's Love,* who '*boldly dare* invade *that heart / Which is anothers right,*' the tempter and his angels seize what they want, with the result that 'Their pinions at pleasure, the clouds can *invade*' (emphasis mine). Among the seventeenth-century definitions of *pinion* we find '*The shaft of a feather; a quill.*'[23] Perhaps it is not too fanciful to see this phrase as applying both to the phallus (so that invading the clouds becomes a priapic act) and to the quill (so that invading the clouds becomes a version of achieving the poetic sublime). Like the women in Dryden's erotic songs, whose smiles and actions belie their spoken denials, the woman here is easily susceptible to pleasure. Her oddest phrase – 'I only repent / I deferr'd my content' – may remind us of the trope of deferred pleasure in the songs about orgasm. The concluding *Chorus of both* should remind us of the end of *An Evening's Love;* by persuading the woman to join him in a sung duet, the angel makes her his accomplice and transfers some of his power to her.

Although carefully worked out as theatre, adequately connected to the main plot, and self-consciously expressive of Dryden's opinions about the relative merits of the arts, this dream sequence is certainly less than serious about the great religious issues of temptation and pride. The concluding lines, with their libertine phrases about forbidden joys and enhanced prices, seem more applicable to a London brothel than to the Tree of Life. Here and elsewhere, *The State of Innocence* displays a curious impulse towards travesty, an inclination that Dryden had already indulged in the hilarious, frame-breaking Epilogue he wrote for Nell Gwyn to speak at the end of *Tyrannick Love,* where he encouraged the audience to laugh at the disjunction between Nell's sexual notoriety as mistress to the king and her purity as the princess Valeria in a play celebrating virginity and martyrdom: 'Here *Nelly* lies, who, though she liv'd a Slater'n, / Yet dy'd a Princess, acting in S. *Cathar'n*' (10:193, ll. 29–30).

When confined to prefaces and epilogues, such mockery of his own work had a self-protective function for Dryden, suggesting a cool professional detachment from the heroic passions portrayed in the play itself. But in *The State of Innocence,* the mockery is expressed at the very heart of the drama: Dryden builds a severe criticism of opera into his most

operatic scene. If *The State of Innocence* had been staged, the casting in
the dream sequence might have added another layer of travesty. A leading actress, perhaps Elizabeth Boutell or Rebecca Marshall, would have
played the speaking Eve, but a professional singer in a similar costume
would have come on for the dream sequence. One fascinating possibility is that the singer would have been Anne Reeves, Dryden's own mistress, who seems to have had musical abilities,[24] and who was famous for
her beautiful legs, which she might have shown to advantage in whatever skimpy 'habit' was contrived for the singing Eve.

Even 'A Song for St. Cecilia's Day, 1687,' designed as the text for a
kind of oratorio, draws on some of the conventions we have been examining. Dryden's catalogue of the passions music can 'raise and quell'
replaces the Pythagorean modes with the timbres of various instruments, a modern substitution that was easier for his audience to grasp,
but the examples take on new meaning when we consider them in the
context of the poet's career as a writer of songs:

> The TRUMPETS loud Clangor
>   Excites us to Arms
> With shrill Notes of Anger
>   And mortal Alarms.
> The double double double beat
>   Of the thundring DRUM
> Cryes, heark the Foes come;
> Charge, Charge, 'tis too late to retreat.
>
> The soft complaining FLUTE
> In dying Notes discovers
> The Woes of hopeless Lovers,
> Whose Dirge is whisper'd by the warbling LUTE.
>
> Sharp VIOLINS proclaim
> Their jealous Pangs, and Desperation:
> Fury, frantick Indignation,
> Depth of Pains, and height of Passion,
> For the fair, disdainful Dame.   (3:202, ll. 25–41)

Once more we have the link between military excitement and sexual
excitement, once more a 'fair, disdainful Dame.' But perhaps the most
striking detail is the mention of 'dying notes.' As Dryden certainly knew,

Fig. 14.4. Excerpt from 'The soft complaining Flute'[26]

wrenching dissonances had been used since the Renaissance to set references to 'dying,' whether the action implied was actual death or *le petit mort* of orgasm. Examples abound in composers like Gesualdo and Monteverdi, who seem to have been at least as interested as Dryden in the link between pleasure and pain.[25] One of the most common 'madrigalisms' was a convention treating a falling half-step in a melody line as a signifier for sorrow or death. Composers soon discovered that if they harmonized such a melodic moment in a way that left the higher pitch still sounding in another line, they could increase the effect through that powerful dissonance, which could appear as a direct clash of two adjacent pitches – or as a major seventh, the interval one half-step less than an octave, the same interval outlined melodically in Smith's song. By resolving such dissonances, they could produce a simulacrum of the motion from pain to pleasure, from tension to release.

The first composer to set the 'Song,' Giovanni Baptista Draghi, was probably not an expert speaker of English, but he knew the conventions. Each time the voice articulates the word 'dying,' Draghi provides a falling half-step, and the first flute part also frequently repeats that interval, producing an unsettling series of dissonances, as shown in fig. 14.4.

The first of the 'dying' chords, which we might describe as an F-minor chord with both the seventh and the sixth sounding, is one of the most dissonant simultaneities I have found in any European composition of the seventeenth century. Even though Draghi resolves it quickly, passing through two progressively less dissonant chords on the way to a triad, that chord remains a remarkable instance of the power of harmony, the very power denied to poetry by the fact of its articulating only one sound at a time. I have argued elsewhere that Dryden sought in this poem to limit the composer's options, dictating the orchestration by mentioning specific instruments, and constructing rhythms so strong and unambiguous as to require certain musical metres.[27] At one level, he probably hoped to show that poetry could achieve by itself many of the effects traditionally attributed to music. Still, Dryden's lifelong link between music and the erotic, even when he presented it as temptation or travesty, was nonetheless an acknowledgment of the power of music. His character Ismeron explains to Zempoalla that art (in this case music) does not give new passions, but may increase old ones. As a man susceptible to the power of the erotic and a poet gifted with 'nicety of hearing,' Dryden has left us in his songs a body of work that can certainly increase old passions; if we are open to the expressive beauty of these songs, we may find them able to give us new passions as well.

Notes

1 From the Epistle Dedicatory to Congreve's edition of *The Dramatick Works of John Dryden* (1717), excerpted in *Dryden: The Critical Heritage*, ed. James and Helen Kinsley (London: Routledge 1971), 265.

2 Dianne Dugaw, '"Critical Instants": Theater Songs in the Age of Dryden and Purcell,' *Eighteenth-Century Studies* 23, no. 2 (1990), 157–81.

3 All five books of this important series are now available as *Choice Ayres, Songs, and Dialogues*, ed. Ian Spink, 2 vols. (London: Stainer and Bell 1989), each of the five original volumes separately paginated.

4 Cyrus Day, *The Songs of John Dryden* (Cambridge: Harvard University Press 1932), xii.

5 *The Rehearsal* (London 1672), II.v.19.

6 *The Works of John Dryden*, ed. E.N. Hooker, H.T. Swedenberg, Jr, et al., 20 vols. (Berkeley: University of California Press 1956–2000), 15:9. All citations of

Dryden follow this edition (hereafter cited as *California Dryden*). I refer to
poems by line number; to plays by act, scene, and line; and to prose by volume and page.

7 I follow the facsimile in *Choice Ayres, Songs, and Dialogues*, ed. Spink, 1:35. A
performance of this song may be found on the accompanying disk, band 1.

8 An extant warrant orders 'the Master of the Great Wardrobe to prouide and
deliuer to Thomas Killigrew Esqr to the value of forty pounds in silke for to
cloath the Musick for the play called the Indian Queen.' L.C. 5/138, f. 15,
printed in *The London Stage*, Part 1, 74. 'The Musick' was the term for the
instrumentalists who played between the acts and accompanied the songs.
Later in the same year, the twenty-four string players of 'the King's Musick'
were split into two bands of twelve to play at the theatres. See Andrew Ashbee, *Records of English Court Music*, Vol. I. (1660–85) (Snodland, Kent:
Andrew Ashbee 1986), 59–61.

9 *The Indian Queen* is a collaboration between Dryden and Howard, but scholars have long attributed the songs to Dryden, correctly in my opinion. As
Day points out (142), the similarity between the musical episodes in the two
'Indian' plays weighs in favour of Dryden's authorship of the songs in *The
Indian Queen*; the echoes of this passage in *King Arthur* are further evidence
of Dryden's authorship. Ismeron's 'powerful Charm' is printed in italics, a
normal convention for a song, but there is no stage direction indicating that
he sings, as there is for the later song 'supposed sung by Aerial-Spirits.' Sens-
ing the musical possibilities of Ismeron's lines, Purcell set them to music for
the 'operatic' *Indian Queen* of 1695. Curtis A. Price, arguing that the text for
this version is very carefully cut, surmises that 'Dryden, who had many dealings with Purcell in the early nineties, may have undertaken the revision
himself, since it is so expertly made'; *Henry Purcell and the London Stage* (Cambridge: Cambridge University Press 1984), 126. Andrew Pinnock disagrees,
pointing to sundry ineptitudes in the cut version; see his 'Play into Opera:
Purcell's *The Indian Queen*,' *Early Music* 18 (1990), 3–21.

10 Dryden's song in *The Conquest of Granada*, Part I, which begins *'Beneath a
myrtle shade / Which Love for none but happy Lovers made'* (III.i.198–9), is closely
modelled on Cowley's 'The Despair,' which begins 'Beneath this gloomy
shade / By Nature onely for my Sorrows made.' See *The Mistress*, Vol. 2 of *The
Collected Works of Abraham Cowley*, eds. Thomas O. Calhoun, Laurence Hey-
worth, and Allan Pritchard (Newark: University of Delaware Press 1993), 43–
4. All the extant settings of Cowley's lyrics have now been recorded by The
Consort of Musicke, Anthony Rooley, Director, Musica Oscura CD 070986.

11 *The Siege of Rhodes*, ed. Ann-Mari Hedback (Uppsala: Acta Universitatis Upsa-
liensis. Studia Anglistica Upsaliensia, 14 1973), 4. For a fuller discussion, see

James A. Winn, 'Heroic Song: A Proposal for a Revised History of English
Theatre and Opera, 1656–1711,' *Eighteenth-Century Studies* 30 (1997), 113–37.

12 E.E. Duncan-Jones has identified five lines of French verse that the young
poet foisted into the dedicatory Epistle to Lord Buckhurst printed with *An
Essay of Dramatick Poesie* in 1668. The source, long imagined to be some
unpublished bit of society verse, turns out to be the *Ballet Royal de la Nuit* of
Isaac Benserade (1612–91), first performed and printed in 1653. As Duncan-
Jones points out, Buckhurst had been in France in the later 1650s and
attended similar musical performances; Dryden evidently expected him to
recognize the passage. For our purposes, the most exciting conclusion to be
drawn from this finding is that Dryden had detailed knowledge of Benserade
by 1667 – indeed, sufficient knowledge to have more or less memorized
some lines. See 'Dryden, Benserade, and Marvell,' *Huntington Library Quar-
terly* 54 (1991), 73–8.

13 Anyone inclined to doubt that Dryden and his contemporaries regarded
swords as phallic should read the scene in the Dryden-Davenant *Tempest* in
which Miranda '*wipes and anoints the Sword*' of Hippolito in an attempt to
cure his wound (V.ii).

14 I should think it more likely that Humfrey's setting was used in a revival than
in the original production, since he was abroad from 1664 until 1667. The
music was first printed in Playford's *Choice Ayres, Songs, & Dialogues, The Second Edition* (1675), a year after Humfrey's death.

15 *The Diary of Samuel Pepys: A New and Complete Transcription*, ed. Robert Latham
and William Matthews, 11 vols. (London: Bell 1970–83), 7:529 (15 November 1667).

16 I follow the facsimile in *Choice Ayres, Songs, and Dialogues*, ed. Spink, 1:66. A
complete performance of this song may be found on the accompanying disk,
band 2.

17 As Price explains in *Henry Purcell and the London Stage*, 297–8, the score for
King Arthur has been reconstructed from a series of fragmentary and conflicting manuscripts. The music for these lines may simply be lost; alterna-
tively, Purcell may have chosen not to set this stanza, preferring the second
song for the two sirens.

18 As James G. Turner pointed out to me when this paper was read in Los Angeles, it is difficult to determine at what date the verb 'come' begins to have the
experiencing of orgasm as one of its meanings. The *OED*, s.v. 'come,' sense
17, gives an example of 'come off' with that meaning, dated to 1650, though
printed much later. It may well be that passages like this one helped establish
that meaning.

19 *The Music in King Arthur*, ed. Margaret Laurie (Sevenoaks, Kent: Novello

1972). I have omitted the editorial realizations of the bass lines and the added dynamics. A complete performance of this song may be found on the accompanying disk, band 3.

20 Verbal details in 'Ah, fading joy' and the plot situation in *King Arthur* also link both scenes with the Bower of Bliss in Spenser's *The Faerie Queene*, where Guyon is tempted by naked damsels in a fountain, then by ravishing music:

> The ioyous birdes shrouded in chearefull shade,
> Their notes vnto the voyce attempred sweet;
> Th'Angelicall soft trembling voyces made
> To th'instruments diuine respondence meet:
> The siluer sounding instruments did meet
> With the base murmure of the waters fall:
> The waters fall with difference discreet,
> Now soft, now loud, vnto the wind did call:
> The gentle warbling wind low answered to all. (2.12.71)

I follow the text given in *Poetical Works*, ed. J.C. Smith and E. de Sélincourt (Oxford: Clarendon Press 1910).

21 'An Allusion to Horace' in *The Poems of John Wilmot, Earl of Rochester*, ed. Keith Walker (Oxford: Blackwell 1984), 99–102, here quoting ll. 61–70.

22 Ibid., ll. 71–4.

23 *OED*, s.v. 'pinion,' sense 3b.

24 See Curtis A. Price, *Music in the Restoration Theatre* (Ann Arbor, Mich.: UMI Research Press 1979), 42, and James A. Winn, *John Dryden and His World* (New Haven: Yale University Press 1987), 533–4.

25 For a much fuller discussion, see James A. Winn, 'Dissonance: 1613–1798,' in *Eighteenth-Century Contexts: Historical Inquiries in Honor of Phillip Harth*, ed. Howard Weinbrot and Peter Schakel (Madison: University of Wisconsin Press 2001), 3–25.

26 My transcription from the manuscript at the Royal College of Music, London. A complete performance of this song may be found on the accompanying disk, band 4.

27 See James A. Winn, '*When Beauty Fires the Blood*': Love and the Arts in the Age of Dryden (Ann Arbor: University of Michigan Press 1992), 129–31. This essay borrows and reworks some material from that book.

chapter fifteen

'Thy Lovers were all untrue': Sexual Overreaching in the Heroic Plays and *Alexander's Feast*

JAMES GRANTHAM TURNER

Momus.	All, all of a piece throughout;
Pointing to Diana	Thy Chase had a Beast in View;
To Mars	Thy Wars brought nothing about;
To Venus	Thy Lovers were all untrue.

(ll. 86–9)

At the very end of the 1700 *Secular Masque*, at the very close of Dryden's writing life, Momus points in turn to the three deities who define the three stages of the century, forcing the entire company to conclude "*Tis well an Old Age is out, / And time to begin a New.*'[1] These words resonate across future fins de siècle down to the present; like other papers in this volume, my own commentary on these lines was occasioned by a conference entitled 'An Old Age Is Out.' Momus divides the seventeenth century into three periods and a hiatus, so that Diana, Mars, and Venus serve as chronotypes or spirits of their age. My particular concern is the age of Venus, who took up her presidency at the Restoration and who resigned, Chronos strongly implies, at the joyless Whig Revolution, leaving him crushed under the weight of the globe. Venus – or, as we would say, Sexuality – certainly seems the right goddess for the restored Stuart court, and the hectic libertinism of the period has been shown (by Maximillian Novak, Warren Chernaik, and myself) to embody the deepest contradictions of the culture.[2] Jean Hagstrum's *Sex and Sensibility* and James Winn's *Beauty Fires the Blood* have established Dryden's central role in the cult of erotic passion, particularly in his serious drama and his literary criticism. But Momus's song leaves some questions unanswered. Why does he dismiss Venus along with the other deities, *all of a piece throughout*? Why the fatal proviso that the entire enterprise proved 'untrue'?

On the positive side, the *Secular Masque* conceives Venus in the spirit of Lucretius's invocation to *De Rerum Natura*, as a cosmic force of sweetness and renewal; in Britain as in Rome, Venus heals the wounds of civil war, 'repair[s]' the damage done by Mars in a kind of georgic cycle of destruction and fertility. As in the celebrated song 'Fairest Isle, all Isles Excelling,' the benevolent realm of Eros merges into a sentimental vision of Stuart England. At century's end, however, this rosy myth must be retrospectively declared 'untrue' because the hereditary principle had failed to bring political harmony; as Chronos pointedly laments, the world weighed light on his shoulders during Venus's reign, but the 'Queen of Beauty' has already left the earth, banished like Mary of Modena after the cataclysm of 1688. We could also infer from Momus's words that the age of Eros was untrue to itself precisely *because* it was true to the rest of that troubled century, 'all of a piece' with the previous periods because, having taken a libertine form, sexuality resembled too much the stylized predation of hunting and the outright aggression of war. Dryden himself did much to promote this cult of venereal conquest: when Peter Hughes wrote his classic article 'Erotic Heroism and the Implosion of Texts,' he found his title 'Wars within Doors' ready-made in *All for Love*.[3] 'Cymon and Iphigenia,' the last of the *Fables*, might confirm that Dryden remained deeply divided about the militant or 'heroic' assertion of upper-class sexual privilege. It begins with the most rapturous tribute to the civilizing and creative power of Love, a reaffirmation of the driving idea that 'When Beauty fires the Blood ... Love exalts the Mind'[4] (7:514, l. 41), the source of Winn's title and the central principle of Dryden's erotic aesthetics. But this civilizing process working through Cymon leads inexorably to rape and violence, a descent only *partly* explained as an image of William III's conquest of England.

We might say then that the *practice* of Venus was 'untrue' to its own idealized form. I want to suggest in this essay, however, that it is not the gross abuse of heroic love but its idealization that propels Dryden into the realm of untruth. The crucial change that defined the Restoration age of Venus, and rendered it 'all of a piece' with war and hunting, was the advent of what I call the libertine sublime: lawless, violent sexuality could now be conceived as awesome rather than absurd. Concentrating on the heroic plays, I will trace affinities between the erotic bravado of

Dryden's protagonists and the critical language used to praise great poets including Dryden himself. This erotic-aesthetic nexus leads to another poem of globalized, all-powerful, epoch-making Eros: *Alexander's Feast*. The central incantation of that later ode – 'None but the Brave deserves the Fair'[5] – takes on a new and more lurid light when juxtaposed with the overblown Morat in *Aureng-Zebe*, characterized as 'too much a Brave.'[6] I shall also, more briefly, discover parallels in the unpublishable obscene verse by Rochester ('The Disabled Debauchee') and by his less talented imitators (Oldham's Pindaric *Sardanapalus*, the anonymous mock drama *Sodom*).

In the most obvious sense, Momus's 'untruth of lovers' refers once again to libertine inconstancy – the sort of casual serial promiscuity that Dryden himself had impersonated in comedies like *Secret Love*, where Celadon modestly claims that 'I can live with as few Mistresses as any man: I desire no superfluities; onely for necessary change or so; as I shift my Linnen.'[7] But the Celadon type is actually quite constant in inconstancy, committed to a kind of truth-telling and to a kind of imperturbable truth-to-self that rules out fidelity – at least before the fifth act, when the traditional marriage plot kicks in. In this way he provides the comic counterpart to those romance heroes of absolutely inflexible constancy that populate Dryden's heroic dramas. In both extremes of character, sheer dramatic verve – truth to their own performativity – pushes them off the scale of quotidian realism and truth to conventional morality.

If rakes like Celadon are too true to be good, then romantic overreachers like Almanzor in *The Conquest of Granada* are too good to be true. Mary Evelyn, in a famous letter recording her response to that titanic play, found Almanzor more suited for a Utopia than for the Restoration stage, and felt it surprising that 'one born in the decline of morality should be able to feigne such exact virtue.'[8] Dryden's dilemma is nicely encapsulated in this remark: he sincerely wanted to create a new synthesis of love and heroism for the new age of Venus – but what models were available? The 'Heroic Furors' of Renaissance Platonism were long outmoded, and the impossibly virtuous love heroes of romance were undermined, or at least rendered deeply ironic, by the hegemonic court culture of Charles II and the 'decline of morality' it hastened. Seeing Almanzor emerge from the Green Room, Mrs Evelyn could see only hyperbolic fiction, the 'feigning' of a poet debauched by what he himself later called a 'lubrique and adult'rate age.'[9] Even when he is most deeply immersed in the theatre world, Dryden seems acutely aware of the fictiveness lurking at the heart of erotic representation. I find this in his backhanded and ambiguous compliment to Nathaniel Lee, his sometime collaborator and rival in creating extravagant eroto-maniac heroes:

> Such praise is yours, while you the Passions move,
> That 'tis no longer feign'd; 'tis real Love:
> Where Nature Triumphs over wretched Art;
> We only warm the Head, but you the Heart.[10]

At once sincere in his admiration for Lee's 'Heroic' efforts and aware of their absurdity, Dryden assigns emotive, passionate writing to the ani-mal realm of nature, excluding his fellow dramatist both from the cold-ness of cerebration and from the professional self-validation of the real artist ('*We* only warm the Head'; my emphasis). Grammar further desta-bilizes the compliment, since the 'it' that hovers between 'feigned' and 'real love' refers logically to Dryden's 'praise' rather than Lee's achieve-ment. Above all, Dryden assumes with Mary Evelyn that endeavours to move the passions will probably just increase the sense of fictiveness: only a miracle of nature makes it seem 'no longer feigned' but 'real Love.'

The heroic drama raises the spectre of artificial language betraying real love. But Momus's sweeping dismissal might also derive from the opposite problem, as articulated by Lucretius in the fourth book of *De Rerum Natura* – a passage that conspicuously contradicts the glorious invocation to 'sweet Venus' in Book I. Momus can therefore refute Venus by throwing her own book at her. When Lucretius turns from cos-mic Eros to human sexual passion he finds it fundamentally and philo-sophically 'untrue' at its core, an empty or, in Dryden's word, 'vain' illusion that can never be satisfied. Reproductive sex and transient lust pose few problems for Lucretius, but intense, burning, devouring, obsessive sexual love for another individual – precisely the heroic love that drives Dryden's most romantic characters – is nothing but a 'simu-lacrum' and a delusion. Paradoxically, Dryden translated this passage of Lucretius into the most 'luscious *English*' for his own pleasure, as if poetic language can yield the delights that real bodies eternally deny.[11]

In an earlier version of this argument, I proposed that, in the view of contemporaries and in his own self-presentation, Dryden played a cen-tral role in the 'libertine sublime' and the 'libertine refurbishment of the traditional equivalence of Eros and creativity.' By this I meant that he helped to transfer the heroic conception of Eros, evolved in French court circles and influenced by the novels of Scudéry and the philosophy of Descartes, from virtuous love to fully sexual passion unrestrained by morality. As I put it then, 'fire, excess, height, greatness, "sublimity," the intensity of pleasure and refinement of taste that combine in the word "gust" – all these pass from courtly Amour to bravura sexual performance in word and deed.'[12] To the modern reader, the most familiar example would be the 'greater Gust' and 'diviner Lust' with which King David conceived Absalom, the 'vigorous warmth' with which he scattered his seed throughout the land.[13] In his own time it was Dryden's heroic plays – whatever ironic distance and *sprezzatura* he tried to establish between himself and them – that served as the vehicle for this love cult and the occasion to apply it to his own creativity. The Prologue to the most outrageous of them, *Tyrannick Love*, sums up his erotic poetics in what amounts to the rapist's creed: '*Poets, like Lovers, should be bold and dare.*'[14]

It would be wrong to call Dryden a libertine in the personal sense, for he never poured himself body and soul into what Rochester called 'Love raised to an extreme,'[15] and always retained a certain non-committal moderation expressed in the form of his couplets and the measure of his language. (He may have abandoned rhyme because 'Passion's too fierce to be in Fetters bound,'[16] but the fetters are always present.) Nevertheless, he still loved to dramatize characters reaching for extreme states of feeling associated with nobility. He fed this cult of erotic sublimity, tumult, and fire – or what I will call a 'pyrotechnics' of sexuality – not only because it fitted the fashions of the Restoration court and its extravagant mistresses, but also (more importantly) because it provided a vocabulary to praise his own creative genius. Turning sex into aesthetics sidestepped the problem of Lucretian 'untruth' lurking at the core of real love. At the same time, Dryden the dramatist of flesh and blood never lost his sense that one extreme could loop into the other, from the sublime to the ridiculous. Sexual extremity leads to self-cancellation, to self-immolation in the noble characters, and to histrionic self-parody in the absurd ones. Libertine heroes tend to disappear in a puff of stage smoke.

'Love,' as Queen Isabel proclaims in *The Conquest of Granada*, is a 'Heroique Passion' apparently unique to the aristocracy, since it finds 'No room in any base degenerate mind.'[17] At the same time it is dramatized as an all-consuming, elemental force that 'kindles all the Soul with Honours Fire, / To make the Lover worthy his desire' (I.147–8). Love crowns the structure of elite society, and it destroys all structures in a kind of conflagration; love 'refines' and 'exalts the mind,' yet generates a kind of admirable excess and enlarging frenzy far different from the traditional detachment and self-control of the ruling class. It seems appropriate that Almanzor, the original Noble Savage, should become the textbook example of the heroic lover, impossibly generous, bursting with animal spirits, zigzagging wildly from 'the Lethargy of Love' (III.i.337) to the hyperactive state of 'tempest' and conflagration – exactly as Descartes had described him in his letters to Queen Christina and his treatise *Les Passions de l'âme.* He is thus well matched with Almahide, who despises the 'vulgar good' and 'dull' blessings of her inert fiancé after discovering that with Almanzor 'love all strife, / All rapid, is the Hurrican of life' (V.i.371–2). Like the Portuguese Nun she detests tranquillity, and measures both Eros and nobility as a burst of energy – a 'gust' in the meteorological as well as the aesthetic sense.[18]

Mary Evelyn found Almanzor improbably virtuous in comparison with the debauchery of the age, but for many critics his chief appeal lay in an erotic energy that made moral criteria irrelevant or oxymoronic. Dryden himself advertises the 'excessive and overboyling' aspect of Almanzor, defining his purpose by pointing out that a perfect hero 'who never transgresses the bounds of moral vertue, would shine but dimly in an Epick poem.'[19] This line of self-justification in turn prompts Dr Johnson's remark that in Almanzor 'all the rays of romantick heat, whether amorous or warlike, glow ... by a kind of concentration'; for Johnson, Almanzor is 'above all laws ... exempt from all restraints,' and this generates an effect that he calls 'majestick madness' or 'illustrious depravity.'[20] Other commentators perceived all too great a similarity between Dryden's amorous overreachers and the upper-class hooligans of contemporary London. *The Whores Rhetorick* builds an entire episode around the actor who plays Almanzor and takes his character from the stage to the brothel, and *The Conquest of Granada* is repeatedly burlesqued in *Sodom,* whose absolute monarchs declare their 'boundless' sexual ambitions in ponderous, closed couplets. I argued in my 'Libertine Sublime' essay that the death-defying sexual exhibitionism of characters like Morat and Antony brings them quite close to their counterparts in *Sodom* and *Sardanapalus,* who embrace an orgasmic death in the flames of divine destruction. Ned Ward's Libertine, looking back over the Restoration, praises the heroic drama for promoting the absolute power of sexuality, teaching ambitious mistresses to enslave the king to their desire, 'mak[ing] the Head subservient to the Tail.'[21]

Dryden's supporters extract the same sexual charge from his heroic lovers but convert it into critical currency. One defender justified the 'violence' and 'rapture' of Almanzor as essential to the 'masculine beauty' of the high style. In the decorous 1690s Dryden's talents – expressing his 'boundless Mind' and 'Vast Ideas' – were still thought to culminate in erotic stimulation:

> Thy charming Numbers do our Souls inthrall,
> The Rigid melt, and we turn Lovers all;
> The *Cupids* dance in ev'ry Ladies eye,
> Who reading Love as they were acting, die.[22]

Lord Bolingbroke brings out these sexual implications in almost pedantic detail: like a sultan in his harem, Dryden copulates 'vigour[ously]' with all nine of the 'wishing Muses,' while avoiding the 'stale thing' of a 'Poetick Wife' (which might have diminished his Fancy and put out his 'Fire'); this undecayed performance even in old age proves that 'Sublime your Fancy, boundless is your Mind.'[23] These compliments refashion Dryden as his own Almanzor, introduced in *The Conquest of Granada* with the same formula: 'Vast is his Courage; boundless is his mind' (I.i.253).

Reckless and magnificent statements of love ideology resonate throughout Dryden's tragedies. Like Otway and Lee, he replaces what Mary Evelyn called 'exact virtue' with an equally 'Utopian' worship of energy in both heroes and villains. 'Desire' is called 'the vast extent of humane mind.' 'Love' confers 'a God-like liberty,' for 'Love is the freest motion of our minds.' Even the old rise to the rhetoric of glorious freedom, lifting them momentarily from absurdity. The antinomian and libertarian energies of the English Revolution are transferred to the boudoir, so that 'Love scorns all ties but those that are his own,' 'wondrous' beauty 'justifies Rebellion' and dissolves the 'Sin' of 'looking on it.'[24] Jean Hagstrum liked to emphasize the tender *sensibilité* of Dryden's lovers, but it is their sexual overreaching – their romantic heat and illustrious depravity, in Johnson's words – that give them their allure. Colley Cibber vividly recalls the effect of these titanic performances, which filled the audience with 'trembling Admiration' – 'admiration' of course meaning awestruck astonishment rather than moral approval.[25] *The Conquest of Granada* brought to a high pitch Dryden's mix of imperious libido, tempestuous energy, and Orientalist absolutism, and he keeps it boiling in his later plays. For the Emperor Muley-Moluch in *Don Sebas-*

tian, love is an awesomely destructive power, a 'Hurrican of Soul' and 'a greater King' even than himself,[26] though he still declares his *tendresse* with a suitably regal ferocity: '[I] Love thee implacably, yet hate thee too; / Wou'd hunt thee bare-foot, in the mid-day Sun ... / T'enjoy thy Love, and once enjoy'd, to kill thee' (II.i.444–7).

His victim Almeyda is quite unimpressed by these threats and mocks their 'false courage,' prompting the thwarted Emperor to escalate them: 'there's a new gust in Ravishment, / Which I have never try'd' (II.i.496–7). Even the noble Don Sebastian has his moment of Titanism in the face of the prohibition on incest: 'I shou'd break through Laws Divine, and Humane, / And think 'em Cobwebs, spred for little man' (V.i.629–30). This later play continues the ranting, thunder-defying gesture of Anthony, Oedipus, and Morat, so easily parodied in *Sodom*.

But the extremity of 'romantick heat' and heroic declamation – typified by the frustrated Empress Nourmahal in *Aureng-Zebe* –generates a melange of sublimity and absurdity, revealing what thin partitions divide them. This Indian Phaedra obsessed with her virtuous stepson evokes a 'higher' love that sweeps away all restraint, overrides all but its own laws, attaches itself only to the highest object, and 'fills the Senses' with a joy 'so great' that the strings of life are overstretched and break (IV.i.122–6). Desire is a force that propels her beyond 'sense,' beyond ethics, beyond even the boundaries that separate sublimity from bathos: 'That Sovereign power all guilt from action takes, / At least the stains are beautiful it makes' (III.i.368–9).

As in the *Secular Masque*, Venus establishes an absolute dominion, but in Nourmahal's dream-vision she does this by appealing to the heroic ideology of transgression: 'Mean Soul! and dar'st not gloriously offend?' (IV.i.114). In her final desperation, believing the prince to be dead, she admits 'the glorious sin, and the more glorious flame,' and pretends that, like Semiramis or Muley-Moluch, she would merely have quenched her fires and flung away his slaughtered body (V.i.296). All her sensual energy flows into revenge and death; she will watch her rival's death throes like a voyeur or a stage audience, with 'full gust' (V.i.312) – an apt phrase to describe the spirit of both Nourmahal and her author, excited to produce splendid fictions of absolute desire.

In the heroic drama as in obscene parodies like *Sodom* and *Sardanapalus*, the desires of both lovers and authors tend towards a consummation in fire. When the frustrated queen Cuntagratia in *Sodom* longs to 'fire the world' and satisfy her 'love of Glory' as she 'spend[s] at each melting pore,' the parody departs only a few degrees from the original 'glorious flame.' Oldham's Sardanapalus likewise dies 'Revelling in Fire, / At every Pore dripping out Scalding Lust, / With all [his] Strength collected in one Thrust,' copulating on his own suicidal funeral pyre.[27] Fire is both the sublimating principle of creativity and the force of *Eros maniaque* that seizes upon the characters. Both these meanings come together in Aureng-Zebe's defence of the imaginative component of love:

> If Love be Vision, mine has all the fire
> Which, in first Dreams, young Prophets does inspire:
> I dream, in you, our promis'd Paradice,
> An Age's tumult of continu'd bliss. (I.i.378–81)[28]

Some critics feel that these speeches deliberately critique the vanity of illusion, making Dryden a consciously antiheroic dramatist, and certainly Aureng-Zebe's conditional construction ('*If* Love be vision'; my emphasis) leaves open this Momus-like possibility. Indamora had indeed proposed that love is an 'airy' illusion created by the imagination and opinion – but this is her counsel of despair, not her heartfelt belief. Aureng-Zebe's response, like the rest of the play, reasserts the authenticity of true desire and invokes fire as a kind of epistemic guarantee.

Fire is associated not with illusion but with excess, intensity, 'tumult,' and noble vastness of mind. Aureng-Zebe himself is consumed by a love that 'mounts and rowls about my stormy mind, / Like Fire that's born by a tempestous Wind,' and this fire image kindles a blaze of rhetorical 'tumult' that signals the contradictory physiology of desire: in quick succession he weeps, burns, 'rushes on' Indamora to 'stifle' and 'eat' her, pushes her away so he can 'gaze' at her, and then 'invades' her with 'torrents of joy' (IV.ii.252). Here as in the obscene versions, the fire of libertine sublimity meets the hydraulic Cartesian body to produce a scalding, spurting climax. Symptoms taken from Lucretius, particularly the 'devouring' impulse and the flood imagery, are offset by the idea of an unstoppable conflagration, in an attempt to dispel the Lucretian shadow of futility and 'untruth.' As Aureng-Zebe prepares for the final scene he swells again with pyrotechnic zeal, both emotionally and metrically – 'With Glory, and with Love, at once I burn: / I feel th'inspiring heat, and absent God return' (IV.ii.221–2). His half-brother and rival Morat expires in an ecstacy of redemptive love for Indamora, feeling 'enlarg'd' like 'a blazing Fire, / Fed from the Brand,' and his faithful

Melesinda literalizes this amorous death in the act of suttee: 'I'll seek his breast, and kindling by his side, / Adorn'd with flames, I'll mount a glorious Bride' (V.i.634–5).[29]

Nourmahal once again provides both a comic and a heroic version of this pyrotechnic trope, in the mad scene that becomes her dying speech. She brings to a climax the literal and metaphorical burning thematized throughout the play – for example, in her scornful parallel of Indamora to the 'fatal *Helen*' who 'set the World on fire' (V.i.257–8) – and characteristically pushes it towards grotesque extremity. Her husband is reduced to an underfilled firework ('he'll but whiz, and strait go out' [V.i.650]), but her astonishing description of poison at work – flames streaming from mouth and nostrils, a Miltonic 'burning Lake' that 'rowls and flows' through her entire body (V.i.694), a 'Brain-pan' that 'glows' in the heat (V.i.656) – conveys some of the terror of the Great Fire of London, even though Dryden himself never witnessed it.[30] (*Annus Mirabilis* had associated the Fire with 'crafty Courtezans' [1:93], and here tenor and vehicle are reversed.) Later theories of the sublime derived it from the response to vast natural objects, which provoke contrary emotions of helplessness and exultation; the Restoration taste for imperious and incendiary desire may derive from a similar response, not to storms and mountains, but to two great spectres of the human environment, absolute monarchy and urban conflagration.

If Dryden's intention *was* to satirize rather than to emulate the erotic sublime, this was not noticed by his contemporaries. Whether they praised or pilloried the result, they assumed that he aimed to create an impression of 'Flame and Power,' that his own art emulated rather than critiqued the pyrotechnics of his theatrical lovers. For some, indeed, his ability to create characters of amorous intensity, and thereby to involve and stimulate the audience, verged upon the titanic: 'Sure you have gain'd from Heav'n *Promethean* Fire, / To form, then kindle Souls into Desire.'[31]

'Kindling' once again serves as the creative means and the erotic effect, as if text and response had fused together in the heat. Such flatterers pick up the critical language that Dryden himself uses to define the highest literary achievement: it is 'When Beauty *fires* the Blood' that 'Love exalts the mind' and invents the arts. As he said of Lucretius, 'Masculine' thoughts and a 'Masculine' style denote a 'fiery temper' and a 'sublime and daring Genius.'[32] If 'Poets like lovers should be bold and dare,' then the poet-critic records the effect of this daring on the receiver: Horace 'may Ravish other men,' Dryden admits, but '*Juvenal* is of a more vigorous and Masculine Wit; he gives me as much Pleasure as I can bear, he fully satisfies my Expectation.'[33] John Dennis echoes this perverse spin on the erotic-poetic parallel when he declares his 'Love' for Dryden, 'who has so often given me all the pleasure that the most Insatiable Mind can desire'; like Almahide in *The Conquest of Granada* he attests that Dryden has 'raised [my Soul] to Transports which made it contemn Tranquillity,' and like Lord Bolingbroke he praises the charms of Dryden's Muse, inexhaustible though 'long and often Enjoy'd.'[34]

This preoccupation with erotic/poetic heroism, which promotes the criteria of energy and transgression over those of prudential 'rule' and 'exact virtue,' helps to explain the affinity between high and low genres in the literary system of the Restoration, and the curious ambiguity of Dryden's place within it. At the 'abject' end of this spectrum, mock heroics like *Sardanapalus* and *Sodom* borrowed the pomp of Dryden's language and the sublime confidence of his sex-crazed princes, who defy the gods and end their life in an orgasmic blaze of literal and metaphoric fire. The high literary panegyrics of Dennis and Bolingbroke rework the sexual-critical theme of an earlier lampoon on Dryden's authorial self-presentation, which pretends to celebrate 'the *Dildo* of Mr *Dryden's* Muse, so neatly applied to the females of the Town,' and 'the Intrigue that Mr *Dryden* endeavours to hold with the World.' Hostile contemporaries loved to puncture Dryden's claims with bathetic lines from his own tragedies: he promised 'Flame' and gave them earth ('cold, dry, and heavy'); he promised 'an Intrigue with the World' and delivered a wooden dildo or a 'Dry Bob,' as Rochester put it – meaning an attempt at penetration without ejaculation, 'dry' in the sexual as well as the discursive sense.[35]

Dryden participated in an age of compromised and problematic heroism, an age ostensibly devoted to love as boundless as the mind, but severely and sometimes ludicrously limited by modernity, 'sense,' and worldliness – its sublime aspirations continually punctured by what Peri Bathous would later call the 'A-la-mode' and the 'Prurient.'[36] He became the object as well as the source of satire, attacked by his contemporaries for slavish immersion in the causes and fashions of his day, and for the incoherent mixture of impressiveness and absurdity in his life and his work. George Farquhar's remarks on Dryden's chaotic funeral in 1700 captured this uncontrolled quality and set the pattern for subsequent criticism of the heroic plays: his burial, 'a kind of rhapsody ... mostly burlesque,' was like his life; reversing Momus's final judgment in the *Secular Masque* ('All, all of a piece throughout'), Farquhar declares the life, the work, and the funeral 'variety and not of a piece; the quality and mob, farce and heroicks, the sublime and ridicule mix'd in a piece – great Cleopatra in a hackney coach.'[37]

But the ambiguity of erotic heroism can hardly have escaped Dryden's own awareness, skilled as he was in staging serious and comic versions of the trope side by side. It should be possible to find a late text that embodies the interconnection of the 'sublime' and the 'ridicule,' somewhere between the full-blooded admiration of desire and the final dismissal of Venus as 'all of a piece' with idiotic pastoralism and futile militarism. Dryden's tribute to 'the power of mighty Love' should culminate in a treatment both anarchic and ennobling, both absolutely Olympian and destructively over-performative. Like court culture itself in the age of Venus, high-libertine desire should be figured as '*both* classical and grotesque, both regal and foolish, high and low,'[38] its 'Fire' at once refining and arsonistic. This precarious double act is achieved, I suggest, in *Alexander's Feast*.

'Love' takes its place *among* the passions excited in turn by Timotheus's heroic virtuosity, but it also serves as the universal passion, the component that drives every other affect to excess. The opening tableau gives equal billing to the triumphant Alexander and the grand courtesan Thais (or 'Lais' in the first printing, as if one courtesan were the same as another). The transition from Mars to Venus at first appears effortless and appropriate, an unthinking celebration of the heroic ethos: 'Desert in Arms' *should* be crowned with roses and myrtles, since 'None but the Brave deserves the Fair' (l. 15). The skipping repetitions of 'happy' and 'brave' discourage any sense that the Fair might be a mere whore and the Brave nothing but a bravo or Hector. (The unreclaimed Morat, in the early stages of *Aureng-Zebe*, is dismissed as 'too much a Brave' [I.i.98]). But Alexander's burning of Persepolis did carry these low associations. Rochester's Disabled Debauchee, no longer able to smash windows and couple with link-boys, uses his reminiscences to 'inspire' the next generation of libertines with such 'Heat' that they 'long some ancient church to Fire.' In Dryden's own *Mr. Limberham*, the bawdy farce he claims to have co-authored with Charles II himself, the rioters Aldo and Woodall cry in their drunken enthusiasm 'burn, ravish, and destroy ... We'll have a Night on't; like *Alexander*, when he burnt *Persepolis*.'[39] Alexander's feast resembles a Rochesterian 'frolick' in its violence and drunkenness as well as in its heroic aspirations.

'Love' officially occupies only part of one stanza, the fifth, where *Lydian* Measures' sooth the soul to 'Pleasures' as soporific as the rhyme. The lyric transition from the futility of war to the god-given benefit of Eros, embodied by the 'lovely *Thais*' who sits beside him, anticipates the Venus stanza in the *Secular Masque* even down to the phrasing: Venus murmurs 'Take me, take me, while you may' (l. 76) and Timotheus warbles 'Take the Good the Gods provide thee' (l. 106). But Alexander's response brings us back to the problematic heroic mode. He does not simply 'take' Thais like a ripe fruit or a cup of wine, which only two stanzas earlier had likewise brought infantile rhythms and sweetly simple 'Pleasure' after the 'Pain' of war. Instead he adopts the stricken posture of the Romance lover, 'sighing' and 'looking' ad infinitum and thereby revealing his 'Pain' (just what 'Pleasure' is supposed to relieve). The covert parallel of sex and drinking – a standard trope of low-libertine braggadocio epitomized in 'The Disabled Debauchee' – becomes explicit when the 'vanquished victor' passes out on her breast, 'with Love and Wine at once oppress'd' (l. 114).

'Vanquished victor' further implicates war in this triangle of stimulants, and reminds us that the symptoms of Love, Wine, and War can mutate into one another with alarming rapidity. Bacchus enters in stanza 3 with trumpets and drums and exits in stanza 4 in the 'glowing Cheeks [and] ardent Eyes' of Alexander's drunken bravado (l. 70), when, uncannily like the Disabled Debauchee, he 'Fought all his Battails o'er again' (l. 67). Thus Dryden prepares for Alexander's final mutation, when Timotheus's fortissimo rouses him from his baby-like sleep on Thais's breast into the furious revenge that sets fire to the city, passing once again from torpor to frenzy, or from what Almanzor would call Lethargy to Hurricane. At the climactic moment, Thais too mutates from cuddly pillow to guerrilla leader, from Venus into Mars, initiating the blaze that reads as a metaphorical extension of her own sexual fire; indeed it is Thais, and not Alexander, who actively '*fir'd another* Troy' '*like another* Hellen' (l. 154), becoming the grammatical subject of the verb and the historical agent of the event. So 'Love' in the Restoration sense – the aggrandized libido manifested in the titanic debauchee, the monarch-lover, and the absolute mistress who sets the 'Tail' above the 'Head' – extends far beyond its confines in the fifth stanza, dominating the final orgy of destruction just as it dominated the very opening of Timotheus's song, which narrates Alexander's conception by Jupiter in the guise of a dragon: 'Such is the Pow'r of mighty Love' (l. 27). Like Dryden himself in *Absalom*, Timotheus begins with a quasi-pornographic allusion to sudden copulation as the stamping of an image, royal and divine.[40] As he seduces Olympias, Jove moves 'Sublime on Radiant Spires' (l. 29) like the snake in *Paradise Lost*, 'sublime' in the literal but also in the Longinan aesthetic sense, and this 'power' of heightened desire is clearly transferred to the poet-lyrist, who does not merely flatter Alexander but 'ravishe[s]' his ears.

'Love' in this poem cannot be said to exist apart from 'the Power of Music,' but I would argue that the reverse is also true, that in Dryden's ode neither musical nor poetic power can exist except as modulations of Eros. Timotheus controls the sequence and stage-manages the emotions with an almost cynical detachment and satisfaction in his craft. Even while Alexander is dissolving in pity for the fallen Darius, 'The Mighty Master smil'd to see / That Love was in the next Degree' (ll. 93–4). The ostensible reason is psychological, since 'Pity melts the Mind to Love' (l. 96; we are not sure whether this is the narrator's comment or the soliloquy that accompanies Timotheus's anticipatory 'smile'). But he clearly exults in his power to do the melting and burning, to make the passions transitive and work them on a passive Alexander. The modes and moods are mixed, and he is the mixer. Alexander proves that the greatest lovers 'are all untrue,' their passion not only destructively pyrotechnic but inauthentic, changeable, contingent, in this case literally instrumental. But Timotheus proves that 'mighty Love' transformed by 'Art' cleaves to its own truth. In Dryden's final stanza the power of this music is epitomized as the power to 'swell the Soul to rage, or kindle soft Desire' (l. 160), a chiasmus that intermingles the affects of rage and desire by associating both with an arousal that is both swelling and kindling – that is, precisely the heroic version of erotic passion expanded in the drama and applied by critics to Dryden's own genius, that '*Promethean* Fire, / To form, then kindle Souls into Desire.'

The final introduction of St Cecilia no doubt means to trump this pagan fiction with Christian hagiography; love 'all untrue,' as Momus would say, is defeated by the organ of true religious art that begins a new age. Nevertheless, the effect of the conclusion is to equate the two myths, the two halves of a divided crown or closed circle: Timotheus raises a mortal to the false heaven of the libertine sublime; Cecilia learns to sustain the same seductive sounds and thereby to draw a supernatural being down to earth. But this had already been achieved by the descent of Jove to Olympias, drawn down by 'the pow'r of mighty Love.' The same 'pow'r of mighty Love' is celebrated right up to the final works of 1700, *Cymon* and the *Secular Masque*, but at the same time gives us an ugly picture of the loves of the mighty. Beauty fires the blood; Thais fires the city. Venus ruled the night and lightened the weight of the world; Venus is an empty lie. As always, Dryden has it both ways.

Notes

1 *The Works of John Dryden*, ed. E.N. Hooker, H.T. Swedenberg, Jr, et al., 20 vols. (Berkeley: University of California Press 1956–2000), 16:273, ll. 96–7. Subsequent references will be to this edition (hereafter cited as *California Dryden*) and will appear in the text with line numbers.

2 See, among others, Maximillian E. Novak, 'Margery Pinchwife's "London Disease": Restoration Comedy and the Libertine Offensive of the 1670s,' *Studies in the Literary Imagination* 10 (1972), 1–23; Warren Chernaik, *Sexual Freedom in Restoration Literature* (Cambridge: Cambridge University Press 1995); James Grantham Turner, 'The Properties of Libertinism,' in Robert Purks Maccubbin, ed., *'Tis Nature's Fault: Unauthorized Sexuality during the Enlightenment* (Cambridge: Cambridge University Press 1988), and *Libertines and Radicals in Early Modern London: Sexuality, Politics and Literary Culture, 1630–1685* (Cambridge: Cambridge University Press 2003); Jean H. Hagstrum, *Sex and Sensibility: Ideal and Erotic Love from Milton to Mozart* (Chicago: Chicago University Press 1980); James Anderson Winn, *'When Beauty Fires the Blood': Love and the Arts in the Age of Dryden* (Ann Arbor: University of Michigan Press 1992). At the December 2000 conference, Winn argued that the eroticism of Dryden's songs fully satisfies Rochester's criteria for libertine poetics ('songs and lyrics mannerly obscene').

3 Peter Hughes, 'Wars within Doors,' *English Studies* 60 (1979), 402–21.

4 *California Dryden* 7:514, l. 41.

5 Dryden, *Alexander's Feast. The Poems of John Dryden*, ed. James Kinsley, 4 vols. (Oxford: Clarendon Press 1958), 3:1428, l. 15. Subsequent references are to this edition and will be cited parenthetically by line number.

6 *California Dryden* 12:I.i.98. Subsequent references are to this edition and are cited parenthetically in the text.

7 *California Dryden* 9:I.ii.13–15. Subsequent references are to this edition and will be cited parenthetically in the text.

8 Mary Evelyn, Sr, letter to Bohun (1671), in John Evelyn, *Diary*, ed. William Bray (London: Bickers 1879), III:57.

9 Dryden, 'To the Pious Memory of the Accomplisht Young Lady Mrs. Anne Killigrew.' *California Dryden* 3:111, l. 63.

10 Dryden, 'To Mr. Lee on His *Alexander.*' *California Dryden* 1:107, ll. 33–6.

11 Dryden, Preface to *Sylvae. California Dryden* 3:12.

12 'The Libertine Sublime: Love and Death in Restoration England,' *Studies in Eighteenth-Century Culture* 19 (1989), 146–63, esp. 103, 105.

13 Dryden, *Absalom and Achitophel, California Dryden* 2:5, l. 8.

14 *California Dryden* 10:134, l. 12.

15 Rochester, l. 26. In *Works*, ed. Harold Love (Oxford: Oxford University Press 1999), 28.

16 Dryden, Prologue to *Aureng-Zebe. California Dryden* 12: 1.9.

17 Dryden, *The Conquest of Granada, Part I. California Dryden* 11:I.i.145–6. Subsequent references are to this edition and will be cited parenthetically in the text.

18 Though Almanzor is inscribed within the conventions of Romance rather than libertinism, it is obvious that Dryden has his sexual energy in mind (cf. 9), where he threatens a feeble rival that on his wedding night 'the thought of me shall make thee impotent.' The (almost certainly) fictional Portuguese Nun grows to 'detest the tranquillity in which I lived before I knew you'; J.G.L. de Guilleragues, *Chansons et Bon Mots, Valentins, Lettres Portugaises*, ed. Fréderic Deloffre and Jacques Rougeot (Geneva: Droz 1972), 159.

19 Dryden, Preface to *The Conquest of Granada. California Dryden* 11:6.

20 *Dryden: The Critical Heritage* (hereafter cited as *DCH*), ed. James and Helen Kinsley (London: Routledge 1971), 286.

21 Ned Ward, *The Libertine's Choice*, 2nd ed. (London: H. Hills 1709), 10; cf. *The Whores Rhetorick, Calculated to the Meridian of London, and Conformed to the Rules of Art* (London: G. Shell 1683), 97–9, and *Sodom* [full title *Sodom and Gomorah*], in Harold Love, ed., *The Works of John Wilmot, Earl of Rochester* (Oxford: Oxford University Press 1999), esp. 303 ('Thus in the Zenith of my lust I reigne: / I eat to swive and Swive to eat againe'), 304 ('May your most gracious Pr--- and Cods be still / As boundless in their pleasure as your will'), 312 ('Who would forsake or shun the charming faire / Whose eyes are C--ts and every glance a haire?'). Despite these and other echoes of heroic drama, the author(s) of *Sodom* mostly confine themselves to the songs and stage effects that the average theatre-goer might best remember; the most striking of these is the travesty of 'Ah Fading Joy' and its fountain setting from *The Indian Emperour* (306) – a scene that, as Winn vividly demonstrated in his presentation to the December 2000 conference, was already very erotic.

22 *DCH* 97.

23 *DCH* 100, 208, 222.

24 Dryden, *Aureng-Zebe.* 12:177; 184–5; *The Spanish Fryar. California Dryden* 14:151, 155. Torrismond's speech (155) reduced Jeremy Collier to par-

oxysms of rage (*DCH* 233), but he fails to recognize the ironic context – Torrismond is using these arguments to persuade the Queen *against* an evil deed she has decreed.

25 *DCH* 193; cf. Hobbes's theory that heroic literature must 'raise admiration, principally, for three Vertues, Valour, Beauty, and Love,' in his Preface to the *Odyssey* (1675), in *Critical Essays of the Seventeenth Century*, ed. Joel E. Spingarn, II (Oxford: Clarendon Press 1908), 68.

26 *California Dryden* 15:II.i.40, 57. Subsequent references are to this edition and will be cited in the text parenthetically.

27 *Sodom and Gomorah* 309; *The Poems of John Oldham*, ed. Harold F. Brooks with Raman Selden (Oxford: Clarendon Press 1987), 350. Julia Kristeva interprets the fascination with fire in seventeenth-century drama as an expression of 'the extravagant superiority of baroque man,' suspending reality and defying the godhead in a purely momentary triumph (thus 'the fire that swallows Don Juan is the same fire that carries off the baroque scenery'); 'Eros maniaque, Eros sublime,' in *Histoires d'amour* (Paris: Denoël 1983), 251–2 (following Jean Rousset, *L'Intérieur et l'extérieur: essai sur la poésie et sur la théâtre au XVIIe siècle* (Paris: J. Corti 1968).

28 Dryden exploits the Orientalist myth that Islam offers its believers endless copulation in Heaven; cf. Derek Hughes, *Dryden's Heroic Plays* (London: Macmillan 1981), 143–4 and passim.

29 This Morat-Melesinda death scene (12:240, 247) is parodied in *Sodom and Gomorah*: as Pricket is 'dyeing in venerall fire' he too turns away from his faithful companion to his forbidden love ('Here on my fathers breast I will expire, / Ram'd to the top with an unknown desire'), but his sister-lover Swivia still resolves to be 'warm'd' with him and 'perish in his Armes' (314).

30 The Fire also provides Almanzor and Almahide with an elaborate and pedestrian simile to discuss their love: he should have blown up selected buildings to save others, he does not have enough stock to start rebuilding, etc. For the connection to Milton's Hell, see Blair Hoxby's 'Dryden's Baroque Dramaturgy: The Case of *Aureng-Zebe*' in this volume.

31 *DCH* 47 (Bayes in *The Rehearsal* praises his own 'Flame and Power'); Theophilus Parsons, commendatory poem to *Cleomenes* (*California Dryden* 16:83); ironically, the Promethean fire idea had been used, quite sincerely, by Richard Flecknoe (*DCH* 38).

32 Dryden, Preface to *Sylvae*. *California Dryden* 3:10.

33 Dryden, *Discourse of Satire*. *California Dryden* 4:63.

34 *The Critical Works of John Dennis*, ed. Edward Niles Hooker (Baltimore: Johns Hopkins Press 1943), 2:384.

35 *DCH* 76, 77, 185, 118.

36 See my 'Pope's Libertine Self-fashioning,' in David B. Morris, ed., Special Issue on Alexander Pope, *The Eighteenth Century: Theory and Interpretation* 29 (1988), 123–44, esp. 125.

37 *DCH* 242.

38 Peter Stallybrass and Allon White, *The Poetics and Politics of Transgression* (Ithaca: Cornell University Press 1986), 101–2.

39 *California Dryden* 14:61. See Winn, *Beauty Fires the Blood,* 89, for the king as Dryden's 'parcell poet' in *The Kind Keeper, or Mr. Limberham*; Rochester, *Works,* 541 (cf. variant reading 'such thoughts,' 45).

40 Implied when King David 'Scatter'd his Maker's Image through the Land' (2.1.10); cf. the would-be adulterous Emperor in *Aureng-Zebe* (how dare Arimant 'Intrench on Love, my great Prerogative? / Print his base Image on his Sovereign's Coin? / 'Tis Treason if he stamp his Love with mine,' (II.i.129–31) and *Sodom and Gomorah* ('My laws shall Act more pleasures than Command / And with my Prick I'le governe all the land,' 303), both texts earlier than *Absalom*. For the 'circular' relation between this mythic opening and the Christian ending, see William Fitzgerald, *Agonistic Poetry: The Pindaric Mode in Pindar, Horace, Hölderlin, and the English Ode* (Berkeley: University of California Press 1987), 124–9.

Index